Cameron Fuller
John Joyner
Andy Dominey

System Center Operations Manager 2007 R2

UNLEASHED

SUPPLEMENT TO
SYSTEM CENTER
OPERATIONS
MANAGER 2007
UNLEASHED

SAMS 800 East 96th Street, Indianapolis, Indiana 46240 USA

System Center Operations Manager 2007 R2 Unleashed

Copyright © 2010 by Pearson Education, Inc.

ISBN-13: 978-0-672-33341-5
ISBN-10: 0-672-33341-4

The Library of Congress Cataloging-in-Publication Data is on file.

Printed in the United States of America

Second Printing April 2010

Trademarks

All terms mentioned in this book that are known to be trademarks or service marks have been appropriately capitalized. Sams Publishing cannot attest to the accuracy of this information. Use of a term in this book should not be regarded as affecting the validity of any trademark or service mark.

Warning and Disclaimer

Every effort has been made to make this book as complete and as accurate as possible, but no warranty or fitness is implied. The information provided is on an "as is" basis. The authors and the publisher shall have neither liability nor responsibility to any person or entity with respect to any loss or damages arising from the information contained in this book or from the use of it.

Bulk Sales

Sams Publishing offers excellent discounts on this book when ordered in quantity for bulk purchases or special sales. For more information, please contact:

U.S. Corporate and Government Sales

1-800-382-3419

corpsales@pearsontechgroup.com

For sales outside of the U.S., please contact:

International Sales

international@pearson.com

Editor-in-Chief
Karen Gettman

Executive Editor
Neil Rowe

Development Editor
Mark Renfrow

Managing Editor
Kristy Hart

Project Editor
Anne Goebel

Copy Editor
Water Crest Publishing, Inc.

Indexer
Lisa Stumpf

Technical Editor
Rory McCaw

Publishing Coordinator
Cindy Teeters

Book Designer
Gary Adair

Contents at a Glance

Table of Contents

Foreword

To all of our customers…In 2000, Microsoft acquired a technology license for the software that became Microsoft Operations Manager (MOM) 2000 and later MOM 2005. In ten years, things have changed. Long gone are those days where applications lived on standalone web servers; instead there is a new era of distributed applications, spread across multiple devices including both Windows and non-Windows platforms. This is the reality of the data center, and it is where Microsoft needs to be for our customers.

When designing System Center Operations Manager 2007, we realized we needed to answer some questions on how to tie all this together and create relationships between objects that constructed these applications. Messaging, for example, consists of many parts, like storage, servers, services, and devices. On the same note, we needed to build and enhance native management packs for key workloads such as SharePoint, SQL Server, and Active Directory—applications business critical to the success of our customers.

Operations Manager 2007, the successor to MOM 2005, allowed the server to take a back seat in the monitoring space and brought to light a new notion of monitoring objects. This required some fundamental architectural changes; for example, management packs are no longer in binary format, but rather XML. This required customers to reinvest in management pack authoring and tooling because, architecturally speaking, our design was so different, and most legacy management packs couldn't convert cleanly. Making big investments in performance and scale was paramount, including the number of agents supported per management group and management server. We extended scale for URL monitoring in bulk by adopting the Bulk URL Editor (BUE) tool. We added process monitoring and extended functionality around service monitoring, and provided SLA reports and dashboards—key to enabling our customers to have the "big picture" overview of service management.

We always envisioned monitoring the data center and to achieve this needed to reach our Unix and Linux operators. We had to meet this group in the middle and decided to build our agent on open source technologies, namely OpenPegasus. In non-traditional Microsoft fashion, we open sourced our providers and are working toward submitting our changes to the OpenPegasus group for integration into their code. Today, OpsMgr 2007 R2 supports over 19 non-Windows platforms, including Red Hat and Solaris. We needed to make it easy to find and import management packs from the console—so with the R2 release you can now import and install management packs using the integrated web service that automatically resolves dependencies on the fly. Users missed the MOM 2005 capability to right-click an alert and create a notification subscription—we added it. Users wanted the ability to view the Health Explorer from the Web console—we added that. Users wanted an Override summary to help manage their overrides—we added this as well.

Our Microsoft Management Pack ecosystem continues to thrive with over 100 application and server management packs, including key workloads such as Exchange, SQL, BizTalk, Hyper-V, Windows Server, IIS, and SharePoint. The external ISV partners are steadily growing in numbers. Solutions such as management packs, connectors, and tools help our customers monitor applications like Oracle, SAP, MySQL, VMWare, JBoss, and Apache; devices like Cisco, APC, and Juniper; and hardware from IHVs. These connect to all sorts of other enterprise management products, help desks, and much more. We do this to enable you to have the best monitoring environment possible using the Microsoft platform!

—*Justin Incarnato, Microsoft*

Preface

System Center Operations Manager (OpsMgr) 2007, released in March 2007, was a complete rewrite of the Microsoft Operations Manager 2005 product, monitoring Windows operating systems and applications. Unlike MOM 2005, Operations Manager 2007 focuses on the health of applications and components, as opposed to looking at the status of individual servers.

Its first service pack (March 2008; released just as *System Center Operations Manager 2007 Unleashed* was published) smoothed out some of the more glaring problems introduced with the base release. In May 2008, Microsoft announced the Cross Platform Extensions (X-Plat) for OpsMgr 2007 as part of a second service pack anticipated for 2009. The X-Plat capabilities enable monitoring non-Windows platforms (Linux/Unix), incorporated into the OpsMgr interface.

Microsoft later decided to bundle X-Plat with other enhancements and bug fixes into a R2 release, publicly announced at TechEd/ITForum in November 2008, and released on May 22, 2009. These other enhancements include, but are not limited to, the following:

- Windows 2008, IIS 7, and SQL Server 2008 platform

- Updated management packs for monitoring operating systems, services, and applications

- New templates for ease of use

- Improved process monitoring and maintenance mode support

- Additional functionality for the Web console, now able to access the health explorer to drill-down into health of individual components

- A more intuitive reporting interface, making it easier to generate reports

- Performance enhancements

This work, a supplement to *System Center Operations Manager 2007 Unleashed*, provides in-depth reference and technical information about Microsoft System Operations Manager 2007 including its R2 release, as well as information on other products and technologies on which its features and components are dependent.

Chapter 1, "Introduction and What's New," takes up where the original *System Center Operations Manager 2007* ended, bringing you up to date on changes with SP 1 and introducing the R2 release. Chapter 2, "Unix/Linux Management: Cross Platform Extensions," jumps into the most publicized change in R2: those cross platform extensions that allow Unix/Linux management. Chapters 3, "Operations Manager 2007 R2 and Windows Server 2008," and 4, "Using SQL Server 2008 in OpsMgr 2007 R2," discuss using Windows Server 2008 and SQL Server 2008 in OpsMgr 2007 R2.

The next set of chapters discusses intertwined technologies. Chapter 5, "PowerShell Extensions for Operations Manager 2007," covers PowerShell and the OpsMgr Shell, Chapter 6, "Management Solutions for Small and Midsize Business," looks at management approaches for smaller-sized businesses, and Chapter 7, "Operations Manager and Virtualization," discusses virtualization.

The last two chapters take a "deep dive" into several areas of Operations Manager 2007. This includes authoring, discussed in Chapter 8, "Management Pack Authoring," and high availability, business continuity, the new Visio add-in, ACS in-depth, and targeting, covered in Chapter 9, "Unleashing Operations Manager 2007." These topics are presented by subject-matter experts in each area.

In keeping with being supplemental to *System Center Operations Manager 2007 Unleashed*, Appendix A, "OpsMgr R2 by Example," is an update of the *OpsMgr by Example* series published with the first book, and Appendix B, "Reference URLs," updates reference URLs, with nearly 250 useful links. Several chapters reference additional online content, which is described in Appendix C, "Available Online." You can download the online content from http://www.informit.com/store/product.aspx?isbn=0672331179.

System administrators in both Windows and Linux/Unix platforms should be interested in learning about the cross platform monitoring capabilities. The material will continue to be of interest for those shops that have not yet migrated from MOM 2005 to OpsMgr 2007, and the new material in this book will be of interest to those who previously purchased *System Center Operations Manager 2007 Unleashed*.

About the Authors

Kerrie Meyler, Operations Manager MVP, is an independent consultant and trainer with more than 15 years of Information Technology experience, including work as a senior technical specialist at Microsoft. Kerrie is the lead author of *Microsoft System Center Operations Manager 2007 Unleashed* (Sams, 2008), *System Center Configuration Manager 2007 Unleashed* (Sams, 2009), and *Operations Manager 2005 Unleashed* (Sams, 2006). She participated in the alpha walkthrough for Microsoft Certification Exam 70-400, "Configuring Microsoft System Center Operations Manager 2007." Kerrie has presented at numerous Microsoft conferences, including TechEd 2007 and MMS 2009.

Cameron Fuller, Operations Manager MVP, is a Principal Consultant for Catapult Systems, an IT consulting company and Microsoft Gold Certified Partner. He focuses on management solutions, with 15 years of infrastructure experience. Cameron is co-author of *System Center Operations Manager 2007 Unleashed* (Sams, 2008) and *Microsoft Operations Manager 2005 Unleashed* (Sams, 2006), and a contributor to *System Center Configuration Manager 2007 Unleashed* (Sams, 2009). Cameron has presented at numerous Microsoft conferences, TechEd 2005/2007/2008, and MMS 2008/2009.

John Joyner, Operations Manager MVP, is a senior architect at ClearPointe, a provider of remote server management and hosted Network Operations Center (NOC) services based on Operations Manager to customers and partners around the world since 2001. John is a co-author of *System Center Operations Manager 2007 Unleashed* (Sams, 2008) and contributing author of *Microsoft Operations Manager 2005 Unleashed* (Sams, 2006). John presented on Microsoft systems management technologies at the Worldwide Partner Conference Denver 2007, ITForum Barcelona 2007, and MMS 2008. He was the Track External Advisor for the Virtualization track at TechEd 2009.

Andy Dominey, Operations Manager MVP from 2006 to2009, is currently working as a Principal Operations Manager Consultant at 1E, a Microsoft Partner specializing in Windows Management. Andy is a contributing author to *System Center Operations Manager 2007 Unleashed* (Sams, 2008) and co-authored *Microsoft Operations Manager 2005 Field Guide* (Apress, 2006). Andy has written various magazine articles and hosted TechNet webcasts highlighting the technology. He has also worked with Microsoft, making substantial contributions to high-availability aspects of OpsMgr 2007. Andy co-presented with Kerrie at MMS 2009.

Dedication

To Justin Incarnato, the heartbeat of the OpsMgr community.
—With deep thanks from Kerrie, Cameron, John, and Andy

Acknowledgments

This book would not be possible without the help of many individuals. The authors would like to thank (in alphabetical order) Jeremiah Beckett, Justin Incarnato, Cleber Marques, Steve Rachui, Marco Shaw, Alexandre Verkinderen, and Pete Zerger for assisting with content. Thanks also to Raymond Chou, Maarten Goet, Barry Shilmover, Marnix Wolf, and Alexey Zhuravlev for their input, and Rory McCaw for being our technical editor. And of course, thanks to the entire OpsMgr product team at Microsoft and our fellow Operations Manager MVPs!

In addition, we would like to thank ClearPointe Technology for the use of lab equipment supporting the environment used throughout this book, and Roger Myers from Sun Systems both for his loan of Sun equipment and for his assistance with debugging the OpsMgr deployment in Unix/Linux.

Thanks also go to the staff at Pearson, in particular to Neil Rowe, who has worked with us since *Microsoft Operations Manager 2005 Unleashed* (Sams, 2006).

We Want to Hear from You!

As the reader of this book, *you* are our most important critic and commentator. We value your opinion and want to know what we're doing right, what we could do better, what areas you'd like to see us publish in, and any other words of wisdom you're willing to pass our way.

You can email or write me directly to let me know what you did or didn't like about this book—as well as what we can do to make our books stronger.

Please note that I cannot help you with technical problems related to the topic of this book, and that due to the high volume of mail I receive, I might not be able to reply to every message.

When you write, please be sure to include this book's title and author as well as your name and phone or email address. I will carefully review your comments and share them with the author and editors who worked on the book.

Email: feedback@samspublishing.com

Mail: Neil Rowe
Executive Editor
Sams Publishing
800 East 96th Street
Indianapolis, IN 46240 USA

Reader Services

Visit our website and register this book at informit.com/register for convenient access to any updates, downloads, or errata that might be available for this book.

CHAPTER 1

Introduction and What's New

In March 2007, Microsoft released System Center Operations Manager (OpsMgr) 2007, developed under the codename Microsoft Operations Manager (MOM) V3. OpsMgr 2007 is completely re-architected and is a total rewrite from its MOM 2005 predecessor. In fact, it is so much of a rewrite that many longtime MOM 2005 administrators and fans feared the worst for the new version in terms of stability and performance—and there were definitely some early issues with the released to manufacturing (RTM) build. However, OpsMgr 2007 has come of age, as evidenced by Gartner Group's July 2009 Magic Quadrant for IT Event Correlation and Analysis report (https://h10078.www1.hp.com/bto/download/Gartner_Magic_Quadrant_IT_Event_Corr_Analysis.pdf), which, similar to their December 2007 report (http://mediaproducts.gartner.com/reprints/microsoft/vol10/article2and3/article2and3.html), places Operations Manager 2007 R2 firmly in the Challengers quadrant (see Figure 1.1).

The gist of the Gartner report is that OpsMgr 2007 contains some major enhancements in comparison to the functionality in MOM 2005, with a focus in monitoring Windows environments. Gartner notes that the R2 release adds non-Windows management, but suggests it still has a way to go when managing non-Microsoft IT elements. This appears to be at least in part because Microsoft relies on third parties to provide management packs to monitor non-Microsoft applications. Microsoft provides the technology to manage Unix/Linux operating systems, but in terms of application monitoring chooses to focus on its own applications such as Exchange, SQL Server, Active Directory, and Internet Information Services. (See Chapter 2, "Unix/Linux Management: Cross Platform Extensions," for a discussion on Unix/Linux integration.)

System Center Operations Manager 2007 Unleashed, the predecessor to this book, was published in February 2008, just as Microsoft released OpsMgr 2007 Service Pack (SP) 1. Although that book tried to the best of its ability to cover all the improvements in the service pack by discussing enhancements as of the SP 1 Release Candidate (RC), Microsoft added several changes to the released version that were not in the RC. Therefore, this book takes up where the previous leaves off—with a summary of the SP 1 changes, an in-depth look at the R2 release, and a "deep dive" into some of the key capabilities of OpsMgr 2007 through Cumulative Update 2 (CU2) for R2.

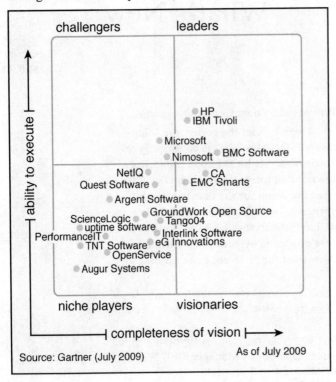

FIGURE 1.1 Gartner's Magic Quadrants for IT Event Correlation and Analysis, December 2007

This chapter highlights the changes to Operations Manager 2007, beginning with the release of SP 1.

Licensing Updates

There are two areas to be cognizant of regarding licensing and OpsMgr 2007 R2—licensing for the System Center Server Management Suite and licensing of cross platform applications. The next sections discuss this information.

Licensing Changes to the System Center Server Management Suite

In conjunction with the R2 release, Microsoft is changing licensing for the System Center Server Management Suite. Here are the products included in this suite:

- ► System Center Operations Manager 2007
- ► System Center Operations Manager 2007 R2
- ► System Center Data Protection Manager 2007
- ► System Center Virtual Machine Manager 2008
- ► System Center Virtual Machine Manager 2008 Management Server License

The July 2009 changes to Server Management Suite licensing include the following:

- ► The System Center Server Management Suite Enterprise (SMSE) offering changes from an unlimited operating system environment to a four-system operating system environment, limited license, with a corresponding 20 percent price decrease.

- ► A new suite offering System Center Server Management Suite Datacenter (SMSD) includes the same products as SMSE, but is licensed per processor and provides for managing an unlimited number of operating system environments.

OpsMgr 2007 will continue to use Standard and Enterprise Server management licenses (MLs). Here is when you do not need a ML:

- ► Any Operating System Environments (OSEs) running instances of the server software on your licensed servers
- ► Any OSEs in which no instances of software are running
- ► System Center Data Protection Manager 2007
- ► Any devices functioning only as network infrastructure devices (OSI Layer 3 or below)
- ► Any devices for which you are exclusively performing out-of-band management

Microsoft provides the following links with more detailed information. You will want to check them for updates:

- ► **Product Licensing Web and Product Use Rights—**
  http://www.microsoftvolumelicensing.com/userights/PUR.aspx.

- ► **Operations Management Licensing—**
  http://www.microsoft.com/systemcenter/operationsmanager/en/us/operations-management-licensing.aspx.

- ► **Pricing and Licensing—**
  http://www.microsoft.com/systemcenter/operationsmanager/en/us/pricing-licensing.aspx.

- ►

Licensing of Cross Platform Applications

The other area of consideration is whether cross-platform monitoring requires a Standard or Enterprise ML. According to Microsoft, if an application is monitored, the license required is Enterprise ML regardless if it is a Microsoft or non-Microsoft application. As an example, if you are just monitoring a Linux server, you need a Standard ML. If that Linux Server is running a Bridgeways MP for MySQL, you must purchase an Enterprise ML to monitor the application. This also means that should you create a monitor that monitors an application process or service (on any operating system), you would need to purchase an Enterprise ML to license it correctly.

New in Service Pack 1

Service Pack 1 is available from Microsoft both as a standalone executable file for upgrading an existing OpsMgr 2007 installation, and a slipstreamed installation enabling you to install both OpsMgr 2007 and the service pack at the same time. Both versions are available for x86 and x64 (32- and 64-bit) computer systems. The link at http://technet.microsoft.com/en-us/opsmgr/cc280350.aspx lets you download the slipstreamed evaluation copy of SP 1 and the SP 1 upgrade bits for existing installations.

Those bugs fixed with the SP 1 release are listed in Knowledge Base (KB) article 944443, at http://support.microsoft.com/default.aspx/kb/944443. In addition, Microsoft now has an update rollup for SP 1, available at http://www.microsoft.com/downloads/details.aspx?FamilyID=05d7785d-fe69-48bc-8dfa-72a77c8936bf&displaylang=en. This combines previous hotfix releases for SP 1 with additional fixes and support of SP 1 roles on Windows 7 and Windows Server 2008 R2. The update also provides database role and SQL Server Reporting Services upgrade support from SQL Server 2005 to SQL Server 2008.

SP 1 Highlights

OpsMgr 2007 SP 1 updates and enhancements include the following:

► Improved performance and stability for alerts, overrides, and searches:

> ► Improved fetching capabilities have increased the performance of alert views.

> ► Alert row selection is up to three times faster than in the base release.

> ► Search improvements enable the ability to perform advanced searches across monitors and rules by their overrides.

► Support for Simple Network Management Protocol (SNMP) v1 network devices. The base release supported SNMP v2 only. The discovery wizard allows you to select which SNMP version to use.

► Capability to export Operations Manager 2007 diagrams to Microsoft Visio XML Diagram (VDX) file format.

▶ A Visio button is located on the toolbar in the diagram view. Diagram layouts can be saved and are remembered when that view is selected again.

▶ Support for copy and paste (CTRL C and CTRL V functions) from the Alert details pane.

▶ Support for earlier versions of email servers, correcting an issue that could result in malformed data in the subject line of email notifications.

▶ Ability to copy views from an existing management pack to an unsealed management pack.

▶ Overrides Summary Box enables you to view overrides for an object.

▶ Ability to use scripts with diagnostic tasks.

▶ Incorporates the OpsMgr VSS Writer Service, enabling you to create shadow copies.

▶ Ability to publish reports to multiple locations—for example, Microsoft Windows SharePoint Services websites.

▶ Ability to view performance data through the Operations Manager Web console, with filters for desired performance counters to ease searching and navigation.

▶ Increase in the number of command notifications that can be handled simultaneously from 5 in OpsMgr 2007 SP 1 to 200 in the R2 release. This is configurable in the Registry by creating a key at HKEY_LOCAL_MACHINE\ Software\Microsoft\Microsoft OperationsManager\3.0\Modules\Global\ Command Executer\AsyncProcessLimit REG_DWORD:0x0000000a. Note that every command notification triggered will start a monitoringhost.exe process on the root management server (RMS); this can lead to memory and processor issues if you do not have enough memory and processor power to support it.

▶ New discoveries and views added to the Audit Collection Services (ACS), along with new monitors and alerts to track the health of ACS collectors.

▶ Support for clustering the ACS database.

Gateway Enhancements

With the base release of OpsMgr 2007, gateway servers only supported a maximum of 200 agents, making them unsuitable for any purpose other than monitoring DMZs and small untrusted networks. Beginning with SP 1, gateways have been tested to 800 agents and, depending on the hardware configuration and WAN link specifics, could theoretically support many more. Although management servers are able to support up to 2,000 servers since SP 1, gateways are a welcome alternative in complex, distributed environments, as they forward compressed data from multiple agents to a management server using a sustained connection; the management server then manages the connection to the database. More information on how gateway servers can help in a distributed environment is available in Chapter 9, "Unleashing Operations Manager 2007."

Clustered RMS Enhancements

With SP 1, Microsoft tried to make the RMS recovery story a bit better. New with the
OpsMgr 2007 architecture, the RMS is a single point of failure; one approach to allevi-
ate that is to cluster the RMS. However, if your clustered RMS failed in the RTM release and you then promoted a management server to become the RMS, you were
unable to later repromote the failed cluster to the RMS role. This was remedied in
SP 1. See Chapter 9 for a discussion on RMS high availability.

RMS Encryption Key Backup

One of the more vocal criticisms of the OpsMgr 2007 RTM was its single point of failure with the RMS. If the RMS fails and there is no backup of the encryption key, you
must reinstall the entire management group! SP 1 adds the Secure Storage Backup
Wizard at the end of the OpsMgr setup process, displayed in Figure 1.2, providing a
backup the RMS encryption key.

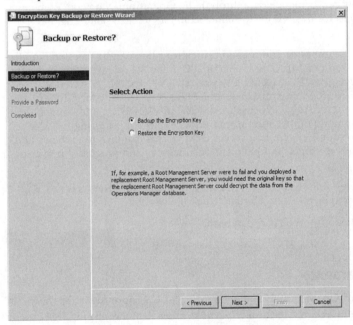

FIGURE 1.2 Option to back up RMS key after OpsMgr installation

You will use this key if you need to recover an Operations Manager management
group; without a copy of the key, you cannot recover your Operations Manager environment. Prior to SP 1, there was no automated process to back up the encryption key.

OpsMgr 2007 SP 1 also introduces a CREATE_NEWKEY command switch to make
recovery easier. Details on this application are available on the Manageability Team

Blog at http://blogs.technet.com/smsandmom/archive/2007/12/05/opsmgr-2007-what-if-i-lose-my-rms-encryption-key.aspx.

The best practice is to back up your RMS key, so accept the default configuration at the completion screen to start the Encryption Key Backup or Restore Wizard. The wizard first displays an introduction screen, and then asks if you want to back up or restore the key, as shown in Figure 1.3.

The wizard continues by asking where to back up the RMS key, asks for a password, and then completes the process. It is highly recommended to store a copy of the backup key on your other management servers so it is local in the event of an emergency. Also, ensure that the password for the key is stored with the key; otherwise, you will not be able to restore the key.

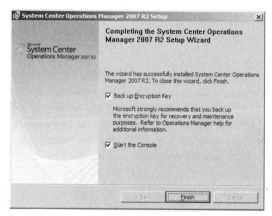

FIGURE 1.3 Encryption Key Backup or Restore Wizard

R2 Highlights and Capabilities

The Gartner Group report on OpsMgr 2007, referenced at the beginning of this chapter, notes the product's greatest weakness to be its lack of monitoring non-Microsoft platforms. Historically, Operations Manager 2007's strength is in monitoring the Windows environment and lessens when managing non-Microsoft IT systems and devices, whether using Microsoft or third-party add-ons to provide management capabilities. Enter the R2 release—which incorporates cross-platform monitoring!

At the Microsoft Management Summit (MMS) in 2008, Microsoft's annual conference on managing the Windows platform, Microsoft announced the upcoming enhancement of cross-platform monitoring, also known as X-Plat. Not only was OpsMgr going to change to encompass monitoring of non-Windows platforms, but the code would be open source. To add some humor to what was a seismic shift in direction by the company (pigs would fly!), Microsoft distributed pigs…with wings, an illustration of which is displayed in Figure 1.4.

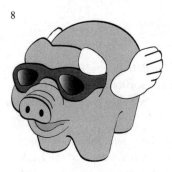

FIGURE 1.4 Pigs flew when Microsoft announced cross-platform monitoring for OpsMgr.

X-Plat was initially going to be part of a service pack; however, at TechEd-Europe in November 2008, Microsoft announced that X-Plat and other changes would be bundled into an R2 release.

In addition to extending OpsMgr 2007 monitoring capabilities to Unix and Linux environments using the familiar Operations Manager console, R2's integration with System Center Virtual Machine Manager (VMM) 2008 enables maximizing availability of virtual workloads. But that's not all—in addition to getting a facelift with new skins (see Figure 1.5), the R2 release includes numerous other performance and functionality enhancements. R2 also resolves quite a few bugs and incorporates a number of hotfixes— see KB article 971410 at http://support.microsoft.com/kb/971410/ for the list.

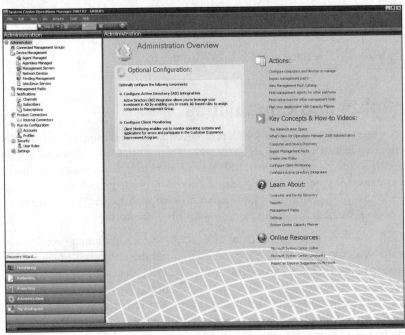

FIGURE 1.5 The new skin of the R2 Operations console

NOTE: RENAMED COMPONENTS AND SERVICES

As part of the OpsMgr R2 release, Microsoft has renamed the Operations Manager Command Shell to Operations Manager Shell. The three Windows services used in OpsMgr deployments are renamed as well:

▶ The OpsMgr SDK Service is now System Center Data Access.

▶ The OpsMgr Health Service became System Center Management.

▶ The OpsMgr Config Service is System Center Management Configuration.

Successive chapters of this book cover in detail many of the new features in R2, with the remainder of this chapter discussing those topics not discussed elsewhere.

Importing Management Packs

Both MOM 2005 and OpsMgr 2007 support downloading management packs (MPs) from the System Center Management Pack Catalog (http://pinpoint.microsoft.com/en-US/systemcenter/managementpackcatalog) using a web browser outside the Operations Manager console. New with R2 is the capability to download MPs within the Administration node in the console. To download management packs from the OpsMgr console, perform the following steps:

1. In the OpsMgr console, navigate to Administration -> Management Packs. From the Actions pane on the right side, select the Download Management Packs task to open the Download Management Packs wizard.

2. The first screen of the wizard asks you to select a local folder in which to store the downloaded management packs. Click on the Browse button to browse to a folder such as c:\Management Packs.

3. Now, click the Add button in Figure 1.6 to find the management packs you want to download.

4. When selecting management packs, the search criterion in the View section of the Select Management Packs from Catalog page enables you to select one of the following search options:

   ▶ All management packs in the catalog

   ▶ Updates available for installed management packs

   ▶ All management packs released within three months

   ▶ All management packs released within six months

   For this example, the search is for updates to installed management packs. Figure 1.7 shows the results.

5. You can expand the categories to see the specific management packs available within each area. Click on the Add button in Figure 1.7 to select specific management packs.

FIGURE 1.6 Select the Add button to add management packs to the download list.

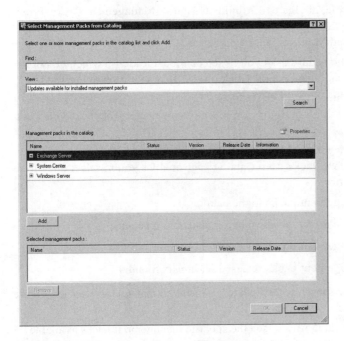

FIGURE 1.7 The list of installed management pack updates shows updates for Exchange, System Center, and Windows.

If there are dependencies on other management packs or versions, you will be alerted to this in the download wizard and can select to download those to resolve the issue. Should a management pack contain potentially harmful content, it will alert you to this as well and allow you to view that content.

6. Complete your selection, and then select OK to view the download list and begin the download. Figure 1.8 shows the download list for the Hyper-V 2008 management pack.

7. After downloading the management packs to disk, you can use the Import Management Packs task in the Actions pane to import the management packs into your management group.

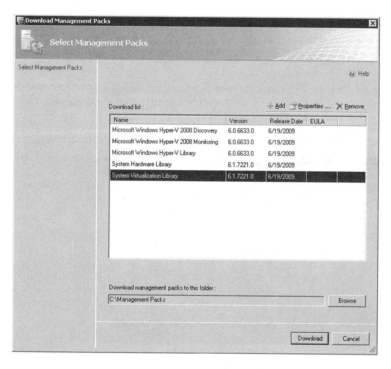

FIGURE 1.8 The list of management packs to download

New and Updated Templates

A *template* serves as a starting point. OpsMgr 2007 provides templates for several object types to help make it easier to create custom objects. R2 brings additions and enhancements to the templates existing in the RTM and SP 1 releases of OpsMgr 2007. The next sections discuss the Process Monitoring Template, Windows Service Management Pack Template, and OLE DB Management Pack Template. You will find the list of Management Pack templates in the Authoring node of the Operations Manager console. This list will vary based on the management packs loaded into your management group. Other templates new to R2 include Unix/Linux LogFile and Unix/Linux

Service. To initiate the wizard for any of the Management Pack templates, right-click on that template, choose Add Monitoring Wizard, and then select the monitoring type.

Process Monitoring Template

Prior to R2, there were ways to monitor processes, but they were a bit clunky and required custom monitors and scripts. The authors of *System Center Operations Manager 2007 Unleashed* have firsthand experience with this, as they wrote a process monitor available with that book! The new Process Monitoring template enables you to specify a number of criteria when monitoring a process, as follows:

▶ Defining scenarios both for processes you want and for unwanted processes.

▶ Targeting a group; this narrows the scope of the monitor.

▶ Specifying the minimum and maximum number of process instances and duration, and choosing to generate an alert if the process runs longer than that duration.

▶ Generating an alert if CPU usage or memory usage exceeds a specified threshold, and indicating the number of consecutive samples that should exceed a threshold before generating an alert.

Figure 1.9 shows part of the configuration of a monitor created using this template.

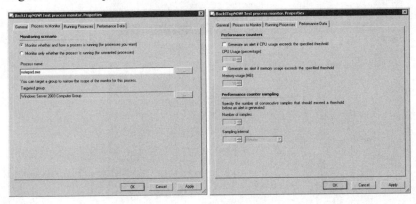

FIGURE 1.9 Using the OpsMgr 2007 R2 Process Monitoring template

Windows Service Management Pack Template

The Windows Service template lets you discover and monitor a Windows service by doing little more than typing in the service name. This template was first available with the RTM version of OpsMgr 2007 and performs the following two functions:

▶ Creates a new class (target) for your service

▶ Creates a discovery to find instances of that new class

The RTM release had several issues, as follows:

▶ There was no support for wildcards, although Brian Wren's article at http://blogs.technet.com/brianwren/archive/2008/03/07/using-wildcards-with-the-windows-service-template.aspx presents a solution replacing the discovery with a WMI discovery module providing wildcard support.

▶ The template only enabled you to select services created with SERVICE_WIN32_OWN_PROCESS; monitoring other services required creating a unit monitor.

The R2 version enables wildcard entry to select multiple, similarly named services.

OLE DB Management Pack Template

Enhancements to the OLE DB template allow operators to identify the database and set thresholds for connection, query, and fetch times (see Figure 1.10), and to type or paste a custom query to run against the remote OLE DB data source. You can use this template to simulate synthetic transactions from a user perspective.

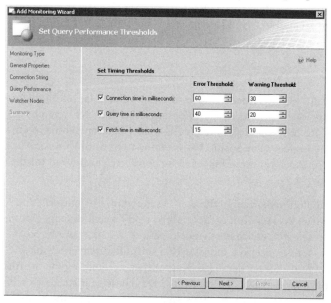

FIGURE 1.10 Setting Timing Thresholds in the OLE DB Management Pack template

Note that if you created an OLE DB monitor using an earlier release of OpsMgr 2007, you must upgrade it to the new template before saving any additional changes to the monitor. Open the Properties page to upgrade the template automatically; then click OK at the end of the upgrade process.

User Interface

Operations console performance is greatly improved in R2. Here are the areas where improvements are most evident:

- ► Opening new views in the monitoring space

- ► Pivoting between views

- ► Selecting multiple items in the Results view and rendering the Details pane more quickly

- ► Indicating that a view is in the progress of loading

Other interface enhancements include the Overrides Summary and a search tool to assist in creating dashboard views:

- ► The Overrides Summary View enables you to view all rule and monitor overrides for sealed and unsealed management packs, and you can customize it by grouping items by multiple column headers.

- ► When you create a dashboard view, you populate the different panes in the dashboard with individual, existing views. The R2 release provides a search tool you can use to find the views you want quickly. The search also includes views that you have created in My Workspace.

Run As

With Operations Manager 2007 R2, Microsoft added distribution and targeting features for Run As Accounts and Run As Profiles. When you associate a Run As Account with a particular Run As Profile, R2 lets you target the profile to any class available in Operations Manager and see the logical relationship between the two. Both Run As Account distribution and Run As Account targeting must be correctly configured for the Run As Profile to work properly.

You can specify which computers will receive the Run As Account credentials. You can choose to distribute the Run As Account credentials to every agent-managed computer (less secure) or only to selected computers (more secure). As an example, say you have a script that runs as a response to a monitor or a script that performs some level of monitoring against a SQL Server database. Rather than associating the profile with the agent, you can choose to associate the profile with a database instance or with the SQL Server Database Engine for that agent. This enables you to target the profile by group, object, or instance class. Chapter 9 discusses how targeting works. For additional information on Run As Profiles and Run As Accounts, see http://technet.microsoft.com/en-us/library/bb735423.aspx.

IIS 7 and ASP.NET 64-Bit Apps

R2 adds support for monitoring Internet Information Services (IIS) 7, without having to enable the backward compatibility APIs or legacy management features. Operations Manager 2007 R2 also discovers and monitors 64-bit ASP.NET applications running on IIS servers.

Large-Scale Monitoring of URLs

R2 now supports up to 2,000 URL monitors per management server. The overall capacity of URL monitors increases commensurately for the management group.

Maintenance Mode

R2 streamlines the process of placing a computer and all its related objects into maintenance mode, as follows:

▶ You can put an entire computer into Maintenance mode—This automatically puts the Health Service and the associated Health Service watcher into maintenance mode, which suppresses all alerts on that computer.

▶ Management pack authors can specify what should be included in an alert and how it is formed when a monitor comes out of maintenance mode.

▶ Alerts are generated on HealthService heartbeat failures after exiting out of maintenance mode.

32-Bit Performance Counter Support on 64-Bit Systems

When running 32-bit applications on a 64-bit operating system (OS), unless the pre-R2 OpsMgr agent is 32-bit, you cannot monitor those applications. However, if you are running the 32-bit agent, you will not be able to monitor 64-bit applications or the OS itself. OpsMgr 2007 R2 incorporates a module change, allowing management packs to query the 32-bit registry hive on a 64-bit Windows installation to perform discoveries successfully. This change is also available in a SP 1 hotfix.

Configuration Manager (ConfigMgr) 2007 is one example of a 32-bit application that has trouble being monitored in a 64-bit environment prior to OpsMgr 2007 R2. The ConfigMgr 2007 management pack for OpsMgr 2007 R2 is updated to take advantage of the new discovery method. ConfigMgr 2007 SP 2 will also have native 64-bit performance counters added.

Web Console (Health Explorer)

R2 adds the Health Explorer to the Web console, giving the Web console operational parity with the Operations Manager console for monitoring capabilities. Figure 1.11 displays the Web Health Explorer for one of the servers in the domain used in this book: Odyssey.com.

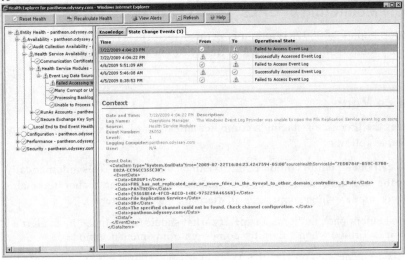

FIGURE 1.11 Viewing the Health Explorer using the R2 Web console

Notification Subscription Wizard

R2 totally restructures the notification feature, making it easier to set up notifications. The Notifications folder in the Administration node contains folders for Channels, Subscribers, and Subscriptions:

▶ A notification is sent by channels; examples are SMTP, instant messaging, or command.

▶ Subscribers are the entities that receive a notification; an example is user@odyssey.com.

▶ Subscriptions describe what the subscriber will be notified of and the schedule for those notifications.

As before, you can create new channels and subscribers prior to configuring a subscription. However, the New Subscription Wizard enables creating new channels and subscribers if the one you want to use does not already exist. Figure 1.12 displays the Notification Subscription Wizard. After specifying the notification criteria, you can create new subscribers or select existing ones.

The next step of the wizard enables you to create a channel.

R2 also provides the capability to create a new subscription directly from an alert and to add the parameters from the selected alert to an existing subscription. This significantly improves efficiency and reduces human error in remembering and incorrectly typing the required string!

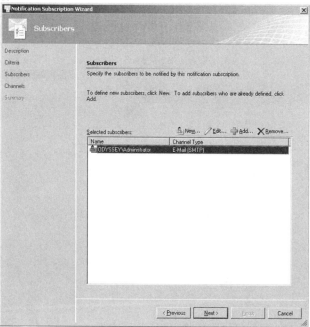

FIGURE 1.12 The R2 Notification Subscription Wizard

Service Level Monitoring

You can use the Service Level Tracking Wizard to define thresholds known as Service Level Objectives (SLOs), enabling you to classify monitors and rules to compare the availability and performance of monitored applications. In the Authoring node of the Operations console, navigate to Management Pack Objects -> Service Level Tracking to define thresholds for a Service Level Agreement (SLA) and create SLOs to represent this SLA. Figure 1.13 displays the Service Level Objectives page of the Service Level Tracking Wizard:

► The threshold definition for Availability is created using a Monitor State SLO (see Figure 1.14).

► The Threshold definition for Performance is created with a Collection Rule SLO (see Figure 1.15).

After creating these thresholds, the Service Level Tracking Summary Report will compare SLO thresholds with monitored data from the OpsMgr Reporting database.

NOTE: SERVICE LEVEL TRACKING PREREQUISITES

Using Service Level Tracking requires an OpsMgr 2007 R2 environment implemented with OpsMgr Reporting and defined service levels to ensure proper representation in reports and dashboards.

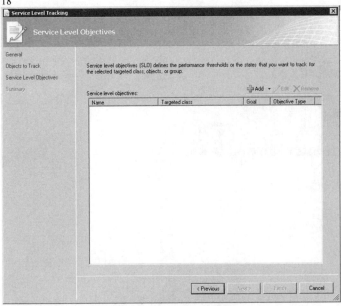

FIGURE 1.13 Adding a Service Level Objective while creating a SLA

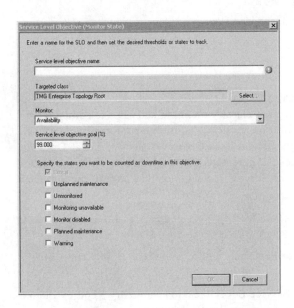

FIGURE 1.14 Define the thresholds to track.

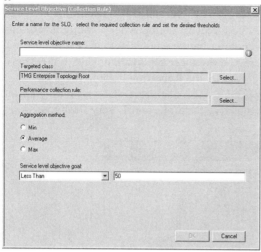

FIGURE 1.15 Define the Collection Rule for the Service Level Objective.

THE SERVICE LEVEL DASHBOARD

Service Level Dashboard (SLD) 2.0 is a Solution Accelerator. Solution Accelerators are tools with best practices used by Microsoft, its customers, and partners that provide prescriptive guidance. The Dashboard was introduced with OpsMgr 2007 SP 1 and is enhanced in R2 with version 2.0. Here are the new features:

▶ Monitoring in near real time (2–3 minutes)

▶ Integration with Windows SharePoint Services (WSS) 3.0 and Microsoft Office SharePoint Server (MOSS) 2007

▶ Utilization of OpsMgr 2007 R2 Service Level Objectives

▶ New metrics include Mean Time To Repair (MTTR) and Mean Time Between Failures (MTBF)

Here are the prerequisites to install SLD 2.0:

▶ Operations Manager 2007 R2 (with OpsMgr Reporting)

▶ WSS 3.0 SP 1 or MOSS 2007 SP 1

▶ SQL Server 2005 SP 2 or higher or SQL Server 2008

▶ Microsoft .NET Framework 3.5 and Internet Explorer 6.0 or higher

To download a step-by-step guide and the SLD 2.0 installation files, see http://www.microsoft.com/downloads/details.aspx?FamilyId=1d9d709f-9628-46a8-952b-a78f5dd2bdd9.

Reporting Enhancements

R2 adds a number of long-awaited and requested features for reporting users and authors, as follows:

► **Service Level Tracking Reporting**—The "Service Level Monitoring" section discussed how R2 provides Service Level Tracking. After creating thresholds, you can run the tracking reports comparing thresholds with state and performance data collected by the system. To run these reports, navigate to the Microsoft Service Level Report Library under the Reporting node in the OpsMgr console. The Service Level Tracking Report compares SLOs with the monitored data. The Service Level Objective Detail Report is very flashy, and is displayed in Figure 1.16.

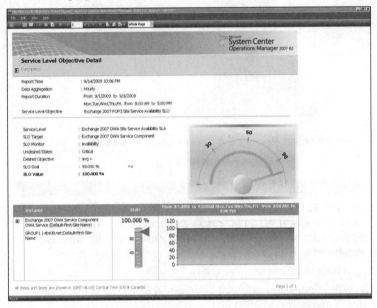

FIGURE 1.16 Service Level Tracking Objective Detail Report

► **Saving Reports to a Management Pack**—You can save reports to an existing management pack, enabling you to share a report using a specific set of parameters. See http://technet.microsoft.com/en-us/library/dd789017.aspx for details. As mentioned in this reference, a management pack with a saved report to another management group using a different data warehouse requires you to save the report again for it to function properly.

► **Report Object Picker**—Object picker enhancements allow searching and filtering by name or class of object, making it easier to find the objects needed to retrieve data. Filter settings are applied under the Options button for both the Add Objects and Add Group functions, and the feature enables you to select only certain (meaningful) classes of objects. Figure 1.17 illustrates this using a report in the SQL Server 2008 management pack. The Options button was selected in the previous dialog, bringing up the SQL 2008 DB Engine as the only valid object to select for this report.

This feature has the most value when the list of supported classes is defined in a management pack. However, only newer releases of management packs take advantage of this capability.

> ► **Authoring Console Support**—The Authoring console now includes a Reporting space, exposing all available reporting elements.

> ► **Enhanced Most Common Events Report**—R2 adds multi-selection parameters to this report.

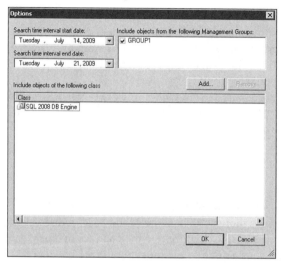

FIGURE 1.17 The R2 Report Object Picker automatically displays the objects of interest for you to select.

Recalculating and Resetting Monitor States

The Health Explorer includes the ability to force the agent to recalculate the health of a particular monitor. One of the most common uses for this is when you want to confirm that the action that you took actually fixed the problem. If the management pack is correctly implemented, all you need to do is select the unit monitor in Health Explorer and click on the "Recalculate Health" button.

Health Explorer also includes a Reset Health button. The behavior of these buttons has varied during the different updates of OpsMgr 2007, and has pretty much been a moving target:

> ► At OpsMgr 2007 RTM, the interface only had a Reset button, which actually did a Recalculate, but only if on-demand detection was defined by the management pack. It did not do a Reset (for further information, see Chapter 14, "Monitoring with Operations Manager," in *System Center Operations Manager 2007 Unleashed*).

> ► SP 1 added a Recalculate button. The Recalculate button had a similar issue to the Reset button in RTM, as it actually worked only when there was on-demand detection. The Reset button worked as expected, and changed the monitor state to healthy regardless of its current state (even if it was already in a healthy state).

▶ R2 continues to have both the Reset and Recalculate buttons, and Recalculate works more accurately than it did in SP 1.

Power Consumption Monitoring

A new Power Management Library MP enables you to monitor power consumption for each computer or a group of computers. Monitored systems must be running Windows Server 2008 R2 or Windows 7. Additional information is available at http://technet.microsoft.com/en-us/library/dd789061.aspx. See http://www.windowsservercatalog.com/results.aspx?&chtext=&cstext=&csttext=&chbtext=&bCatID=1333&cpID=0&avc=10&ava=0&avq=30&OR=1&PGS=25&ready=0 for the current list of supported hardware.

Summary

Operations Manager 2007 R2 brings "fit and finish" to the 2007 release. The R2 enhancements are quite substantial, perhaps more so than some of the "R2" releases with previous Microsoft server products. This chapter highlighted the changes in OpsMgr 2007 SP 1 and R2. The next chapter discusses one of the most publicized enhancements in R2: Cross Platform Extensions.

## CHAPTER 2

Unix/Linux Management: Cross Platform Extensions

Cross Platform Extensions, also referred to as *CrossPlat* (or X-Plat), is perhaps the most highly touted and anticipated feature of Operations Manager 2007 Release 2 (R2). First announced at the Microsoft Management Summit in 2008 with the fanfare of flying pigs, CrossPlat enables you to monitor Unix platforms using the Operations Manager (OpsMgr) console and tools. This chapter looks at how the CrossPlat capabilities enable you to monitor non-Microsoft environments. This incorporates a discussion of supported platforms, discovery, system monitoring including distributed applications and using the Health Explorer, and some of the more significant management packs and connectors.

Supported Platforms and Requirements

Microsoft's CrossPlat enhancements in OpsMgr 2007 R2 allow you out of the box to monitor some of the more significant Unix and Linux platforms. Table 2.1 lists the platforms supported by CrossPlat and prerequisites. For additional information and updates, check http://technet.microsoft.com/en-us/library/dd789030.aspx. For those platforms not supported by the R2 release, Microsoft has published the CrossPlat providers on codeplex (http://scx.codeplex.com/) as OpenSource (MS-PL license). Although this does not include the entire stack, it can be combined with any Common Information Model Object Manager (CIMOM) and a WS-Management (WSMan) layer to port to the platform you want to support. You would have to write a management pack for that platform as well.

TABLE 2.1 Cross Platform Operating System and Dependencies

Platform	Required Package	Description	Minimum Version
IBM AIX 5L 5.3	OS Version	Version of Operating System	AIX 5.3, Technology Level 6, Service Pack 5
	xlC.rte	XL C/C++ Runtime	9.0.0.2
	openssl. base	OpenSSL Libraries; Secure Network Communications Protocol	0.9.8.4
IBM AIX 6.1	OS Version	Version of Operating System	AIX 6.1; any technology level and service pack
	xlC.rte	XL C/C++ Runtime	9.0.0.5
	openssl. base	OpenSSL Libraries; Secure Network Communications Protocol	0.9.8.4
HP-UX 11i v2 IA 64	HPUX-BaseOS	Base OS (Operating System)	B.11.23
	HPUX-BaseAux	HP-UX Base OS Auxiliary	B.11.23.0706
	HPUX BaseAux. openssl	OpenSSL Libraries; Secure Network Communications Protocol	A.00.09.07I.003
	PAM	Pluggable Authentication Modules	Part of the core operating system components on HP-UX
HP-UX 11i v2 PA-RISC	HPUX11i-OE	HP-UX Foundation Operating Environment	B.11.23.0706
	OS-Core.Minim umRun-time.CORE-SHLIBS	Compatible development tools libraries	B.11.23
	HPUX-BaseAux	HP-UX Base OS Auxiliary	B.11.23.0706
	HPUX BaseAux. openssl	OpenSSL Libraries; Secure Network Communications Protocol	A.00.09.07I.003
	PAM	Pluggable Authentication Modules	Part of the core operating system components on HP-UX
HP-UX 11i v3 PA-RISC	HPUX11i-OE	HP-UX Foundation Operating Environment	B.11.31

	OS-Core.Mini-mumRun-time.CORE-SHLIBS	Specific IA emulator libraries	B.11.31
	openssl/Openssl.openssl	Open SSL Libraries; Secure Open Communications Protocol	A.00.09.08d.002
	PAM	Pluggable Authentication Modules	Part of the core operating system components
HP-UX 11i v3 IA64	HPUX11i-OE	HP-UX Foundation Operating Environment	B.11.31.0709
	OS-Core. Minimum Runtime. CORE-SHLIBS	Specific IA emulator libraries	B.11.31
	SysMgmt Min. openssl	Open SSL Libraries; Secure Open Communications Protocol	A.00.09.08d.002
	PAM	Pluggable Authentication Modules	Part of the core operating system components
Red Hat Enterprise Linux ES Release 4	glibc	C Standard Libraries	2.3.4-2
	Openssl	OpenSSL Libraries; Secure Network Communications Protocol	0.9.7a-43.1
	PAM	Pluggable Authentication Modules	0.77-65.1
Red Hat Enterprise Linux Server release 5.1 (Tikanga)	glibc	C Standard Libraries	2.5-12
	Openssl	OpenSSL Libraries; Secure Network Communications Protocol	0.9.8b-8.3.el5
	PAM	Pluggable Authentication Modules	0.99.6.2-3.14.el5
Solaris 8 SPARC	Required OS patch	PAM memory leak	108434-22
	SUNWlibC	Sun Workshop Compilers Bundled libC(sparc)	5.8,REV=99.06.09

	SUNW libms	Sun Workshop Bundled Shared libm (sparc)	5.8,REV=99.10.21
	OpenSSL	SMCossl (sparc) Sun does not provide a version of OpenSSL for Solaris 8 SPARC. A version is available from Sunfreeware.	0.9.8h
	PAM	Pluggable Authentica-tion Modules SUNWcsl, Core So-laris, (Shared Libs) (sparc)	11.8.0,REV=2000.01. 08.18.12
Solaris 9 SPARC	Required OS patch	PAM memory leak	112960-48
	SUNWlibC	Sun Workshop Compil-ers Bundled libC (sparc)	5.9,REV=2002.03.18
	SUNW libms	Forte Developer Bun-dled Shared libm (sparc)	5.9,REV=2001.12.10
	OpenSSL	Pluggable Authentica-tion Modules SUNWcsl, Core So-laris, (Shared Libs) (sparc)	11.9.0,REV=2002.04. 06.15.27
Solaris 10 SPARC	Required OS patch	PAM memory leak	117463-05
	SUNWlibC	Sun Workshop Compil-ers Bundled libC (sparc)	5.10;REV=2004.12. 22
	SUNW libms	Math and Microtasking Libraries (Usr) (sparc)	5.10;REV=2004.12. 22
	SUNW libmsr	Math and Microtasking Libraries (Root) (sparc)	5.10;REV=2004.11. 23
	SUNWlcslr	Core Solaris Libraries (Root) (sparc)	11.10.0;REV=2005. 01.21.15.53
	SUNWcsl	Core Solaris Libraries (Root) (sparc)	11.10.0;REV=2005. 01.21.15.53
	OpenSSL	SUNopenssl-libraries (Usr) Sun provides OpenSSL libraries for Solaris 10 SPARC; they are bun-dled with the operating system.	11,10.0;REV=2005. 01.21.15.53

	PAM	Pluggable Authentication Modules SUNWcsr Core Solaris, (Root) (i386)	11.10.0,REV=2005.01.21.16.34
SUSE Linux Enterprise Server 9 (i586)	OS Patch lib gcc-41.rpm	Standard shared library	41-4.1.2_20070115-0.6
	OS Patch lib stdc++-41.rpm	Standard shared library	41-4.1.2_20070115-0.6
	Openssl	OpenSSL Libraries; Secure Network Communications Protocol	0.9.7d-15.10
	PAM	Pluggable Authentication Modules	0.77-221.1
SUSE Linux Enterprise Server 10 SP2 (i586)	glibc-2.4-31.30	C Standard shared library	2.4-31.30
	Openssl	OpenSSL Libraries; Secure Network Communications Protocol	0.9.8a-18.15
	PAM	Pluggable Authentication Modules	0.99.6.3-28.8
SUSE Linux Enterprise Server 11 (i586)	glibc-2.9-13.2	C Standard shared library	2.9-13.2
	PAM	Pluggable Authentication Modules	pam-1.0.2-20.1

Preparing to Discover Unix/Linux Computers

There are several steps to perform before attempting to deploy OpsMgr agents onto Unix or Linux systems. Most OpsMgr administrators (including the authors!) will want to start by immediately running the discovery and start getting some agents installed. However, you will learn the hard way that this usually will not work. Therefore, do not pass go and do not collect $200 before performing the steps in the next sections.

Name Resolution

Each of the systems you want to discover with OpsMgr must be able to resolve their Internet Protocol (IP) address to their host name. Figure 2.1 shows an example of what occurs if you attempt to discover a system via IP address and are unable to resolve the host name.

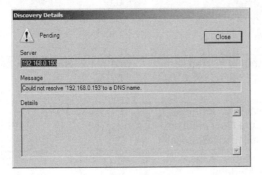

FIGURE 2.1 Discovery failure due to name resolution

To avoid this issue, determine those Unix/Linux systems you will be monitoring prior to performing the discovery, and if necessary add the appropriate records within the DNS Manager Microsoft Management Console (MMC) application to the DNS zone, as shown in Figure 2.2. When you create DNS records, they need to match the host name of the system. See the section "Notes on Unix Commands" for commands to determine the host name of the Unix/Linux system.

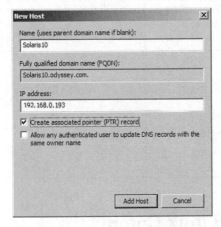

FIGURE 2.2 Creating a DNS record

Account Information Gathering

To discover and deploy the CrossPlat agent, you will need a username and password for those systems to which you are deploying the agent. You will also need to know the superuser password, used by OpsMgr during the agent installation process. Figure 2.3 shows the dialog where this is specified to perform discovery on Unix/Linux systems.

You can select to run discovery as a superuser account (default) or as a regular user account and then specify the root password. The root account typically does not have access rights to log in via Secure Shell (SSH), which is the approach OpsMgr uses to deploy the CrossPlat agent. The CrossPlat agent installation executes the scripts using the `su` command (see the "Notes on Unix Commands" section for details on this command) as part of the installation process. Generally, you will be required to provide a user name and password and the root password for the system.

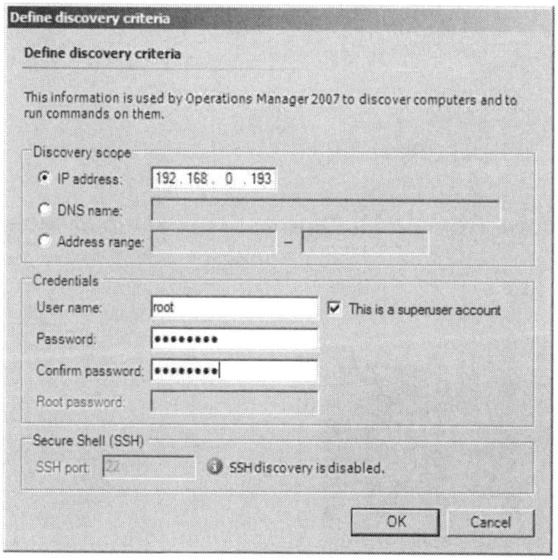

FIGURE 2.3 Specifying the credentials to discover Unix/Linux systems

Update WinRM

Before OpsMgr can discover any Unix/Linux systems, you must configure WinRM to allow Basic Authentication. Figure 2.4 shows the error message that occurs if you attempt to discover prior to making this configuration change.

To update WinRM, log in as an administrator to the root management server (this requires use of Run As Administrator if using User Account Control or UAC—see Chapter 3, "Operations Manager 2007 R2 and Windows Server 2008," for more details on Windows 2008 and UAC). The command to make this configuration is as follows:

```
Winrm set winrm/config/client/auth @{Basic="true"}
```

Figure 2.5 shows the successful results of this command.

After configuring WinRM to allow Basic Authentication, you can configure the accounts the CrossPlat systems will use.

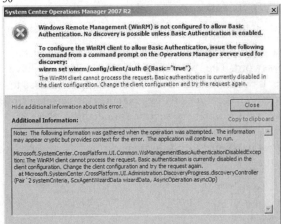

FIGURE 2.4 Error on discovering with Windows Remote Management not set to allow Basic Authentication

```
Administrator: Command Prompt                                    _ □ ×
Microsoft Windows [Version 6.0.6001]
Copyright (c) 2006 Microsoft Corporation.  All rights reserved.

C:\Users\administrator.ODYSSEY>winrm set winrm/config/client/auth @{Basic="true"
}
Auth
    Basic = true
    Digest = true
    Kerberos = true
    Negotiate = true
    Certificate = true


C:\Users\administrator.ODYSSEY>_
```

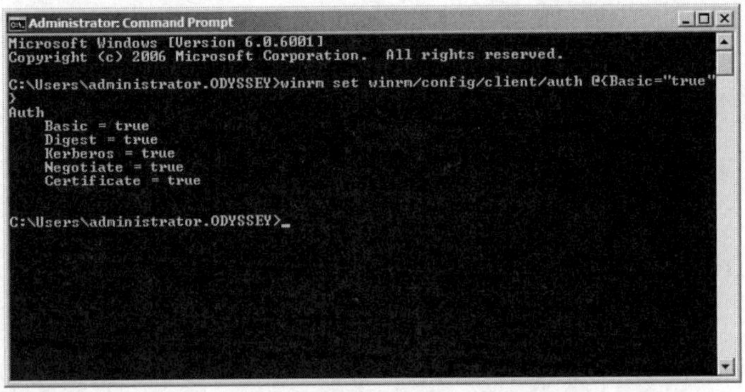

FIGURE 2.5 Configuring WinRM to allow Basic Authentication

Configuring Accounts and Profiles

There are two accounts that must be defined as part of the CrossPlat functionality: the Unix Action account and the Unix Privileged account. Open the OpsMgr console -> Administration -> Run As Configuration -> Profiles to define a Run As profile for both the Unix Action account and the Unix Privileged account. You will need to configure a Run As profile for each of these accounts. The Unix Action account should be a basic account used for low-security activities on the Unix/Linux systems it is specified for.

TIP: CROSS PLATFORM DEPLOYMENT IN LEAST PRIVILEGE MODE

CrossPlat uses two accounts—the Unix Action account and the Unix Privileged account:

▶ The Unix Privileged account needs to be root; it is used to install the agent. The agent must be running as root; however, tasks will run using the credentials of the user requesting the task. This prevents a non-privileged account from running a task that requires privileges. The Privileged account is used for any required privileged process or tasks such as diagnostics, recoveries, agent removal, and reading secure log files.

▶ The Unix Action account is a regular login account that can be created with the useradd command. Anything that does not specifically require root permissions uses the Unix action account.

In summary, actions that require root use root, but if the command does not require root, it uses the Unix Action account.

Perform the following steps to create the Unix Action account:

1. Right-click on the Unix Action account (shown in Figure 2.6) under Profiles and then open Properties, which starts the Run As Profile Wizard for the Unix Action account.

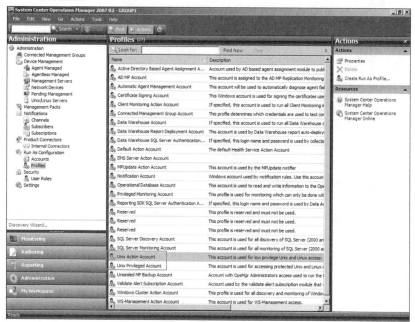

FIGURE 2.6 Profiles in OpsMgr including the Unix Action account and the Unix Privileged account

2. After the introduction screen, Figure 2.7 displays the first screen of the wizard, showing the General Properties of the Unix Action account. Continue to the Run As Accounts screen, click Add, and then select a new account. This process launches the Run As Account Wizard displayed in Figure 2.8.

3. For this account, specify the Run As Account type as Basic Authentication (although there are other options that include Windows, Community String, Simple Authentication, Digest Authentication, Binary Authentication, Action Account, for CrossPlat monitoring, this must be Basic Authentication) and a display name of **Unix action account**. On the next screen, define the account name and password for the Run As account you are creating, as shown in Figure 2.9.

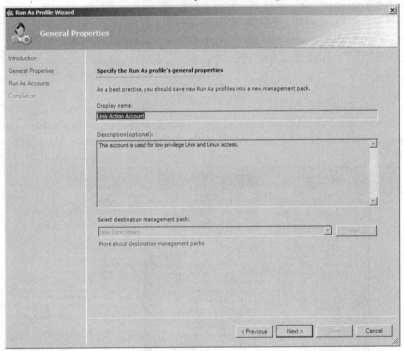

FIGURE 2.7 General properties of the Unix Action account profile

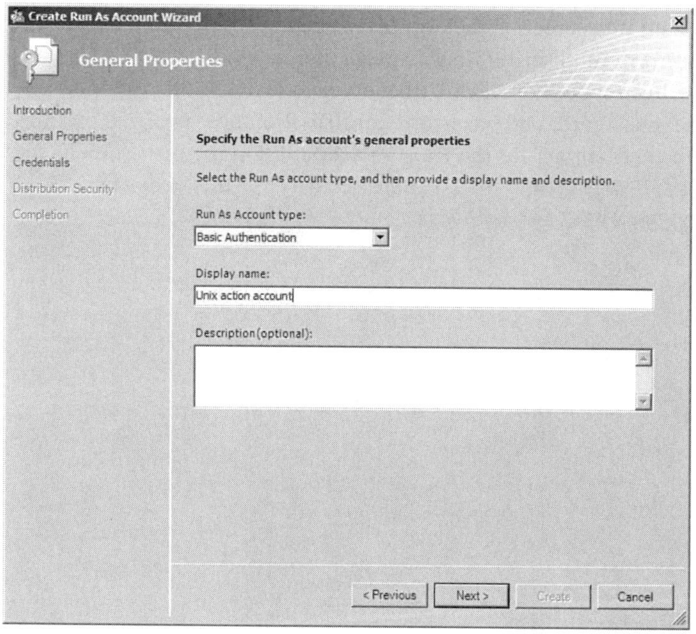

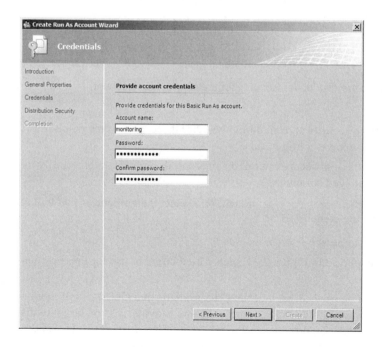

FIGURE 2.8 Defining general properties for the Unix Action account

FIGURE 2.9 Defining the credentials for the Unix Action account

The account name on this screen is the non-privileged account that exists on the Unix system to perform monitoring. In this particular case, the requirement was to create a monitoring account on each Unix server to provide this functionality. The account name, password, and password confirmation are specified on this screen to define the credentials for the Run As account. On the next screen (see Figure 2.10), you will define how to distribute security for this account.

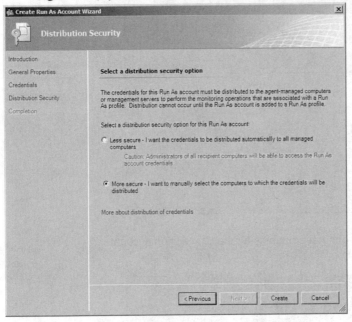

FIGURE 2.10 Defining the distribution security for the Unix Action account

4. At the distribution security screen, define whether these credentials will be stored in a less- or more-secure configuration:

    ▶ With the less-secure option, the credentials are sent automatically to all managed computers.

    ▶ With the more-secure approach, you select the computers that will receive the credentials.

    The more-secure approach is recommended.

5. At the screen displayed in Figure 2.11, pick which target to use for these credentials.

    This account will be used on each of the Unix systems that OpsMgr will monitor, so for this environment, the Unix Computer Group provides a good target to distribute the credentials. To provide additional granularity, different Unix Action accounts can be created and targeted on an object (or smaller group) level. Figure 2.12 shows the targeting of the Run As account just created.

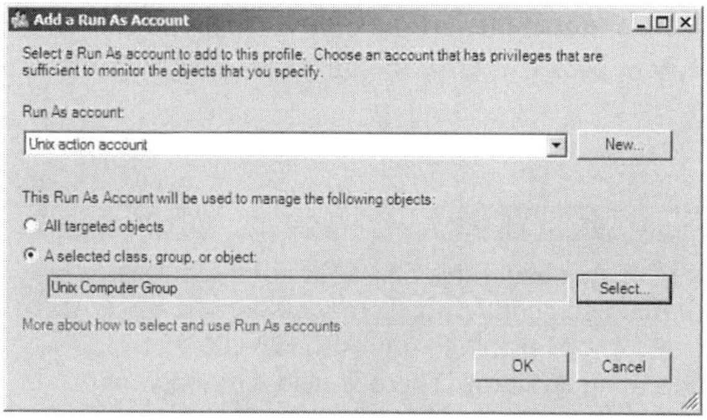

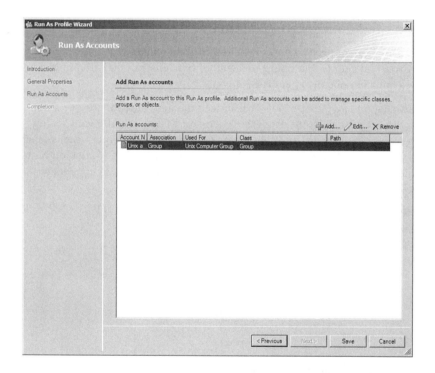

FIGURE 2.11 Selecting the target for the Unix Action account

FIGURE 2.12 Summary of the credentials for the Run As account

After completing this process, your next step is to define the Unix Privileged account. The Unix Privileged account must be a privileged account, as it is used for activities requiring a higher level of authority than the Unix Action account.

The process to define this Run As account is similar to that used for the Unix Action account, but start the process by right-clicking the Unix Privileged account and going to Properties. When you reach the screen to define the credentials (shown in Figure 2.9), specify the root (or other high-privilege) account and password.

36

With the Unix Action account and Unix Privileged account configured, you can import the appropriate Unix/Linux management packs and then begin discovering Unix/Linux systems.

TIP: MANAGEMENT PACK GUIDES FOR UNIX

Microsoft is creating management pack guides for the Cross Platform Operating systems, available at http://technet.microsoft.com/en-us/library/ee346642.aspx. At the time of writing this chapter, guides are available for the AIX, HP-UX, Red Hat Linux, Solaris, and SUSE Linux Operating Systems. There is also a management pack guide for Cross Platform Audit Control Services; see Chapter 9, "Unleashing Operations Manager 2007," for additional information.

Importing the Unix/Linux Management Packs

Technically, you are not required to import the Unix/Linux management packs prior to deploying the CrossPlat agents, but doing so ahead of time ensures that all monitoring for the agent is available once the agent is deployed.

Chapter 1, "Introduction and What's New," discussed the new functionality available to import management packs directly from the Microsoft Management Pack Catalog rather than downloading and then installing them. To add the management packs, open the Operations Console -> Administration -> Management Packs. Right-click on Management Packs and choose Download Management Packs. Click Add to connect to the catalog, as shown in Figure 2.13.

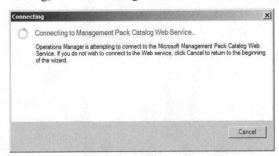

FIGURE 2.13 Connecting to the MP catalog

Clicking Add starts the connection to the Management Pack Catalog Web Service shown in Figure 2.13. Connecting to the management pack catalog requires Internet connectivity to function but can be run on any system with the Operations Manager console installed. In secure environments, servers generally do not have Internet connectivity so you may need to use a workstation with the OpsMgr console installed to download management packs.

By filtering on Cross Platform based upon all management packs in the catalog (see Figure 2.14), you will see the four high-level groups CrossPlat management packs are currently split into, as follows:

► AIX

► HP

► Linux

► Solaris

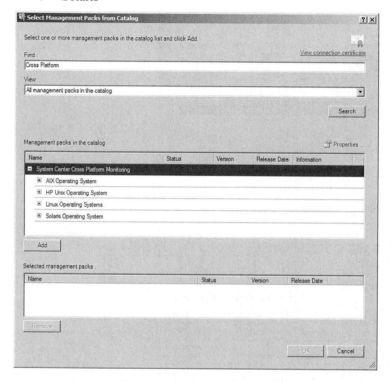

FIGURE 2.14 Filtering based on the keywords of Cross Platform

You can expand any of the groups displayed in Figure 2.14 to list the specific management packs available for that platform. Figure 2.15 lists management packs and their installed status for the HPUX Operating System Library. The Unix/Linux agent files are stored under the %*ProgramFiles*%\System Center Operations Manager 2007\AgentManagement\UnixAgents folder, and range from approximately 7MB–20MB (shown in Figure 2.16).

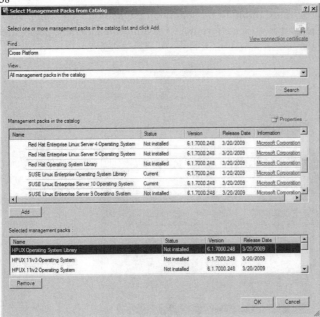

FIGURE 2.15 Selecting management packs from the catalog

FIGURE 2.16 UnixAgents files on the management servers

After specifying the management packs to import, they are added to OpsMgr, as shown in Figure 2.17.

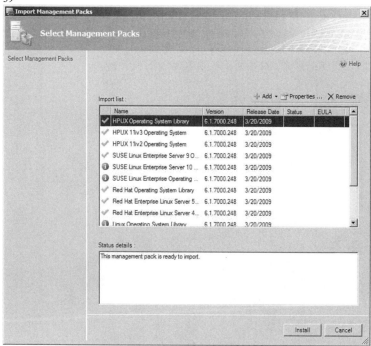

FIGURE 2.17 Importing management packs

Up to this point, you have been preparing to discover the Unix/Linux systems. You have worked through name resolution, gathered account information from the Unix systems, updated WinRM, configured accounts and profiles, and imported the Unix/Linux management packs. All of this work is in preparation to discover these systems in your environment, discussed in the next section.

Discovering and Monitoring Unix/Linux Computers

With all the required prep work completed, the actual process to discover Unix/Linux systems should be straightforward. The next step is to discover the systems, which you will do in the OpsMgr console Administration node at Device Management -> Agent Managed.

Discovering

To discover Unix/Linux systems, perform the following steps:

1.   Right-click on the Agent Managed folder and choose the discovery wizard. The wizard defaults to Windows computers, but select the Unix/Linux computers option, as shown in Figure 2.18.

FIGURE 2.18 Unix/Linux computers discovery type

2.   After specifying that you want to discover Unix/Linux computers, you need to define the discovery method.

Choose the management server you will use to perform the discovery (Hydra was used in this environment for Odyssey.com). The option is also available to Enable SSH-based discovery. This option is unchecked by default as it sends the user name and password to the remote systems you specify. In this case, the option is checked as the OpsMgr administrators know and are responsible for each of the Unix systems. You must define the discovery criteria, so click on the Add button shown in Figure 2.19.

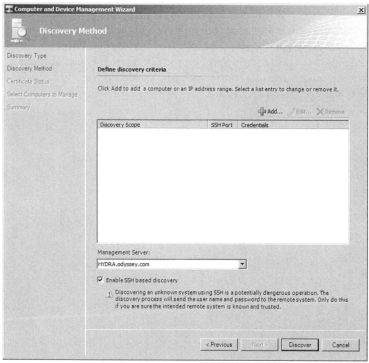

FIGURE 2.19 Defining the discovery method

3.   There are a variety of different methods available to discover Unix/Linux sys-
      tems. You can discover for a range of IP addresses, for a specific DNS name, or
      a specific IP address (all shown in Figure 2.20).

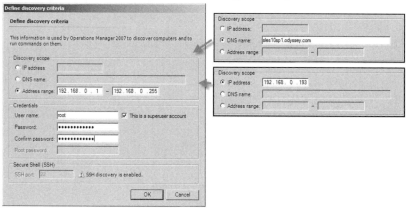

FIGURE 2.20 Defining the discovery criteria

4.	As discussed in the "Account Information Gathering" section, there are situations where the root account will not be able to log in via SSH, which is necessary for OpsMgr to deploy the CrossPlat agent. If this is true for your systems, you must specify the credentials to use, as shown in Figure 2.21. Here the user account name and password (and password configuration) provided is used to access the system via SSH, and privileged scripts are run with the root account password specified.

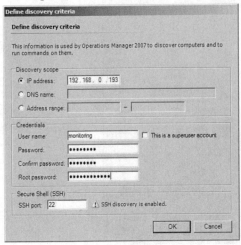

FIGURE 2.21 Discovery using both a monitoring account and the root account

5.	The information specified on the Define discovery criteria screen is populated to the Discovery Method screen displayed in Figure 2.22. Figure 2.22 specifies performing a discovery for the entire 192.168.0.x address range.

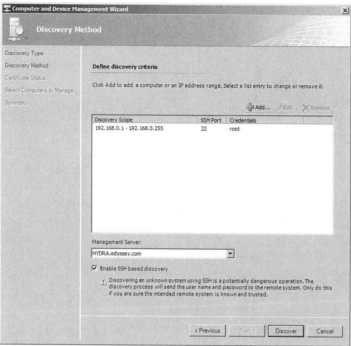

FIGURE 2.22 Discovery method for the 192.168.0.x network address range

6. The discovery process identifies each of the systems fitting the discovery criteria (in this case, the IP address range from 192.168.0.1 to 192.168.0.255 or 255 potential computers). It then scans each of the systems and identifies those that are discoverable. Figure 2.23 shows the discovery in progress.

7. When the discovery process completes, the wizard displays the results of the discovery as shown in Figure 2.24, which shows that OpsMgr found and identified one SUSE Linux system for agent installation.

8. Check the option to install on the identified system (see Figure 2.24), and the computer and device management wizard continues to the Summary screen where it deploys the agent, installs the agent, and signs the agent. If all works correctly, the Summary screen will indicate a successful deployment of the agent. Figure 2.25 shows this progression.

After deploying the agent, it will be visible in the Operations Manager console in the Monitoring -> Unix/Linux Servers section. A number of errors may occur when deploying the CrossPlat agent; see the "Common Agent Deployment Errors" section of this chapter for further information.

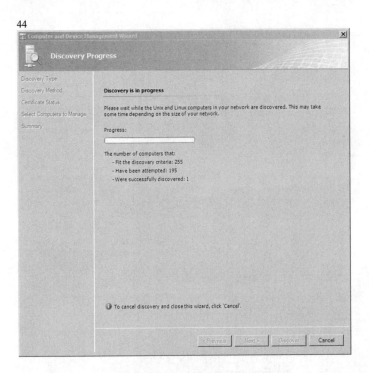

FIGURE 2.23 Discovering the 192.168.0.x network address range

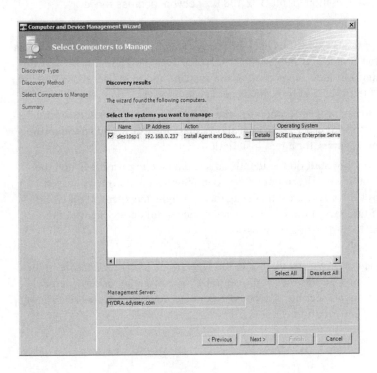

FIGURE 2.24 Discovery results

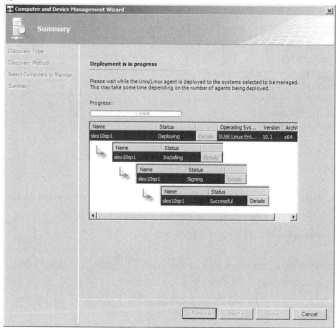

FIGURE 2.25 Unix/Linux agent deployment

Manually Installing the CrossPlat Agent

There are situations where you may need to deploy the CrossPlat agent manually. Examples of this include unsupported versions of Unix/Linux or systems where an SSH connection cannot be established. This section will perform a manual deployment to a Solaris 10 system called Solaris10 when DNS resolution name was defined but actually named hadji on the Unix system itself. (Any Johnny Quest fans out there?)

Perform the following steps to perform the manual installation:

1. Install FTP server on a Windows server; add the Unix agent installation files to the FTP share; then connect from the Unix system and perform an FTP get of the files.

    To get the files from the FTP server, log into the Unix system (either via SSH or locally connected via a null modem cable with HyperTerm or another Windows terminal emulator), as follows:

    ```
    Start the ftp client: ftp
    Open (ip address): Open 192.168.0.209
    Username: administrator
    Password: password
    Set the transfer type to binary: Binary
    Get (filename): get scx-1.0.4-248.solaris.10.sparc.pkg.Z
    ```

    Figure 2.26 displays this process.

```
ftp> open 192.168.0.209
Connected to 192.168.0.209.
220 Microsoft FTP Service
Name (192.168.0.209:LOGIN): administrator
331 Password required for administrator.
Password:
230 User administrator logged in.
Remote system type is Windows_NT.
ftp> binary
200 Type set to I.
ftp> get scx-1.0.4-248.solaris.10.sparc.pkg.Z
```

FIGURE 2.26 FTP get files

2.   Once the file is locally available on the Unix/Linux system, you will need to un-
      compress the file. For this file, the syntax would be as follows:

      uncompress scx-1.0.4-248.solaris.10.sparc.pkg.Z

3.   Once the file is uncompressed, you can install the package using pkgadd: (when
      prompted to with the y/n to install, choose y):

      pkgadd -d scx-1.0.4-248.solaris.10.sparc.pkg MSFCscx

4.   Next, verify the package installed by using the pkginfo command:

      pkginfo -l MSFCscx

      Figure 2.27 shows an example of how a successful installation looks when veri-
      fying the installation with the previous command (pkginfo -l MSFCscx).

```
# pkginfo -l MSFTscx
   PKGINST:  MSFTscx
      NAME:  Microsoft system center cross platform.
  CATEGORY:  system
      ARCH:  sparc
   VERSION:  1.0.4-248
   BASEDIR:  /
    VENDOR:  http://www.microsoft.com
      DESC:  Provides monitoring capabilities to the heterogenous platform
    PSTAMP:  20090423-2332
  INSTDATE:  Jul 25 2009 12:37
    STATUS:  completely installed
     FILES:      623 installed pathnames
                  35 directories
                 536 executables
               34316 blocks used (approx)

#
```

FIGURE 2.27 Successful manual agent installation

After verifying the installation, the next step is to verify that the agent is running. You
can use the svcs command, as follows:

svcs scx-cimd

If the results of this command indicate a state of **online** as shown in Figure 2.28, the CrossPlat agent monitoring (`scx-cimd`) service is running.

```
# svcs scx-cimd
STATE            STIME    FMRI
online           12:38:42 svc:/application/management/scx-cimd:default
#
```

FIGURE 2.28 CrossPlat agent running on Solaris.

After manually adding the Unix/Linux system, you will need to complete the discovery process by accessing the OpsMgr console and discovering the system to which you manually installed the agent (see the "Discovering" section of this chapter for details). Figure 2.29 shows a successful discovery process.

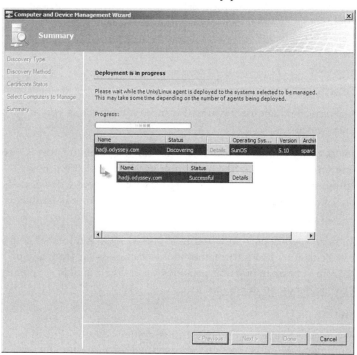

FIGURE 2.29 Discovering the manually installed agent

The syntax of the commands you will use vary depending upon the version of Unix/Linux to which you are deploying the agent. This particular example showed the syntax for a Solaris 10 Unix system. Additional syntax examples for Red Hat, SUSE, HP-UX, and AIX are available at http://technet.microsoft.com/en-us/library/dd789016.aspx.

There are situations where you may need to uninstall the CrossPlat agent, such as when re-installing to create a new certificate. In the following example, an issue occurred when the agent was deployed manually to a system named Solaris10 but the actual machine name was hadji. To address this situation, remove the agent using the following syntax:

```
pkgrm MSFTscx
```

Additional details on situations where agent names do not match are available in the "Common Agent Deployment Errors" section of this chapter.

TIP: DEPLOYING THE CROSSPLAT AGENT TO UNSUPPORTED PLATFORMS

With the large number of variations of Unix/Linux that exist, there are also a large number of versions not currently supported by CrossPlat. The user community is investigating solutions such as this article, which discusses deploying the OpsMgr CrossPlat agent on Ubuntu: http://www.muscetta.com/2009/05/30/installing-the-opsmgr-2007-r2-scx-agent-on-ubuntu/ .

Notes on Unix Commands

This section discusses several fundamentals you will want to remember as you deploy agents to Unix and Linux systems.

Remember to use telnet to verify connectivity to the Unix/Linux system on port 22 (see Chapter 3 for details, but telnet is not installed by default in Windows 2008). Few things are more frustrating than spending hours debugging why an agent will not deploy than to later find out the management server you are deploying from is unable to reach the Unix/Linux agent on port 22.

For those who have not been staying current working in Unix/Linux, a refresher course on basic commands may be useful. The information in this section is far from a comprehensive list of Unix/Linux commands, but it provides several commands frequently used when debugging CrossPlat agent deployment:

▶ **Root command.**

▶ To execute privileged commands on Unix/Linux systems, you will need to access the root command. Do this through `su root` (and then provide the password for root). Here is an example:

```
su root
```

▶ Use `ifconfig` to show address information and turn on network interfaces.

▶ Showing the IP address information for the system:

```
ifconfig -a
```

▶ Setting the IP address information for the system: `ifconfig` "interface type" "ip address" "subnet mask" "broadcast address." For example:

```
ifconfig hme0 192.168.0.193 netmask 255.255.255.0 broadcast 192.168.0.255
```

Turning on a network interface: `ifconfig` "interface name" up. For example:

```
ifconfig hme0 up
```

▶ **Specifying the DNS server.**

▶ To specify the DNS server, edit the /etc/resolv.conf file with the domain and name server information. As an example, to set the name servers to 192.168.0.230 and 192.168.0.231, here is the syntax for the odyssey.com domain:

```
domain odyssey.com
nameserver 192.168.0.230
nameserver 192.168.0.231
```

▶ **Creating directories.**

▶ To make a directory: `mkdir` (directory). For example:

```
mkdir /export/home
```

▶ **User maintenance.**

▶ To create a user: `useradd -d /export/home/`**(name)** `-m -s /bin/ksh -c` "(name)" (name). Example of syntax:

```
useradd -d /export/home/Admin -m -s /bin/ksh -c "Admin" Admin
```

▶ To configure the account password: `passwd` (username). Sample syntax:

```
passwd Admin
```

▶ Then enter the password for the user specified.

▶ To add a user to a group: `usermod -G` (group) (username). This syntax adds a user (Admin) to a group named root:

```
usermod -G root Admin
```

▶ **Rebooting a system.**

▶ To reboot down a Unix/Linux system, you need to sync twice and then `init` it to the correct level. Sample syntax:

```
Sync; sync; init 6
```

▶ **Restarting SSH.**

▶ Here is the command to restart `ssh`: `svcadm restart` (service):

```
svcadm restart ssh
```

Again, this is far from a comprehensive list, but if you do not have access to Unix/Linux administrators, these may be useful during your agent deployment process. For additional information on Unix commands, see
http://en.wikipedia.org/wiki/List_of_Unix_utilities.

Common Agent Deployment Errors

During a CrossPlat agent deployment, you may encounter errors that need to be resolved. This section includes a number of errors with the error message that occurs with the recommended method to address the error:

▶ Issue: The certificate Common Name (CN) does not match.

▶ or

▶ Issue: The SSL certificate contains a common name (CN) that does not match the hostname.

▶ Resolution: When performing a manual installation, you may have created a fully qualified name for the system that did not match the system's actual fully qualified name (as in the installation in this chapter). In this case, the certificate will not match the actual fully qualified host name. To resolve this, perform the following steps:

1. Uninstall the CrossPlat agent (see the "Manually Installing the CrossPlat Agent" section for details).

2. Delete the certificate stored under /etc/opt/microsoft/scx/ssl named scx-key.pem.

3. Change your DNS resolution so that the name used to connect to the system will match the actual system name.

4. Now, re-deploy the agent manually as discussed in the "Manually Installing the CrossPlat Agent" section of this chapter.

▶ Another option is to just re-issue the certificate and restart the CrossPlat agent, discussed at http://technet.microsoft.com/en-us/library/dd891009.aspx.

▶ Issue: The certificate is invalid; please select the system to install a new certificate.

▶ Resolution: For this situation, you will have to uninstall the CrossPlat agent, delete the certificate, and re-deploy the CrossPlat agent.

▶ Issue: The certificate signing Operation Failed.

▶ or

▶ Issue: The certificate for this system is not valid.

▶ or

▶ Issue: The certificate is invalid; please select the system to issue a new certificate.

▶ Resolution: These can occur when there are issues connecting to the Unix system on the SSH port. Use telnet from the management server to the SSH port to verify connectivity; if connectivity is not available, debug this issue and then re-create the certificate.

▶ Issue: Could not transfer the discovery script.

or

▶ Issue: Could not create secured folder.

▶ Resolution: Many different connectivity issues can cause this, including IPTABLES blocking the connection, SSH not running on the client system, or as occurring during our testing if an invalid user account/password combination were specified when discovering the Unix/Linux system.

▶ Issue: Could not resolve "w.x.y.z" to a DNS name.

▶ Resolution: Name resolution is not available for the IP address specified. Create a record in the DNS server for the fully qualified name of the Unix/Linux system.

▶ Issue: Agent installation failed.

▶ Resolution: OpsMgr was able to connect to the remote system but was not able to successfully use the root credentials to run the pkgadd command. Verify the root password, and if this continues to fail, attempt a manual CrossPlat agent installation.

▶ Issue: Unable to install agent and discover computer instance into Operations Manager.

▶ Resolution: SSH is disabled on the Unix/Linux system. Either enable SSH or manually install the CrossPlat agent.

▶ Issue: Alerts generated about "Secure Reference Override Failure."

▶ Resolution: The Run As profiles were not properly defined for the CrossPlat management packs. See the "Configuring Accounts and Profiles" section of this chapter for details.

Additional information on troubleshooting issues with CrossPlat is available at http://technet.microsoft.com/en-us/library/dd891012.aspx.

Additional Reference Material on CrossPlat

Although this chapter attempts to provide as much information as possible about the CrossPlat functionality, a variety of additional resources are available online to supplement your CrossPlat information. In addition to resources in Appendix B, "Reference URLs," here are some suggested resources.

Blogs and Blog Entries

Here are some blog postings you will want to see:

▶ **Anders Bengtsson**—http://contoso.se/blog/?p=712

▶ **Bridgeways on CrossPlat**—http://blog.xplatxperts.com/

- **Daniele Muscetta CrossPlat**—http://www.muscetta.com/tag/xplat/

- **David Allen CrossPlat Field Notes**—
  http://wmug.co.uk/blogs/aquilaweb/archive/2009/07/21/opsmgr-r2-xplat-
  agent-deployment-field-notes.aspx

- **Ops-Mgr's Hyper-V/OpsMgr and Unix**—http://ops-
  mgr.spaces.live.com/blog/cns!3D3B8489FCAA9B51!538.entry

- **Ops-Mgr's CrossPlat Gateway to Linux in the Datacenter**—http://ops-
  mgr.spaces.live.com/blog/cns!3D3B8489FCAA9B51!857.entry

Webcasts

There are several webcasts of interest, including the following:

- **Monitoring CrossPlat with OpsMgr R2**—
  http://www.microsoft.com/events/series/detail/webcastdetails.aspx?seriesid=3
  7&webcastid=5558

- **Microsoft discussion on CrossPlat**—
  http://mschnlnine.vo.llnwd.net/d1/edge/1/8/8/2/opsmgrr2_edge.wmv

Websites or Download Links

There are also a number of websites and downloads available that cover CrossPlat, as
follows:

- **CrossPlat MP authoring**—http://technet.microsoft.com/nl-
  nl/library/dd919155(en-us).aspx

- **Datasheets from Microsoft**—Linux Systems with Operations Manager 2007
  Cross Platform Extensions, Datasheet- System Center Operations Manager
  2007 Cross Platform Extensions

- **List of online documentation specific to CrossPlat**—
  http://myitforum.com/cs2/blogs/rtrent/archive/2009/06/22/locations-of-
  opsmgr-2007-cross-platform-specific-documentation.aspx

- **Microsoft's CrossPlat and Interoperability Solutions**—
  http://technet.microsoft.com/en-us/opsmgr/cc677004.aspx

- **Microsoft's CrossPlat security account information**—
  http://technet.microsoft.com/en-us/library/bb432133.aspx

- **Microsoft's deploying Unix/Linux agents**—http://technet.microsoft.com/en-
  us/library/dd788943.aspx

- **Microsoft overview of CrossPlat in R2**—
  http://download.microsoft.com/download/8/8/B/88BBD053-14A7-442E-8066-
  0EE84231EC0E/SC_OpsMgr2007_R2-CrossPlat.pdf

Monitoring (Where Do You Find Everything?)

After successfully deploying the CrossPlat agent to Unix/Linux systems, your next logical question may be "Where do you find these agents in the OpsMgr console?" The cross platform agents integrate seamlessly within the OpsMgr console. The first place to verify successful deployment of CrossPlat agents is in the Administration node, at Administration -> Device Management -> Unix/Linux Servers. Figure 2.30 shows two Unix/Linux systems (one SunOS, one SUSE Linux) integrated into the Administration node of the Operations Manager console.

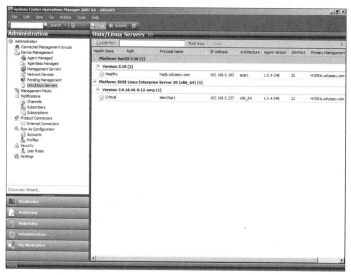

FIGURE 2.30 Unix/Linux systems displayed in the Administration node

After verifying the agents have deployed successfully, you can check on the status of these servers within the Monitoring node, at Monitoring -> Unix/Linux Servers. Figure 2.31 shows two Unix/Linux systems integrated into the Monitoring node of the Operations Manager console.

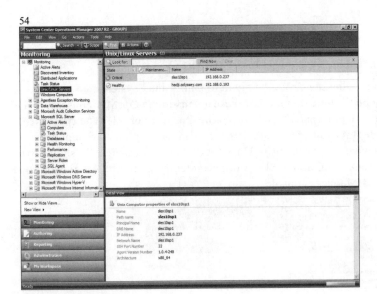

FIGURE 2.31 Unix/Linux systems viewed in the Monitoring node

Integrating Unix/Linux Computers in OpsMgr

There is much more to monitoring cross platform systems than just providing a heart-beat and an up/down status. CrossPlat monitoring has taken and integrated the same types of monitoring that were available on Windows operating systems and provides these for Unix/Linux systems as well. The CrossPlat agents are integrated not only in the Operations Manager console but also in components such as the Health Explorer. The next sections provide examples of this integration.

OpsMgr Console

Figure 2.32 shows the Solaris Computer Diagram view, which includes the health of the various sub-components of the server. The other views at this level provide health for the other components, such as logical disks, network adapters, physical disks, over-all server health, and a view for the operating system performance counters. This closely mirrors the views provided when monitoring Windows servers.

There are also sub-folders under this node, providing information that is more detailed. Figure 2.33 shows the logical disk bytes per second performance counters for the So-laris system. As with other views in OpsMgr 2007, you can display this information for a period of time that ranges up to the amount of time the performance data is retained in the Operational database. (The default is 7 days.)

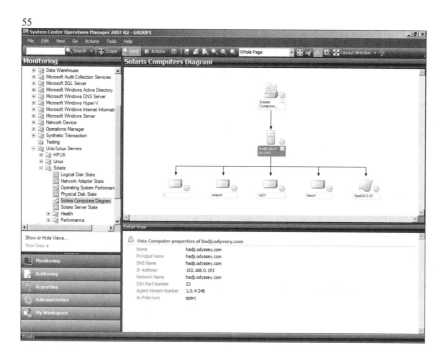

FIGURE 2.32 Solaris Computers Diagram view

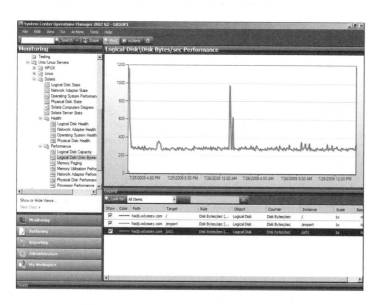

FIGURE 2.33 Solaris logical disk performance

Figure 2.34 shows the network performance counters for the same Solaris system split between the number of bytes received, sent, and total. Similar to other views in OpsMgr, you can display this information for multiple systems within this view. Because this environment is monitoring a single Solaris system, these views show the single system for these counters.

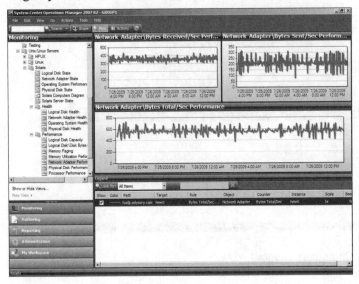

FIGURE 2.34 Solaris network performance

Health Explorer

The Health Explorer is a core component of Operations Manager. It provides a simple way to investigate issues on a system using a logical drill-down approach. Figure 2.35 shows that Unix/Linux systems are integrated fully with the same core components available in the Health Explorer for Windows systems (Availability, Configuration, Performance, and Security).

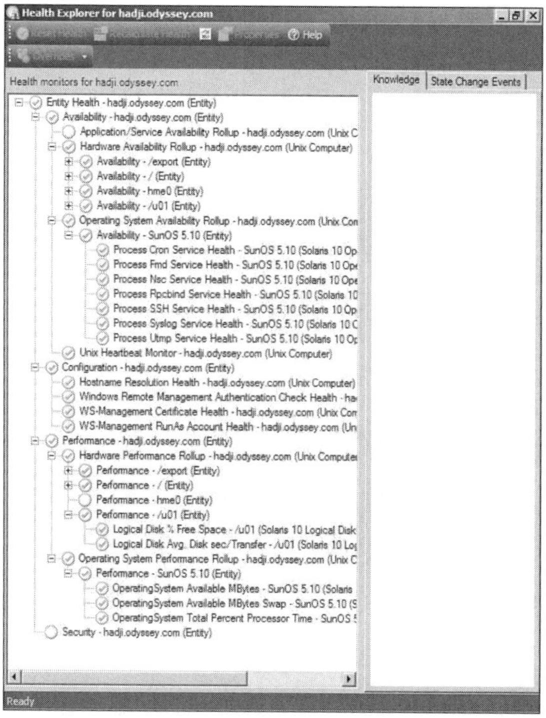

FIGURE 2.35 Solaris Health Explorer

The core concept regarding CrossPlat integration with OpsMgr is *consistency*. The OpsMgr and CrossPlat development teams used the same approaches to provide those views, performance counters, and status that are used with the Windows platform management packs. This makes using the same tool (OpsMgr) intuitive as it provides the same functionality in the same way for Unix/Linux systems as with Windows server systems.

Reports

When you select a Linux server in the Linux Server State view folder, the Actions pane will show a dozen targeted Unix computer reports available for on-the-fly generation. Figure 2.36 displays the seven-day memory performance history (pages per sec) report for the hadji computer:

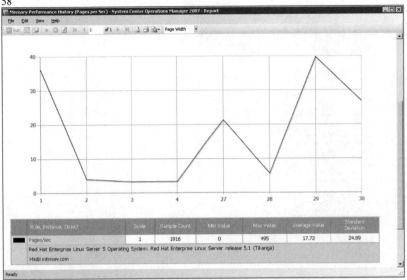

FIGURE 2.36 Report on memory performance history

Tasks

An additional benefit to the CrossPlat release is the addition of a small collection of Unix Computer tasks, which are available in both the Operations and Web consoles. These tasks are as follows:

► **Memory Information**—System paging and swap data.

► **Run VMStat**—A report on virtual memory statistics, paging block I/O, traps, system, and CPU usage.

► **Top 10 CPU Processes**—Listing of the top 10 processor-intensive processes on the Unix system.

Figure 2.37 shows an example listing the top 10 CPU processes on a Linux server run from the OpsMgr Web console.

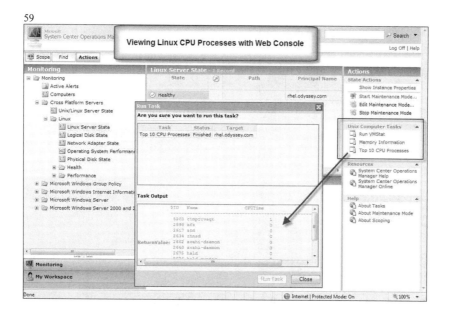

FIGURE 2.37 Unix top 10 CPU processes task

Integration with Distributed Applications

Distributed Applications are one of the most powerful and unfortunately among the least-utilized functions of Operations Manager 2007. You can create distributed applications within the Operations Manager console in the Authoring node, at Authoring -> Distributed Applications. To create a new distributed application, right-click and choose Create a New Distributed Application.

For more details on distributed applications within Operations Manager, see Chapter 19, "Distributed Applications," of *System Center Operations Manager 2007 Unleashed*, and Chapter 9 in this book.

In terms of CrossPlat, interest in Distributed Applications is from the perspective of how you can integrate Unix/Linux systems within these applications. Figure 2.38 shows how new component groups can be added using the Unix Supported agents.

The addition of CrossPlat extensions creates OpsMgr objects for monitored components of discovered Unix/Linux computers. This expands the universe of objects available to use within distributed applications (DAs) to include Linux disks, processors, network interfaces, and other components. As an example, you can create a DA that contains two components of classes: Windows 2008 logical disks and Linux logical disks. This DA represents the health of the logical disks of all the web farm members, regardless of their operating system.

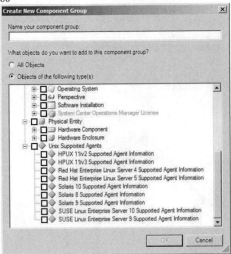

FIGURE 2.38 Component groups with Unix Supported platforms

Two relationships are defined in Figure 2.39: Web Server Farm Logical Disks Uses Linux Logical Disk, and Web Server Farm Logical Disks Uses Windows 2008 Logical Disk. Figure 2.39 is a screenshot of the distributed application, which is open in the Distributed Application Designer.

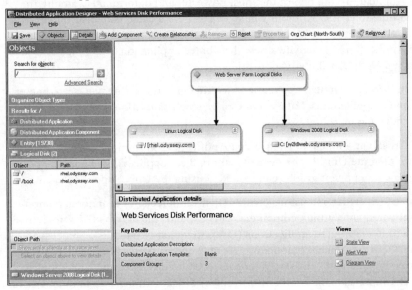

FIGURE 2.39 Example of a distributed application with CrossPlat and Windows components

By creating a Performance view targeting the DA you created, you can assess aggregated logical disk performance across Windows and Linux members of a web server farm. Figure 2.40 shows OpsMgr performance monitoring with both CrossPlat and Windows components in a single view.

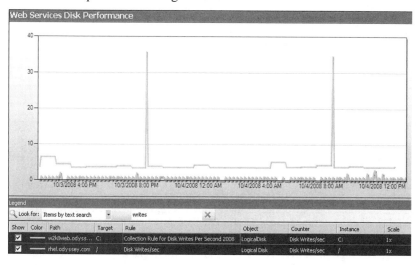

FIGURE 2.40 Performance monitoring with both CrossPlat and Windows components

Operations Manager's integration of CrossPlat is seamless and intuitive to work with once you are familiar with OpsMgr and is not dependent upon heavy familiarity with Unix/Linux operating systems. However, monitoring the operating system is only the first major step toward providing full management for non-Windows systems. Monitoring through Bridgeways and Novell management packs extend OpsMgr's reach into these areas, providing an extremely comprehensive monitoring solution regardless of the platforms involved. The next sections of this chapter discuss management packs, templates, and connectors used to enhance the CrossPlat experience.

Bridgeways Management Packs

Bridgeways provides a number of different management packs designed to work natively with the OpsMgr product, further extending monitoring beyond the operating system and into the application layer on Unix/Linux systems. They offer a healthy list of management packs, with more planned for 2010. Table 2.2 lists the Bridgeways roadmap as of early February 2010.

TABLE 2.2 Cross Platform Management Packs Roadmap

Timeframe	Management Pack	Status
Q3 2003	VMware v1.1	Released
	Apache Tomcat	Released
	JBoss	Released
Q4 2009	JMX Custom Template	Released
	Blackberry Enterprise Server 4.0/5.0	Released
	IBM DB2	Released
	Oracle ASM	Released
Q1 2010	IBM WebSphere	Beta
	Oracle/BEA WebLogic	Beta
	Oracle RAC	Contact Bridgeways
	VMware 1.2	Contact Bridgeways
Q2 2010	IBM MQ	Contact Bridgeways
	Oracle ESB	Contact Bridgeways

When deployed to agent-managed Unix/Linux (or Windows) systems, these management packs provide the same deep and granular level of monitoring you have come to expect from the Exchange or Active Directory management packs, and work seamlessly from the Operations console. The management packs usually require very little configuration; those that do typically just need a provider installed on the Unix/Linux system for the management pack to communicate with the application. For example, the Oracle management pack requires installing an Oracle provider on the managed system, and the VMware management pack communicates with ESX and/or Virtual Center using a Windows service and a small configuration UI.

The next sections discuss several of the available Bridgeways management packs—the VMware ESX and Apache management packs.

The Bridgeways VMware ESX Management Pack

Monitoring VMware with OpsMgr has always been somewhat challenging and required installing a third-party add-on or management pack of some sort. There have been a number of different solutions including nWorks (now a subsidiary of Veeam and previously discussed in Chapter 22, "Interoperability," of *System Center Operations Manager 2007*) and eXc Software's (now owned by Quest) virtual agents. Bridgeways recently stepped firmly into the fray with their version of the VMware ESX management pack.

Managing VMware can be difficult. ESX uses a variation of Linux but it is stripped down and unable to support installing an agent. This requires using another method to connect to VMware; third-party solutions such as Bridgeways utilize the powerful VMware Application Programming Interface (API). To connect to this API, the Bridgeways management pack uses a Windows service and a small configuration interface. The service connects to a VMware ESX host or the Virtual Center server, and interacts with both VMware and OpsMgr.

The management pack itself provides an extremely deep level of monitoring, perhaps a little too much for some! Fortunately, from the authors' personal experience, Bridgeways VMware personnel are extremely knowledgeable and quite happy to guide you through tuning their management pack, ensuring you get the most from your investment.

Installing the management pack is straightforward. Here is what it entails:

- ▶ Install the Windows service.
- ▶ Install the configuration console.
- ▶ Install the management pack itself.

If you are installing the Bridgeways management pack in a large or complex environment or one with a large number of ESX hosts, consider a dedicated server for hosting the VMware Windows service. The service processes a large amount of data and may cause performance degradation if installed on a management server or the RMS. As the Windows service communicates directly with the RMS, provision extra resources to the RMS when you design your environment to account for the added overhead of the VMware management pack. This chapter does not cover the process to install the management pack as that is documented in the Bridgeways installation guide, but looks at various aspects of the management pack and the different levels of monitoring it provides.

After importing the VMware management pack, you must establish a connection with the ESX host(s) or Virtual Center. Do this using the VMware Management Administrator tool, displayed in Figure 2.41.

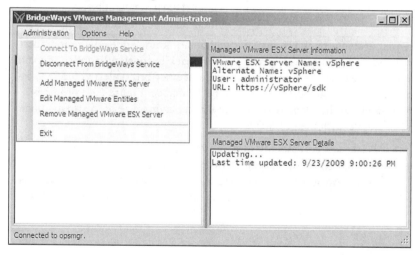

FIGURE 2.41 The VMware Management Administrator

NOTE: USE VIRTUAL CENTER TO COMMUNICATE WITH VMWARE INFRASTRUCTURE

VMware's EULA states that wherever possible you should use Virtual Center for interaction with the VMware infrastructure. With that in mind, the authors recommend connecting through Virtual Center if present.

After you successfully add a VMware server or Virtual Center instance, it will take some time for the data to appear in the OpsMgr console. This will vary based on the number of ESX servers, or the size of your infrastructure if connecting to Virtual Center. Typically, everything is populated within an hour or two. Once initial population of the data completes, the management pack functions in real-time, similar to many other management packs.

Adding VMware ESX Server or Virtual Center server requires an account with sufficient access rights to VMware. Table 2.3 lists the minimum rights identified in the Bridgeways VMware ESX management pack installation guide.

TABLE 2.3 Privileges Required for the Bridgeways VMware ESX Management Pack

Function	Privileges
Monitor the VMWare ESX environment.	System.View System.Read on all entities System.Anonymous
Perform host operations.	Host.Config.Maintenance
Perform virtual machine operations.	VirtualMachine.Interact.PowerOff VirtualMachine.Interact.Reset VirtualMachine.Interact.Suspend

The VMware management pack provides a vast level of knowledge, even more than available within Virtual Center, as the management pack is constantly collecting and analyzing performance data from the infrastructure in an effort to alert you of any issues and provide recommendations to improve performance. Figure 2.42 provides a glimpse into the depth of the management pack by displaying one of the many diagram views that are available with the product.

As the diagram view delves very deeply into the VMware infrastructure, it could be difficult to locate the root cause of an issue. However, because the Bridgeways management pack utilizes OpsMgr native functionality, you can use the problem path tool from within the diagram view to assist in locating an issue, as shown in Figure 2.43.

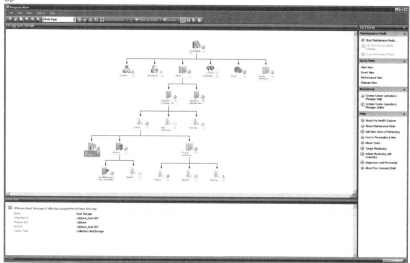

FIGURE 2.42 Diagram view

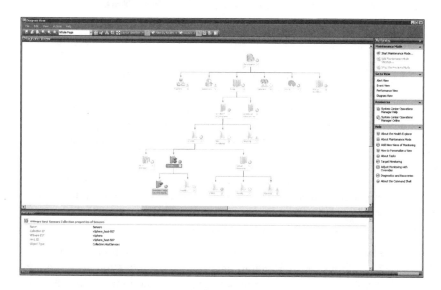

FIGURE 2.43 Diagram view with problem path tool

In addition to using the diagram view for troubleshooting, you can use the health explorer. The Health Explorer, shown in Figure 2.44, illustrates the depth of the management pack. This example shows a write request failure condition of one of the VMware storage disks.

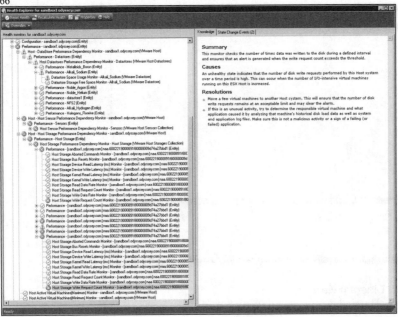

FIGURE 2.44 Health Explorer

One of the unique and very beneficial features of the Bridgeways VMware management pack is the large number of dashboard views, making it extremely easy to view related and dependent data on a single screen. This minimizes the need to navigate to multiple locations in the console to obtain the information you need. Figure 2.45 shows an example of the datacenter dashboard, which displays both the datacenter state and the datacenter active alerts on one screen.

Bridgeways also utilizes dashboard views to view performance data, letting you quickly visualize comparative performance from a single pane of glass. Figure 2.46 provides an example of a performance dashboard, which depicts the Virtual Machine VCPU Metrics of multiple machines using a single screen.

The Bridgeways VMware management pack provides the ability to monitor your VMware infrastructure alongside your operating system and application layer, and provides performance reporting and analysis and configuration recommendations that are either not present or very difficult to locate and utilize in ESX and Virtual Center. Overall, the Bridgeways VMware management pack is certainly one the authors recommend for monitoring VMware with OpsMgr 2007 R2.

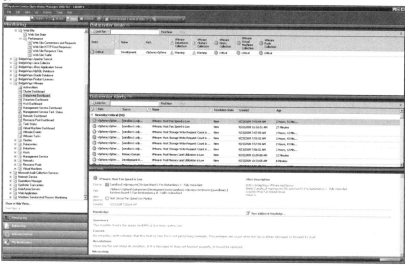

FIGURE 2.45 The datacenter dashboard displays datacenter state and active alerts.

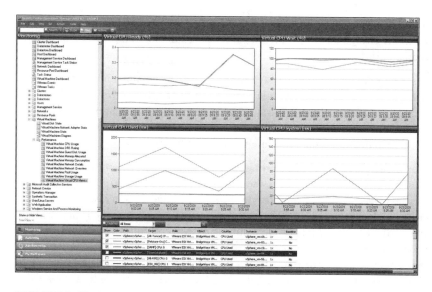

FIGURE 2.46 The performance dashboard enables simultaneously viewing metrics of multiple machines.

The Bridgeways Apache Management Pack

As the "Bridgeways Management Packs" section mentioned, Bridgeways provides a number of management packs for non-Microsoft applications such as Oracle, Black-Berry Enterprise Server, and Apache. This section takes a more detailed look at the Apache management pack.

Like the majority of the Bridgeways management packs for non-Windows applications, the Apache management pack requires a provider installed on the Unix/Linux system, which will collect data. Here are the basic steps to install the management pack:

1.   Run the Setup program.

2.   Import the newly extracted management packs.

3.   Ensure the Unix Run As profiles are configured.

4.   Install the Apache provider on the Unix/Windows Apache servers.

5.   Install the mod_bridgeways_probe on the Apache servers.

6.   Configure the management pack.

This chapter does not cover the installation process for the management pack; this is documented in the Bridgeways-provided installation guide included when you purchase the management pack.

Although installing the Bridgeways Apache HTTP Server management pack is somewhat manual, the process of installing the provider and mod_bridgeways_probe is made easier by a set of console tasks to automate the installation. Just be sure you execute the Bridgeways Apache MP installation program on the management server managing the Unix machine on which you intend to install the provider.

To run the task, navigate in the Monitoring node of the Operations console to the Unix/Linux computer view and execute the Install Bridgeways Provider–Apache HTTP Server task against the Apache server. Figure 2.47 shows this task. Next, install the mod_bridgeways_probe, which is essential to transmit Apache data to the Bridgeways Apache provider. Install this module similar to how you installed the provider—navigate to the Web Server State view in the Bridgeways Apache HTTP Server management pack and run the Install Bridgeways Provider–Apache HTTP Server task against the newly discovered web server. It may take several moments to discover the web server. You will need to restart the Apache HTTP Server application when installing the mod_bridgeways_probe, which will render all websites unavailable for a short time. Schedule this installation during a maintenance window if possible.

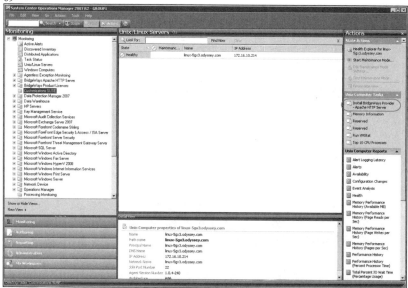

FIGURE 2.47 Install Apache Provider task

After installing the module, there are two components to configure, as follows:

► **DataProvider.conf file**—Configure to match the configuration of your environment.

► **Apache HTTP Server**—Verify that the server responds on IP address 127.0.0.1.

After completing these steps, the management pack begins monitoring the web server and all configured websites.

The management pack contains a number of monitors and performance collection rules to assist with monitoring and maintaining the Apache HTTP Server. These include monitoring for server availability, performance of requests per second coming into the server, and collecting data for website access and web server performance. Figure 2.48 shows one of the graphs available with the Apache HTTP Server management pack.

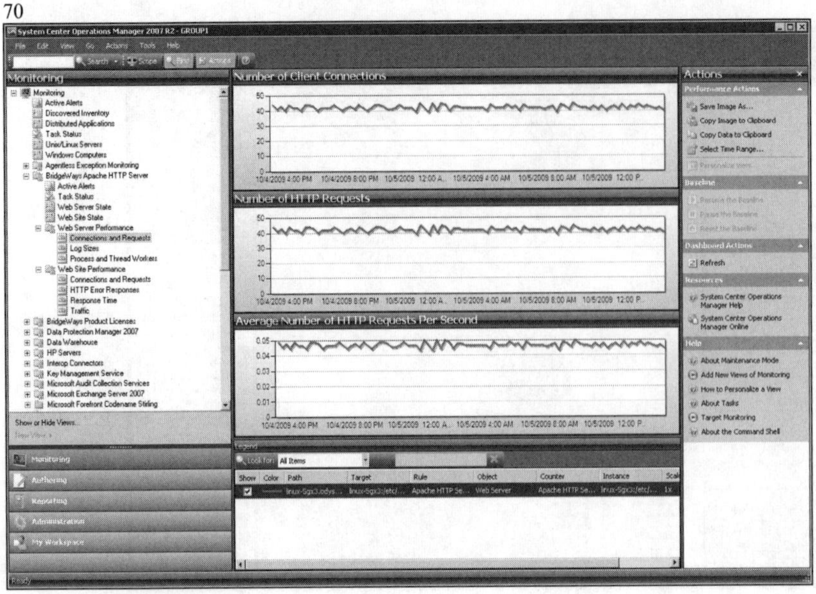

FIGURE 2.48 Apache web server MP graph

Novell SUSE Management Pack

OpsMgr 2007 R2's cross platform monitoring component enables natively monitoring a number of different Unix/Linux flavors out of the box. One such flavor is Novell SUSE Enterprise Linux. Let's look at the SUSE Linux management pack, including the monitoring provided out of the box, plus what's possible with custom SUSE agent scripts.

The SUSE management pack, similar to the other Unix/Linux management packs, monitors the core operating system environment such as the disk volumes, CPU performance, memory allocation, and network adapter state. The health of core system processes (referred to as *services* within OpsMgr) are monitored as well.

When you deploy the agent and configure the Run As accounts and Run As profiles, the SUSE server and its components are discovered and visible in the console, as shown in Figure 2.49. After installing the agent, creating the Run As accounts and profiles, and discovering the systems, additional objects will appear in the console. If you open the diagram view, you will see these objects displayed, as shown in Figure 2.50.

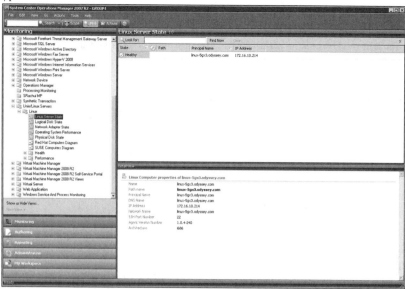

FIGURE 2.49 Viewing the SUSE system in the Monitoring node

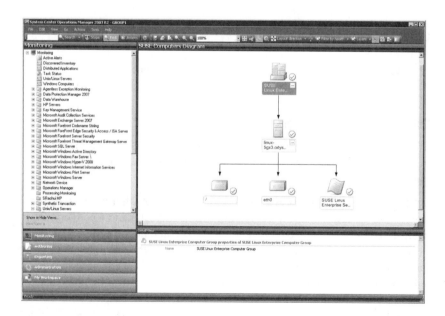

FIGURE 2.50 The Linux SUSE server and its components viewed in the diagram view

Figure 2.51 shows the Health Explorer for the SUSE server with the different monitors that exist out of the box. The Health Explorer shows that the SUSE management pack monitors various components for availability and performance. The management pack also monitors the SUSE agent on the server and the ability for the management server to successful connect and authenticate to the agent. Validity of the Run As accounts on the server is also verified. In addition to the objects visible in the Health Explorer, the SUSE management pack contains a number of pre-defined Diagnostic and Recovery actions. The next sections look at several of these—the tasks for logical disk volume recovery and cron service recovery.

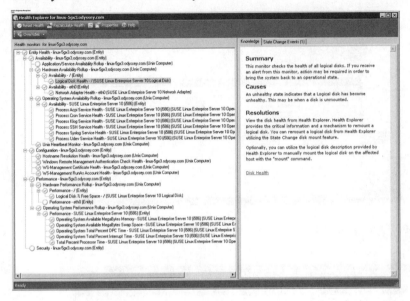

FIGURE 2.51 Monitors installed with the Linux SUSE management pack

Logical Disk Volume Recovery

Similar to the diagnostic and recovery actions in the Windows OS management pack to automate problem resolution, the SUSE management pack comes with a number of predefined actions.

Navigate to the SUSE logical disk monitor (through either the Authoring pane or the Health Explorer) and open the monitor properties. The Diagnostic and Recovery tab shows pre-configured tasks, displayed in Figure 2.52. The diagnostic action runs by default and provides additional information about the status of the drive that is in error. However, the recovery task that attempts a remount of the volume is disabled by default. To enable automatic re-mounting of un-mounted volumes, simply right-click the recovery task and enable it using an override. You can see the command that the diagnostic and recovery actions execute by looking at the properties of each task. The diagnostic action runs the df -k command against the failed volume, and the recovery action runs the mount command. The df -k command is used to calculate the amount of free disk space, displayed in the state change events tab in the Health Explorer to aid with troubleshooting.

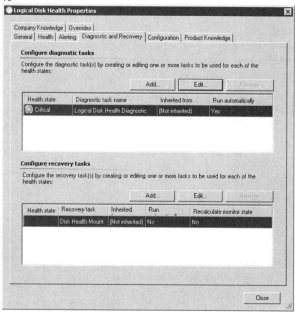

FIGURE 2.52 Diagnostic and recovery tasks

Cron Service Recovery

Cron service recovery is similar in nature to logical disk recovery; although, as it applies to a service (or process), the commands executed by the diagnostic and recovery actions are different. Once again, the diagnostic action probes the status of the service and is enabled by default, and the recovery action (again disabled by default) will attempt to restart the service if stopped. In this case, the diagnostic action runs the `service cron status` command. To see the output generated and how the recovery action works, stop the cron service on the SUSE server. Perform the following steps:

1. Enable the recovery action; right-click it and then enable it for the linux-5gx3 server in this case.

2. Stop the cron service on the SUSE server; verify that the recovery action is successful.

3. To connect to the server, you can use PuTTY to establish a remote SSH connection. PuTTY is a free telnet/SSH client. Running the executable presents the screen shown in Figure 2.53. Input the IP address or hostname of the server and verify the connectivity method, which is SSH in this case. Click Open to establish the connection.

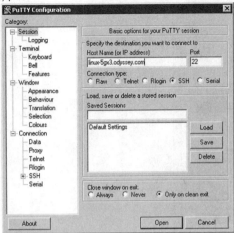

FIGURE 2.53 Using PuTTY to connect to the Linux system

4. The first time you connect to a machine, you are prompted with the dialog shown in Figure 2.54. This asks whether you trust the machine and want to add its rsa2 key fingerprint to the PuTTY cache. Select Yes.

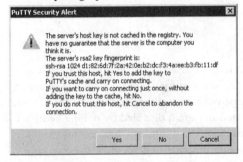

FIGURE 2.54 PuTTY warning dialog

5. Now, input a login account and password to access the machine. After logging in, run the `service cron status` command to see the output you will see in the state change events tab in OpsMgr once you stop the service. Figure 2.55 shows the output in the Odyssey environment.

6. Run the `service cron stop` command, stopping the service. If you check back within OpsMgr, after several moments (the default interval for the monitor is 300 seconds) the server state is now critical, the Health Explorer shows the CRON service is critical, and the diagnostic has run successfully, displaying the status of the service as shown in Figure 2.56.

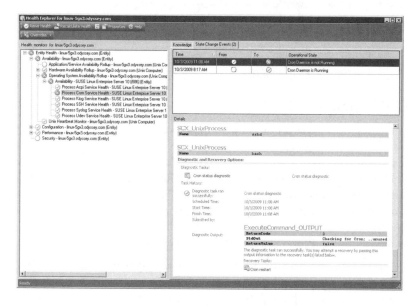

FIGURE 2.55 Cron service status

FIGURE 2.56 Showing cron in a critical state

7. The next time the monitor checks, the status returns to healthy; if you look at the Health Explorer, you can see where the recovery action ran to restart the service, as displayed in Figure 2.57.

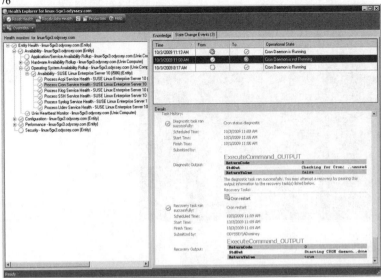

FIGURE 2.57 Cron shows as restarted

Performance Collection

In addition to using monitors to detect the state of the server, the SUSE management pack contains performance collection rules that collect performance data to assist in the monitoring and resolution of issues with SUSE servers. Various pieces of performance data from CPU, memory, disk, and network traffic are collected, including Disk Read, Writes, and Transfers per second, % Processor Interrupt Time, and % Used Swap Space. As with other management packs, you can display this data using performance views in the Operations console or a report. Figure 2.58 shows an example of a dashboard view displaying the Processor performance over the past 24 hours.

Figure 2.59 displays the reports available for the SUSE management pack, which are a combination of configuration and performance reports. You can also execute generic reports such as the availability report and the generic performance and alert analysis reports against Unix/Linux agent-managed machines.

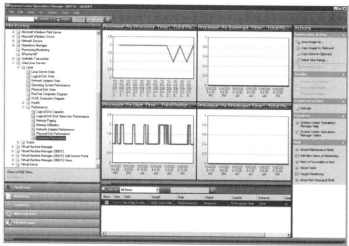

FIGURE 2.58 Processor performance over the last 24 hours

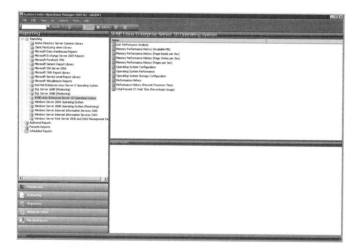

FIGURE 2.59 Reports

Custom Scripting in the SUSE Management Pack

You can create your own custom scripts for monitoring. This section discusses the process to create a basic file monitoring script and a monitor that shows a critical state if the file does not exist.

The process for creating custom scripts to execute against Unix/Linux machines in OpsMgr is relatively simple but not that straightforward. Start by creating a custom monitor type based on the Microsoft.Unix.WSMan.Invoke.ProbeAction module type. You can either use the Authoring console or an XML editor to type the code manually. This example targets the monitor at the Microsoft.Unix.Computer class and sets it to disabled by default; you would enable it for specific machines by using an override. It should be noted that although it should be possible to modify this example for any Unix/Linux system, it was designed and tested on the IBM AIX platform and therefore may not work as intended on other platforms.

Here are the three components that make up this script monitor:

- ► The script
- ► The monitor type
- ► The monitor itself

Perform the following steps:

1. Create the script. This example uses a simple bash script that checks for the existence of a file and outputs a 0 if the file exists and a 1 if not. Here is the script:

   ```
   #! /bin/bash

   if [ ! -f "$filename" ]
   then
   echo 1
   else
   echo 0
   fi
   ```

2. Replace the `$filename` argument in step 1 with the filename you want to check. You could also use a variable here, but this particular example will keep things simple. As an example, replace `$filename` with `testfile`, which will be the file created and deleted for the test.

3. Save the file as a .sh script and copy it to the Unix/Linux server. An easy way to copy the file is SFTP using WinSCP. For this example, PuTTY was used to log into the server, and the following commands were run to create the script folder and file for testing:

   ```
   md tmp
   cd tmp
   >testfile
   ```

4. Run the `ls` command to verify the file exists. Here is the generated output, confirming that the test file was created and the script was located in the correct place:

   ```
   chk_file_exist.sh      testfile
   ```

5. Create the custom management pack containing the monitor type and monitor. Instructions for creating custom management packs are in Chapter 8, "Management Pack Authoring," of this book and Chapter 23, "Developing Management Packs and Reports," of *System Center Operations Manager 2007 Unleashed*.

6. Use the following eXtended Markup Language (XML) code to create the monitor type:

```
<MonitorTypes>
      <UnitMonitorType ID="Custom.Unix.FileMonitoring.RunScript.MonitorType"
Accessibility="Internal">
         <MonitorTypeStates>
           <MonitorTypeState ID="Error" NoDetection="false" />
           <MonitorTypeState ID="OK" NoDetection="false" />
         </MonitorTypeStates>
         <Configuration>
           <xsd:element minOccurs="1" name="TargetSystem" type="xsd:string" />
           <xsd:element minOccurs="1" name="Command" type="xsd:string" />
           <xsd:element minOccurs="1" name="Interval" type="xsd:integer" />
         </Configuration>
         <OverrideableParameters>
           <OverrideableParameter ID="Command" Selector="$Config/Command$"
ParameterType="string" />
           <OverrideableParameter ID="Interval" Selector="$Config/Interval$"
ParameterType="int" />
         </OverrideableParameters>
         <MonitorImplementation>
           <MemberModules>
             <DataSource ID="Scheduler" TypeID="System!System.Scheduler">
               <Scheduler>
                 <SimpleReccuringSchedule>
                   <Interval Unit="Seconds">$Config/Interval$</Interval>
                   <SyncTime />
                 </SimpleReccuringSchedule>
                 <ExcludeDates />
               </Scheduler>
             </DataSource>
             <ProbeAction ID="RunScript"
TypeID="MicrosoftUnixLibrary!Microsoft.Unix.WSMan.Invoke.ProbeAction">
                 <TargetSystem>$Config/TargetSystem$</TargetSystem>
                 <Uri>http://schemas.microsoft.com/wbem/wscim/1/
cim-schema/2/SCX_OperatingSystem?__cimnamespace=root/scx</Uri>
                 <Selector />
                 <InvokeAction>ExecuteCommand</InvokeAction>
                 <Input><![CDATA[ <p:ExecuteCommand_INPUT
xmlns:p="http://schemas.microsoft.com/wbem/wscim/1/cim-
schema/2/SCX_OperatingSystem"><p:command>$Config/Command$</p:command><p:timeout
>10
</p:timeout></p:ExecuteCommand_INPUT> ]]></Input>
             </ProbeAction>
             <ConditionDetection ID="CDOK"
```

```
TypeID="System!System.ExpressionFilter">
                <Expression>
                  <SimpleExpression>
                    <ValueExpression>
                      <XPathQuery Type="Double">//*[local-name()="StdOut"]
                      </XPathQuery>
                    </ValueExpression>
                    <Operator>Equal</Operator>
                    <ValueExpression>
                      <Value Type="Double">0</Value>
                    </ValueExpression>
                  </SimpleExpression>
                </Expression>
            </ConditionDetection>
            <ConditionDetection ID="CDError"
TypeID="System!System.ExpressionFilter">
                <Expression>
                  <SimpleExpression>
                    <ValueExpression>
                      <XPathQuery Type="Double">//*
[local-name()="StdOut"]
                      </XPathQuery>
                    </ValueExpression>
                    <Operator>Equal</Operator>
                    <ValueExpression>
                      <Value Type="Double">1</Value>
                    </ValueExpression>
                  </SimpleExpression>
                </Expression>
            </ConditionDetection>
          </MemberModules>
          <RegularDetections>
            <RegularDetection MonitorTypeStateID="Error">
              <Node ID="CDError">
                <Node ID="RunScript">
                  <Node ID="Scheduler" />
                </Node>
              </Node>
            </RegularDetection>
            <RegularDetection MonitorTypeStateID="OK">
              <Node ID="CDOK">
                <Node ID="RunScript">
                  <Node ID="Scheduler" />
                </Node>
              </Node>
            </RegularDetection>
          </RegularDetections>
```

```
        </MonitorImplementation>
    </UnitMonitorType>
</MonitorTypes>
```

The code creates a monitor type that runs a custom script (configured in step 8) and shows a critical state if it detects a "1" as output from the script and OK if the output is "0." The "//*[local-name()="StdOut"]" line collects the output from the script.

7. Use the following XML to add the newly created monitor type to the Language-Pack sections:

```
<DisplayString ElementID=
    "Custom.Unix.FileMonitoring.RunScript.MonitorType">
    <Name>File Monitoring Run Script Monitor Type</Name>
    <Description />
</DisplayString>
```

8. Create the monitor. This is straightforward, as you configured all the complicated items when creating the monitor type. You can use either XML or the Authoring console to create the monitor. If using the Authoring console, create a custom monitor and select the newly created monitor type, as shown in Figure 2.60.

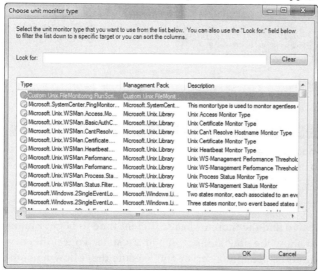

FIGURE 2.60 Creating a custom monitor

9. There are several options to configure after creating the new monitor. The most important is the option specifying the script to run. In the Configuration tab displayed in Figure 2.60, configure the Command property as sh tmp/chk_file_exists.sh, which will execute the command. From this dialog, configure the health state and if the monitor generates an alert.

10. Save the management pack, import it into your management group, and create an override on the new monitor to enable the monitor for the Unix/Linux server. Figure 2.61 displays the override screen; this screen shows that although the monitor supplies the default command, you can override it here if you want.

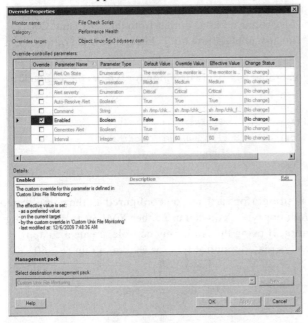

FIGURE 2.61 Override properties

NOTE: ADJUSTING THE MONITOR INTERVAL

The interval set in this example for the monitor is 60 seconds for demonstration purposes. You may need to increase this for a production environment to avoid potential performance issues.

11. Once the override is created and the monitor has sufficient time to begin running, the Health Explorer will show the new monitor in a green state. To test this new monitor, connect back to the Unix/Linux server and execute the following commands:

```
cd tmp
rm testfile
```

This deletes the testfile file, which you can verify by running the ls command and ensuring that the file is no longer present. As the monitor is set to a very frequent interval, the health state of the server should very quickly turn to critical.

12. After verifying that the monitor works, you can recreate the file if necessary and verify that the monitor returns to a healthy state.

Now let's look at another feature delivered with CrossPlat: management pack templates.

Management Pack Templates

In addition to the rules and monitors provided with the Unix/Linux management packs, the R2 release includes a number of new management pack templates specifically designed for Unix/Linux. These are discussed in the next sections.

Unix/Linux Log File Template

The Log File template does exactly as its name suggests and enables you to configure monitoring of a log file hosted on a Unix/Linux server. As with other management pack templates, creating a new log file monitor is simple and wizard based. Choosing to create a new log file monitor presents the standard rule/monitor creation dialogs where you provide the log file monitor a name and select a management pack in which to store it. Click Next to open the dialog shown in Figure 2.62, where you will configure the log file monitor:

▶ **Target**—Select either a specific Unix/Linux computer or a computer group to target the monitor.

▶ **Name and location**—Manually enter the name and location of the log file to monitor. The format of this test will depend on which version of Unix/Linux you are targeting but will be similar to the `/tmp/logfile` format.

▶ **Expression**—Configure the expression (in regular expression format) to monitor for in the log file. The Expression Test section enables you to test the regular expression you just created against a sample line of text you input, which replicates what is found in the log file. Figure 2.62 also displays an example of a successful test.

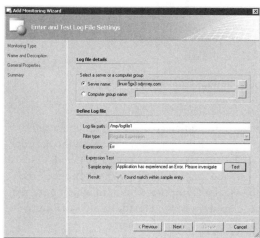

FIGURE 2.62 Log file monitor configuration screen

After correctly configuring the log file monitor, click Next and Finish to save the monitor.

Unix/Linux Service Template

The Unix/Linux Service template also ships as part of OpsMgr 2007 R2. This template works similarly to the Windows Service monitoring template, enabling you to monitor the availability of a specific service (sometimes referred to as a *process*) running on a Unix/Linux server.

After choosing to create the new template and assigning it a name and destination management pack, proceed to the service details dialog shown in Figure 2.63. From this screen, select a source server for the service or process. This server does not necessarily have to be the server you ultimately monitor but must be actively running the service; during the next stage, the wizard connects to the server and enumerates the running services to make it easier to select the appropriate one for monitoring. Figure 2.64 shows the server selection screen.

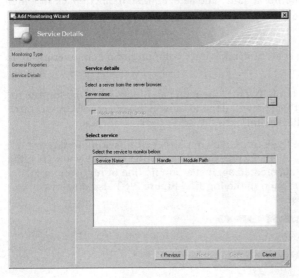

FIGURE 2.63 Service details in the service template dialog

After clicking OK on Figure 2.64, the wizard immediately begins to enumerate the services, displaying the dialog shown in Figure 2.65. Here you can select the appropriate service for monitoring; Figure 2.65 shows the sftp-server service selected. Click the Create button to monitor the service on only the single server selected, or check the Apply to Computer Group checkbox and select a Computer Group to which to target the monitor. Once the monitor is created, it appears in the Health Explorer (Figure 2.66); if the service stops, the monitor displays an unhealthy state.

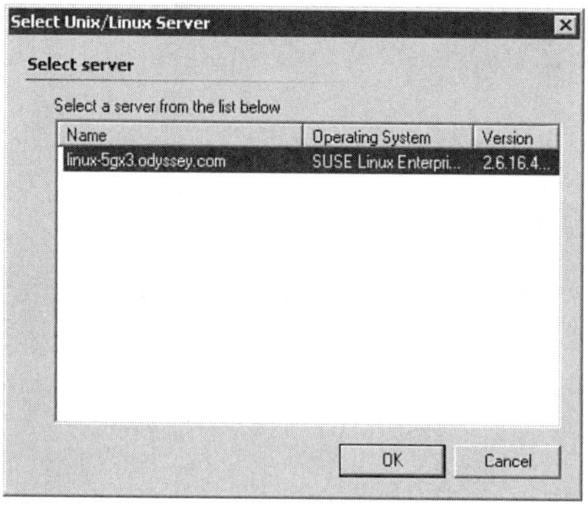

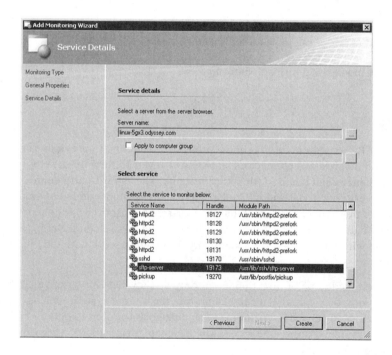

FIGURE 2.64 Server selection screen

FIGURE 2.65 Select a service for monitoring

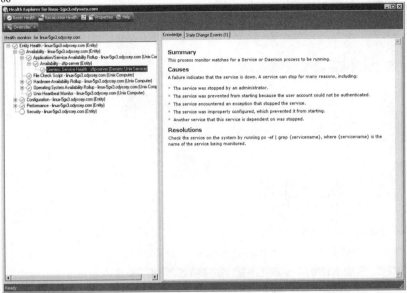

FIGURE 2.66 Service monitor in the Health Explorer

Connectors

New to OpsMgr 2007 R2 are native bi-directional product connectors. In previous versions, third-party vendors provided connectors, enabling OpsMgr to forward data to other monitoring appliances and helpdesk ticketing systems. These third-party connectors were quite often very functional and worked exceptionally well, but added to the cost and complexity of implementation. With the R2 release, Microsoft has designed and built a number of native connectors provided free of charge. These connectors, completely integrated with the product, are specifically designed to work with the OpsMgr architecture.

The connectors are designed to be bi-directional; not only do they send alerts and alert data to the remote system, they can also receive data from the remote system such as ticket number and such. You can also synchronize any change to the alert in either OpsMgr or the remote system. At the time of writing this chapter (Q1 2010), Microsoft provides the following connectors:

► Operations Manager 2007 R2 Connector for IBM Tivoli Enterprise Management Console

► Operations Manager 2007 R2 Connector for HP Operations Manager (formerly HP OpenView Operations)

► Operations Manager 2007 R2 Connector for BMC Remedy Action Request System (ARS)

► Operations Manager 2007 R2 Universal Connector

This list addresses major third-party systems, although a number are currently unavailable—NetCool being an example. Microsoft will continue developing additional connectors and will concentrate on these in terms of industry adoption. In the interim, connectors remain available from Quest Software (formally eXc) for systems not provided by Microsoft. The Quest connectors add additional cost, and often are not as integrated as the native connectors are.

Microsoft also provides a universal connector. This offers the capability to connect those systems currently without native connectors available. The universal connector passes data from OpsMgr into a specific, documented format accessible using custom code. This enables a developer to write the code necessary at the connected system end to communicate and pass data to and from the OpsMgr connector framework. To aid this process, documentation that comes with the universal connector describes the process to create custom code for a third-party system and includes an example to make writing this code easier.

The Microsoft connectors are native to the product and free of charge, although they do not come on the OpsMgr 2007 R2 installation media. Download them from http://www.microsoft.com/downloads/details.aspx?FamilyID=592e4143-c5c8-4270-9a7a-cd0a31ab3189&displaylang=en.

To illustrate implementing connectors, this section looks at the process to install and configure the IBM Tivoli Enterprise Management Console (TEC) connector. Start by downloading the connector package and extracting the files, and then perform the following steps:

1. Install the TEC side of the connector. You can either run an .msi file on a TEC system hosted in Windows or install the components manually on a Unix system. Instructions to install these components are in the accompanying product documentation, but in the Odyssey environment where TEC is hosted on AIX, the following commands installed the core components and the connector (assuming the connector files were copied to /tmp/):

    ```
    gzip -d /tmp/scx-1.0.4-248.aix.5.pcc.lpp.gz
    installp -X -d /tmp/ scx-1.0.4-248.aix.5.ppc.lpp scx.rte
    gzip -d /tmp/scinterop-6.1.7000-58.aix.5.3.pcc-unv.lpp.gz
    installp -X -d /tmp/scinterop-6.1.7000-58.aix.5.3.ppc-unv.lpp MSFTscinterop-pUnv.rte
    ```

2. Next, install the Windows side of the connector. Open the index.html file from the root of the extracted folder, which launches a web page with links to all the necessary components. Figure 2.67 shows this web page.

3. Because this is configuring the IBM TEC connector on an x86 machine, select the connector service (32-bit) from the IBM Tivoli Enterprise Console section (the first section). Clicking the link opens a Windows Explorer window in the file location. Run the SciConnectorSetup_x86.msi file as a user with Operations Manager Administrator rights. This wizard also creates a database, so ensure that the credentials used to run the wizard have sufficient rights on the SQL Server to create databases.

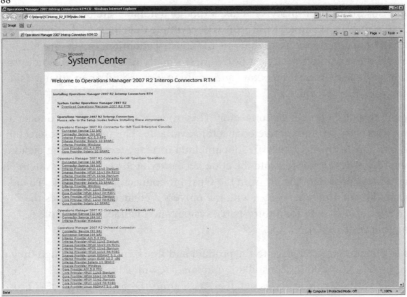

FIGURE 2.67 HTML connector installation page

3. Click Next on the Welcome screen. Accept the licensing agreement and click Next again.

4. Select the appropriate connector components depending on the system you are connecting to. Figure 2.68 shows the components selected in this example. Click Next to continue.

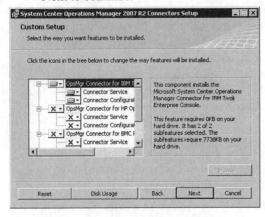

FIGURE 2.68 Selected components

5. Now, configure the location of the SQL Server database used by the connector. This new database created by the wizard has the default name of **SCInterop**. It is best to host this database on the same server hosting the OperationsManager database. Thunder is selected in this case, as this server also hosts the OperationsManager database. Figure 2.69 shows the selections. Click Next to continue.

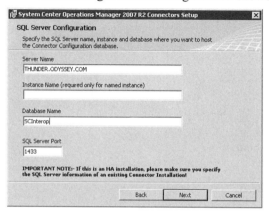

FIGURE 2.69 Database configuration dialog

6. Now, configure a service account to run the connector service. This account requires System Center Data Access and System Center Management Configuration permissions to the management group. For simplicity of configuration, you may simply opt to add this account to the Operations Manager Administrators group.

    This example uses a newly created OM_TEC service account, shown in Figure 2.70. In addition, if you are configuring the connector for high availability (that is, multiple connector servers), you can check the Install Connector as a High Availability Service checkbox on this screen to indicate that this server will act as a connector failover server. Click Next to continue; then Install on the next dialog to install the connector service and connector.

7. When the connector completes installation, a dialog appears with one option available: Configure IBM Tivoli Enterprise Console Connector. Click this option to configure the connector settings.

8. Clicking the button presents the screen shown in Figure 2.71. In this dialog, enter the name of the RMS, the name of the Tivoli TEC server, and the credentials used to access the TEC server. These credentials are often the same as those you specified in the Unix Privileged account Run As Profile. Clicking Configure prompts you to test the connection to validate that the server is reachable.

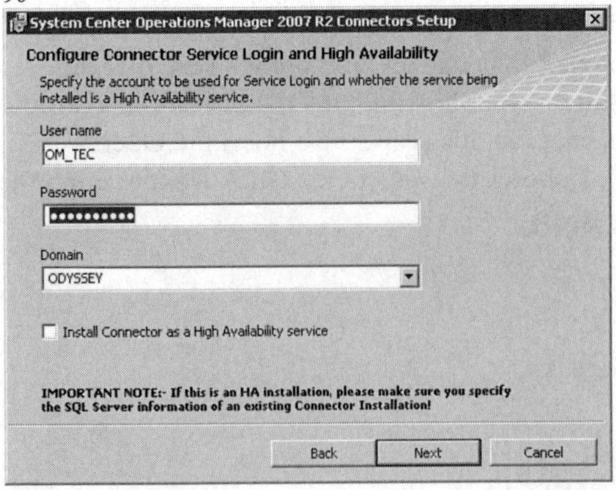

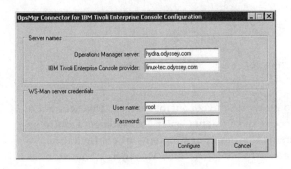

FIGURE 2.70 Configure the service account

FIGURE 2.71 Connector configuration dialog

9.   Next, create and install certificates at each end of the connector to enable the TEC end and the OpsMgr end to communicate. A dialog appears at the end of the setup process and prompts you to create these certificates; you can have the wizard create them for you automatically, which is recommended.

10. Once Setup is complete, open the Operations console; in the Administration node, navigate to Product Connectors to finalize the connector configuration. Figure 2.72 shows the new connector present. Right-click the connector; then select Properties to complete the configuration.

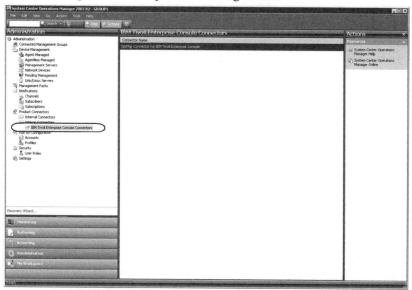

FIGURE 2.72 The TEC connector visible in the Operations Console

▶ The TEC Server tab (selected in Figure 2.73) is where you configure basic connector communication. Configure additional TEC servers to connect to as required, and specify if the connector is bi-directional with the Receive Updates.... and Send Updates.... checkboxes.

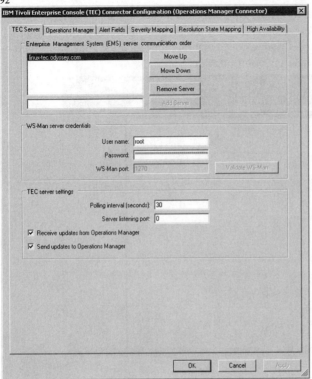

FIGURE 2.73 The TEC Server tab

▶ Use the Operations Manager tab (see Figure 2.74) to configure the Operations Manager end of the connector, including the servers to connect to and the order they are used, and various polling settings to fine-tune the way the connector sends data to the remote system.

▶ The Alert Fields tab (see Figure 2.75) enables you to further configure the different alert fields to send from OpsMgr to TEC, although the alerts shown in Figure 2.77 are configured by default.

▶ The Severity Mapping tab (see Figure 2.76) is also configured out of the box but can be tweaked as required to ensure that alerts raised in OpsMgr create tickets in TEC with the correct severities.

▶ The Resolution State Mapping tab (see Figure 2.77) is similar to the Severity Mapping tab, except here you configure how the resolution states map to TEC. These are initially configured at a basic level. If required, you can create new resolution state mappings from this screen, although you may first need to custom resolution states within OpsMgr.

▶ Finally, use the High Availability tab to configure the failover settings for the connector servers if you configured the connector servers for high availability.

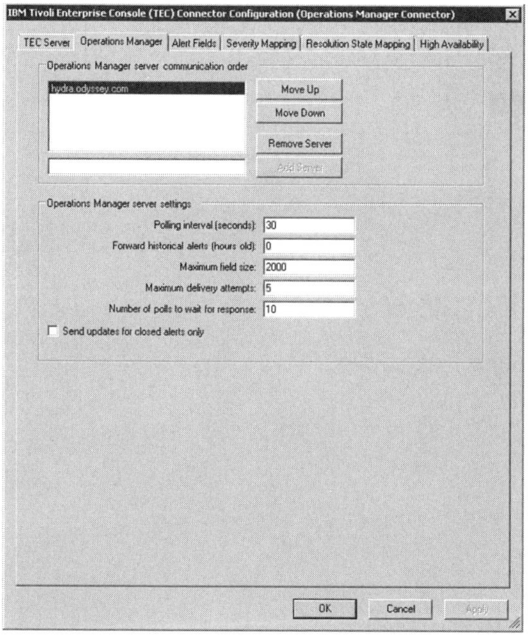

FIGURE 2.74 The Operations Manager tab

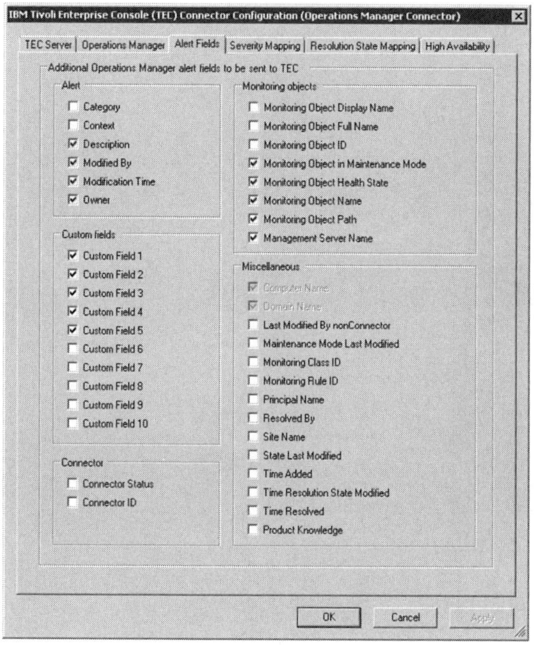

FIGURE 2.75 The Alert Fields tab

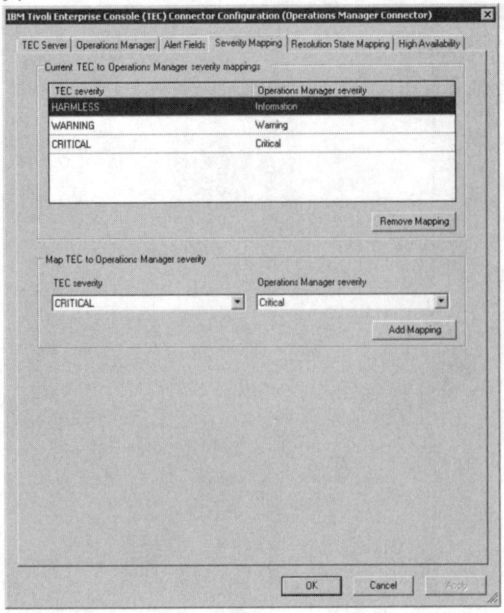

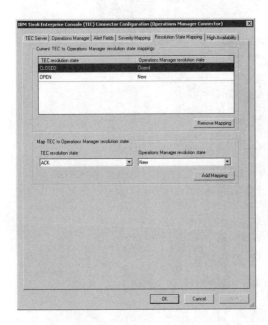

FIGURE 2.76 The Severity Mapping tab

FIGURE 2.77 The Resolution State Mapping tab

11. After configuring the connector, create a subscription to the connector to enable the connector to discern which alerts to forward to TEC. More information on creating subscriptions is in Chapter 1. If desired, you may also right-click any alert and choose to forward it manually.

12. Once the connector is configured, you can view its status in the monitoring pane shown in Figure 2.78. The status of the connector is monitored by the TEC Interop Connector management pack, which is automatically imported when you install the connector.

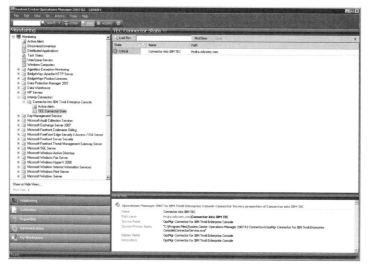

FIGURE 2.78 Monitoring pane view of the connector

13. The final step is ensuring that TEC is aware of the alert and can process it. For this to happen, you must create a number of classes in TEC—this is most easily accomplished by running the System_Center_Interop_Configure_TEC_Task on the TEC server. Additional information is available in the installation guide accompanying the connectors.

14. After configuring the connector, alerts can forward from OpsMgr to TEC; once the alert is successfully forwarded, information from TEC, such as the ticket ID, is passed back to OpsMgr and appended to the alert (if configured).

Although this chapter focused on the TEC connector, configuring the ARS and HPOM connectors is similar, and you will find detailed installation and configuration instructions in the documentation accompanying the connector software.

Summary

This chapter incorporated a discussion of the OpsMgr Cross Platform Extensions, which is perhaps the most widely known enhancement incorporated in the OpsMgr 2007 R2 release. The next two chapters look at the core platform components, and discuss installing and using OpsMgr 2007 R2 on Windows Server 2008 and SQL Server 2008.

## CHAPTER 3

Operations Manager 2007 R2 and Windows Server 2008

Windows Server 2008 brings a number of new features to the Microsoft server platform. Server 2008 includes enhancements to Active Directory—adding the ability to define password requirements on a more granular level (fine-grained password policies), restart domain services, and provide enhanced security through deploying read-only domain controllers. The introduction of Server Core provides a minimal footprint version of the Windows operating system that is more secure and requires fewer outages to apply patches. Server 2008 also adds improved clustering through new options such as the majority node cluster, and enhances virtualization capabilities with Microsoft's release of Hyper-V.

Although many of these features do not directly affect System Center Operations Manager (OpsMgr), some have an impact—these will be the focus of this chapter. This chapter discusses how OpsMgr 2007 Release 2 (R2) functions with Windows Server 2008. Topics include the following:

▶ The impact of several of the new Windows 2008 capabilities—such as the Windows Firewall, server roles, and Hyper-V—on an OpsMgr deployment.

▶ The effect of Windows Server 2008's new features on how you deploy OpsMgr.

▶ How to upgrade to OpsMgr 2007 R2.

▶ Other considerations when deploying OpsMgr into a Windows 2008 environment.

Installing Operations Manager 2007 R2

The process to install Operations Manager 2007 R2 requires effective planning and follows the same installation procedures as the

Operations Manager 2007 Released to Manufacturing (RTM) and Service Pack (SP) 1 releases. For details, refer to Chapter 4, "Planning Your OpsMgr Deployment," and Chapter 6, "Installing Operations Manager 2007," in the predecessor to this book, *System Center Operations Manager 2007 Unleashed* (Sams, 2008). OpsMgr 2007 R2 does not add new components, and the order to install OpsMgr components is unchanged since Operations Manager 2007 RTM. Install the components in the following order to:

1. Operations Database Server

2. Root Management Server, Operations Console, and Web Console Server

3. Management Servers

4. Reporting Server and Data Warehouse Server

5. ACS Database Server and ACS Collection Server

6. Gateway Servers

7. Agentless Exception Monitoring

8. Operations Manager Agents

9. ACS Forwarders

The big changes related to installing Operations Manager 2007 R2 are hotfixes required for Windows Server 2008 systems, new prerequisites, the Windows Firewall, what happens once installation completes, and the effect of Windows Server 2008 roles and features on Operations Manager 2007. The next sections discuss these changes.

Hotfixes

Three hotfixes are required on Windows Server 2008 systems that will run OpsMgr components. Applying the hotfixes before installing Operations Manager decreases the possibility of difficult debugging issues after completing your deployment:

▶ **Hotfix 951327**—Systems running the OpsMgr console must have this hotfix installed. The hotfix (http://support.microsoft.com/kb/951327) addresses issues where the Operations Manager console may crash when opening the Health Explorer on either Windows Vista or Windows Server 2008.

▶ **Hotfix 952664**—All Windows Server 2008 (or Vista) systems running Operations Manager 2007 components must install hotfix 952664. This hotfix (at http://support.microsoft.com/kb/952664) fixes problems where the Event Log service may stop responding due to a deadlock condition.

▶ **Hotfix 953290**—All Windows Server 2008 (or Vista) systems running Operations Manager 2007 components must install this hotfix. The hotfix (available at http://support.microsoft.com/kb/953290) fixes issues where an application may crash if legacy methods are used to query performance values.

If you have a large number of Server 2008 systems, you may want to use an automated deployment mechanism to deploy these hotfixes to systems requiring them. See a good write-up on how to use System Center Configuration Manager (ConfigMgr) 2007 to deploy at http://ops-mgr.spaces.live.com/blog/cns!3D3B8489FCAA9B51!1285.entry/.

These hotfixes are included in Windows 2008 Service Pack 2. See the "Windows Server 2008 SP 2" section of this chapter for additional details.

Prerequisite Changes

Prerequisites for the Operations Manager R2 components have not changed significantly since the RTM release. The only change is the additional requirement to deploy Ajax extensions to incorporate the Health Explorer with the Web console. Figure 3.1 shows the OpsMgr prerequisite checker failing by not finding the Ajax extensions.

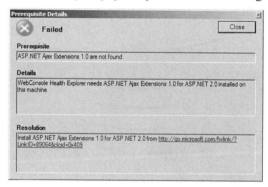

FIGURE 3.1 Ajax extension 1.0 prerequisite failed

The Ajax 1.0 extensions are available for download at http://go.microsoft.com/fwlink/?LinkID=89064&clcid=0x409. After downloading the extensions, the installation process is straightforward with a welcome screen, acceptance of license agreements, the installation itself, and a completion screen with an option to display the release notes.

Roles and Features

Windows Server 2008 introduces server roles and features. These simplify the process to add functions to a server, decrease the footprint of what is installed by default, and improve firewall integration:

> ► A *server role* installs the software required for a major function such as a Directory Services domain controller, DNS server, DHCP server, Hyper-V (virtualization), or Web server. Roles are installed without downloading additional software, and modify the firewall to allow communication on whatever ports necessary for the application to function.

> ► A *feature* provides smaller pieces of functionality. Examples include Group Policy Management, Network Load Balancing, Remote Assistance, and the Telnet Client. Features are installed without downloading or adding software.

Web Server Prerequisite for the OpsMgr Web Console

Server 2008 server roles and features change how you install Operations Manager prerequisites. As an example, the World Wide Web service is a prerequisite for the Web console installation. You will add this using the Server Manager application (which starts by default unless turned off in Windows 2008), displayed in Figure 3.2.

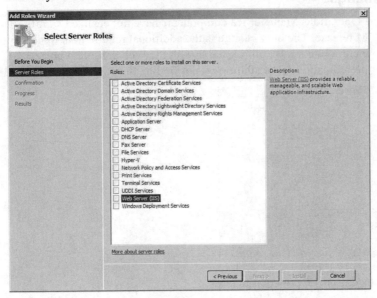

FIGURE 3.2 Select the checkbox to add the World Wide Web prerequisite through server roles.

TIP: WEB CONSOLE PRIOR TO R2

Installing the Web console for Operations Manager versions prior to R2 on Windows 2008 requires hotfix 954049, available at http://support.microsoft.com/kb/954049/.

Installing the Web Server (IIS) server role is intuitive but requires selecting a set of additional services, including the following:

▶ IIS 6 metabase compatibility

▶ IIS WMI compatibility

▶ Static content

▶ Default document

▶ Directory browsing

▶ HTTP errors

▶ ASP.NET

▶ .NET extensibility

- ► ISAPI extensions
- ► ISAPI filters
- ► Request filtering

After adding these services, take the defaults for the remainder of the installation process. This includes a confirmation screen, process indicator, and a results page summarizing the addition of the server role.

TIP: SQL SERVER 2008 REPORTING SERVICES

The reporting services functionality in SQL Server 2008 has changed such that web components are no longer a requirement for installing SQL Reporting Services (SRS). See Chapter 4, "Using SQL Server 2008 in OpsMgr 2007 R2," for more information on SQL Server 2008 and Operations Manager 2007.

.NET Framework Prerequisite for the OpsMgr Web Console

The .NET Framework is another OpsMgr prerequisite requiring the use of server roles to install on Windows Server 2008. To add this prerequisite, use the Server Manager application, displayed in Figure 3.3.

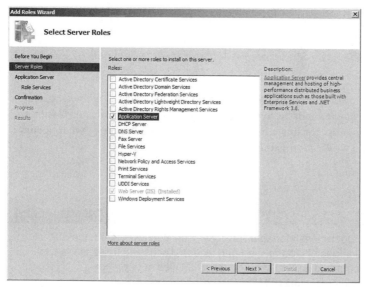

FIGURE 3.3 Adding the ASP .NET 2.0 prerequisite through server roles

Complete adding the Application Server role by taking the defaults through the remainder of the installation process; this includes a confirmation screen, a process indicator, and a results page summarizing the addition of the server role.

Windows PowerShell Installation for the OpsMgr Console

Windows PowerShell is a prerequisite to install the Operations Manager Shell. Install PowerShell in Windows Server 2008 by adding a feature, as shown in Figure 3.4.

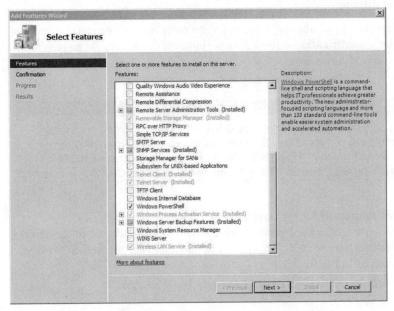

FIGURE 3.4 Adding the PowerShell prerequisite through server features

You can also install PowerShell using the command prompt and `ServerManagerCMD` command. This command cannot be run while adding other server roles or features. Figure 3.5 shows the syntax for this command, with an example first of what occurs if you run this command while adding another role:

```
ServerManagerCMD -I Powershell
```

TIP: INSTALLING OPSMGR SP 1 ON WINDOWS 2008

If you are installing Operations Manager 2007 SP 1 on Windows 2008, the authors have written a series of blog articles and videos discussing lessons learned during the installation process. You can find these articles at http://ops-mgr.spaces.live.com/blog/cns!3D3B8489FCAA9B51!768.entry.

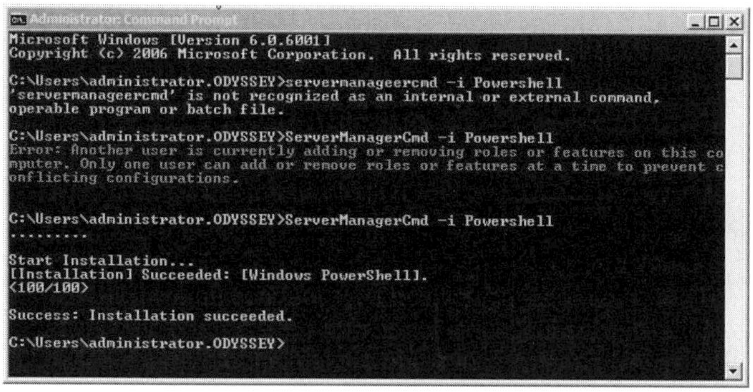

FIGURE 3.5 Adding the PowerShell prerequisite using the command line

The Windows 2008 Firewall

The Windows 2008 Firewall is a significant advancement compared to what was available with Windows Server 2003. In Windows 2008, you can leave the firewall active, install roles or applications that provide their own firewall exceptions, and the applications will function without firewall-related issues.

Although Operations Manager 2007 R2 does not install as a Windows 2008 server role, it automatically integrates with the Windows 2008 Firewall and makes the firewall changes required for the management application to be functional. However, underlying applications used with OpsMgr 2007 R2 may not make the firewall changes needed to work properly, as discussed in the next sections.

SQL Server Port Requirements

SQL Server 2005 and 2008 installations do not integrate with the Windows 2008 Firewall to configure those ports used for connectivity with other systems connecting to the database. As an example, the default instance of SQL Server requires TCP port 1433 as an inbound connection. To determine if firewall changes are needed, log into the server and use telnet to connect to port 1433 on the local system. If port 1433 responds locally but does not respond when attempting to connect from a remote system, the firewall is most likely blocking the connection.

> **TIP: TELNET ON WINDOWS 2008**
>
> Telnet is not installed by default on Windows 2008. Use the Server Manager application to add the Telnet Client feature.

To provide remote connectivity to the SQL databases (including the Operations database, data warehouse, and ACS database) first open port 1433 on each database server. Operations Manager does support running SQL on a port other than the default port of 1433. If you have changed your SQL server port, create the firewall rule as discussed next but specify the port that you configured SQL Server to use. (Chapter 4 provides additional information on dynamic ports with SQL Server 2008.) Perform the following steps using the Windows 2008 Server Manager application:

1.   Navigate to Configuration -> Windows Firewall with Advanced Security -> Inbound Rules.

2.   Right-click, and create a new rule.

3.   Add a new inbound rule for TCP port 1433 (shown in Figure 3.6), which allows the connections for all the profiles.

4.   Name the rule, as shown in Figure 3.7.

A good discussion on configuring the Windows Firewall to allow SQL Server access is available at http://msdn.microsoft.com/en-us/library/cc646023.aspx. The article covers the ports used by SQL Server, firewall troubleshooting, and configuring the Windows Firewall. Additional references on this topic are at http://technet.microsoft.com/en-us/library/cc540430.aspx and http://technet.microsoft.com/en-us/library/cc540431.aspx. SQL Server also uses UDP port 1434 to provide the connectivity required for the SQL Server Browser Service. The process to create this rule is the same as shown in Figures 3.6 and 3.7; select UDP port **1434** and name the rule **SQL Server Browser Service** to make it easy to identify.

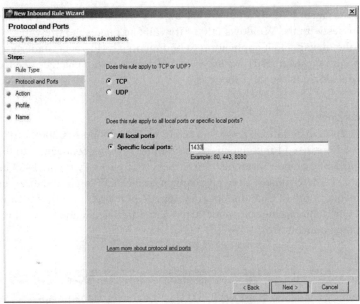

FIGURE 3.6 Defining the port information for SQL connectivity

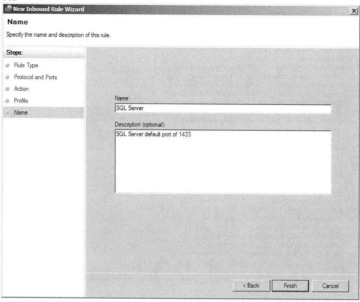

FIGURE 3.7 Providing name and description information for SQL connectivity

TIP: ADDING THE SQL PORT FIREWALL RULE VIDEO

A good video that steps through the configuration to create a firewall rule for SQL server on port 1433 is available at http://ops-mgr.spaces.live.com/blog/cns!3D3B8489FCAA9B51!710.entry.

Reporting Server Port Requirements

SQL Server 2008 Reporting Services no longer requires the World Wide Web service. Adding the Web Server (IIS) server role creates a rule allowing inbound connectivity to the required ports. However, because this prerequisite is no longer required for SQL Server 2008 Reporting Services, you must modify the firewall to allow communication with the reporting server. To configure the firewall to allow HTTP and HTTPS connections, open the Server Manager application and navigate to Configuration -> Windows Firewall with Advanced Security -> Inbound rules. Create the HTTP and HTTPS inbound firewall connections using the processes discussed in the "SQL Server Port Requirements" section of this chapter, using TCP port 80 and TCP port 443 inbound, with the results shown in Figure 3.8.

TIP: AUTOMATICALLY ADDING THE HTTP AND HTTPS RULES

If you add the Web Server (IIS) server role and then remove it, Windows will automatically generate the HTTP and HTTPS inbound rules and deactivate them when the Web Server (IIS) server role is removed. You can re-activate these rules by right-clicking each and choosing Enable Rule.

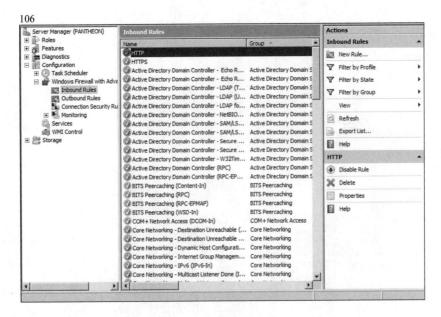

FIGURE 3.8 Configuring firewall rules for reporting services

You will want to test port connectivity as discussed in the "SQL Server Port Requirements" section, but this time testing ports 80 and/or 443 instead of 1433. Verify connectivity locally on port 80 and/or 443, and then compare the results when connecting
via a remote server. If the system responds locally but does not respond when attempting to connect from a remote system, the firewall is probably blocking the connection.

CAUTION: STOPPING THE FIREWALL SERVICE

Do NOT stop the Windows Firewall service via either the cmdline (`net stop`
`"Windows Firewall"`) or services snapin (services.msc). Stopping this service
while the firewall is still active locks down all inbound communication, meaning
that you cannot connect to the system from any port and or reach it via ping.

To disable the firewall, use the Server Manager application; navigate to Configuration –> Windows Firewall with Advanced Security, right-click, and go to Properties. Change the firewall state to Off.

After Installation

When the RMS installation completes, the final screen of the wizard shows a checkbox
to backup the RMS key. R2 includes new service names (see Table 3.1) and an updated
version of the OpsMgr agent. When installing on Windows Server 2008, User Account
Control (UAC) introduces changes you need to consider when running OpsMgr 2007
R2 on this platform. Here is additional information on these areas.

Encryption Key Backup

One of the changes with Operations Manager 2007 SP 1 is an installation step to back up the RMS key. After completing a root management server installation, the installation process has a checkbox to back up the encryption key. This enhancement is discussed in Chapter 1, "Introduction and What's New." You will also want to back up the SQL Reporting Server encryption key. For details, see Chapter 12, "Backup and Recovery," in *System Center Operations Manager 2007 Unleashed.*

Service Name Changes

When installing System Center Operations Manager 2007 R2, notice that the service names have changed from the names used in the RTM and SP 1 versions of Operations Manager 2007. Table 3.1 shows the service names for each version of OpsMgr 2007.

TABLE 3.1 Operations Manager Service Names

OpsMgr 2007 RTM and SP 1	OpsMgr 2007 R2
OpsMgr SDK Service	System Center Data Access
OpsMgr Health Service	System Center Management
OpsMgr Config Service	System Center Management Configuration

Agent Version Changes

Table 3.2 shows the various releases of Operations Manager 2007 and the associated version number. These version numbers are especially useful when determining the agent versions installed on your systems. See the version number displayed in the OpsMgr console, under Administration -> Device Management -> Agent Managed.

TABLE 3.2 Operations Manager Version Numbers

OpsMgr 2007 Version	Version Number
OpsMgr 2007 RTM	6.0.5000.0
OpsMgr 2007 SP 1	6.0.6278.0
OpsMgr 2007 R2 RC	6.1.7043.0
OpsMgr 2007 R2 RTM	6.1.7221.0

User Account Control

User Account Control is enabled by default on Windows Server 2008 systems. Microsoft designed UAC to improve the security of the Windows operating systems by limiting application software to run under standard user privileges rather than administration-level privileges. However, UAC can affect Operations Manager.

Here's an example of what can happen: A situation occurred where after installing the Operations Manager console on Windows Server 2008, the OpsMgr administrator could not log into the console. The error message stated that the account did not have sufficient privileges to log into the console (the exact message was "The user Domain\User does not have sufficient permission to perform the operation").

This was puzzling, as the user account belonged to both the local administrators and the Operations Manager administrators groups. Eventually, the administrator resolved the issue—by right-clicking the OpsMgr console icon and choosing Run as administrator, the Operations Manager console connected without issues. What was most confusing about this issue was although it looked like a permissions error, the user account actually had the access rights required but was not running the application with administrator rights—as UAC was running it with standard user privileges!

TIP: HOW TO DISABLE UAC

Although not recommended, another option to avoid these types of issues is disabling UAC. Do so by running MSCONFIG; on the Tools tab, check the Disable UAC option. After rebooting, UAC is disabled on the system.

Another challenge with UAC is its effect on the Operations Manager RTM and SP 1 Web consoles. UAC may cause the Web console not to display pages correctly. You may experience one or more of the following symptoms:

► The Web console will not open.

► The My Workspace page will not display.

► Performance views will not display.

Hotfix 954049 (http://support.microsoft.com/kb/954049/) resolves these issues. The MOM team blog at http://blogs.technet.com/momteam/archive/2008/12/17/installing-web-console-on-windows-server-2008.aspx provides additional information.

One of the command-line tools Operations Manager uses is the gateway approval tool (Microsoft.EnterpriseManagement.GatewayApproval.exe). When running this tool on Windows Server 2008, you must log in as an OpsMgr administrator and right-click when opening the command prompt to run it as an administrator, shown in Figure 3.9. If you do not run this tool with the Run as administrator option, it will hang and eventually time out. When running any command-line program for OpsMgr in Windows 2008 with UAC installed, it is highly recommended to run it as an administrator.

FIGURE 3.9 Opening the command line with the Run as administrator option

There are a variety of changes to consider when installing and running Operations Manager 2007 on Windows Server 2008. However, what if you installed Operations Manager 2007 on Windows Server 2003 and now want to migrate to OpsMgr 2007 R2 on Server 2008? The next section of this chapter discusses upgrade considerations.

Upgrading to Operations Manager 2007 R2

Three different scenarios exist when deploying Operations Manager R2. The first is a new installation, discussed earlier in this chapter in the "Installing Operations Manager 2007 R2" section. A fresh installation is the simplest and cleanest approach but is only likely to occur when newly deploying Operations Manager or implementing a replacement OpsMgr infrastructure. The other options vary depending upon your current OpsMgr configuration. Here are the available upgrade paths to OpsMgr R2:

► OpsMgr 20007 SP 1 -> OpsMgr 2007 R2

► OpsMgr 2007 RTM -> OpsMgr 2007 SP 1 -> OpsMgr 2007 R2

► OpsMgr 2007 R2 Eval -> OpsMgr 2007 R2

The process required to upgrade each of these configurations will vary based on the current operating system and the intended operating system for your OpsMgr 2007 R2 deployment. These are discussed here as two different operating system scenarios: currently running on Windows 2008, and currently running on Windows 2003.

Upgrading to OpsMgr 2007 R2—Currently on Windows 2008

Microsoft supports Operations Manager 2007 SP 1 on the Windows Server 2008 platform. If your current OpsMgr environment is on Windows 2008, the upgrade is relatively simple. Prior to upgrading, you will want to perform the following processes:

► Back up the current OpsMgr environment (see Chapter 12 in *System Center Operations Manager 2007 Unleashed* for details).

► Document current usernames and passwords for accounts used for OpsMgr.

► Document the OpsMgr servers and the order that the upgrade will occur.

► Document any agents in a gray state because their upgrade will probably fail.

► Verify that the Operations Manager database has at least 50% free space, or increase its size to provide 50% free space.

► Back up the encryption key.

► Disable all connector subscriptions and notification subscriptions. (Optionally, notification subscriptions can be backed up by exporting the management pack they were created in.)

► Uninstall all stand-alone Operations Manager 2007 SP 1 Operations consoles.

After completing the pre-upgrade processes, launch the Operations Manager 2007 R2 installation media (see Figure 3.10).

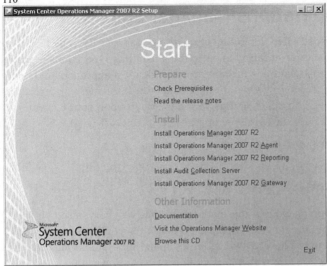

FIGURE 3.10 Operations Manager 2007 R2 Setup splash screen

Similar to the Operations Manager 2007 base installation, the splash screen includes options to install Operations Manager, an agent, reporting components, and audit collection services. The R2 screen adds a gateway server option.

Here is the order of components to upgrade:

1.   Root management server (which also upgrades the Operations Manager database).

2.   Reporting server. (Remove the OpsMgr agent before upgrading.)

3.   Standalone OpsMgr consoles.

4.   Management servers.

5.   Gateway servers.

6.   OpsMgr agents. (Approve agents pushed from the Operations Manager console, or deploy the new version of the agent to those systems deployed manually, such as via Configuration Manager.)

7.   Web console.

8.   ACS collector and ACS database.

9.   Import the latest management packs (MPs) with the new MP import wizard.

As you select each component to upgrade, Operations Manager indicates an upgrade of that component is available by displaying the upgrade checkbox screen in Figure 3.11.

TIP: DEPLOYING THE OPSMGR AGENT WITH CONFIGMGR

Configuration Manager can automate deploying Operations Manager components. One of the more common uses of ConfigMgr is deploying the Operations Manager agent to server systems. The OpsMgr blog has a good article (available at http://ops-mgr.spaces.live.com/blog/cns!3D3B8489FCAA9B51!1034.entry) with information on deploying the OpsMgr agent with Configuration Manager.

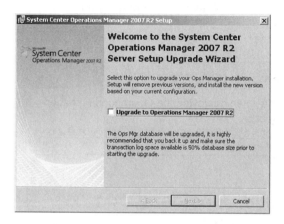

FIGURE 3.11 The Setup screen to upgrade OpsMgr 2007 R2

After upgrading the components, re-enable those subscriptions and connectors you disabled prior to the upgrade. Additional information on upgrading to Operations Manager 2007 R2 is available at http://technet.microsoft.com/en-us/library/dd362729.aspx.

Upgrading to OpsMgr 2007 R2—Currently on Windows 2003

Here is the recommended approach to upgrade an OpsMgr environment running on Windows 2003 to Windows 2008 and Operations Manager 2007 R2:

1. Install on new equipment to a different management group name (see the "Installing Operations Manager 2007 R2" section of this chapter).

2. Configure the agents to report to both management groups.

3. After replicating functionality in the new management group, decommission the original Operations Manager environment.

Upgrading to OpsMgr 2007 R2—Known Issues

There are two issues to be aware of when upgrading from OpsMgr 2007 SP 1, as follows:

▶ If you configured your Operations Manager database to grow as needed without limit (autogrow), the upgrade process changes this setting back to not allow any growth. You can change this setting back to allow unrestricted growth after the upgrade completes; however, the best practice approach for the OpsMgr database is to not enable autogrow.

► Customized notification formats have new channel names, such as smtp<*guid*>. For details, see Knowledge Base (KB) article 971233, available at http://support.microsoft.com/kb/971233/. You can avoid this issue by exporting the management pack in which the notifications were stored, performing the upgrade of OpsMgr, and then re-importing the notifications management pack.

TIP: INSTALLING OR UPGRADING THE OPSMGR AGENT FROM THE COMMAND LINE

A large number of options are available when deploying the Operations Manager 2007 agent. See the MOM Team blog at http://blogs.technet.com/momteam/archive/2009/07/08/windows-agent-install-msi-use-cases-and-commands.aspx for information.

Additional Windows 2008 Considerations

Items to consider if deploying OpsMgr in a Windows Server 2008 environment include Server 2008 SP 2 or R2, Server Core, and Server 2008-specific management packs.

Windows Server 2008 SP 2

Microsoft released Windows Server 2008 SP 2 on June 30, 2009. Service Pack 2 includes the hotfixes listed earlier in the "Hotfixes" section of this chapter (951327, 952664, and 953290), eliminating the need to deploy these patches on Windows Server 2008 systems running SP 2. Windows 2008 SP 2 is supported for each of the Operations Manager components according to the documentation at http://technet.microsoft.com/en-us/library/bb309428.aspx. For additional information on changes in Windows Server 2008 SP 2, see http://technet.microsoft.com/en-us/library/dd335036(WS.10).aspx.

Windows Server 2008 R2

Windows Server 2008 R2 was released to manufacturing in July 2009, and is supported by OpsMgr SP 1 and R2. http://support.microsoft.com/kb/974722 describes support for Server 2008 R2 and Windows 7. The article also discusses several known issues. Additional details on the features and functions of Windows Server 2008 R2 are available at http://www.microsoft.com/windowsserver2008/en/us/r2.aspx.

Server Core

Windows Server 2008 introduces a new edition of Windows Server with a smaller footprint, known as *Server Core*. Server Core does not have the typical graphical user interface components of Windows, enabling it to be more fully secured; the small codebase it uses requires fewer patches, leading to fewer outages for applying patches.

Operations Manager 2007 R2 supports deploying the OpsMgr agent to Windows 2008 Server Core systems but does not support deploying any other Operations Manager 2007 components on Server Core. You can deploy agents using the standard agent deployment methods and validate that the agent is running by using the `net start` command, which shows the services installed on the server. Figure 3.12 shows the results of this command on a system running Server Core. Note that the System Center Management service is listed, indicating that the Operations Manager agent is deployed on that system.

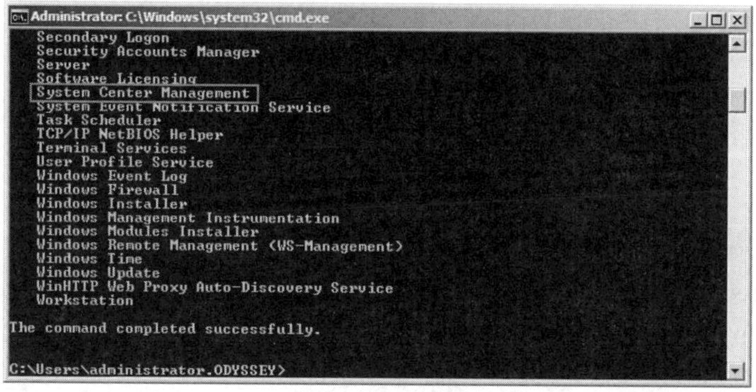

FIGURE 3.12 Windows 2008 Server Core running the Operations Manager 2007 R2 agent

Figure 3.13 displays the Health Explorer for a system running the Server Core operating system (OS), showing that Server Core systems integrate seamlessly with Operations Manager 2007 R2.

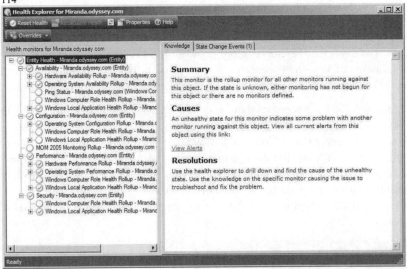

FIGURE 3.13 Server Core integrated into the Health Explorer

Windows Server 2008 Updated or New Management Packs

Windows Server 2008 required updates to a number of existing management packs and several new management packs. These management packs include Windows Server 2008 Operating System, Dynamic Host Configuration Protocol (DHCP), Internet Information Services, Microsoft Cluster Services (MSCS), Domain Name Service (DNS), Group Policy, Active Directory (AD), Application Server, Terminal Services (TS), Network Load Balancing (NLB), Windows Deployment Services, Fax Server, Print Server, Clustering, Hyper-V, and System Center Virtual Machine Manager (VMM). Three of these management packs can directly affect how you will design Operations Manager, as follows:

▶ Clustering

▶ Hyper-V

▶ VMM

The next sections discuss these management packs.

Windows Server 2008 Clustering

Windows clustering historically required a shared drive called a *quorum*; this determined the node in the cluster owning the resources of the cluster. Windows 2008 includes new functionality to provide a *witness-based* quorum. A witness-based quorum consists of multiple nodes that can own the resource, and another node that watches the nodes of the cluster. As an example, a cluster could have two nodes sharing resources and a third node monitoring the nodes of the cluster. Microsoft Cluster Services integrates this new functionality to provide monitoring for these types of clusters.

Cluster monitoring in Operations Manager 2007 provides the functionality required to discover clusters and their resources and integrate the clusters into OpsMgr. The Windows 2008 Cluster management pack matches the functionality available in the Windows 2003 Cluster management pack and adds additional functionality to match the new clustering functions available in Windows Server 2008.

Chapter 9, "Unleashing Operations Manager 2007," contains additional information on Windows 2008 clustering and any high-availability impacts on OpsMgr 2007.

Hyper-V

Windows Server 2008 adds Hyper-V as the new Windows-based virtualization platform. Major enhancements from Virtual Server 2005 R2 include multiple processor support, increased memory support, and increased disk performance. Hyper-V also helps virtual machines from one host system to another with minimal downtime using the Quick Migration feature; Windows Server 2008 R2 enhances this functionality with a faster migration method called *Live Migration*. The Hyper-V management pack integrates functions to monitor your Hyper-V servers within the Operations Manager console. Chapter 7, "Operations Manager and Virtualization," discusses additional information regarding Hyper-V. You can also check the web at http://www.microsoft.com/windowsserver2008/en/us/hyperv-main.aspx.

TIP: SAVING DRIVE SPACE ON VIRTUAL SERVERS

Environments with a large number of virtualized servers often use relatively small C: drives to minimize storage requirements. (There is no reason to provide a 128GB drive on a virtual system if you can store it in 30GB.) This approach enables you to run a large number of virtual guests with a limited amount of disk space. It also means that the operating system drives must be as clean as possible. If you are running out of free space on a Vista, Windows 7, or Server 2008 virtualized system, consider removing the hibernation file. This file is automatically created and allocates space equal to the amount of installed memory. Most virtuals are not hibernated—they either have their state saved or shut down. Remove the hibernation file using the `powercfg -h off` command from the command line. As with other UAC items (see the "User Account Control" section for details), this command will fail unless you open the command prompt with administrator rights.

VMM

System Center Virtual Machine Manager provides the ability to manage both Hyper-V and ESX hosts in a single console. VMM also includes PRO tips, which can remediate issues on virtual resources using pro-enabled management. In addition, VMM provides a library for virtuals and can quickly provision new machines and perform physical-to-virtual migrations. See Chapter 7 for more information on VMM and PRO tips, or on the web at http://www.microsoft.com/windowsserver2008/en/us/hyperv-main.aspx.

Summary

This chapter discussed how Windows Server 2008 affects Operations Manager and focused on initial installation on Windows Server 2008. It also discussed additional factors to consider when upgrading to Operations Manager R2 on the Windows Server 2008 platform, and included a discussion about additional items to consider when using Operations Manager 2007 with Windows Server 2008. The next chapter discusses using SQL Server 2008 in Operations Manager 2007 R2.

Using SQL Server 2008 in OpsMgr 2007 R2

SQL Server is an integral component of a functional OpsMgr management group. This chapter discusses specifics of installing and upgrading SQL Server 2008 for the System Center Operations Manager (OpsMgr) 2007 Release 2 (R2) environment. The focus is on what's new when using SQL Server with OpsMgr 2007 R2, including core database support and architectural changes for the OpsMgr Reporting component to work with SQL Server 2008. Also discussed is upgrading a SQL Server 2005 database installation to SQL Server 2008, and database maintenance and optimization approaches to use to keep your OpsMgr databases up and running. The chapter includes useful SQL queries to retrieve agent and management pack information, determine the noisiest monitor in the database, and assist with database maintenance.

The chapter does not discuss how to design, plan, and implement SQL Server or your OpsMgr components; this is discussed in the predecessor to this book, *System Center Operations Manager 2007 Unleashed* (Sams, 2008), in Chapter 4, "Planning Your Operations Manager Deployment," Chapter 5, "Planning Complex Configurations," and Chapter 6, "Installing Operations Manager 2007."

Core OpsMgr Component Support

With OpsMgr 2007 R2, Microsoft has updated database component supportability. The OpsMgr 2007 R2 database components now natively support SQL Server 2008. Table 4.1 lists supported SQL Server configurations for OpsMgr 2007 R2.

118

TABLE 4.1 Core OpsMgr Component Support

Operations Manager Component	Software Requirement	Notes
Operations Manager Database	SQL 2005 Enterprise and Standard with Service Pack (SP) 1, SP 2, or SP 3, or SQL 2008 Standard or Enterprise with SP 1	SQL collation must be SQL_Latin1_General_CP1_AS; no other collation configurations are supported.
Operations Manager Data Warehouse	SQL 2005 Enterprise and Standard with SP 1, SP 2, or SP 3, or SQL 2008 Standard or Enterprise with SP 1	
Reporting Server	SQL 2005 Reporting Services with SP 1, SP 2, or SP 3, or SQL 2008 Reporting Services with SP 1	.NET Framework 3.0.
Audit Collection Database	SQL 2005 Enterprise and Standard with SP 1, SP 2, or SP 3, or SQL 2008 Standard or Enterprise with SP 1	

NOTE: SQL SERVER 2005 INSTALLATION REQUIRED FOR OPSMGR 2007 SP 1

The OpsMgr 2007 SP 1 core components require SQL Server 2005 Standard or Enterprise Edition with SP 1, SP 2, or SP 3 during installation; Microsoft does not support a new OpsMgr 2007 SP 1 installation on the base release of SQL Server 2008. To install OpsMgr 2007 SP 1 on a SQL 2008 server, install SQL 2005 first; then upgrade to SQL 2008 SP 1. Here are some references for additional information on supported configurations for OpsMgr 2007 SP 1:

▶ http://technet.microsoft.com/en-us/library/dd819933.aspx.

▶ Chapter 4 of *System Center Operations Manager 2007 Unleashed*.

▶ http://support.microsoft.com/kb/958170 discusses the limits of support of SQL Server 2008 for OpsMgr 2007 SP 1.

▶ http://support.microsoft.com/kb/971541 describes how SP 1 adds support for upgrading SQL 2005 to SQL 2008 SP 1.

Microsoft SQL Server comes in seven editions: Compact, Express, Workgroup, Web, Standard, Enterprise, and Developer. Of these seven, you must use either the Standard or Enterprise editions with OpsMgr. Here are the differences between the two supported versions:

▶ **Standard Edition**—This edition supports 32-bit and 64-bit hardware, up to four multicore processors, memory limited by operating system, unlimited database size, support of failover clustering for two nodes, log shipping, and database mirroring. It is intended for large datasets and production loads.

► **Enterprise Edition**—Enterprise Edition supports 32-bit and 64-bit hardware, an unlimited number of multicore processors, memory limited by operating system, unlimited database size, failover clustering up to 16 nodes, log shipping, and database mirroring. This edition is intended for the largest and most demanding online transaction processing (OLTP) environments, data analysis, and data warehousing systems.

Often asked is whether to use SQL Server Standard or Enterprise Edition with OpsMgr 2007. Enterprise Edition is strongly recommended in high-volume Audit Collection Services (ACS) environments because it reduces the chance of lost security events (discussed in the "Database Maintenance with Standard and Enterprise Editions" section). Although not as necessary for the Operational database and data warehouse, there are several reasons for considering SQL Server Enterprise Edition in your environment. Here are some benefits to consider:

► Enterprise Edition supports parallel index operations, hot-add CPU and memory, parallel DBCC operations, table and index partitioning (should you want to implement that), online index operations, and online page and file restores.

► Enterprise Edition is better when handling over 500GB of data, which can be useful for the OpsMgr data warehouse. Standard Edition runs on a maximum of four CPUs, whereas Enterprise can handle an unlimited number of CPUs (based on the version of the underlying OS). The additional hardware capabilities provide room for growth in larger shops.

The article at http://www.microsoft.com/sqlserver/2008/en/us/editions-compare.aspx provides additional information on the different SQL Server 2008 editions. The differences between SQL Standard and Enterprise can affect your OpsMgr components and OpsMgr environment in the areas of high availability and maintenance, discussed in the next sections.

High Availability with Standard and Enterprise Editions

From a high-availability perspective, both Standard and Enterprise editions support failover clustering. However, there are several differences, as follows:

► SQL Server Standard Edition supports up to two clustered nodes—for the OpsMgr databases, those can be configured as active/passive.

► SQL Server Enterprise Edition supports up to 16 clustered nodes. SQL Server Enterprise Edition also supports online indexing, support for hot-add memory and CPU, database snapshots, and online page and file restore.

NOTE: OPERATING SYSTEM REQUIREMENTS WHEN CLUSTERING SQL SERVER

When clustering, the operating system (OS) must be running Windows Server Enterprise or Datacenter.

With the current architecture of OpsMgr, the Operational database and root management server (RMS) are single point of failures. Should one of these components fail, monitoring will stop until the failing component is recovered. If your organization requires high availability and cannot tolerate failures, you will need to ensure that your OpsMgr environment can tolerate a simultaneous failure of different OpsMgr components such as the RMS, gateway servers, management servers, and OpsMgr databases. These topics and the steps to cluster the RMS are discussed in Chapter 9, "Unleashing Operations Manager 2007."

When clustering the OpsMgr database, take into account that workflows write simultaneously to the OpsMgr database and the data warehouse. Should the data warehouse fail, the OpsMgr database will also encounter issues, affecting the performance of your entire management group. If you cluster the OpsMgr database, clustering the OpsMgr data warehouse as well is strongly recommended. Chapter 10, "Complex Configurations," in *System Center Operations Manager 2007 Unleashed* discusses the mechanics of creating an OpsMgr database cluster and the available redundancy options.

Database Maintenance with Standard and Enterprise Editions

In terms of database maintenance, the edition of SQL Server used affects how the system (or in this case, the different OpsMgr components) behave during the daily database maintenance window. This is particularly true for the ACS database, which supports both SQL Server 2005 and 2008 Standard or Enterprise editions. The ACS collector queue stores events received from ACS forwarders before sending those events to the ACS database. The number of events in the queue increases during periods of high-audit traffic, or when the ACS database is not available to accept new events, such as during database purging. As part of daily maintenance (normally at 2:00 AM), those database partitions with time stamps outside the data retention schedule (14 days by default) are dropped from the ACS database. The two SQL Server editions behave differently during this activity:

- ▶ SQL Server Enterprise Edition continues inserting processed security events but at only 30% to 40% of the regular insertion rate.

- ▶ With Standard Edition, security event insertion halts and events queue up on the ACS collector until database maintenance is completed.

  The ACS collector is configured to queue 262,144 events by default. Although this seems to be a large number of events, if several servers (forwarders) are sending security events, you may quickly reach the limit. You can reduce the number of events by carefully configuring the maintenance window for the daily database maintenance. Pick a timeframe when there is the least amount of user and application activity on the network.

Chapter 15, "Monitoring Audit Collection Services," of *System Center Operations Manager 2007 Unleashed* includes an in-depth discussion of how to monitor ACS collector performance. The chapter discusses which performance counters to monitor and the registry keys to change to tune ACS collector performance.

The Operations database runs various maintenance tasks. These include the following:

- ▶ Discovery Data Grooming (2:00 AM)

> ► Partitioning and Grooming (12:00 midnight)

> ► Detecting and Fixing Object Space (every 30 minutes)

> ► Auto Resolving Alerts (4:00 AM)

These are in addition to a daily backup job you should configure and schedule for all OpsMgr databases and significant system databases, such as Master and MSDB (for additional information on backups, see Chapter 9 of this book and Chapter 12, "Backup and Recovery," in *System Center Operations Manager 2007 Unleashed*). The Data Warehouse database also performs optimizations, reindexing, and grooming. The "Database Maintenance" section discusses the necessary types of maintenance.

WINDOWS SERVER CORE AND SUPPORT FOR SQL SERVER

Windows Server Core is a new SKU with Windows Server 2008. This installation option enables you to install the smallest possible footprint of an operating system and provides a minimal environment that reduces maintenance, management requirements, and attack surface. With Windows Server 2008 R2, Microsoft added .NET Framework to Server Core. This opens the possibility of installing SQL Server 2008 on a Windows Server 2008 Server Core R2 server, although this is currently unsupported! For additional information, see http://www.nullsession.com/2009/06/02/sql-server-2008-on-server-core-2008-r2/.

Setup

The next sections discuss considerations when planning your installation of SQL Server 2008 for OpsMgr 2007 R2. These include choosing a drive configuration and upgrading your OpsMgr databases from SQL Server 2005 to SQL 2008. This chapter does not focus on how to upgrade SQL Server itself, but covers the steps to perform on your OpsMgr 2007 data before and after upgrading SQL Server.

Topics discussed also include choosing your SQL collation and configuring memory limits. Chapter 3, "Operations Manager 2007 R2 and Windows Server 2008," discusses configuration changes for the Windows 2008 Firewall. Not covered here is how to install a new OpsMgr 2007 environment. For procedures to install OpsMgr, check Chapter 3, along with Chapter 6 in *System Center Operations Manager 2007 Unleashed*.

Hardware Best Practices

The Operational database is often a performance bottleneck. All OpsMgr data either comes from SQL Server or goes to SQL Server, which is why you need to size and configure your SQL disks appropriately—the faster the disks, the better the performance. This section discusses database hardware recommendations specific for an OpsMgr environment. These guidelines are based on observations by the authors during multiple OpsMgr deployments.

64-bit hardware and a 64-bit operating system are highly recommended for your database environment. Using 64-bit hardware enables you to increase memory beyond 4GB. Even if your deployment does not currently require over 4GB, 64-bit hardware provides room for growth should memory requirements later change.

Here are some considerations for disk and file placement:

- ► At least three disks are recommended, as follows:
    - ► One disk for OS; one disk for OpsMgr and SQL; one disk for transaction log.
    - ► Redundant Array of Inexpensive Disks (RAID) 10 is highly recommended.

- ► Here is the ideal configuration:
    - ► Install the RMS and Operational database on different systems.
    - ► Install the Operational database and data warehouse on different systems. Similar to its updates of the Operational database, OpsMgr 2007 writes data almost in real time to the data warehouse, making its load similar to that on the Operational database.
    - ► If there are many concurrent reporting users, place the OpsMgr reporting server on a different system from the data warehouse. This will increase performance, as running reports that query large data ranges or targeting many objects demand additional resources.
    - ► Configure the database server with one disk for OS, one disk for SQL, one disk for TempDB, and one disk for transaction logs.
    - ► Use multiple database files for databases. (For each CPU, you will want to dedicate from 25% of a file to the entire physical file.)
    - ► Use multiple files for TempDB (number of files equal to CPUs).

Use multiple physical files for your databases to increase physical I/O operations. The more I/O SQL Server performs at a disk level, the better your database performance. If you use separate database physical files, verify that the files have the same initial size and growth settings. If they are of different sizes, SQL Server tries to fill the physical file with the most free space first to maintain an equal amount of free space within all the files. If the files are of identical size, writes are distributed across the various database files, improving performance.

Here is a preferred drive configuration:

- ► Do not place database data files in the same drive as the operating system.
- ► Place transaction logs and database data files on separate drives. The transaction log workload consists of mostly sequential writes; putting the transaction logs on a separate volume allows that volume to perform I/O more efficiently. A single two-spindle RAID 1 volume is sufficient for most environments when handling very high volumes of sequential writes.
- ► Place the TempDB database on its own drive.

► Resize TempDB and its transaction log to be 20% of the total size of the Operational database and data warehouse.

► As a best practice, Microsoft suggests a battery-backed write-caching disk controller for both the Operational database and data warehouse. Testing has shown that the workload on these databases benefits from write caching on disk controllers. When configuring read caching versus write caching on disk controllers, allocate 25% to read caching and 75% of the cache to write caching. When using write-caching disk controllers with any database system, a proper battery backup system can prevent data loss in the event of an outage.

Additional information on design requirements for OpsMgr 2007 R2 is available at http://technet.microsoft.com/en-us/library/bb735402.aspx.

TIP: MOVING TEMPDB ON ITS OWN DRIVE TO INCREASE PERFORMANCE

During a typical SQL Server installation, the TempDB and TempDB transaction log files are installed on the same drive as the other databases. Here is a query to move these files to another drive (D:\data\MSSQLserver\ in this example):

```
USE MASTER
GO
ALTER DATABASE TEMPDB
MODIFY FILE (NAME = TEMPDEV, FILENAME = 'D:\DATA\MSSQLSERVER\TEMPDB.MDF')
GO
ALTER DATABASE TEMPDB
 MODIFY FILE (NAME = TEMPDEV, FILENAME = 'D:\DATA\MSSQLSERVER\TEMPLOG.LDF')
GO
```

Restarting the SQL Server instance will apply your changes.

An OpsMgr 2007 R2 sizing helper spreadsheet is available at http://blogs.technet.com/momteam/archive/2009/08/12/operations-manager-2007-r2-sizing-helper.aspx. This spreadsheet is also on the OpsMgr 2007 R2 installation media. Based on the input you provide, the spreadsheet will give recommendations for RAM, disk configurations, and so on.

NOTE: VIRTUALIZING THE COMPONENTS

Often asked is whether to virtualize the OpsMgr components. Chapter 7, "Operations Manager and Virtualization," discusses this topic.

Upgrading Databases from SQL Server 2005 to SQL Server 2008

As discussed in the "Core OpsMgr Components Support" section, OpsMgr 2007 R2 fully supports SQL Server 2008 for the OpsMgr database and reporting components. If you use SQL Server 2005 for the OpsMgr database components and want to upgrade to SQL Server 2008, you must perform several steps on these components before and after upgrading your SQL Server installation. Note that this chapter does not specifically cover how to upgrade your SQL environment from SQL 2005 to SQL 2008.

Microsoft provides two upgrade tools to facilitate the upgrade process for the SQL Reporting Services (SRS) database—SRSupgradetool.exe and SRSupgradeHelper.msi. You can find the SRSupgradeHelper.msi in the OpsMgr R2 installation media in the \Support folder. The version of SRSupgradetool.exe included with R2 does not work properly; you will need to download the updated version that is available with the Cumulative Update 1 (CU1) for OpsMgr 2007 R2, as discussed in the "SRSupgradetool step 4 may encounter errors when running SRSupgradetool.exe /postupgrade" sidebar in the next section.

When you are ready to upgrade your SQL 2005 environment, make sure you are prepared. Every upgrade has an impact, so ensure that you have good backups of the databases, the SQL Server itself, and all other OpsMgr components as well. If you have servers with a dedicated SQL role, such as a separate SQL reporting server, you will need to back up these servers as well. Here is the upgrade order for upgrading the OpsMgr components from SQL Server 2005 to SQL Server 2008:

1. Back up all databases and the SRS encryption key.
2. Upgrade all OpsMgr database components to OpsMgr 2007 R2:
    ► Operational database
    ► Data warehouse
    ► ACS database
3. Upgrade the Operational database to SQL Server 2008.
4. Upgrade the data warehouse to SQL Server 2008.
5. Upgrade the ACS database to SQL Server 2008.
6. Run SRSupgradetool prior to upgrading SRS (instructions in the next section).
7. Upgrade the SRS database to SQL Server 2008.
8. Run SRSupgradetool again, and then run SRSupgradeHelper.
9. Apply Service Pack 1 to all components running SQL Server 2008.

CAUTION: SRSUPGRADETOOL.EXE WILL NOT RUN ON SQL 2008 SP 1

Do not upgrade the SRS database to SQL Server 2008 SP 1 until completing all these steps. SRSupgradetool.exe will not run on SQL 2008 SP 1.

The next sections discuss the two tools provided to facilitate the upgrade process for the SRS database.

SRSupgradetool.exe

Begin by running the CU1 version of SRSupgradetool.exe on your SQL Server Reporting Services server. SRSupgradetool.exe saves and restores three configuration files previously modified when you installed OpsMgr 2007 Reporting. You must run this tool prior to upgrading the SRS database server to SQL Server 2008, as the SQL 2008 installation detects the custom OpsMgr security extensions and blocks the upgrade until they are removed. Perform the following steps:

1. Run the following from a command prompt:

    ```
    SRSUpgradeTool.exe /InstanceName:<instance> /Action:PreSQLUpgrade
    ```

    Where *<instance>* is the SQL instance containing the SRS database. If you chose the default instance name during SQL Reporting Services installation, the instance name is MSSQLSERVER.

TIP: SRSUPGRADETOOL WILL NOT RUN FROM A MAPPED DRIVE OR THE INSTALLATION CD

You cannot run SRSupgradetool.exe from a mapped drive or even the installation CD. You will need to copy it to a local drive. This is because it is a .NET tool. If you receive an error similar to the one here, you are not running the tool locally:

```
Error: Request for the permission of type Sys-
tem.Security.Permissions.EnvironmentPermission,
mscorlib, Version=2.0.0.0, Culture=neutral, PublicKeyToken=b77a5c561934e089'
failed..
```

2. Restart the SRS service, validate the configuration by using the Reporting Services Configuration Manager tool, and review each setting. Check the SRS (see Figure 4.1) by browsing to the report manager URL (http://<computername>/reports<_instance>).

3. Upgrade the SRS instance from SQL Server 2005 to SQL Server 2008 released to manufacturing (RTM). These steps are not included in this chapter.

4. After upgrading SQL Server, run SRSupgradeTool again to update the registry entries for OpsMgr 2007 R2 Reporting to the new SQL Server Reporting Services location. Run the following from the command prompt:

    ```
    SRSUgradeTool.exe /InstanceName:<Instance> /Action:PostSQLUpgrade
    ```

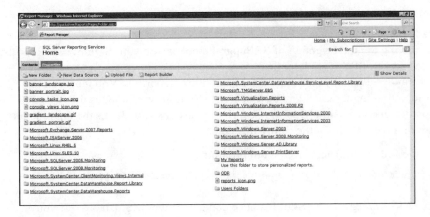

FIGURE 4.1 Connect to SRS.

SRSUPGRADETOOL STEP 4 MAY ENCOUNTER ERRORS WHEN RUNNING SRSUPGRADETOOL.EXE /POSTUPGRADE

If you run SRSupgradeTool.exe /InstanceName:*<Instance>*
/Action:PostSQLUpgrade using the version supplied with the R2 media, you may
receive the following error:

```
D:\SupportTools\i386>srsupgradetool.exe /InstanceName:MSSQLSERVER
/Action:PostSQLUpgrade

Microsoft System Center Operations Manager 2007 R2 -- Upgrade SQL Reporting

Server Preparation Tool

(C) Copyright 2000-2006 Microsoft Corp.

getSQLInstanceVersion: SRS Server is: XXXX.

getSQLInstanceVersion: SRS Instance is: MSSQLSERVER

getSQLInstanceVersion:  Actual SRS reg location is:

SOFTWARE\Microsoft\Microsoft

SQL Server\MSRS10.MSSQLSERVER\Setup

SQL Instance reg location is MSRS10.MSSQLSERVER

SRS version is 10.0.1600.22

SRS Report Server folder is C:\Program Files\Microsoft SQL

Server\MSRS10.MSSQLSERVER\Reporting Services\ReportServer\.

Error: Failed while updating registry entry for reporting code MSI component
```

Microsoft has confirmed this is a problem with the R2 release of SRSupgrade-
Tool, and has released an updated version of the SRSupgradeTool with CU1 for
OpsMgr 2007 R2. You can download Cumulative Update 1 from
http://www.microsoft.com/downloads/details.aspx?FamilyID=05d30779-2ddc-
48dc-aa91-a23167ee2cad&displaylang=en. Once downloaded, you will find the
updated SRSupgradeTool in the \Support folder; use the appropriate platform file
of this tool instead of the tool supplied in the OpsMgr 2007 R2 media.

SRSupgradeHelper.msi

The last tool to run is SRSupgradeHelper.msi. This tool moves the OpsMgr Reporting configuration files to the new SRS folder and sets the SQL Server reporting services configuration.

Run the following command from a command prompt:

```
Msiexec /i SRSUpgradeHelper.msi DATAREADER_DOMAIN=<Domain>
DATAREADER_USER=<datareaderuseraccount> MGSERVER=RMSserver
SRS_SERVER=<SRSServer\instance>
```

NOTE: OPSMGR 2007 R2 NEEDS SQL SERVER 2008 WITH SERVICE PACK 1

After completing these steps, apply SQL Server 2008 SP 1 (if you have more than one instance, the service packs must be applied for each instance). Microsoft requires SQL Server 2008 SP 1 to use SQL Server 2008 with OpsMgr 2007 R2. The service pack resolves some report rendering issues.

Post-Upgrade Steps

There are several post-installation steps after upgrading your OpsMgr 2007 components and upgrading SQL to SQL Server 2008. These steps are necessary only if upgrading to OpsMgr 2007 R2 and not for new installations.

OpsMgr 2007 SP 1 had an issue where the localized text table continued to grow. This was primarily caused by converted Microsoft Operations Manager (MOM) 2005 management packs, such as the Exchange 2007 management pack, running many backward-compatibility scripts. The issue was each event wrote additional data to the localized text table, which is not groomed. Over time, the Operational database continued to grow, negatively affecting OpsMgr performance. This problem is documented at several places, including the following:

- ▶ http://blogs.technet.com/kevinholman/archive/2008/10/13/does-your-opsdb-keep-growing-is-your-localizedtext-table-using-all-the-space.aspx

- ▶ http://scug.be/blogs/scom/archive/2009/09/14/cleaning-the-localizedtext-table-after-scom-upgrade-to-scom-2007-r2.aspx

OpsMgr 2007 R2 resolves the issue that kept the localizedtext table growing. However, you will need to run a SQL query to clean up the localizedtext and publishermessage tables. The cleanup script (cleanup.sql) can be found in the online content included with this book and at http://technet.microsoft.com/nl-nl/library/dd789073(en-us).aspx, where you will also find a complete post-installation checklist.

CAUTION: SQL SERVER 2008 SECURITY CHANGES

SQL Server 2008 adds several security improvements, as follows:

- ▶ The BUILTIN\Administrators no longer has sysadmin rights by default on new SQL Server 2008 installations. Only the SQL Server agent and SQL Server service are granted sysadmin rights by default.

▶ For Windows Server 2008 installations, User Account Control (UAC) will be a consideration. Chapter 3 provides additional information on this.

For more information on SQL Server 2008 security changes, see http://msdn.microsoft.com/en-us/library/cc280562.aspx.

SQL 2008 Reporting Services

With the R2 release, OpsMgr 2007 R2 Reporting supports SQL 2008 Reporting Services (with SP 1). A key differentiator from SQL 2005 SRS is that SRS 2008 no longer needs Internet Information Services (IIS) installed on the SQL Server system. SRS 2005 uses IIS mainly for client authentication, port 80 listener, and process hosting. SRS 2005 is not easy to manage; this was particularly true if you had several IIS applications running on the SQL Server at the same time. SRS 2008 does not have a dependency on IIS, which also gives it a performance gain. IIS has a simple model for thread, memory, and state management; it was not built to serve reports with enormous amounts of data simultaneously. The new on-demand processing model used with SRS 2008 ensures that no report executions will run out of memory. Not requiring IIS is also advantageous for those organizations wanting to use only Apache web servers or with a security policy not allowing a web server on the same system as SQL Server.

The data warehouse and reporting server components can be separated and installed on separate servers. When installing the reporting roles separately on a SQL 2005 server, you will only need to install IIS on the SRS server and not on the server with the Data Warehouse component. After installing SRS 2008, you must configure it so you can install OpsMgr Reporting. Perform the following steps:

1. Start the SQL Reporting Server Manager and connect to your SRS instance, shown in Figure 4.2.

FIGURE 4.2 Connect to the reporting server instance.

2. Next, specify the virtual directory and TCP port 80 (see Figure 4.3).

3. Configure a new database by selecting Change Database, as shown in Figure 4.4.

4. Create a new database.

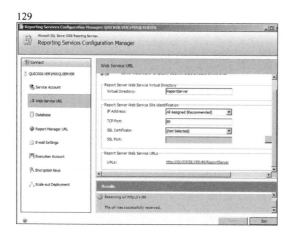

FIGURE 4.3 Specify the virtual directory.

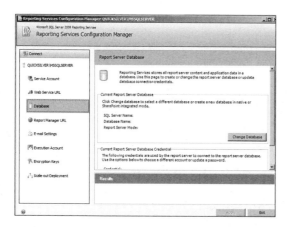

FIGURE 4.4 Select Change Database.

5.   Select the database server and authentication type (see Figure 4.5). Ensure that you have sufficient rights when selecting the current user. Use the Test Connection button to validate the connection.

6.   Enter a database name as shown in Figure 4.6; this typically is **ReportServer**. Ensure that you select Native Mode and not SharePoint Integration Mode. OpsMgr reporting does not support SharePoint mode; additional information is available in the Microsoft knowledgebase at http://support.microsoft.com/kb/946419.

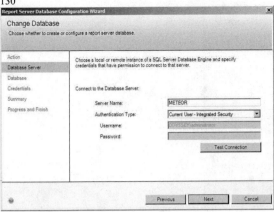

FIGURE 4.5 Connect to the database server.

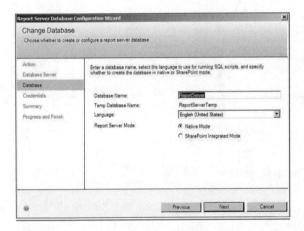

FIGURE 4.6 Enter the SRS database name, language, and report server mode.

7. Specify the credentials of an existing account and enter an authentication type; this can be Windows, SQL, or service credentials. The specified account is granted permissions automatically to access the report server database.

8. Review the Summary page (see Figure 4.7 for an example using the Quicksilver server), and select Finish.

Now you are ready to install OpsMgr 2007 R2 Reporting (covered in Chapter 6 of *System Center Operations Manager 2007 Unleashed*).

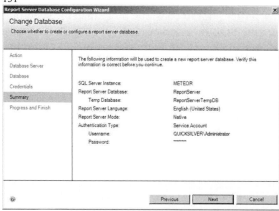

FIGURE 4.7 The summary page for configuring SRS

TIP: TOP OPSMGR REPORTING INSTALLATION ISSUES

Microsoft has released a document discussing the most common reporting installation issues. If you have issues installing the Reporting component, check
http://technet.microsoft.com/en-us/library/dd883295.aspx.

Post-Installation Steps for SQL Server

After installing SQL Server, there are several post-installation steps and checks to verify that you have a fully functional and healthy SQL Server environment to support
your OpsMgr management group. The next sections discuss these configurations.

Configure SQL Memory Limits

Configure the SQL maximum memory limit such that the OS and other applications
have at least 2GB RAM available. Ideally, allocate as much memory as possible to
SQL Server without causing the operating system to swap. Use the following formula
to calculate the amount of memory you can allocate to your SQL Server instance:

```
Maximum SQL Server Memory = Amount of memory in server - 2GB for operating system -
memory required for other applications
```

As an example, if SQL Server is installed on a system with 16GB of memory and no
other applications, you could configure the SQL maximum memory limit to 14GB. By
design, SQL Server continually uses more and more memory. The SQL Server buffer
pool is a caching feature that caches pages in RAM rather than disk, which is slower.
The buffer pool uses all available memory allocated to SQL Server. If SQL Server
consumes all available RAM, the operating system will have inadequate memory and
SQL Server will run as if it is memory constrained. This causes CPU usage to go up,
disk I/O to rise as Windows begins paging, and query response time to increase

drastically. To prevent the SQL server buffer pool to consume more than the specified allowed amount of memory, configure the SQL max server memory usage by instance using the sp_configure system stored procedure or with SQL Management Studio. In SQL Management Studio, configure the maximum server memory option by opening the Server Properties page and specifying an amount for Maximum server memory (in MB:), as displayed in Figure 4.8.

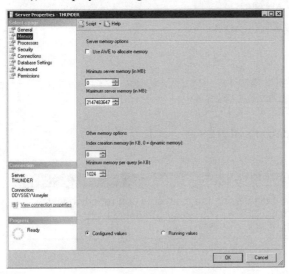

FIGURE 4.8 Configure maximum server memory.

Dynamic Port Allocation and Configuring the OpsMgr Database to Listen on a Specific TCP/IP Port

A default SQL Server installation enables dynamic port addressing. The default instance listens on TCP Port 1433. Named instances use a dynamic port, which is determined when the SQL Server service starts. If another service is using that port, SQL continues looking until it finds a free port.

When using dynamic ports, the SQL Server Browser service will ensure that applications such as OpsMgr are able to connect to the SQL Server database when a port number changes. The SQL Server Browser service translates an instance name into a port number and provides the discovery service for applications to find the instances on the server.

When clustering a multiple instance SQL Server, you may want to set each named instance to listen to a specific unused port. In addition, if your reporting server and RMS are separated by a firewall (which is not recommended), you will need to configure SQL Server and the OpsMgr database to use a static port. See http://technet.microsoft.com/en-us/library/cc540431.aspx for more information.

To configure SQL Server to listen on a specific TCP/IP port and not use dynamic port allocation, you must disable dynamic port allocation on the SQL Server, edit the

DBO.MT_ManagementGroup table, and edit the Registry on the RMS. Perform the following steps:

1.   Configure SQL Server with a static port:

      ► Open SQL Server Configuration Manager.

      ► Expand SQL Server Network Configuration in the left pane.

      ► Expand Protocols for *<instance>*.

      ► Open the TCP/IP Protocol Properties and click the IP addresses tab.

      ► In the IPn section, delete the 0 in the TCP Dynamic Ports.

      ► In the IPAll section, delete the port number in the TCP Dynamic Ports.

      ► In the IPAll section, insert a static port in the TCP port dialog box.

      ► Restart the SQL Server service.

2.   Enter the new static port in the dbo.MT_ManagementGroup table:

      ► Open SQL Management Studio and expand the Operational database.

      ► Right-click the dbo.MT_ManagementGroup table and select Update to query.

      ► Update the column titled CommunicationPort <guid> with the new static port.

3.   Edit the Registry on the RMS:

      ► Open Regedit (Start -> Run -> **Regedit**).

      ► Expand HKEY_LOCAL_MACHINE\Software\Microsoft\Microsoft Operations Manager\3.0\setup.

      ► Edit the DatabaseServerName. Add a comma and a space, followed by the static port number.

      ► Restart the System Center Data Access service.

      ► Check the Operations Manager log for EventID 26331, The SDK service reestablished database connectivity.

Operations Manager 2007 R2 Reporting

In addition to supporting SQL 2008 SP 1 for OpsMgr reporting (discussed in the "Core OpsMgr Component Support" section), OpsMgr 2007 R2 reporting incorporates many new capabilities. These include architectural changes and enhancements, discussed in the next sections.

Architecture

OpsMgr data warehouse data collection processes are implemented as OpsMgr 2007 workflows. Here are the two types of workflows:

▶ **Synchronization workflows**—These transfer data from the Operational database to the data warehouse.

▶ **Collection workflows**—Collection workflows transfer data from the agent to the data warehouse in parallel with transferring the same data to the Operational database. These processes write data that does not change once collected (state change events, performance samples, and general events).

Note that because the same workflow is writing data to both databases, if one database is having issues, it will affect the other as the data sources are waiting for acknowledgment of the data write generated to both.

In MOM 2005, real-time updates to the MOM reporting database were not as critical as the operational database, as the reporting database was updated nightly at 1:00 AM from the operational database by a daily DTS job that transferred data from the MOM database to the MOM reporting database. With the re-architecture of OpsMgr, the workflows write data to both databases, so if clustering your Operations database is a business requirement, you should also cluster your data warehouse. Otherwise, if your OpsMgr data warehouse is broken, your clustered OpsMgr database may encounter some issues, as it will wait for acknowledgment of the data write generated by the workflows and written simultaneously to both databases.

Figure 4.9 depicts these workflows.

Synchronization workflow has all workflows
running on the RMS.

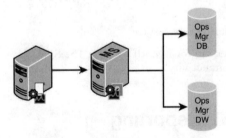

Data Collection workflow has the same
workflow writing data to the Operational
database and data warehouse, through the
management server.

FIGURE 4.9 Data warehouse workflows

As previously discussed in the "SQL 2008 Reporting Services" section, SQL Server 2008 no longer uses IIS with SRS. However, OpsMgr 2007 Reporting is designed to use the services provided by IIS. See http://support.microsoft.com//kb/958170 for background information on this issue in the OpsMgr 2007 SP 1 environment. To work-around this limitation in R2 with SQL Server 2008, the OpsMgr development team wrote an OpsMgr-specific module to replace the functionality previously provided with SRS.

Enhancements

Operations Manager 2007 R2 Reporting incorporates many new features, including the following:

- ► Object Picker
- ► Saving reports to a management pack
- ► Report authoring support in the R2 Authoring console
- ► Multiple selection parameters for most common events

The next sections discuss these topics.

Object Picker

The Object Picker will filter down search results when targeting objects within a report. The Object Picker module can only be utilized by those management packs where a list of supported classes is defined; this includes the native Exchange 2007 management pack, SQL Server management pack, Windows Server management pack, and several others; not all management packs take advantage of this capability yet.

The object-oriented structure of OpsMgr 2007 can make it challenging to know which object or class to target when running a report. (See Chapter 9 for additional information on targeting.) The OpsMgr data warehouse contains many classes, objects, and related information. However, not every object can be used in any report, and picking the incorrect object results in an empty report. The solution here is the new Object Picker module (see Figure 4.10), which will show only relevant classes for that particular report. This enhances the search functionalities when targeting classes in a report.

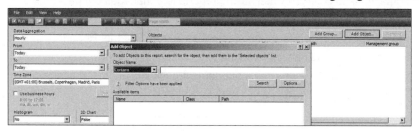

FIGURE 4.10 Using the Object Picker

Saving Reports to a Management Pack

R2's ability to save custom reports to a management pack lets you share custom reports within your organization. OpsMgr 2007 SP 1 let you save reports to Favorites and

Published Reports, but other report users could not access those reports due to the reporting security model (see the sidebar "Share Reports with Other Users in OpsMgr 2007" for a workaround with SP 1).

When you save a report in the OpsMgr console, it is saved under the My Reports folder in SQL Server SRS; reports in that folder are accessible only by the creator of the report. To share a newly published report, move it to a custom folder within SRS that is available to all users. Perform the following steps:

1.   In Internet Explorer, open the SRS home page (http://<servername>/reports).

2.   On the SRS home page, click New Folder, enter a name for the folder, and then click OK.

3.   Back on the home page, select the My Reports folder.

4.   Open the My Reports folder of the respective author.

5.   Select Properties of the published report.

6.   On the General page, select Move and select the custom folder you just created. Click OK.

7.   Do the same for the corresponding report's *.rpdl file.

8.   In the OpsMgr console, expand the Reporting node and select the custom folder you just created.

All users are now able to see your published report.

When you save reports to a management pack in R2, OpsMgr deploys them automatically when you import the management pack, enabling you to share reports with others easily.

NOTE: RESTRICTIONS ON SAVING REPORTS TO MANAGEMENT PACKS

Here are some items to consider when saving reports to a management pack:

▶   You cannot save a report to a management pack from Authored Reports.

▶   You can save a report to a management pack from Favorite Reports.

▶   Only administrators can save reports to a management pack.

▶   You cannot import reports in a management pack into another management group if it uses a different OpsMgr data warehouse.

Authoring Reports Support in the Authoring Console

The OpsMgr Authoring console, enhanced for R2, now supports writing reports (see Figure 4.11). Although this does not include an integrated editor for editing Report Definition Language (RDL) files or editing the Reporting Parameter Definition Language (RPDL), you will find all other report elements supported, such as scripts, resources, linked reports, reports, data warehouse datasets, and so on. For additional information on authoring management packs and using the Authoring console, see Chapter 8, "Management Pack Authoring."

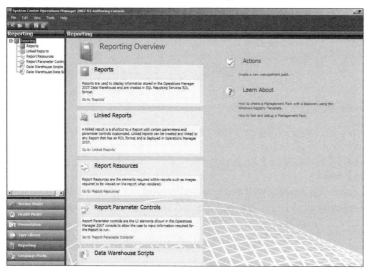

FIGURE 4.11 Authoring reports from the R2 Authoring console

Improved Search Interface for Performance Reports

When running a performance report from the Microsoft Generic Report Library, R2 adds additional fields to the search dialogs (see Figure 4.12). Previously, it was not always clear when distinguishing rules with the same name from each other.

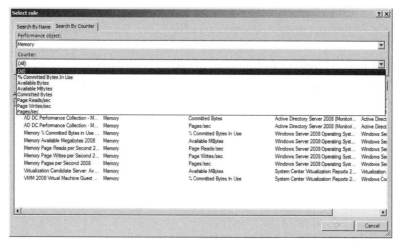

FIGURE 4.12 Parameters when running a performance report

Multi-Selection Parameters for Most Common Events

The Multi-Selection Parameters for Most Common Events capability, displayed in Figure 4.13, enables you to create a custom report showing the most common events based on certain criteria such as Event Log Parameters and Event Source.

FIGURE 4.13 Multi-Selection Parameters for the Most Common Events

Service Level Tracking Reports

Using Service Level Tracking reports will show whether you are meeting the configured Service Levels Objectives (SLOs) for the selected service levels. You must author or configure Service Level Tracking prior to running these reports. For more information on Service Level Tracking, see Chapter 1, "Introduction and What's New."

Securing Reports

R2 also enables you to use the Operations console to create Report Operator roles and secure your reports. The console previously did not have the capability of creating a custom Report Operator role, and you had to use PowerShell. See Chapter 11, "Securing Operations Manager 2007," of *System Center Operations Manager Unleashed*, for a description of this process. R2 makes it easier to create a custom Report Operator role and secure your reports. Perform the following steps:

1. Open the Administration node in the Operations console.

2. In the User Role section, right-click and select New User Role -> New Report Operator role.

3. Give the new Report Operator role a name and select Add Users.

4. Right-click the new Report Operator role and copy the Globally Unique Identifier (GUID) needed for securing the reports.

5. Open SRS by browsing to http://localhost/reports.

6. Select the Properties tab.

7. Click the New Role Assignment and paste the GUID of the custom Report Operator role.

8. Save your changes.

Database Maintenance

The next sections discuss maintenance jobs you should run on a regular basis and those jobs automatically performed to keep your OpsMgr databases up and running. SQL database administrators typically create a SQL maintenance plan to run basic maintenance such as UPDATE STATISTICS, DBBC DBREINDEX, BACKUP, and so on, running those daily or weekly at night. However, OpsMgr 2007 already includes several database maintenance jobs, such as reindexing and grooming (Chapter 12 of *System Center Operations Manager 2007 Unleashed* includes a discussion of grooming).

Ensure that your database maintenance jobs do not conflict with the OpsMgr built-in maintenance jobs and schedules. Microsoft created these maintenance jobs and schedules to ensure that OpsMgr will maintain acceptable SQL performance, even if you do not configure additional maintenance jobs. Because some organizations do not have a dedicated SQL team to configure and maintain the databases, the OpsMgr development team made the OpsMgr databases fully self-maintaining. Kevin Holman has a very good blog posting on the types of SQL maintenance to perform at http://blogs.technet.com/kevinholman/archive/2008/04/12/what-sql-maintenance-should-i-perform-on-my-opsmgr-databases.aspx.

Confirm that you have the most current SQL Server management pack installed to monitor your OpsMgr databases. The SQL Server management pack helps you check the performance data, availability, and configuration of your SQL databases, SQL agents, engine instances, and so on. Tuning particulars of the SQL Server management pack are included in Appendix A, "OpsMgr R2 by Example."

TIP: INSTALL SQL-DMO ON SQL SERVER 2008

When using the SQL Server management pack to monitor your SQL 2008 servers, you must install SQL distributed management objects or the SQL-DMO feature. Some scripts still rely on SQL-DMO to query information from SQL Server. Because Microsoft has removed SQL-DMO from SQL Server, you will need to download and install it separately from http://www.microsoft.com/downloads/details.aspx?familyid=228DE03F-3B5A-428A-923F-58A033D316E1&displaylang=en.

Operational Database Maintenance

The Operational database is one of the core components of your OpsMgr infrastructure, and you will want to ensure that it is always running smoothly. The next sections discuss actions you can take to keep the database performing optimally.

Maintaining Operational Database Free Space %

Always keep an eye on database free space. If the database is full, collected agent information is not inserted into the Operational database, collected reporting data is not inserted into the OpsMgr data warehouse, and monitoring of your datacenter stops. In addition to the SQL database free space monitor (which has thresholds of 20% and 10%) in the SQL management pack, there is a special Operational Database Free Space % monitor targeted at the System Center Operations Manager Operational Database Watcher. This monitor contains specific free space thresholds for the OpsMgr database. The thresholds for the OpsMgr database are set to 40% and 20% free space, which you should not change. As a best practice, ensure that there is at least 40% of free space is available for maintenance jobs, such as reindexing, to have enough space to run.

CAUTION: MONITORING FREE SPACE ON THE DATA WAREHOUSE

Because the OpsMgr data warehouse does not have a specific monitor with special thresholds to keep an eye on the free space of the data warehouse, you will need to use the free space monitors of the SQL management pack.

Optimizing Indexes

Microsoft includes reindexing the OpsMgr databases as part of the product. The Optimize Indexes rule for the operational database, displayed in Figure 4.14, is targeted at the RMS. This rule runs daily at 2:30 AM (see Figure 4.15), which cannot be modified. This means you must ensure that no other SQL maintenance jobs run at 2:30 AM.

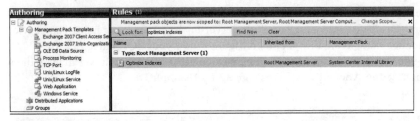

FIGURE 4.14 The Optimize Indexes rule

FIGURE 4.15 The Optimize Indexes rule runs daily at 2:30 AM.

The Optimize Indexes rule executes the stored procedure p_OptimizeIndexes stored procedure, as shown in Figure 4.16.

FIGURE 4.16 The Optimize Indexes rule executes the stored procedure p_OptimizeIndexes.

The stored procedure p_OptimizeIndexes calls another stored procedure, dbo. DomainTableIndexOptimize, which runs numerous optimizations, such as rebuilding indexes if necessary, updating statistics, reorganizing the indexes, and so on. Figure 4.17 shows the syntax of DomainTableIndexOptimize.

```
USE [OperationsManager]
GO
/****** Object:  StoredProcedure [dbo].[p_OptimizeIndexes]    Script Date: 09/12/2009 16:06:52 ******/
SET ANSI_NULLS ON
GO
SET QUOTED_IDENTIFIER ON
GO
ALTER PROCEDURE [dbo].[p_OptimizeIndexes]
AS
BEGIN
    SET NOCOUNT ON

    DECLARE @Err int
    DECLARE @DatasetId uniqueidentifier

    SET @DatasetId = '94BE6DB6-EB7E-4C76-9BF5-7569DFE54F96'

    EXEC @Err = DomainTableIndexOptimize
        @DatasetId                              = @DatasetId
        ,@MinAvgFragmentationInPercentToOptimize = 30
        ,@TargetFillfactor                       = 80
        ,@BlockingMaintenanceStartTime           = '00:00'
        ,@BlockingMaintenanceDurationMinutes     = 1440
        ,@MinAvgFragmentationInPercentToReorg    = 15
        ,@NumberOfIndexesToOptimize              = 0

    IF (@Err <> 0)
        GOTO Err

    RETURN 0
Err:
    RETURN 1
END
```

FIGURE 4.17 SQL syntax for the p_OptimizeIndexes stored procedure

Run this next SQL query against the OperationsManager database to determine when the p_OptimizeIndexes stored procedure ran (normally every day), the time to

142

complete, and the average fragmentation of the tables before and after running the stored procedure:

```
select * from DomainTable dt
 inner join DomainTableIndexOptimizationHistory dti

on dt.domaintablerowID = dti.domaintableindexrowID

ORDER BY optimizationdurationseconds DESC
```

TIP: THE OPTIMIZATION JOB SHOULD ONLY TAKE A FEW SECONDS

Pay particular attention to the OptimizationDurationSeconds column in the p_OptimizeIndexes query. This column shows how long the optimization ran. In a normal healthy environment, this should only take a few seconds.

The Operational database is heavily used, and data modifications such as UPDATE and INSERT occur constantly. These data modification operations can cause table fragmentation, which will give you poor query performance and increased disk activity. To display the fragmentation information of the tables in the OperationsManager database, run the following DBCC command:

```
DBCC showcontig with fast
```

Figure 4.18 shows output from running this command.

Notice the Local scan fragmentation and the Scan density values in Figure 4.18:

► The scan density value should be as high as possible; the scan density is 100% if everything is contiguous and less than 100% when there is fragmentation.

► The local scan fragmentation value shows the table fragmentation level; this should be close to zero, although values between 0% and 10% are acceptable.

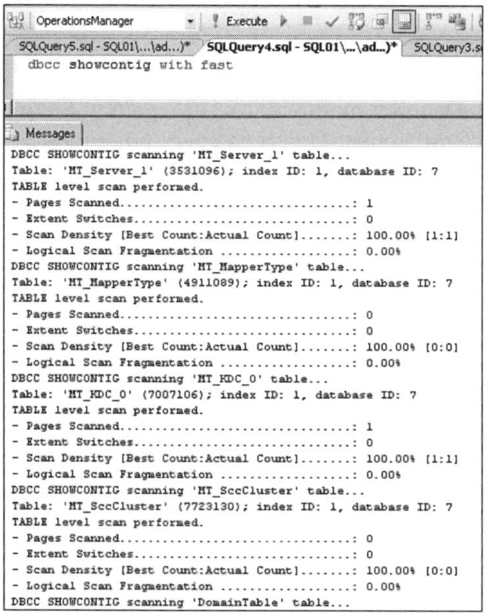

FIGURE 4.18 DBCC SHOW CONTIG with FAST

Here is a query you can use to rebuild the index to reduce fragmentation (the query is also available as online content as Reindex_Database.sql):

```
USE OperationsManager
go
SET ANSI_NULLS ON
SET ANSI_PADDING ON
SET ANSI_WARNINGS ON
SET ARITHABORT ON
SET CONCAT_NULL_YIELDS_NULL ON
SET QUOTED_IDENTIFIER ON
SET NUMERIC_ROUNDABORT OFF
EXEC SP_MSForEachTable "Print 'Reindexing '+'?' DBCC DBREINDEX ('?')"
```

NOTE: DBCC DBREINDEX IS AN OFFLINE OPERATION

Although DBCC DBREINDEX—used in the previous query—does a better job than DBCC INDEXDEFRAG to reduce fragmentation, the tables that are reindexed are not accessible during DBREINDEX. DBCC DBREINDEX is an offline operation and faster when there is a high level of fragmentation.

Data Warehouse Maintenance

Similar to the Operational database, the OpsMgr data warehouse is fully self-maintaining. The Standard Data Warehouse Data Set maintenance rule, seen in Figure 4.19, is responsible for maintaining the data warehouse. This runs every 60 seconds.

This rule calls the stored procedure dbo.StandardDatasetMaintenance, which calls several other stored procedures, as follows:

► dbo.StandardDatasetOptimize

► dbo.StandardDatasetGroom

► dbo.StandardDatasetAggregate

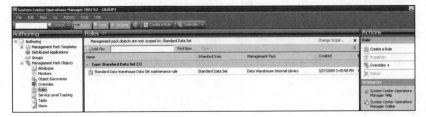

FIGURE 4.19 Standard Data Warehouse Data Set maintenance rule

---

NOTE: YOU CANNOT RUN THE STANDARD DATA WAREHOUSE DATA SET MAINTENANCE RULE MORE THAN ONCE EVERY 60 SECONDS

Although you can override the Standard Data Warehouse Data Set maintenance rule to run more frequently than every 60 seconds, a built-in control mechanism in the stored procedure for the maintenance rule prevents it from running more often than every 60 seconds.

One of the stored procedures called by the maintenance rule is dbo.StandardDatasetOptimize, responsible for indexing. If the average fragmentation in percent is between 10% and 30%, OpsMgr reorganizes the index. If fragmentation is over 30%, the index is rebuilt.

Here is a query (Optimization_results.sql with the online content) that determines the optimization results:

```
USE OperationsManagerDW
GO
select basetablename, optimizationstartdatetime, optimizationdurationseconds,
     beforeavgfragmentationinpercent, afteravgfragmentationinpercent,
     optimizationmethod, onlinerebuildlastperformeddatetime
from StandardDatasetOptimizationHistory sdoh
inner join StandardDatasetAggregationStorageIndex sdasi
on sdoh.StandardDatasetAggregationStorageIndexRowId =
sdasi.StandardDatasetAggregationStorageIndexRowId
inner join StandardDatasetAggregationStorage sdas
on sdasi.StandardDatasetAggregationStorageRowId =
```

```
sdas.StandardDatasetAggregationStorageRowId

ORDER BY optimizationdurationseconds DESC
```

This query displays the optimization method applied to which table, and levels of fragmentation before and after the optimizations jobs, as seen in Figure 4.20.

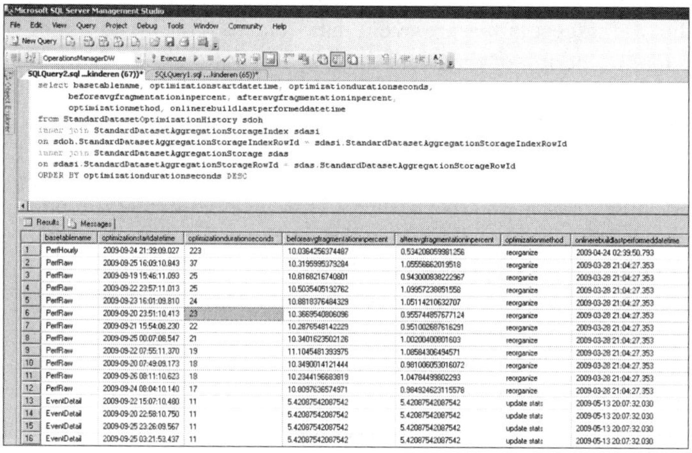

FIGURE 4.20 Data warehouse optimization results

Useful SQL Queries

When the Operations console or Operations Manager Shell does not provide enough information regarding database health and performance, you want to dive directly into the databases themselves. As an example, to clean up old state changes events for disabled monitors, change grooming settings, or know which monitor generates the most noise, use a SQL query to request that data from the Operational database or data warehouse. Kevin Holman has a posting on useful SQL queries (http://blogs.technet.com/kevinholman/archive/2007/10/18/useful-operations-manager-2007-sql-queries.aspx), and this chapter covers the most important and useful queries.

The "largest table" query is used often, particularly if you have performance problems. One of the most important ways to boost OpsMgr console performance is reducing the size of the Operational database. Unlike MOM 2005, OpsMgr 2007 no longer has a hard database limit of 30GB; however, the size of this database directly affects the speed of your console. Alexandre Verkinderen describes this at http://scug.be/blogs/scom/archive/2009/05/28/optimizing-the-performance-of-your-opsmgr-console-and-reducing-db-size.aspx. You can run this query on both the Operational database and the data warehouse to determine the table using the most space:

```
SELECT so.name,
8 * Sum(CASE WHEN si.indid IN (0, 1) THEN si.reserved END) AS data_kb,
Coalesce(8 * Sum(CASE WHEN si.indid NOT IN (0, 1, 255) THEN si.reserved END), 0) AS
index_kb,
```

```
Coalesce(8 * Sum(CASE WHEN si.indid IN (255) THEN si.reserved END), 0) AS blob_kb
 FROM dbo.sysobjects AS so JOIN dbo.sysindexes AS si ON (si.id = so.id)
WHERE 'U' = so.type GROUP BY so.name  ORDER BY data_kb DESC
```

Examine the results of the largest table query and determine what is using the space in your databases and why. As an example, if you run the query on the data warehouse database and discover that the largest tables are event data-related tables, you might consider changing the retention period of the event data. By default, raw event data is retained for 100 days; but it is of little value if you do not use that information for reporting or advanced event analysis.

If you recently upgraded from OpsMgr 2007 to OpsMgr 2007 R2, the LocalizedText table may be your largest table. Verify this by running the largest table query; then run the cleanup.sql script described in the "Post-Installation Steps for SQL Server" section. If other tables are using a tremendous amount of disk space, investigate which management pack, rule, object, and so on is responsible. Here is a SQL query (Noisiest_Monitor.sql in the online content for this book) to determine which monitor is the noisiest in the database and will eventually need some fine-tuning:

```
select
datepart(year, timegenerated) AS Year, datepart(month, timegenerated) AS Month,
datepart(day, timegenerated) AS Day, MonitorName, count(*) AS TotalStateChanges
from statechangeevent with(nolock)
inner join state with(nolock) on statechangeevent.stateid = state.stateid
inner join basemanagedentity with(nolock) on state.basemanagedentityid = baseman
agedentity.basemanagedentityid
inner join managedtype with(nolock) on basemanagedentity.basemanagedtypeid =
managedtype.managedtypeid
inner join monitor with(nolock)
on monitor.monitorid = state.monitorid and monitor.IsUnitMonitor = '1'
group by datepart(year, timegenerated), datepart(month, timegenerated), date-
part(day,
timegenerated), monitorname
order by TotalStateChanges DESC
```

Operational Database SQL Queries

Specific queries available to use with the Operational database include listing groups, retrieving agent information, and checking the database version. Remember to run these against your Operations Manager database.

Listing Groups

When authoring reports, rules, monitors, or entire management packs, you probably will want to know the groups to which this computer belongs. Running the following query (Listing_Groups.sql in the online content) lists all groups for a given computer:

```
Use OperationsManager
GO
SELECT SourceMonitoringObjectDisplayName AS 'Group'
FROM RelationshipGenericView
WHERE TargetMonitoringObjectDisplayName like ('%computername%')
AND (SourceMonitoringObjectDisplayName IN
(SELECT ManagedEntityGenericView.DisplayName
FROM ManagedEntityGenericView INNER JOIN
(SELECT      BaseManagedEntityId
FROM            BaseManagedEntity WITH (NOLOCK)
WHERE        (BaseManagedEntityId = TopLevelHostEntityId) AND (BaseManagedEntityId NOT
IN
(SELECT      R.TargetEntityId
FROM            Relationship AS R WITH (NOLOCK) INNER JOIN
dbo.fn_ContainmentRelationshipTypes() AS CRT ON R.RelationshipTypeId =
CRT.RelationshipTypeId
WHERE        (R.IsDeleted = 0)))) AS GetTopLevelEntities ON
GetTopLevelEntities.BaseManagedEntityId = ManagedEntityGenericView.Id INNER JOIN
(SELECT DISTINCT BaseManagedEntityId
FROM            TypedManagedEntity WITH (NOLOCK)
WHERE        (ManagedTypeId IN
(SELECT      DerivedManagedTypeId
FROM dbo.fn_DerivedManagedTypes(dbo.fn_ManagedTypeId_Group()) AS
fn_DerivedManagedTypes_1))) AS GetOnlyGroups ON
GetOnlyGroups.BaseManagedEntityId = ManagedEntityGenericView.Id))
ORDER BY 'Group'
```

Agent Information

As in earlier releases of OpsMgr 2007, you may have to apply a variety of patches to the OpsMgr agents. This query returns the patches previously applied on the agents:

```
select bme.path AS 'Agent Name', hs.patchlist AS 'Patch List'
from MT_HealthService hs
inner join BaseManagedEntity bme on hs.BaseManagedEntityId = bme.BaseManagedEntityId
order by path
```

Alternatively, to view all agents missing a specific hotfix, run the following query and change the KB number (954049 in the example) in the query:

```
select bme.path AS 'Agent Name', hs.patchlist AS 'Patch List'
from MT_HealthService hs
inner join BaseManagedEntity bme on hs.BaseManagedEntityId = bme.BaseManagedEntityId
where hs.patchlist not like '%954049%'
order by path
```

Management Group Information

To check which version of OpsMgr your database is on, say after upgrading from OpsMgr 2007 SP 1 to OpsMgr 2007 R2, run the following query:

```
SELECT * FROM __MOMManagementGroupInfo__
```

If the value in the DBVersion column is 6.1.####.#, where # is a positive integer, the OpsMgr database has been upgraded successfully. Table 4.2 lists the database versions.

TABLE 4.2 Database Versions in OpsMgr 2007

OpsMgr Version	DB Version
OpsMgr 2007 RTM	6.0.5000.0
OpsMgr 2007 SP1	6.0.6278.0
OpsMgr 2007 R2	6.1.####.#

Data Warehouse Database SQL Queries

Specific queries for the data warehouse include determining the amount of alerts and performance data. Use the following queries as a base to start authoring reports. For more information on developing reports, refer to Chapter 23, "Developing Management Packs and Reports," in *System Center Operations Manager 2007 Unleashed*.

Alerts

This query returns all raw alert data from the OpsMgr data warehouse. Use this command with WHERE statements to build your reports.

```
select * from Alert.vAlertResolutionState ars
inner join Alert.vAlertDetail adt on ars.alertguid = adt.alertguid

inner join Alert.vAlert alt on ars.alertguid = alt.alertguid
```

The next query shows the top-ten most common alerts and the computers on which they occur:

```
SELECT top 10
     RepeatCount,AlertName,vManagedEntity.DisplayName
  FROM [OperationsManagerDW].[Alert].[vAlert]
  INNER JOIN vManagedEntity
    ON Alert.vAlert.ManagedEntityRowId = vManagedEntity.ManagedEntityRowId

order by RepeatCount desc
```

Performance

The next SQL query returns the performance data for the logical disk, network interface, system, processor, and memory for all Windows computers. Use this (General_Performance_Overview.sql with the online content) to build a general performance overview report, as displayed in Figure 4.21:

```
SELECT vManagedEntityTypeImage.Image, Perf.vPerfDaily.DateTime,
Perf.vPerfDaily.SampleCount, Perf.vPerfDaily.AverageValue,
Perf.vPerfDaily.MaxValue, Perf.vPerfDaily.MinValue,vManagedEntity.Path,
vPerformanceRuleInstance.InstanceName,
```

```
vPerformanceRule.ObjectName, vPerformanceRule.CounterName,
vManagedEntityType.ManagedEntityTypeDefaultName
FROM   Perf.vPerfDaily INNER JOIN
vManagedEntity ON Perf.vPerfDaily.ManagedEntityRowId =
vManagedEntity.ManagedEntityRowId
INNER JOIN
vManagedEntityType ON vManagedEntity.ManagedEntityTypeRowId =
vManagedEntityType.ManagedEntityTypeRowId
LEFT OUTER JOIN
vManagedEntityTypeImage ON vManagedEntityType.ManagedEntityTypeRowId =
vManagedEntityTypeImage.ManagedEntityTypeRowId
INNER JOIN
vPerformanceRuleInstance ON vPerformanceRuleInstance.PerformanceRuleInstanceRowId =
Perf.vPerfDaily.PerformanceRuleInstanceRowId
INNER JOIN
vPerformanceRule ON vPerformanceRuleInstance.RuleRowId = vPerformanceRule.RuleRowId
WHERE objectName in ('LogicalDisk', 'Network Interface', 'Processor','Memory') and
 (counterName like '%Processor Time%' or counterName like '%Free MegaBytes%'
or counterName like '%Free Space%' or counterName like '%Available Mem-
ory')and(vManagedEntityType.ManagedEntityTypeDefaultName LIKE N'%Server%')
```

	Memory						Processor		
	% Committed Bytes In Use			Available MBytes			% Processor Time		
	Average Value	Min Value	Max Value	Average Value	Min Value	Max Value	Average Value	Min Value	Max Value
Fireball.ody ssey.com	24.85	24.71	24.98	462.11	453.22	470.90	96.98	94.60	98.44
Mission.ody ssey.com	42.00	41.57	42.45	243.92	225.74	258.91	3.22	0.83	7.84
Hornet.odys sey.com	50.95	50.74	51.16	456.74	420.22	486.91	4.67	2.82	7.89
Hurricane.o dyssey.com	49.42	49.23	49.61	895.87	865.89	935.21	9.86	4.47	21.17
Hydra.odyss ey.com	37.00	36.81	37.18	165.12	147.82	186.14	6.60	4.89	9.26
Meteor.odys sey.com	37.28	37.12	37.47	246.86	239.33	253.76	0.98	0.83	1.16
pantheon.o dyssey.com	37.89	37.70	38.06	186.43	180.90	191.57	0.78	0.60	1.08

FIGURE 4.21 General Performance Overview Report

Miscellaneous SQL Queries

The next sections discuss several miscellaneous SQL queries. These include checking
the status of the SQL broker, reindexing the database, and maintaining the transaction
logs.

SQL Broker

The OpsMgr database requires that the SQL broker is enabled. If the broker is not enabled, you will encounter several issues—one of them being the OpsMgr agent discovery hangs. Run the following query to verify your SQL broker is enabled:

```
SELECT is_broker_enabled FROM sys.databases WHERE name = 'OperationsManager'
```

If the result returned is 0, you need to enable the SQL broker. To enable the SQL broker for your OpsMgr database, use the query described at http://scug.be/blogs/scom/archive/2008/11/22/the-sql-server-service-broker-for-the-current-opsmgr-database-is-not-enabled.aspx.

Reindex the Database

Here is a query to rebuild the index and reduce fragmentation:

```
USE OperationsManager
GO
SET ANSI_NULLS ON
SET ANSI_PADDING ON
SET ANSI_WARNINGS ON
SET ARITHABORT ON
SET CONCAT_NULL_YIELDS_NULL ON
SET QUOTED_IDENTIFIER ON
SET NUMERIC_ROUNDABORT OFF
EXEC SP_MSForEachTable "Print 'Reindexing '+'?' DBCC DBREINDEX ('?')"
```

Truncate and Shrink Transaction Log Files in SQL Server 2008

Truncating the transaction logs is not recommended. If you have problems with transaction log space, check the backup policy and recovery model for your databases. For more information on automatically truncating the logs, check Microsoft's MSDN site at http://msdn.microsoft.com/en-us/library/ms189085.aspx.

In versions of SQL Server prior to SQL Server 2008, you can truncate the log file using the following SQL syntax:

```
BACKUP LOG MOM_LOG with Truncate_only
```

This capability no longer exists with SQL Server 2008. Running this command in SQL 2008 gives you the following error:

```
Msg 155, Level 15, State 1, Line 1
'Truncate_Only' is not a recognized BACKUP option.
```

If the database is set to Full Recovery, change it first to Simple Recovery mode (for information on the difference between the two, see Chapter 12 of *System Center Operations Manager 2007 Unleashed*) with the following SQL syntax:

```
USE OperationsManager
GO
ALTER DATABASE OperationsManager
SET RECOVERY SIMPLE

GO
```

Now, shrink the file:

```
DBCC SHRINKFILE (MOM_LOG,1)
GO
ALTER DATABASE OperationsManager
SET RECOVERY FULL

GO
```

NOTE: TRUNCATION DOES NOT REDUCE THE SIZE OF THE LOG FILE

Truncating a log file does not reduce the size of the file; it merely cleans out old transactions. To reduce the size of a log file, you must shrink the log file after truncating it. For information on shrinking database and log files, refer to http://technet.microsoft.com/en-us/library/ms189493.aspx.

Summary

This chapter discussed the SQL Server 2008 environment used by Operations Manager 2007 R2. It included hardware recommendations and discussed the upgrade process and post-installation recommendations for configuring SQL Server, including the additional steps required to upgrade SQL Server 2008 Reporting Services to work properly. The chapter covered the architectural changes and enhancements to OpsMgr 2007 R2 reporting, database maintenance, and useful SQL queries to help maintain the OpsMgr database components. The next chapter discusses automating your OpsMgr environment using the OpsMgr Shell, an OpsMgr-specific implementation of PowerShell.

## CHAPTER 5

PowerShell Extensions for Operations Manager 2007

Although most administrators use the Operations Manager (OpsMgr) console to manage their environment, sometimes you may want to step outside the graphical user interface (GUI); this may be to automate some aspect of your operations or perform something you cannot do within the console itself.

Windows PowerShell, a powerful and flexible scripting and shell language, is Microsoft's next-generation scripting and automation language. Based on Microsoft's .NET Framework, PowerShell runs on Microsoft operating systems beginning with Windows XP and is included with Windows Server 2008 builds. A number of Microsoft products leverage PowerShell to improve administrator control, efficiency, and productivity. As of Microsoft's Fiscal Year 2009 (starting July 1, 2009), PowerShell became part of Microsoft's Common Engineering Criteria (CEC), meaning all Microsoft server products must provide some level of support for PowerShell.

This chapter discusses using PowerShell to automate various tasks and its integration with Operations Manager 2007.

Windows PowerShell Basics

You can use PowerShell interactively by typing commands directly into a console, or by invoking previously written scripts. Some products, such as Microsoft Exchange 2007, provide strong PowerShell support; everything in the Exchange 2007 user interface is possible via PowerShell using the Exchange Management Shell, and numerous wizards in Exchange that perform tasks from the user interface include a screen showing the actual PowerShell code used to carry out that task. You can easily copy and paste these PowerShell commands and create your own automation tasks. Providing this level of support in Exchange for PowerShell necessitated a complete rewriting of the user interface.

Operations Manager 2007 does not provide as high a level of support for PowerShell. Not every task performed through the user interface is available through PowerShell, and wizards do not generate the equivalent PowerShell command to undertake a particular task. Nevertheless, PowerShell is still very useful for scripting and providing automation for OpsMgr 2007.

Installing and Accessing PowerShell

With PowerShell preinstalled in Windows Server 2008, the only action required is to add the Windows PowerShell feature using the Server Manager, shown in Figure 5.1.

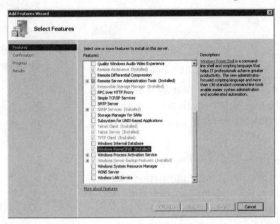

FIGURE 5.1 Adding the PowerShell feature in the Server Manager

Microsoft provides a web download to incorporate PowerShell into older operating systems. Start at the official PowerShell site (http://www.microsoft.com/powershell) to get to the PowerShell location for all supported operating systems and architectures. You will need .NET Framework 2.0 as an installation prerequisite. This is not an issue beginning with Windows Server 2008 Service Pack (SP) 2, as it preinstalls the .NET Framework 2.0 on non-Core installations. (Windows Server 20008 Release 2 [R2] Core includes support for the .NET Framework and Windows PowerShell version 2.) Installing PowerShell does not require a reboot.

To access the PowerShell console, click Start -> Windows PowerShell 1.0 -> Windows PowerShell. This starts the PowerShell console displayed in Figure 5.2. By default, the console has a dark blue background with white lettering.

Note that 64-bit systems have two menu shortcuts to start PowerShell, as follows:

► A shortcut that launches PowerShell in 64-bit mode

► A second link that starts a x86 version of PowerShell

Going into the differences of these versions is beyond the scope of this chapter.

FIGURE 5.2 The default PowerShell console

NOTE: REQUIRING ELEVATED PRIVILEGES

Performing some tasks may require Administrator privileges on Windows Vista, Windows 7, Windows Server 2008, and newer versions of Windows. In this case, right-click the PowerShell link to open it with the appropriate permissions. The typical User Access Control prompt may appear at this point.

In interactive mode, PowerShell parses each command as you key it in. When you type in a command and press the Return key, PowerShell may only return ">>" on a new line. This indicates that either PowerShell needs more information to complete the command or there is a syntax error, which may be as simple as forgetting a quote mark. After fixing the problem, press Enter twice.

PowerShell runs DOS commands, and with appropriate interpreters such as perl.exe or wscript.exe, you can run Perl and VBScript scripts directly from PowerShell. Note that there may be some issues running external commands requiring manipulation of items that PowerShell may try to interpret wrongly—quotation marks being an example.

The next sections discuss general PowerShell concepts, navigation, and structure. The majority of these are in the context of OpsMgr-related tasks, so most of the examples provide code that may only work in the Operations Manager PowerShell console.

General PowerShell Concepts

Let's start with some basic terminology. Here are some of the more important terms:

- ▶ **Console**—The console is the user interface provided to work interactively with PowerShell. Opening the console presents a customizable prompt you can use to enter commands in an interactive fashion with immediate feedback or to run PowerShell scripts. If you are new to PowerShell, using the console interactively is typically the best approach.

- ▶ **Cmdlet**—This term phonetically sounds like command-let, and is the most basic unit or item in PowerShell. Cmdlets are the actual commands typed in that will run in the console. You can use cmdlets alone or to create things more complex, such as scripts. An example is the `Get-Event` cmdlet, discussed in the "Cmdlet Structure" section and used to work with Operations Manager events for all connected management groups.

▶ **Alias**—A number of cmdlets have aliases. Aliases provide the ability to use a shortcut rather then typing the full name of the cmdlet. These are useful for those users coming from different environments with a command-line interface—you can map simple aliases such as `dir` to a PowerShell cmdlet performing a similar task. Some of the more familiar Unix and Linux commands are already in PowerShell, defined as aliases for existing cmdlets.

As an example, an alias for the `Get-ChildItem` cmdlet is simply `dir`. For those new to PowerShell, the cmdlet name `Get-ChildItem` may not seem like a logical choice, but users of other scripting shells such as DOS will definitely recognize `dir`. In addition, another alias for `Get-ChildItem` is `ls`, which should be familiar to any Unix or Linux shell script user.

▶ **Pipeline**—A pipeline is created when cmdlets are chained together, using the pipe character "|". Those objects created by the pipeline are passed from one cmdlet to another in a series. However, you cannot chain together just any set of cmdlets, as each cmdlet needs to know what type of object is passed to it. A simple example of using the pipeline is `Get-Event|Select-Object -Property Description`. Here, `Get-Event` lists all the events, and then `Select-Object` determines the properties to display to the console.

Here are some references for a more thorough discussion of these concepts:

> ▶ http://blogs.msdn.com/powershell/archive/2008/06/17/explaining-objects-to-non-programmers.aspx
>
> ▶ *Windows PowerShell Unleashed, 2nd Edition* (Sams, 2008)

▶ **Provider**—PowerShell has certain data stores presented and navigated in a fashion similar to a file system. In fact, the familiar C: drive found on all Windows-based systems is a PowerShell provider. Using PowerShell, you can navigate or traverse the file system using files and folders. A similar concept applies for other PowerShell providers, such as the Windows registry provider. A number of server products with some form of PowerShell support supply their own application-specific provider, including Operations Manager 2007, Internet Information Services (IIS) 7, Exchange 2007, and SQL Server 2008. This enables you to use the same syntax against the various data stores!

▶ **Snapin**—PowerShell is fully extendable. This extensibility is available as a packaged DLL named a *snapin*. A PowerShell snapin can provide a provider and a cmdlet, or several of each. A snapin may already be registered with PowerShell, but must still be added to the console to have access to those features provided by the snapin. As an example, to have access to the cmdlets for Exchange management, the Exchange PowerShell snapin must be loaded. Similarly, with Operations Manager, the Operations Manager snapin must be loaded for the additional OpsMgr features to be available to the base PowerShell installation.

▶ **Scriptblock**—In PowerShell, a scriptblock is noted by the syntax "{}." This indicates that a set of statements or commands are grouped together into a single block. A simple example of using a scriptblock is `Get-Event|Where-Object{$_.LoggingComputer -eq "some_computer_name"}`. Here the `Get-Event` cmdlet retrieves a list of all events, and is used with the `Where-Object` cmdlet where a scriptblock filters out the number of matches by checking each event for ones with a `LoggingComputer` property matching "`some_computer_name.`"

Basic Navigation and Functionality

Before getting into the more technical details, here are several user-focused enhancements that can make it easier to learn and use PowerShell:

▶ **Tab completion**—In the PowerShell console, you can type the first few letters of a cmdlet; then press the `Tab` key on the keyboard. PowerShell cycles through a list of possible matches on each `Tab` key press. This also applies to parameters (discussed in the "Cmdlet Structure" section) and may apply in some circumstances to finding a file name by repeatedly using the `Tab` key. For example, in the PowerShell console, typing **Get-E**, and then hitting the `Tab` key in a default Operations Manager installation, expands this to `Get-Event`.

▶ **Arrow keys**—Use the arrow keys to undertake various tasks in the console. The up and down arrow keys can be used to cycle through the history of commands you previously entered. You can use the left and right arrow keys to move the cursor along a current command. This can be useful if there is a simple typing error in a particular command—just use the up arrow key to recall the last entered command; then use the left and right arrow keys to modify the command to correct the typing error.

▶ **Function keys**—The function keys provide some useful quick shortcuts, with the most valuable probably the `F7` key. This function key will pop up a menu in the PowerShell console that shows the history of commands executed.

▶ **Escape key**—When typing commands at the PowerShell prompt, you can cancel a typed-in command by pressing the key combination `Ctrl+C`, and completely erase it with the `Escape` key.

▶ **Built-in help**—PowerShell provides extensive built-in help on its commands and on topics as well. The "Getting Started" section discusses this in more detail. For example, typing `Get-Help Get-Command` provides help about the `Get-Command` cmdlet, whereas `Get-Help about_pipelines` covers pipelines.

▶ **Online help**—You can also retrieve up-to-date online help. This is the online PowerShell portal on Microsoft TechNet at http://technet.microsoft.com/en-us/library/bb978525.aspx. The online help currently focuses on PowerShell version 2, so some of the documentation may not apply to systems still running version 1, which is the PowerShell version used with Operations Manager SP 1 and R2.

Cmdlet Structure

A cmdlet is the most basic unit in PowerShell. The naming scheme for cmdlets follows a simple *verb-noun* structure. Probably the most basic verb is `Get`. Typically, you use this verb when retrieving something. The verb is followed by a dash, and then by a noun. As discussed in the "General PowerShell Concepts" section, a good cmdlet for someone new to PowerShell and in the context of Operations Manager-related tasks is `Get-Event`, which is used to retrieve events from all OpsMgr-connected management groups.

If you type `Get-Event` into the PowerShell console (and press `Enter`), PowerShell lists all the events available, as displayed in Figure 5.3.

FIGURE 5.3 Using `Get-Event` to list all events

Although it can be useful to get a full listing of all events, the output typically scrolls by too quickly and is unusable. Cmdlets support *parameters* and associated *values*. Using `Get-Event` as an example, the cmdlet provides a `-Criteria` parameter. When a value is passed with the `-Criteria` parameter, only those events matching the value used for the parameter are listed, as displayed in Figure 5.4.

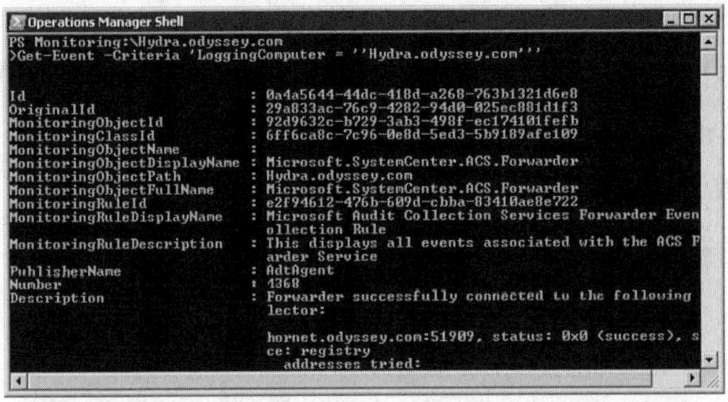

FIGURE 5.4 Using `Get-Event` with `-Criteria`

By default, cmdlets can support many different parameters and values. Parameters do not always have to be explicitly added to the command line, nor do they have to be fully typed, as they can be aliased.

This section has used the `Get-Event` cmdlet as an example and demonstrated the `-Criteria` parameter. Even if the parameter was entered as `-c` with the same value, the output would be the same as Figure 5.4.

Parameter names not only go by their actual names, but can also go by the placement on the command-line. The next section includes a discussion of parameter sets and positioning of parameters, discussed in conjunction with the Get-Help cmdlet.

> **NOTE: CASE INSENSITIVITY**
>
> Unless specified, PowerShell is case insensitive. This means that Get-Event is the same as get-event or even GET-EVENT. Parameters and values are also case insensitive in most cases, but there can be exceptions.

Getting Started

Here are three cmdlets that are very handy when you are new to PowerShell:

▶ **Get-Command**—Retrieves a list of cmdlets.

▶ **Get-Help**—Retrieves help information.

▶ **Get-Member**—Retrieves all the members of objects.

The next sections discuss each of these cmdlets, and the following sections discuss other cmdlets and useful concepts.

Get-Command

Get-Command provides a good way to learn what cmdlets might apply for a particular task. What if you are new to PowerShell and are not sure which command to start with? You can simply type the cmdlet at the PowerShell console, as shown in Figure 5.5. Without any arguments, Get-Command will list all the cmdlets currently loaded.

PowerShell supports wildcards, and using them makes searching for cmdlets relating to a particular task easier to find. For example, to look for cmdlets relating to services, all that is necessary is to pass a particular string like "*service*" to the Get-Command cmdlet to get a listing of all the cmdlets related to Windows Services. Any applications that match the provided value may also be listed.

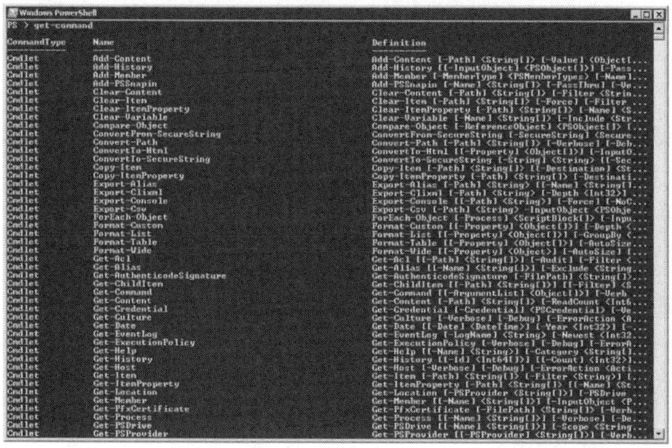

FIGURE 5.5 Get-Command shows a full list of cmdlets.

Get-Help

Get-Help retrieves help information. Get-Help alone simply prints out the help for Get-Help itself. It is commonly used as Get-Help <cmdlet>. As an example, Get-Help Get-Event retrieves the built-in help information for the Get-Event cmdlet.

Get-Help also supports the following parameters:

► **-Default (no parameters)**—Provides basic help information for the cmdlet.

► **-Full**—Gives detailed information for the cmdlet, including all the support parameters, and various details on each. It also provides usage examples.

► **-Detailed**—Provides essentially the same information as –Full.

► **-Examples**—Typically gives various examples of using the cmdlet. There are some third-party products where this parameter does not work as expected, because the associated help files for the cmdlet were not written properly.

Using the –Full or –Detailed parameters provides additional information on parameters. Using Get-Help Get-Event –full provides the following output in the PowerShell console:

```
PS Monitoring:\Hydra.odyssey.com
>Get-Help Get-Event -full

NAME
    Get-Event

SYNOPSIS
    Gets events.
...

    -Id <Guid>
        Specifies the GUID of the event to retrieve.

        Required?                 true
        Position?                 1
        Default value
        Accept pipeline input?    false
        Accept wildcard characters? false

...
```

Here, the cmdlet's built-in help indicates that the –Id parameter is defined as in position 1, which is useful in showing what happens when you explicitly do not define the parameter name. Here's a code snippet to demonstrate this:

```
PS> Get-Event 6f418f92-7fca-43e2-a0bd-f15541bbf7b4
```

Here, the –Id parameter was not explicitly defined on the command line, but because there is an event ID value defined in the first available position, PowerShell automatically assumes this is a value for the –Id parameter.

The value is an ID for an event specific to the test environment used in this scenario. To get a sample ID from another environment, the command `Get-Event|Select-Object -First 1 -Property ID` should get a valid sample value.

For more information on parameters, refer to http://powershell.com/cs/blogs/ebook/archive/2008/10/21/chapter-2-interactive-powershell.aspx#cmdlets-quotgenuinequot-powershell-commands.

Get-Member

`Get-Member` is typically not the first cmdlet introduced to a new PowerShell user. To fully understand this cmdlet and its output, it helps to have a basic knowledge of the Microsoft .NET Framework. Using and understanding `Get-Member` is an advanced topic that is very useful once you understand the basics. Although typical scripting languages just pass simple strings to input/output data, PowerShell uses objects, which are much more powerful. `Get-Member` provides a simple way to get additional information on objects using .NET Reflection, which interrogates objects directly, displaying information about the object's members.

For a more detailed overview of the `Get-Member` cmdlet, check `Get-Help Get-Member`.

Special Variable $_

$_ is a very special variable in PowerShell. It is very powerful and used frequently in PowerShell. In the mindset of objects and pipelines, $_ is the current object in the pipeline.

In its simplest form, $_ might look like this:

```
PS>"Hello"|ForEach-Object {$_}
```

The "Filtering Cmdlets" section looks at the `ForEach-Object` cmdlet in detail. The preceding snippet can be interpreted as follows:

1. Pass the "Hello" string object along the pipeline to the `ForEach-Object` cmdlet.
2. The `ForEach-Object` cmdlet is programmed to accept input from the pipeline, and by definition is set to act on each object that is inputted.
3. Use a scriptblock to define the action to take on each object. In this case, the action is simply to display the current object. The current object is a simple string, so the original string is simply outputted.

Comparison Operators

A very important ability when scripting is the capability to compare one object to another. The comparison can be between a number or string object.

The following code shows what a simple string comparison looks like:

```
PS>"test" -eq "test"
True
PS>
```

Here, the string object "test" is compared with "test"—because these match, the returned Boolean value is simply *True*.

The other common comparison operators are -gt for "greater than" and -lt for "lesser than." Performing comparisons returns a Boolean value of *True* or *False*. This simple return value works with conditional statements, discussed in the "Conditional Statements" section. This only scratches the surface of comparison operators.

PowerShell also supports *wildcards* and the use of *regular expressions*. For information on these concepts, see Get-Help about_comparison_operators, Get-Help about_wildcards, Get-Help about_regular_expressions.

Filtering Cmdlets

Often when working with cmdlets, a *collection* of objects is returned. You may need to filter the collection of returned objects, either to display information to the console or continue to pass the filtered objects along the pipeline. Here are the relevant cmdlets:

► **ForEach-Object (aliases foreach and %)**—Used when a scriptblock needs to be applied to every object as it comes through the pipeline.

► **Where-Object (aliases where and ?)**—Used when a particular criteria needs to be applied to every object as it comes through the pipeline. The result is typically a subset of the original objects passed through the pipeline.

Here are some simple examples of each of these cmdlets.

The following code shows the ForEach-Object cmdlet:

```
PS>"hello","world"|foreach-object{$_.toupper()}
HELLO
WORLD
PS>
```

This shows that by using the ForEach-Object cmdlet, the ToUpper() method is applied to each object in the collection passed along the pipeline.

Next is the Where-Object cmdlet, which you can use to filter out particular objects from the pipeline:

```
PS>get-process|where-object{$_.ws -gt 100MB}
Handles  NPM(K)    PM(K)     WS(K) VM(M)   CPU(s)     Id ProcessName
-------  ------    -----     ----- -----   ------     -- -----------
    526      30   114496    124928   395   273.27   4432 xxx
```

Here, the `Where-Object` cmdlet filters out any process objects where the WS property value (working set) is greater than 100MB. The result is a filtered list of objects that can be passed even further along the pipeline for further processing. (See http://support.microsoft.com/kb/108449 for Microsoft's official description of a working set.)

In some cases, it can be difficult to understand what the information displayed by the console refers to. For example, the output "273.27" in the preceding code output can lead to confusion, as it is unclear what the "CPU(s)" column means. You can use the `Get-Member` cmdlet, introduced in the "Get-Member" section, to help provide useful information on how to retrieve additional information on objects within PowerShell. A simple way to determine what type of object is used is to pipe any command to it, as shown in Figure 5.6.

Note in this figure, the third line of text from the top where "TypeName" is located provides the type of object in this case, which is "System.Diagnostics.Process." One way to determine features of this object is entering that name in a search engine. This usually brings up Microsoft's MSDN documentation as one of the first search results.

FIGURE 5.6 Showing Get-Member output

Although not displayed in Figure 5.6, there is a line that provides information on the "CPU" value, and this appears to be related to `TotalProcessorTime`. From the MSDN documentation, the `TotalProcessorTime` property provides the total processor time for the process. In other words, the PowerShell process has used up a total of 273.27 seconds of total processor (CPU) time.

PowerShell actually recognizes keywords such as "KB," "MB," and "GB" (with more keyword recognition coming in PowerShell version 2). As an example:

```
PS> 1KB
1024
PS> 1MB
1048576
PS> 1GB
1073741824
```

These special values are useful when wanting to change values back to MB or GB.

Using these special formatting tricks can be very valuable with formatting WMI results. The Get-WmiObject is used to work with the Windows Management Instrumentation service. Here's a code snippet that queries the local WMI service to request the Win32_LogicalDisk class:

```
PS>get-wmiobject win32_logicaldisk|where-object{$_.DeviceID -eq "C:"}
```

Figure 5.7 shows the output of the preceding command, which could be presented in a more readable format. The figure also shows a longer example where Format-Table is used to with a calculated property to modify the drive space value so that it is represented in GBs. A feature of the .NET Framework is used to round off the amount.

FIGURE 5.7 Special formatting of disk space values

Here is the code run in Figure 5.7:

```
Get-WmiObject win32_logicaldisk|where{$_.deviceid -eq "C:"}| →
format-table -auto deviceid,drivetype, →
@{label="free";expression={[math]::round($_.freespace/1GB,2)}}
```

Sorting and Selecting Cmdlets

The previous section focused on filtering entire objects before passing them along the pipeline. There are also cmdlets that can select certain properties of an object and only pass those along. In addition, there are cmdlets to sort and group properties together. Here are the relevant cmdlets and examples of each:

▶ **Select-Object (alias select)**—It is possible to limit the number of properties passed along the pipeline. Select-Object has some similarities to the Format-* cmdlets, looked at in the "Formatting Cmdlets" section. You can use this cmdlet to select which specific properties to display, or to select what properties will continue to be passed along a pipeline. Here's an example:

```
PS>get-process|select processname,company
ProcessName                                          Company
-----------                                          -------
AESTSr64                                             Andrea Electronics
AppleMobileDeviceService                             Apple Inc.
audiodg
BCMWLTRY                                             Dell Inc.
...
```

This output demonstrates that rather than have PowerShell display the default properties of this particular object, specific properties are listed that then are displayed on the console.

▶ **Group-Object (alias group)**—You can easily group objects together based on their properties. Consider this example:

```
PS>get-process|group {$_.processname.substring(0,1)}
Count Name                 Group
----- ----                 -----
    3 A                     {System.Diagnostics.Process (AESTSr64),
    1 B                     {System.Diagnostics.Process (BCMWLTRY)}
...
```

This illustration groups all the processes on the system by the first letter of the process' name. Try doing something that powerful in VBScript!

The SubString() method used here is simply a way to get a particular section of a string where the first element is the starting point, and the second element is how many characters to retrieve.

Next, look at an even more advanced example of using grouping:

```
PS>get-process|group {if($_.ws -lt 10MB){"<10MB"} →
elseif($_.ws -lt 20MB){"10MB-20MB"}else{">20MB"}}
Count Name                 Group
----- ----                 -----
   46 <10MB                 {System.Diagnostics.Process (AESTSr64),
   15 10MB-20MB             {System.Diagnostics.Process (audiodg),
    9 >20MB                 {System.Diagnostics.Process (BCMWLTRY),
```

This groups the processes by the value of the WS property. All processes are grouped based on whether that value is less than 10MB, between 10MB and 20MB, or over 20MB in size. The if...elseif..else contained in the script-block is a new concept discussed in the "Conditional Statements" section.

► **Sort-Object (alias sort)**—It is possible to sort objects based on their properties:

```
PS>get-process|sort -desc ws|select -first 10

Handles  NPM(K)    PM(K)      WS(K) VM(M)    CPU(s)     Id ProcessName
-------  ------    -----      ----- -----    ------     -- -----------
    382      68   194924     192324   417    870.02   3768 firefox
    547      47    78008      86888   334     67.52   2660 TweetDeck
...
```

This snippet sorts all the processes based on the value of WS. The -Descending parameter lists the processes from largest to smallest. Next, the Select-Object cmdlet uses the -First parameter to list only the top-ten processes based on the size of WS.

Formatting Cmdlets

Here are four different Format-* cmdlets you can use for formatting objects:

► Format-Custom

► Format-List

► Format-Table

► Format-Wide

Only Format-Table is discussed here; the other cmdlets are left as an exercise for you to read the cmdlets' help details and examples. Using Get-Process to look at the powershell.exe process, the following demonstrates some formatting capabilities of PowerShell; such as being able to easily choose particular properties to display or sizing the columns so they display better. Here is what that looks like:

```
PS>get-process powershell
Handles  NPM(K)    PM(K)      WS(K) VM(M)    CPU(s)     Id ProcessName
-------  ------    -----      ----- -----    ------     -- -----------
    304       6    57120       5696   162      5.98   3752 powershell
PS>get-process powershell|format-table
Handles  NPM(K)    PM(K)      WS(K) VM(M)    CPU(s)     Id ProcessName
-------  ------    -----      ----- -----    ------     -- -----------
    304       6    57120       5696   162      5.98   3752 powershell
PS>get-process powershell|format-table -autosize
Handles NPM(K) PM(K) WS(K) VM(M) CPU(s)    Id ProcessName
------- ------ ----- ----- ----- ------    -- -----------
    330      6 57120  7756   162   6.00  3752 powershell
PS>get-process powershell|format-table -autosize cpu,id
   CPU    Id
```

```
    ---   --
6.03125 3752
PS>get-process powershell|format-table -autosize cpu,id,company
    CPU   Id Company
    ---   -- -------
6.03125 3752 Microsoft Corporation
```

In this example, the following occurred:

1. The code looks at the PowerShell process object, and then pipes that same command to the `Format-Table` cmdlet. The results are the same in this case.

2. Next, the `-AutoSize` switch is provided to the `Format-Table` cmdlet, resulting in the columns being resized into something more manageable. As an example, when only the `CPU` and `ID` of the process display, without using `-AutoSize`, the output is not aligned to the left (this is not shown).

3. Then, using something like `Get-Member` (also not shown), it can be deduced that the process object has a Company property, and that can easily be displayed by passing it to the `Format-Table` cmdlet.

NOTE: USING FORMAT-* CMDLETS

Use the `Format-*` cmdlets only at the end of a pipeline. `Format-*` cmdlets should not be used if any other cmdlets are appended to the pipeline. As an example, consider the following:

```
Get-Process powershell|Format-Table -autosize|Export-Csv C:\my_file.csv
```

This snippet will not work as expected, as the `Format-*` cmdlets change the original objects into another type of object that is no longer useful if passed to additional cmdlets in a pipeline.

Conditional Statements

When creating advanced scripts, you often must decide whether to continue through with different logic in the script or actually exit based on certain conditions. Use conditional statements to make that decision. Two conditional statements are covered, as follows:

► If...Elseif...Else

► Switch

If...Elseif...Else

The "Sorting and Selecting Cmdlets" section provides an example of making a decision based on values using the `Group-Object` cmdlet. This section uses another example making use of variables and adds a *logical operator*. Consider the following:

```
PS>$proc=get-process powershell
PS>$proc

Handles  NPM(K)    PM(K)     WS(K) VM(M)   CPU(s)    Id ProcessName
-------  ------    -----     ----- -----   ------    -- -----------
   1010      11    30024     29964   147     4.62  1836 powershell
PS>if($proc.ProcessName -eq "powershell" -and $proc.CPU -gt 4){"First match"} →
elseif($proc.CPU -gt 4){"Second"}



First
PS>if($proc.ProcessName -eq "powershell" -and $proc.CPU -gt 6){"First match"} →
elseif($proc.CPU -gt 4){"Second"}

Second
```

This code performs the following steps:

1.   The PowerShell process object is saved to a variable, and the variable is displayed in the PowerShell console.

2.   Next, that variable is used, and in particular some of its properties, using a syntax not covered previously—$my_object.my_property. Using the $proc variable enables the properties of the object contained in the variable to be easily accessed with the .my_property notation.

3.   Using a simple conditional statement, the if condition matches when the ProcessName and CPU meet the specified conditions. A logical operator is specified to ensure that both conditions are met. Therefore, as long as the object's ProcessName and CPU are "powershell" and greater than 4, respectively, the condition (two in this example) returns a *True* value, and the associated scriptblock will run.

The general syntax for an if…elseif…else statement is as follows:

```
If(condition)
  {if scriptblock}
Elseif(condition)
  {elseif scriptblock}
Else
  {else scriptblock}
```

The Elseif and Else are optional components to the conditional statement.

A CONDITION MUST RETURN $TRUE

Here is how a condition is evaluated: If the condition returns a True, the script-block associated with that condition will be run. The simplest example of an if statement can be:

```
If($true){"True"}
```

Because the built-in variable $true is equal to *True*, the condition evaluates to True and the scriptblock runs, which displays "True" on the console in this case.

Switch

Another useful statement when making comparisons is the `switch` statement. In certain circumstances, an `If` statement could be used in the place of `switch`, but when you are calculating multiple conditions, using `switch` can make your code easier to follow.

Here is an example using the switch statement that looks at different versions of OpsMgr 2007:

```
Get-Agent| '
Format-Table DisplayName,@{ '
  Label="Version"
  Expression={ '
    Switch ($_.Version){
    "6.0.5000.0" {"RTM"}
    "6.0.6246.0" {"SP1 (RC) "}
    "6.0.6278.0" {"SP1 (RTM) "}
    "6.1.6407.0" {"R2 (Beta1) "}
    "6.1.7043.0" {"R2 (RC) "}
    "6.1.7221.0" {"R2 (RTM) "}
    default {"Other"}
    }
  }
}
```

LINE CONTINUATION CHARACTER

The "`" character is used as a line continuation character in PowerShell.

This code snippet is a slightly modified version of the one shown in the *TechNet Magazine* article on Operations Manager 2007 and PowerShell at http://technet.microsoft.com/en-ca/magazine/2008.08.scom.aspx. It demonstrates using the `Get-Agent` cmdlet, and then passing all the objects to the `Format-Table` cmdlet. From there, the `DisplayName` property is displayed, and a calculated property is used to read the version of each of the agents and transform the numerical value into something more readable.

The output from running this code snippet looks like the following:

```
DisplayName                         Version
-----------                         -------
Mission.odyssey.com                 R2 (RTM)
Tornado.odyssey.com                 R2 (RTM)
Pioneer.odyssey.com                 R2 (RTM)
Quicksilver.odyssey.com             R2 (RTM)
Thunder.odyssey.com                 R2 (RTM)
Meteor.odyssey.com                  R2 (RTM)
Vanguard.odyssey.com                R2 (RTM)

Fireball.odyssey.com                R2 (RTM)
```

The `switch` statement is used in the place of several `if` statements and provides a cleaner looking and more compact script. The `default` keyword is added in case new agent versions are introduced or the script is run elsewhere, to try to account for most versions that would likely be found in a Operations Manager 2007 monitored environment.

For more information, see `Get-Help about_if` and `Get-Help about_switch`.

Thanks to Kevin Holman from Microsoft for pointing out this blog post by Marnix Wolf that details the agent versions used here at http://thoughtsonopsmgr.blogspot.com/2009/05/opsmgr-versions.html.

Looping Statements

There will be occasions where a script will iterate through a number of items or items must run a specified number of times. Here are three looping statements:

- ▶ **For**—Runs a scriptblock a set number of times until a condition is reached.

- ▶ **Foreach**—Runs a scriptblock a set number of times based on the number of objects provided.

- ▶ **While**—Runs a scriptblock while a certain condition remains true.

You typically use the `foreach` statement to iterate through a collection of objects. You can save the collection of objects to a variable before the `foreach` statement, or declare the collection, created in this example by using the `Get-Service` cmdlet, directly within the statement, as shown here:

```
foreach($service in get-service){
  $service.name.toupper()
}
```

This code retrieves a listing of all the services on the local machine, and then goes through each service object to change the `Name` property to uppercase letters.

The basic syntax for the `foreach` statement is as follows:

```
foreach(){
  Scriptblock to run

}
```

Here is a usage scenario specifically relating to OpsMgr with the `Get-Alert` cmdlet. This example updates all current outstanding alerts at the root management server.

```
$alerts=get-alert 'ResolutionState = "0"'
foreach($alert in $alerts){
  $alert.CustomField1="Some event"
  $alert.Update("Update")

}
```

The result of the `Get-Alert` cmdlet for all unresolved alerts is passed to the `$alerts` variable. Next, a `foreach` loop is created to iterate through the collection of alerts, the `CustomField1` property of each alert is updated with a customized string "Some event," and the update is reinserted into the OpsMgr database. This could be useful to automatically update a series of alerts after a network event. With this code as a base, it would be easy to clear these alerts later.

Note that there is a difference between the `ForEach-Object` *cmdlet* and the `foreach` *statement*, which can be a challenge when you are new to PowerShell. You can find a detailed blog post along with an interesting discussion at http://bsonposh.com/archives/327, although it may be a bit advanced.

The `for` and `while` statements were only covered here to provide an overview of their features; they are typically not used in Operations Manager automation scripts. For additional information on the `for` and `while` statements, check `Get-Help about_for` and `Get-Help about_ while`, respectively.

Providers

The "General PowerShell Concepts" section of this chapter introduced the term `provider`. In PowerShell, anything exposed via a provider looks and behaves pretty much like a file system. Using providers enables PowerShell to use similar syntax to that used when accessing files and folders. The Windows Registry is exposed to PowerShell as a provider. In other words, you can transverse the Registry just like a file system!

Figure 5.8 gives an example of walking through the Registry using the `get-location` and `get-itemproperty` cmdlets.

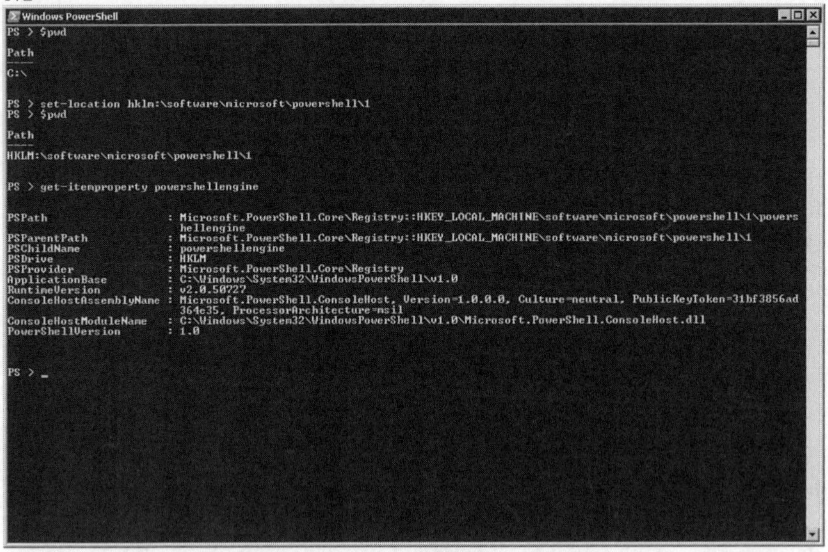

FIGURE 5.8 Looking at the Registry provider

The "Monitoring:\ Provider" section discusses providers again when a special Operations Manager provider is covered. There are other default providers; use the Get-PsDrive cmdlet to list the current providers available.

TIP: LIBRARY OF REGISTRY FUNCTIONS

Shay Levi, PowerShell MVP, provided a useful set of functions to use to easily deal with certain registry tasks, and even remote ones. See a discussion at http://scriptolog.blogspot.com/2007/10/stand-alone-registry-functions-library.html.

Profiles

As you start using PowerShell regularly and become more familiar with its functionality, you may want to save some of your customizations between sessions. Without saving these, closing and reopening the PowerShell console causes your customizations to disappear. You can use profiles to save customizations. The most commonly edited profile is that applying to the current user and host. (The *host* is the PowerShell console seen when starting PowerShell.) Use Notepad to edit the profile:

```
PS>notepad $profile
```

Add to this profile by adding commands, just as you would add them in the console.

NOTE: PROFILE FILE DETAILS

By default, the $profile file does not exist, so Notepad should pop up an error in-dicating the file does not exist, and prompt if you want to create it. Otherwise, if you receive an error, use the command `New-Item $profile -type File -force` to create the file. Several other profiles can be set up in addition to `$profile`. For more information, check `Get-help about_profiles`.

Using the Operations Manager PowerShell Shell

This next part of the chapter focuses on PowerShell use directly applicable to Operations Manager. OpsMgr 2007 provides a PowerShell snapin to access all the Operations Manager PowerShell cmdlets and providers, enabling you to automate many tasks. The snapin is built on the Operations Manager Software Development Kit (SDK). If you are doing any type of advanced Operations Manager development, the Operations Manager SDK is a very complete API for interfacing with Operations Manager. The snapin is provided as additional functionality, meaning all the features of PowerShell itself, such as tab-completion and built-in help, are fully supported.

The Released to Manufacturing (RTM) and SP 1 releases of Operations Manager 2007 referred to the customized PowerShell console as the "Command Shell." Operations Manager 2007 R2 renames the customized console to "Operations Manager Shell."

When you access the Command Shell or Operations Manager Shell, you access the default PowerShell console, which automatically loads the Operations Manager PowerShell snapin. Here are the ways to access the OpsMgr PowerShell console:

▶ **Via the Start menu**—The customized PowerShell console can be easily loaded directly from choosing the appropriate menu item.

▶ **Via the user interface**—The customized PowerShell console can be easily loaded by right-clicking on any computer device and choosing the Windows PowerShell menu item.

▶ **Via the default console**—The default PowerShell console is opened, although none of the Operations Manager features are available by default. The Tech-Net Magazine article at http://technet.microsoft.com/magazine/2008.08.scom.aspx goes into the re-quirements to use the OpsMgr features in this case.

Figure 5.9 shows how you can access PowerShell from the Start menu, and Figure 5.10 accesses PowerShell within the Operations Manager user interface (UI).

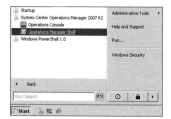

FIGURE 5.9 Accessing PowerShell from the Start menu

FIGURE 5.10 Accessing PowerShell from the user interface

Monitoring:\ Provider

A PowerShell provider (see the "Providers" section of this chapter) is a hierarchical data store providing a user experience similar to looking through a file system—various objects can act like folders, whereas other objects act like files. This provides an easy way to discover objects, especially in the absence of a user interface.

When you access PowerShell using the Operations Manager GUI or the Operations Manager shortcut in the Start menu, the console starts up and you are automatically placed within the Operations Manager Monitoring:\ provider. The provider also places you within the context of the current Operations Manager management server or within the context of the object clicked on. Whereas Figure 5.10 showed starting PowerShell from the GUI and being placed in the context of the management server, Figure 5.11 shows the capability to right-click on any managed device and have a PowerShell console open within the context of that particular device.

FIGURE 5.11 After right-clicking on a device in the user interface

Using providers with Operations Manager 2007 can be quite valuable. Imagine that you do not have access to the Operations console of a particular installation—with the provider, you can make your way progressively through the structure to see the layout of groups and computers.

Logically, traversing the Operations Manager provider looks something like the following: `Monitoring:\Management Server -> Groups -> Computers`

Listing OpsMgr Shell Cmdlets

The OpsMgr RTM release included the `Get-OperationsManagerCommand` function, which listed the cmdlets provided by the Operations Manager snapin. In SP 1 and R2, this became a true cmdlet, providing the ability to use the tab completion feature. Figure 5.12 displays some of the OpsMgr cmdlets.

FIGURE 5.12 `Get-OperationsManagerCommand` cmdlet

Commonly Used Cmdlets

The Operations Manager Monitoring:\ provider provides access to Operations-Manager specific cmdlets. Table 5.1 lists some of the most commonly used Operations Manager cmdlets.

TABLE 5.1 Commonly Used Operations Manager cmdlets by Function

Function	Cmdlet	Description	Example
For admin-istering alerts	`Get-Alert`	Retrieves the alerts either for the entire management server or a particular device.	Get-Alert –Criteria 'ResolutionState = "0"'
	`Get-AlertHistory`	Retrieves the history for a specific alert.	Get-Alert – Id7ff7f1f0-b6ad-470f-b283-2c0dc95c8800|Get-AlertHistory
	`Resolve-Alert`	Resolves the alerts either for the entire management server or a particular device.	Get-Alert –Criteria 'ResolutionState = "0"'|Resolve-Alert
For admin-istering	`Get-Agent`	Retrieves a listing of all the agents on the	Get-Agent|Select-Object –Property

agents			management server.	DisplayName
	`Install-Agent`	Install an agent.	See Get-Help Install-Agent –examples.
	`Install-AgentByName`	Install an agent.	Install-AgentByName meteor.odyssey.com
	`Uninstall-Agent`	Uninstall an agent.	Get-Agent|Where-Object{$_. DisplayName –eq "meteor.odyssey. com"}|Uninstall-Agent
	`Get-AgentPending Action`	Get agent pending actions.	Get-AgentPendingAction
	`Reject-AgentPending Action`	Reject a specified agent pending action.	Get-AgentPendingAc-tion|Where-Object{$_. AgentName –eq "meteor.odyseey. com"}|Reject-AgentPendingAction
For admin-istering manage-ment packs	`Install-Management Pack`	Load the manage-ment pack on the management server. Can also overwrite an existing management pack that has been already loaded.	dir C:\mps\\|Install-ManagementPack
	`Export-Management Pack`	Save a management pack loaded on a management server to a eXtensible Markup Language (XML) file.	Get-ManagementPack| Where-Object{$_.Name –eq "Micro-soft.Windows.Server .2003"}|Export-ManagementPack –Path C:\
	`Uninstall-Management Pack`	Remove a manage-ment pack loaded on a management server.	Get-ManagementPack| Where-Object{$_.Name –eq "Micro-soft.Windows.Server .2003"}|Uninstall-ManagementPack
For admin-istering	`Get-ask`	Retrieve a list of tasks.	Get-Task|Where-Object {$_

tasks			DisplayName –eq "Route Print"}
	`Start-Task`	Start a task.	$task=Get-Task\|Where-Object {$_DisplayName –eq "Route Print"}|Start-Task
	`Get-TaskResult`	Retrieve task results.	Get-TaskResult $task.Id
For administering maintenance windows	`New-Maintenance Window`	Create a maintenance window for a particular object.	New-MaintenanceWindow –StartTime (get-date) –EndTime (get-date). AddHours(1) – Comment "New maintenance window"
	`Get-Maintenance Window`	Retrieve a maintenance window for a particular object.	Get-MaintenanceWindow
	`Set-Maintenance Window`	Change the properties of an existing maintenance window.	Set-MaintenanceWindow –EndTime (get-date)

Remember that `Get-Help` *<cmdlet>* provides additional built-in information on cmdlets. You can also invoke `Get-Help` *<cmdlet>* with the `-Examples` switch to list usage examples.

Get-Alert and Monitoring:\

A perfect example of the usefulness of a provider is combining its features with a cmdlet like `Get-Alert`. Assuming the Operations Manager PowerShell console is loaded and the current context is the management server, running the `Get-Alert` cmdlet without options from this location in the provider will list all alerts for the management server.

In Figure 5.13, the result of Get-Alert is piped to additional cmdlets. `Get-Alert` is sensitive to the current location in the provider where it is invoked. Because the location is at the root management server; the cmdlet will list all alerts for all the computers monitored by this installation. The command in Figure 5.13 can be broken apart a bit, as follows:

1.   The `Get-Alert` cmdlet retrieves all the alerts.

2.   The `Group-Object` cmdlet then groups all the alert objects together, based on the `NetBiosComputerName` property.

3.   Next, the `Sort-Object` cmdlet uses the `-Descending` switch to sort the alert objects by descending order based on the `Count` property.

4.   The `Select-Object` cmdlet uses the `-First` parameter and a value of 5 to return only the first five objects. The first object, or row, represents the alerts for the management server. In this case, the `NetBiosComputerName` property value is blank.

5.   Finally, the `Format-Table` cmdlet uses the `-AutoSize` switch to make the output easier to read and only show the `Name` and `Count` properties.

FIGURE 5.13 Listing all the alerts

Figure 5.14 shows the context or location in the provider changed to a location in the local file system. The `Get-Alert` cmdlet is then run again, only this time an error is returned because is a required parameter is missing. The `Path` parameter is mandatory when using the `Get-Alert` cmdlet. In the example in Figure 5.13, the parameter was not added to the cmdlet as it was automatically filled in due to the current location within the OpsMgr Monitoring:\ provider. This context-awareness is useful as well when dealing with the maintenance mode cmdlets, which also require a `Path` property value.

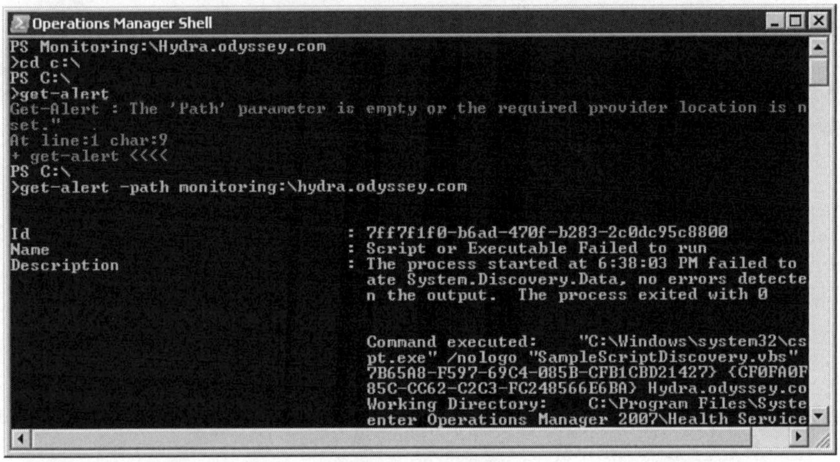

FIGURE 5.14 Showing the context-awareness of `Get-Alert`

Incorporating the Operations Manager SDK

Continuing with the `Get-Alert` cmdlet, let's provide an example of how to use the Operations Manager SDK with PowerShell's ability to access the .NET Framework and basically any .NET assembly.

Running the following code in an Operations Manager PowerShell console will list all the alerts on the local management server, which is the functional equivalent of simply running the `Get-Alert` cmdlet:

```
PS>$mg = New-Object Microsoft.EnterpriseManagement.ManagementGroup("localhost")
PS>$mg.GetMonitoringAlerts()
```

Let's break down the preceding code snippet line-by-line.

In the first line, a connection is made to the local management server by creating an instance of an existing Operations Manager SDK class. Microsoft documents the `Microsoft.EnterpriseManagement.ManagementGroup` class at http://msdn.microsoft.com/en-us/library/microsoft.enterprisemanagement.managementgroup.aspx. From this page on the MSDN site, once a class is found, finding the supported members is as simple as navigating the left-most menu. The `GetMonitoringAlerts` method is listed and its purpose clearly identified.

Here is a code sample in C# code that provides functionality resembling the `Get-Alert` cmdlet:

```
using System;
using System.Collections.ObjectModel;
using Microsoft.EnterpriseManagement;
using Microsoft.EnterpriseManagement.Monitoring;

namespace GetAlert
{
  class Program
  {
    static void Main(string[] args)
    {
      ManagementGroup mg = new ManagementGroup("localhost");
      ReadOnlyCollection<MonitoringAlert> alerts = mg.GetMonitoringAlerts();
      foreach(MonitoringAlert alert in alerts)
      {
        Console.WriteLine(alert.Name);
      }

    }
  }
}
```

This is just a simple example of what you can do using the Operations Manager SDK. The SDK lets you use Operations Manager functionality and data such as alerts in any application based on the .NET Framework. The C# code here is simply displayed for demonstration purposes. For more details on C#, see *C# 3.0 Unleashed* (Sams, 2008). Because PowerShell cmdlets are not provided for all tasks, an advanced PowerShell user can learn how to use the Operations Manager SDK classes to program and automate additional things in Operations Manager.

You may also want to check out http://msdn.microsoft.com/en-us/library/bb449645.aspx. Most examples are provided in the C# and VB.NET programming languages. It is possible to port these programming languages into PowerShell scripts; however, there may be some roadblocks when .NET Generics are required, which may require some advanced techniques like embedding C# or VB.NET code within the PowerShell script.

PowerShell Performance

There are several potential areas of concern in terms of performance, as follows:

▶ PowerShell version 1 includes some routines that were not coded as efficiently as possible, which has been acknowledged by the PowerShell development team.

▶ The PowerShell version 1 installer skipped an important task in ensuring the application starts as quickly as possible. This is an issue specifically when gauging how long it can take powershell.exe to start from fresh.

When running PowerShell scripts in management packs prior to OpsMgr 2007 R2, serious consideration had to be given to performance impacts; for each PowerShell script called, a powershell.exe process would be created using up valuable resources.

PowerShell support is improved with Operations Manager 2007 R2. OpsMgr 2007 R2 uses a feature of the PowerShell API to run its own customized PowerShell host, replacing the powershell.exe process. Using this new model, PowerShell memory and CPU utilization is close to, and sometimes even better than, performance of VBScript scripting. This new feature is geared primarily toward management pack authors and developers.

For more information on the older, and less efficient, method of using PowerShell scripts in management packs, Brian Wren has a blog post at http://blogs.technet.com/brianwren/archive/2008/02/20/running-powershell-scripts-from-a-management-pack.aspx. Brian also posted a follow-up to this article, where he discusses the improvements for using PowerShell scripts with Operations Manager 2007 R2 at http://blogs.technet.com/brianwren/archive/2009/06/04/powershell-scripts-in-a-management-pack-part-2.aspx. http://msdn.microsoft.com/en-us/library/ee809360.aspx is the current portal to the online Microsoft documentation on the new PowerShell features.

TIP: MAKING POWERSHELL START FASTER

A small issue with the PowerShell v1 installer is that a particular task not performed speeds up how quickly the PowerShell console starts up by default. Here is a post on the PowerShell Team blog that leads you through resolving this issue—http://blogs.msdn.com/powershell/archive/2008/09/02/speeding-up-powershell-startup-updating-update-gac-ps1.aspx. Copy and paste the code listing in the blog post into a PowerShell console, and the appropriate actions will be taken. This is not something specific to Operations Manager but to PowerShell v1 in general, so it applies to all PowerShell v1 installations.

PowerShell and Operations Manager Examples

The next sections look at some practical examples of how PowerShell can help with automation and scripting of general Windows and Operations Manager-related tasks.

General PowerShell Examples

The first set of examples looks at general Windows administration tasks. This includes working with the Event Log, accessing Windows services and Windows Management Instrumentation (WMI), and finding files.

Working with the Event Log

There are many examples that demonstrate how PowerShell can help make it easier to accomplish and automate various administrative tasks. One very good illustration is working with the Windows Event log. Presenting and explaining several examples will provide a guide for more complicated pipelines:

▶ An example of querying the local Application log is simple enough:

```
PS>get-eventlog -log application|select -first 10
```

This code gets a listing of the events from the Application event log; the results are piped to the `Select-Object` cmdlet and a parameter is added to only display the first 10 events.

The following retrieves a listing of the top-ten event IDs in the Application event log:

```
PS>get-eventlog application|group eventid|sort -desc count| →
select count,name -first 10|ft -a
```

The Application event log entries are retrieved, grouped by the event ID using the `Group-Object` cmdlet, and then piped to the `Sort-Object`, which has the parameter `-Descending` defined along with the `Count` property. Finally, only the `Count` and `Name` properties are selected (there is a `Group` property that can be a bit confusing), and the `Format-Table` cmdlet with `-AutoSize` is used to left-justify the output.

► This example retrieves all events of the last 25 minutes. If you attempted some of the previous commands, you may have noticed that a `Time` property displays. However, if an attempt is made to retrieve the `Time` property, it fails! The PowerShell designers decided to make things work that way, but there is a way to find a solution, as shown here:

```
PS>get-eventlog application|select -first 1|gm "time"
    TypeName: System.Diagnostics.EventLogEntry#application/ESENT/102

Name                     MemberType Definition
----                     ---------- ----------
GetLifetimeService        Method     System.Object GetLifetimeService()
InitializeLifetimeService Method     System.Object InitializeLifetimeService()
TimeGenerated             Property   System.DateTime TimeGenerated {get;}
TimeWritten               Property   System.DateTime TimeWritten {get;}
```

Here the discoverability features built directly into PowerShell were used to discover the time-based properties available. The `Select-Object` cmdlet was also used so that only one object was passed along the pipeline; otherwise, a considerable amount of information would scroll across the screen. `Get-Member` (alias `gm` in the code snippet) was discussed briefly in the "Getting Started" section of this chapter. By passing "*time*", `Get-Member` will match on any property that has "time" as part of its name.

There is a `TimeGenerated` property available in this particular case. Use the property in the next snippet to retrieve the events from the last 25 minutes using a trick with `Get-Date`:

```
PS>get-eventlog application| →
where {$_.timegenerated -gt (get-date).addminutes(-25)}
```

Once again, all events are retrieved. The collection of objects is passed along to a `Where-Object` cmdlet, which looks at the `TimeGenerated` property of all the objects passed along the pipeline and only passes along those objects generated in the last 25 minutes, as requested.

WHY READING A LOG MAY SEEM SLOW

If you notice a delay when using `Get-EventLog`, it is likely due to the fact that even if only the first ten entries are selected (shown in an example earlier in this section), all the entries in the event log are actually scanned. This may be considered to be inefficient, but is part of the current PowerShell design.

Windows Services and WMI

WMI has been around since Windows NT 4, and there are signs that this technology is around to stay.

Say you needed a script to check all of the services on a local or remote computer. The objective is to have the script check all services with an Automatic start up type, and confirm that those services are actually running. Starting with the cmdlet `Get-Service`, you can see that there does not appear to be anything related to the `startup` property:

```
PS>get-service|select -first 1
```

It is possible that something is hidden by the built-in PowerShell formatting, but looking at all the members of the object in question using Get-Member confirms there is nothing related to the startup type:

```
PS>get-service|select -first 1|gm
```

However, WMI provides a wealth of information about the Windows operating system. You can even use WMI to retrieve the startup property for a service. So, the command now becomes the following:

```
PS>get-wmiobject win32_service| →
where{$_.startmode -eq "Auto" -and $_.state -ne "Running"}
```

This command uses WMI to retrieve a listing of all the Windows services on the local system. The Where-Object cmdlet looks at each object and lists all services where the startup mode is Automatic, but the current status is not *Running*.

NOTE: WMI TERMINOLOGY

Basic terminology in WMI includes class and namespace. Get-WmiObject defaults the namespace value to root\cimv2. Going through a listing of all the classes and namespaces supported by WMI is beyond the scope of this chapter. Note that the listing may change depending on the OS in question.

Using the .NET Framework

To show an advanced example of how PowerShell can take advantage of using the features of the .NET Framework, consider the code you can use to send an email message:

```
# Set the "SMTP smarthost".
$smtpServer = "smtp.server.com"
# Create the mail message object and SMTP connection.
$msg = new-object Net.Mail.MailMessage
$smtp = new-object Net.Mail.SmtpClient($smtpServer)
# Set the properties for the message.
$msg.From = "from@address.com"
$msg.To.Add("to@address.com")
$msg.Subject = "MY SUBJECT"
$msg.Body = "MY TEXT FOR THE EMAIL"
# Send the message.
$smtp.Send($msg)
```

This code uses classes from the .NET Framework to handle creating the email message and send the message. Being able to use some features of the .NET

Framework requires advanced knowledge—the code would be next to impossible to deduce from simply using Get-Member.

Finding Files

Looking for files or folders is a common task. Using the Get-ChildItem cmdlet makes looking for specific files or folders relatively simple. Let's assume that you need to search to recursively look through the file system for files with a certain file name and extension. Here's what you can use:

```
PS>get-childitem C:\ -recurse "*string*.ext"
```

This uses the Get-ChildItem cmdlet and, starting with the C:\ drive, the file system is searched recursively for any files with the name "string" as part of the filename and the extension "ext." The snippet also lists matching folders. To exclude folders, you can use the following syntax:

```
PS>get-childitem C:\ -recurse "*string*.ext"|where-object{!($_.psiscontainer)}
```

This code lists all the matching files and folders; the collection of objects is passed to the Where-Object cmdlet, where the PsIsContainer property is verified. This property returns a *True* for a folder, and *False* for a file. Using the syntax !($_.PsIsContainer) provides the opposite value; when a file goes through the pipeline, its PsIsContainer property is *False*, but using the exclamation reverses this to be *True*. In this case, the scriptblock is actually evaluated as *True*, and the object continues along the pipeline to be displayed.

TIP: THE –NOT OPERATOR

The syntax !($_.PsIsContainer) is equivalent to -not($_.PsIsContainer).

Operations Manager Examples

You now have read a considerable amount of theory and looked at some general examples. The following sections include some practical examples of using PowerShell to script and automate OpsMgr-related tasks.

Agent Settings

In larger environments, it can be difficult to manually confirm or audit a large number of agents to verify they are reporting to the expected primary management server or failover server. PowerShell lets you do this easily. The following code snippet lists all the agents in the current management group by displaying each agent's name, the primary management server they report to, and if they are currently configured for any failover management servers:

```
PS>get-agent| →
format-table -autosize displayname,primarymanagemnetservername, →
@{label="Failover";expression={$_.GetFailoverManagementServers()}}
DisplayName                 PrimaryManagementServerName Failover
-----------                 --------------------------- --------
Mission.odyssey.com         Hornet.odyssey.com          {Hydra.odyssey.com, Hurr...
Tornado.odyssey.com         Hornet.odyssey.com          {Hydra.odyssey.com, Hurr...
Pioneer.odyssey.com         Hornet.odyssey.com          {Hydra.odyssey.com, Hurr...
Quicksilver.odyssey.com     Hornet.odyssey.com          {Hydra.odyssey.com, Hurr...
```

Now, assume you wanted to verify which agents were configured for a specific primary or failover management server. The code required to filter for a primary management server is relatively simple, as follows:

```
PS>get-agent|where{$_.PrimaryManagementServerName -eq "server_name"}
```

To filter for a failover server is slightly more complicated because of how the value for the failover management servers is obtained, and because the result is defined as a collection. The following code shows how you can do this:

```
PS>get-agent| →
where{($_.GetFailoverManagementServers()| →
foreach{$_.PrincipalName}) -contains "server_name"}
```

Getting Alerts

The ability to get alerts is one of the most commonly used features in the OpsMgr Shell. The Get-Alert cmdlet provides this functionality. As discussed in the "Get-Alert and Monitoring:\" section, the Get-Alert cmdlet is location sensitive. Depending on where the cmdlet is invoked, the number of alerts displayed will vary.

Often you will want to filter out alerts based on some type of criteria. An example of filtering alerts is listing only the active alerts, accomplished by filtering alerts with a ResolutionState of zero. Consider the following:

```
PS>get-alert|where-object {$_.ResolutionState -eq 0}
```

On a busy system, running this code is not the most efficient way to list all active alerts. Get-Alert will list all the available alerts, and then pass each of these along the pipeline so the ResolutionState property can be compared to the value of zero.

The more effective way to use the Get-Alert cmdlet is with the -Criteria parameter. As an example, the preceding pipeline would be more efficient if coded as follows:

```
PS>get-alert -criteria 'ResolutionState = "0"'
```

This is much more efficient because the criterion is passed along to the Operations Manager database, meaning only the matching alerts or objects are returned.

Note the differences in the preceding two code listings. The first method has `$_.ResolutionState -eq 0` and the second method has `'ResolutionState = ''0'''`.

The important thing here is where the statement is evaluated. Whereas PowerShell performs an integer comparison in the first case, in the second case, a binary comparison is made at the database level.

TIP: USING THE COUNT PROPOERTY

When dealing with a collection of objects, a quick way to get a count of how many objects are in the collection is with the `Count` property. As an example, use `(Get-Alert).Count.` to get a listing of all the alerts in the current context. The short syntax retrieves the alerts, counts them, and displays the number on the console.

Resolving Alerts

Building on the last example, presume that an event created an alert message storm, requiring a cleanup of all outstanding alerts. Consider the following cmdlet:

```
PS>get-alert -criteria 'ResolutionState = "0"'|resolve-alert|out-null
```

The results of `Get-Alert` are passed to the `Resolve-Alert` cmdlet so all matching alerts have their resolution state changed. The `Out-Null` cmdlet is also appended to the end of the pipeline, ensuring that the pipeline remains silent; otherwise, output would be sent to the console for every alert as it is resolved.

NOTE: USING GET-ALERT

Using the `Get-Alert` cmdlet is not the most efficient way to clear a large number of alerts. This is simply provided as a practical example. The posting at http://www.dario.co.il/blog/?p=350 provides additional information on alternative methods you can use to clear a large number of alerts more efficiently.

A capability very useful for developers is to clear alerts for a specific management pack they are testing. Marco Shaw provides examples in an article in the August 2008 issue of *TechNet Magazine* ("Windows PowerShell in System Center Operations Manager 2007," http://technet.microsoft.com/en-us/magazine/2008.08.scom.aspx) showing how to list alerts with the source management pack name. The following code retrieves all the alerts based on the specified management pack:

```
$mp="System Center Core Monitoring"
Get-Alert |
  # Select the alerts with a PrincipalName and are unresolved.
  Where-Object {$_.ResolutionState -eq '0' -and
    # Determine if this is a monitor-based alert.
    $(if(!($_.IsMonitorAlert)){
# From the MonitoringRuleId property of the object, get the MP info.
      ((Get-Rule $_.MonitoringRuleId).GetManagementPack()).DisplayName -eq $mp
```

```
    }
# This must be a rule-based alert.
    else{
# From the ProblemId property of the object, get the MP info.
      $id=$_.ProblemId
      ((Get-Monitor -criteria "Id='$id'").GetManagementPack()).DisplayName -eq $mp
    })
  }
```

To run this code listing, copy the contents to a .ps1 script file and run it within the OpsMgr Shell. You could also type the code interactively into the console. This code displays a considerable amount of information on the screen, as the -Criteria parameter was not used with Get-Alert. In some cases, using Where-Object seems more intuitive, as in this example.

To resolve the alerts, copy the code to a .ps1 script and pipe the script to the Resolve-Alert cmdlet to clear the alerts, as shown in this next code snippet:

```
PS>./script.ps1|resolve-alert|out-null
```

Changing the Prompt

By default, the prompt provided on the console is a simple PowerShell function of the form:

```
"PS " + $(Get-Location) + "`n" + ">";
```

In some instances, there may be monitored devices that have a dash in their hostname. The Operations Manager provider was not designed to properly handle the dash character, so a device name such as "server-location.domain.com" shows as "server%002dlocation.domain.com."

The prompt is a function, making it highly customizable. Running the following change directly from the PowerShell prompt provides the changes necessary for the dash character to display appropriately:

```
function prompt "PS "+ $(Get-Location).ToString().Replace("%002d","-") + →
"`n" + ">";}
```

To make the change permanent, add that exact line to the profile.

Looking Inside Management Packs

One useful feature PowerShell provides is the ability to look at the contents of a management pack. This snippet of code takes the Microsoft Windows Server 2003 sealed management pack and exports it to XML:

```
PS>get-managementpack| →
where{$_.name -eq "Microsoft.Windows.Server.2003"}|export-managementpack -path C:\
```

The management pack would be copied to C:\Microsoft.Windows.Server.2003.xml based on the command provided.

Using the Operations Manager SDK provides another way to be able to read management pack contents, but without actually needing to first load them into Operations Manager. Boris Yanushpolsky provides an excellent blog post (http://blogs.msdn.com/boris_yanushpolsky/archive/2007/08/16/unsealing-a-management-pack.aspx) where he introduces the PowerShell script:

```
param($mpFilePath,$outputDir)
$assembly = [System.Reflection.Assembly]:: →
LoadWithPartialName("Microsoft.EnterpriseManagement.OperationsManager")
$mp = new-object →
Microsoft.EnterpriseManagement.Configuration.ManagementPack($mpFilePath)
$mpWriter = new-object →
Microsoft.EnterpriseManagement.Configuration.IO.ManagementPackXmlWriter($outputDir)

$mpWriter.WriteManagementPack($mp)
```

Looking at the preceding code snippet line by line:

▶ **Line 1**—This keyword is used at the beginning of a script to enable it to accept script arguments. Two arguments are defined: $mpFilePath and $outputDir. By calling the script with two arguments, those values will automatically be mapped to the $mpFilePath and $outputDir variables used within the script.

▶ **Line 2**—Here, the external .NET functionality is loaded by PowerShell to import all of its members so they can be used in the current session (or script, in this case). If you ran this script from the Operations Manager Shell, this line could be omitted, and the script would still fully function.

▶ **Line 3**—This is where an instance of the Microsoft.EnterpriseManagement. Configuration.ManagementPack class is created and the $mpFilePath variable is passed as a parameter. This class is described at http://msdn.microsoft.com/en-us/library/microsoft.enterprisemanagement.configuration.managementpack.aspx, where the different constructors are defined. In this case, a simple string object is passed as a parameter.

▶ **Line 4**—This is where an instance of the Microsoft.EnterpriseManagement. Configuration.IO.ManagementPackXmlWriter class is created and the $outputDir variable is passed as a parameter. This class is described at http://msdn.microsoft.com/en-us/library/microsoft.enterprisemanagement.configuration.io.managementpackxmlwriter.aspx.

▶ **Line 5**—This is where the contents of the management pack are written to an XML-formatted file using the WriteManagementPack method detailed at http://msdn.microsoft.com/en-us/library/bb438704.aspx.

Boris adapted the code to work with a default PowerShell console, as follows:

```
powershell d:\MpToXml.ps1 →
-mpFilePath:'d:\Microsoft.Exchange.Server.2003.Monitoring.mp' -outputDir:'d:\'
```

Listing MPs and Versions

You can use the `Get-ManagementPack` cmdlet to list all the installed management packs on the system. You can also use this cmdlet to list all the names of the management packs and current version for comparison, shown in Figure 5.15.

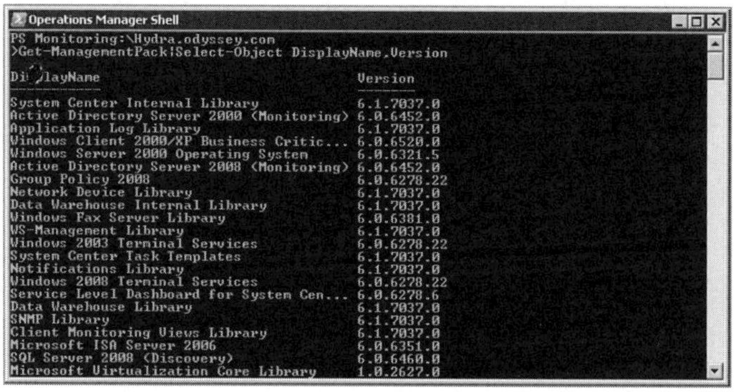

FIGURE 5.15 Listing MP names and versions

The *TechNet Magazine* link referenced in the "Resolving Alerts" section provides additional examples of management pack-related tasks you can perform with PowerShell.

Getting the Rules and Monitors Inside a Management Pack

Something that can also be easily accomplished using PowerShell to list the rules and monitors contained in a management pack is shown in the following code snippet:

```
$mp=Get-ManagementPack|Where-Object{$_.Name -eq "Microsoft.Windows.Server.2003"}
Get-Rule -ManagementPack $mp

Get-Monitor -ManagementPack $mp
```

Here, the first line is used to retrieve the Microsoft Windows Server 2003 management pack object; this is saved into the variable `$mp`. That variable is used as a value passed to the `Get-Rule` and `Get-Monitor` cmdlets. Each of these last two commands retrieves all the rules and monitors respectively from the Windows Server 2003 management pack.

Exporting Alerts to HTML

Consider a requirement to create some type of HTML page displaying all current alerts. You can then copy this to an external source for viewing with a regular web browser. Here's the code to do so:

```
Get-Alert |
  Where-Object {$_.PrincipalName -and
  $_.ResolutionState -eq 0}|ConvertTo-Html > "${home}\alerts.html"
```

To run the code listing, copy the contents into a .ps1 script file and run it in the OpsMgr Shell. You could also type code interactively into the console.

This example takes all the alerts where the `PrincipalName` property is not empty (technically, "null" is empty or even `$null` in PowerShell) and the unresolved alerts, and uses the `ConvertTo-Html` cmdlet to create HTML-based output.

Before piping to `ConvertTo-Html`, you can use the `Select-Object` cmdlet to specify exactly what properties to write to the resulting file. A more involved implementation would produce a table with viewable borders and change the color of each based on severity.

TIP: REDIRECTION OPERATORS

Note the use of the Unix/DOS-style ">" redirect operator. This operator redirects all the output from the pipeline to a file. PowerShell also supports the append operator ">>." However, PowerShell does not currently support using "<" for redirection.

PowerShell Best Practices

Here are tips and techniques constituting some best practices for using PowerShell:

▶ Add comments to your scripts—the more the better! This will definitely help when you or someone else may need to review a script.

▶ Several vendors offer PowerShell script editors (and some are even free!). Using an editor can help with code formatting and coloring, and some editors provide a feature named IntelliSense.

▶ Don't be afraid to ask for help in any online community. There are several places to ask for help, and Microsoft MVPs are always willing to assist.

▶ Some cmdlets support a `-Criteria` parameter. This is more efficient then using the `Where-Object` cmdlet to perform filtering based on properties.

▶ Think about the design of your script; using any of the `Get-*` cmdlets can be time consuming. If you use the same `Get-*` cmdlet more than once in your script, consider changing the first invocation to save everything to a variable, and use that variable later in the script.

▶ Only use `Format-*` cmdlets at the end of a pipeline. If other cmdlets may be appended to the pipeline, remove the `Format-*` cmdlet so other cmdlets in the pipeline can use the objects.

Summary

PowerShell is now part of Microsoft's standards for their server products. This chapter provided a good foundation for those new to PowerShell, and should help to overcome the relatively steep learning curve PowerShell can pose to most IT professionals.

CHAPTER 6

Management Solutions for Small and Midsize Business

Microsoft has tried packaging small and medium business (SMB) solutions for over a decade, beginning with Microsoft BackOffice Server and later BackOffice Small Business Server. These solutions include several enterprise Microsoft applications such as Exchange or SQL Server, scaled down in features and capacity, bundled together with some extra automation and value-add features, and at a discounted price compared to the normal enterprise applications. As the products matured, their value-add automation features have focused on easy-to-use management tools.

Today's packaged SMB offerings fall into the Essentials Business Server Solution (EBSS) family: Essential Business Server 2008 (EBS) and Small Business Server 2008 (SBS). System Center Operations Manager 2007 (OpsMgr) Release 2 (R2) can be deployed in lieu of, or in addition to, the native management features of the EBSS products. This chapter discusses the management aspects of SBS and EBS, which differ from each another in their approach to delivering on a promise of ease of management.

▶ SBS 2008 does not include any native System Center components and features its own "mini" management engine.

▶ EBS 2008 management is built on Essentials 2007, the hybrid SMB management tool based on OpsMgr 2007.

The chapter also includes a preview of System Center Essentials 2010, which is the next version of Essentials. Essentials 2010 offers a fascinating glimpse at how Microsoft is merging various System Center-branded technologies into a unified management console. Essentials 2010 builds on Essentials 2007 by incorporating System Center Virtual Machine Manager 2008 R2 features into the Essentials product. If Essentials 2010 is a predictor of what the next release of OpsMgr may look like, these features will be relevant to everyone in the System Center community.

Windows Small Business Server 2008

Most businesses are small businesses, so any decent market penetration across millions of potential customers will create a reliable, steady following. Microsoft's Small Business Server 2003 version, which had a very attractive price point for small organizations, established SBS as an option for small business.

This part of the chapter discusses the management features and scenarios for SBS 2008. SBS 2008 replaces the broadly deployed SBS 2003 as the Microsoft customer-premise server solution for the very small organization. Although the low price point of the SBS 2003 package made it a good seller, the integration features between the server products in SBS 2003 was not that illustrious. Few used or appreciated the admin wizards and pre-created SBS security groups and such.

In contrast, the integration in SBS 2008 is excellent, eliminating the otherwise complex setup and admin of Windows 2008 X64, Exchange 2007, SharePoint 3.0, Fax services, Certificate services, WSUS, and so on. For Microsoft network owners with fewer than two servers and 75 clients, SBS 2003 and non-SBS 2003 alike, SBS 2008 is a compelling migration option to consider—especially at the very small business end with 25 clients or fewer. Accelerating and error proofing the install and secure operation of these complex technologies are great burdens to take off the small network owner's plate.

The error-free setup of SBS 2008 on an industry standard server with sufficient memory is dramatic. Pre-configured SBS 2008 components allow users to receive Internet email immediately after setup. Every component is correctly configured "out of the box," such as Active Directory user account and Exchange mailbox provisioning, Outlook Web Access (OWA) using a private Certificate Authority (CA), secure Simple Mail Transport Protocol (SMTP) receive connectors, very effective anti-spam and Exchange anti-virus, and much more.

SBS 2008 Native Management Features

Microsoft decided to make SBS management features simple in setup and operation, with as light a resource footprint as possible. Microsoft could have bundled Essentials 2007 as the management engine in SBS 2008, as they did for SBS's big sister, Essential Business Server 2008, covered in the "Windows Essential Business Server 2008" section of this chapter. However, Essentials 2007 had more features than needed in the SBS target environment and higher resource demands than the SBS architects wanted to support. Instead, SBS 2008 includes a brand-new management environment known as the Windows SBS 2008 Monitoring Data Collection Service.

This service is not a modified System Center Management service (named the OpsMgr Health Service pre-OpsMgr R2) but instead is a brand-new mini-management stack developed just for SBS 2008. A local instance of SQL 2005 Express (the instance name is SBSMONITORING) on the SBS 2008 server hosts the management database for the service. Outputs of the service include alerts that appear in the SBS console,

optionally emailed to an administrator. Figure 6.1 is a screenshot of the SBS console ->
Network -> Computers view.

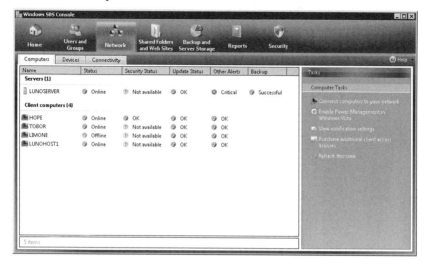

FIGURE 6.1 SBS 2008 console: Computer health view

This particular SBS 2008 network has an SBS server named Lunoserver, three client
computers running Vista, and an additional server using Windows Server 2008. These
computers were connected to the SBS domain by visiting an intranet web site on the
SBS server and running an ActiveX control—joining the computers to the domain and
downloading additional value-add software such as the SBS Vista Gadget, a very simple intranet portal. Clicking through on the Critical Other alerts item for the SBS server
Lunoserver brings up the alert list seen in Figure 6.2. (If you elect to receive email alert
notifications, you will receive the same text displayed in the lower details section of
the alert list.)

It is very simple to extend the native monitoring features of SBS 2008 by adding other
events for alerting. Define alerts in individual exTended Markup Language (XML)
files, placed in a designated folder. As an example, you might want to receive an SBS
alert when the SBS server is restarted. This is a common and important event but not
included as one of the built-in events that generate SBS alerts. You need four pieces of
information to build a custom XML file, as follows:

▶ **Path**—The name of the Windows log in which the event appears, such as the
System log in the case of the server restarted event.

▶ **Provider**—The source of the event as it appears in the appropriate Windows
log, such as EventLog in this example.

▶ **SetEventID**—The numerical Event ID as it appears in the appropriate Windows log, which is 6008 for the server restarted event.

▶ **AlertDefinition ID**—A randomly generated Globally Unique Identifier
(GUID). To generate a unique random GUID, use Microsoft's GuidGen utility
or the online GuidGen service at http://www.guidgen.com/Index.aspx.

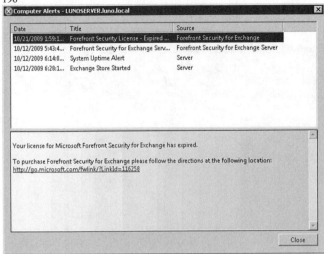

FIGURE 6.2 Viewing the details of an SBS 2008 alert

Using the sample XML code shown here, create the XML file and save it in the *%ProgramFiles%*\Windows Small Business Server\Data\Monitoring\ExternalAlerts folder on the SBS 2008 server (the 64-bit subdirectory, not the 32 bit one):

```
<?xml version="1.0" encoding="utf-8" ?>
<AlertDefinitions>
    <AlertDefinition ID="896e6561-b29d-42b5-b349-a87460c8556f" Default="1" →
Title="Unexpected Shut down" Source="Server">
        <Parameters>
            <Path>System</Path>
            <Provider>EventLog</Provider>
            <SetEventID>6008</SetEventID>
        </Parameters>
    </AlertDefinition>
</Alert Definitions>
```

Like Essentials 2007, SBS 2008 includes a daily report optionally emailed to the SBS administrator's email distribution list. (SBS 2008 adds a more detailed weekly report.) Differences between the Essentials Daily Health Report and the SBS 2008 Summary Network Report include removing the software installed listing for SBS 2008, but adding server uptime, backup, and email usage and mailbox size sections not included with Essentials.

Figure 6.3 shows an actual SBS Summary Network Report open in Outlook 2007. A simple approach to network management for SBS administrators is enabling email notification for alerts and reading the emailed daily and weekly network reports for important issues. When alerted to issues by emailed alerts or by reading the network reports, the administrator can log into the SBS server for further investigation.

FIGURE 6.3 SBS 2008 Summary Network Report emailed daily to the SBS administrator

Remote Operations Manager Scenarios for SBS 2008

Many SBS 2008 owners seek a means to centrally manage multiple SBS networks. A common situation is a chain of small businesses with an independent SBS server at each member location, or an organization acquires another that has a well-established SBS in place. In these scenarios, a network service provider or central Information Technology (IT) department can leverage the native Windows SBS 2008 Monitoring Data Collection Service, with the SBS server emailing the service provider the alerts for follow-up investigation. That might work for a very low-capacity management service with relaxed timeframes for problem resolution. SBS 2008 and EBS both include Remote Web Workplace (RWW); this is a secure way for the service provider to remotely access customer computers for support and service.

Alternately, the SBS 2008 owner (or IT service provider or central IT department supporting the SBS owner) may consider employing additional technology (or partner with a service provider) for deeper monitoring and/or remote management than that provided by the Windows SBS 2008 Monitoring Data Collection Service.

Candidates in the Microsoft management portfolio to provide richer monitoring and management of SBS 2008 are Essentials 2007, Operations Manager 2007, and Remote Operations Manager 2007. Here are the supportable topologies for this scenario:

> ► Essentials 2007 on a second server in SBS 2008 domain; monitor the SBS server with an agent component. Enable Service Provider mode with the Start menu wizard.

▶ OpsMgr gateway server component on a SBS 2008 server or a second server in SBS 2008 domain. Connect to Remote OpsMgr gateway with gateway and MOMCertImport.exe.

▶ OpsMgr agent component on SBS 2008 server and any other computers in SBS 2008 domain. Connect to Remote OpsMgr gateway with agent and MOMCertImport.exe.

Installing Essentials 2007 on the SBS 2008 server is not a valid option. It may be technically possible, but there are too many chances for conflict with the SBS native components, WSUS in particular. The SBS 2008 server should be in its basic configuration as much as possible and administered via the SBS 2008 console to keep everything "in synch" on the SBS network.

Windows Essential Business Server 2008

Having examined SBS 2008, this section focuses on the System Center Essentials 2007 component of EBS. Windows EBS 2008 is a new three-server suite combining database, messaging, directory, file and print, and security/firewall services (an optional fourth server runs SQL Server, which can be 32-bit or 64-bit). Years in development, this product for the mid-market space of up to 300 users or devices is a superset of SBS 2008. The messaging, security, and management server components are split across three servers installed in one multi-phase setup procedure and managed as a group. Think of EBS as a resurrection of the Microsoft BackOffice concept, only this time with a license enforcement mechanism strictly regulating the number of user or device Client Access Licenses (CALs, also known as *seats*) purchased by the organization, up to a maximum of 300 seats.

You may confuse the EBS product with the System Center Essentials product since both include the word "essential." To tell them apart, remember that System Center Essentials uses a plural noun, whereas Essential Business Server takes the singular adjective. EBS 2008 installs Essentials 2007, using it as the management and updating engine for the network. Essentials 2007 is a subset of Operations Manager 2007 and uses the identical binaries and management packs to deliver a tailored SMB experience. The Remote Operations Manager feature of Essentials 2007 is fully functional in Essentials Business Server, providing a convenient means to manage multiple EBS networks.

EBS and Essentials

During setup, System Center Essentials 2007 is installed automatically on the first server built, the management server. The Essentials EBS instance is modified from a default Essentials by adding management packs for Exchange 2007, Forefront Server Security (for Exchange 2007), and Forefront TMG. There is also an EBS management pack primarily used by EBS to perform configuration checks to ensure that the EBS servers and applications remain properly installed and licensed. Essentials agents are automatically deployed to the Security and Messaging servers, and the Essentials product features are pre-configured during EBS install.

The only portion of Essentials setup not fully automated during initial EBS install is configuring the Updating features of Essentials. Launching a task from the menu of EBS post-installation tasks configures these features. After completing EBS setup and the post-configuration tasks, all three EBS servers are fully monitored by the OpsMgr and WSUS components of Essentials.

A goal of the EBS product is shielding the administrator from needing to choose among the various server administration consoles (such as Exchange and Essentials), offering a single top-level administrative interface for all routine network admin activities—the EBS console. Figure 6.4 shows the EBS console displaying the computer health overview. This pane is analogous to the SBS console view of computer health shown in Figure 6.1. In EBS, selecting the View recent critical alerts action launches the Essentials 2007 alerts view filtered for the selected computer.

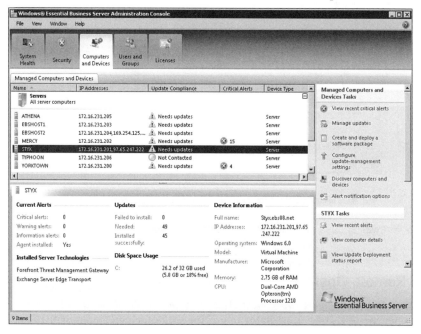

FIGURE 6.4 Overview of computer health in the EBS console

Managing the Threat Management Gateway (TMG) firewall component of EBS is error-proofed by pre-creating applicable custom protocols and access rules needed for Essentials agent -> Management Server (or gateway) communication and for publishing Remote Web Workplace. RWW is included with both SBS 2008 and EBS 2008 to provide easy VPN-free remote access to applications and computers over the Internet using only SSL port 443. Here are the options included in the RWW landing page:

► Change your network password.

► Open Outlook Web Access.

► Launch remote desktop using the TSWeb component of Windows Server 2008.

► Open the customer's SharePoint home page if SharePoint is installed.

Correctly publishing RWW and installing an OpsMgr agent on a firewall can sometimes be difficult tasks to get right without some help. Figure 6.5 shows the automatically created access rules in the TMG firewall configuration that support management features of EBS.

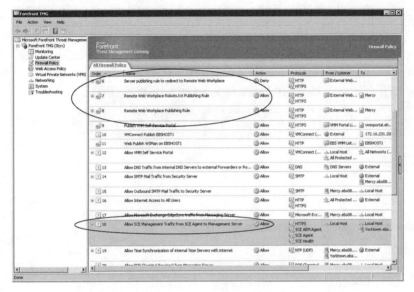

FIGURE 6.5 Firewall access rules that support EBS management

EBS with Remote OpsMgr

Because EBS 2008 includes the full Essentials 2007 product, the Essentials Enable Service Provider Mode feature is available to use for remote management of EBS. Once you connect the local Essentials instance to the service provider facility (by running the Enable Service Provider Mode applet from the Start menu of the EBS management server), the management packs running in the service provider instance of OpsMgr (Remote OpsMgr) are downloaded to the customer Essentials server. For additional information on Remote Operations Manager, see Chapter 21, "Reading for the Service Provider: Remote Operations Manager," in *System Center Operations Manager 2007 Unleashed.* The EBS server is approved in the Remote OpsMgr Operations console after running the gateway approval tool, just like bringing any other customer Essentials server into management. Once the Essentials server is green in the Remote OpsMgr console, you can push Remote OpsMgr agents to the other two EBS servers, and have remote eyes on all three customer EBS servers.

The Remote OpsMgr instance must already have management packs for Exchange 2007 and Forefront Server Security for Exchange loaded. Next, copy the TMG and

EBS management packs distributed with the EBS product and import them into the Remote OpsMgr management group, enabling that management group to monitor all the server technologies in EBS. Hardware vendor and advanced application management packs from the Remote OpsMgr instance (such as Hyper-V Server) are applied to customer servers without needing to modify the EBS instance of Essentials.

Importing the EBS management pack creates a new group type, "Windows Essential Business Server core servers computer group," against which you can target custom views and monitors. Figure 6.6 is a diagram view for a customer EBS group, with captions added to identify each EBS computer role.

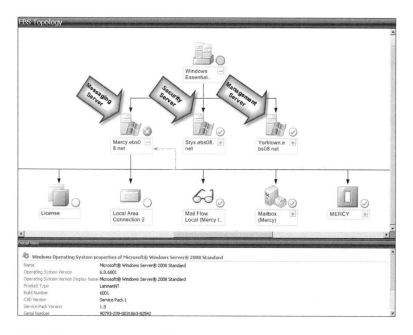

FIGURE 6.6 A customer EBS computer group diagram view in the Remote OpsMgr console

To grant a customer administrator access to his portion of the Remote OpsMgr Web console, scope an Operator role to the appropriate Essentials customer group. To avoid clutter, expose only relevant view folders in the user role's tailored console view. As a customer service, you can create an EBS dashboard view that rolls up the EBS diagram, Exchange 2007 health, IIS website health, and logical disk health. Figure 6.7 shows such a dashboard view open in the Remote OpsMgr Web console as it would be seen by a customer over the Internet.

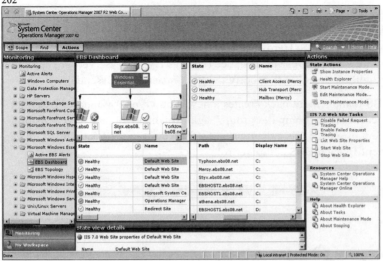

FIGURE 6.7 A custom EBS dashboard view in the Remote OpsMgr Web console

Preview of System Center Essentials 2010

System Center Essentials 2007 was a bold move by Microsoft to release a systems management solution packaged for the small to mid-market space. Essentials 2007 is a hybrid application merging a subset of Operations Manager 2007 with a superset of Windows Server Updating Service (WSUS). Essentials can deploy software and manage updates for Windows servers and clients, as well as monitor and manage computers just like OpsMgr.

Essentials 2007 was limited to managing a maximum of 31 server computers, including the Essentials server and 500 client computers. Essentials is marketed at the IT generalist, who is the key individual supporting most of the technology in a small or medium business (SMB). Using the Essentials console, the SMB administrator can manage health, inventory, updating, and software distribution to all computers on the network.

NOTE: STUDY ESSENTIALS AS A PREVIEW FOR MICROSOFT'S DIRECTION WITH OPSMGR

Microsoft used Essentials previously as a proving ground for next-generation OpsMgr technologies. An early beta of Essentials 2007 preceded test releases of OpsMgr 2007 by almost a year. If a similar product development approach is taking place, with Essentials 2010 an indication of directions for future versions of OpsMgr, expect System Center management software for the datacenter to fold virtualization management into service-level management as deftly as Essentials 2010.

The Essentials design simplifies and right-sizes the otherwise complex installation and configuration of an all-in-one OpsMgr management group. As an example, appropriate management packs for an SMB network are pre-loaded and tuned. The SMB organization benefits from the monitoring features of OpsMgr without the investment costs in hardware, software, and IT staff support that might otherwise be required.

Essentials 2010 takes this consolidated installation and configuration experience to a new level by incorporating all functionality of the Virtual Machine Manager 2008 R2 product into the core Essentials 2010 product. Here is a high-level summary of changes from Essentials 2007:

- ▶ Core monitoring and management features are upgraded from Operations Manager 2007 to Operations Manager 2007 R2, such as the ability to create an inline Notification action from an alert.

- ▶ Additional new features are unique to Essentials 2010, such as a ping monitor and more Essentials reports.

- ▶ There is a redesigned graphical user interface (GUI) with "new look" colors and fonts.

- ▶ There is an increase in the maximum number of managed servers from 30 to 50 (other than the Essentials 2010 server). (There is no change in the maximum of 500 client computers.)

- ▶ The biggest new feature is native support for virtualization by incorporating the feature set of Virtual Machine Manager 2008 R2 into Essentials 2010.

Figure 6.8 is the Computers Overview page of Essentials 2010 shortly after a default installation. It's easy to follow the tip and link on the page to get started with virtualization. Microsoft is making it conceptually straightforward for its SMB customers to deploy virtualization technology for their organizations.

Essentials 2010 Setup Experience

The setup experience for Essentials 2010 over Essentials 2007 is significantly improved. Despite being a more complex product—particularly with the addition of the virtualization management components—the time to install and the number of clicks and decisions to make is notably less. Microsoft has made what looks like good progress in making Essentials 2010 actually "easy to install." Automatic installation of prerequisites worked well; there is little work to prepare the computer to host Essentials 2010.

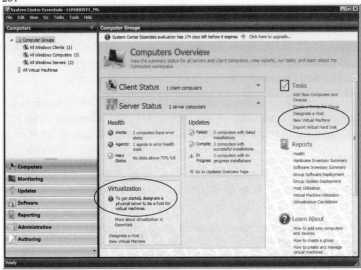

FIGURE 6.8 The Computers Overview page of Essentials 2010 directs you to the Designate a Host task to get started with virtualization.

Essentials 2010 uses SQL Server 2008 Reporting Services as the report generating and display engine. Because this latest version of report server does not depend on or use the local Internet Information Service (IIS), it remedies a source of many Essentials 2007 setup issues. The modular nature of the report service piece is also leveraged to provide some granularity in the basic Essentials 2010 setup. Essentials 2007 was an all-or-nothing install, particularly regarding the complex and troublesome report server setup. Essentials 2010 lets you decline to install the report service piece, reducing the application footprint. You can add reporting later if you change your mind.

Essentials 2010 also lets you de-select the virtualization piece during setup. If you chose not to install this piece, Essentials 2010 resembles the previous version of Essentials in terms of features, plus the updates included with OpsMgr 2007 R2 and an updated "2010" user interface (UI). Based on the pre-release of Essentials 2010, this will be a quicker and smoother administrator experience, with fewer system resource requirements than the previous version. Similar to the report server piece, you can install virtualization later in a modular fashion.

The computer running Essentials 2010, if it has enough memory, storage, and processor resources, can also be running the Windows Server Hyper-V role and act as a primary virtualization host for managed computers (virtual machines, or VMs). Another solution would be to run Essentials 2010 in its own VM, or even two VMs if you elect to host the Essentials databases on an external, pre-existing, or new SQL server.

A final setup innovation in Essentials 2010 is the administrator is warned if any pre-existing group policy objects (GPOs) are detected in Active Directory that would conflict with the built-in Essentials 2010 GPOs, another common source of Essentials 2007 configuration issues. Essentials 2010, like Essentials 2007, uses several GPOs to do things such as push trusted root authority certificates and WSUS settings to managed computers. An inline link lets the installer modify the existing GPO on the spot and proceed with Essentials 2010 setup without interruption.

Using the Essentials 2010 Virtualization Features

Certainly the biggest new feature in Essentials 2010 is the integration of a virtualization management environment into the IT generalist's systems management console. Installing the virtualization piece of Essentials 2010 doesn't merely expose the Virtual Machine Manager (VMM) console in a new pane. All virtualization-relevant tasks and tools are rendered in a context-appropriate and comfortable manner. In the pre-release version of Essentials 2010 on which this preview is based, no dedicated VMM-style console appears to be installed.

Designating a host on the network that is already a virtualization host will bring the virtual machines running on the host into the Essentials console. Figure 6.9 shows VM Lunoserver running as a guest on host computer Lunohost1. The Virtual Machine Remote Control (VMRC) protocol is used to render the live console view of the VM inset into the center details pane. Selecting a virtual machine in the Essentials Computers pane exposes applicable virtualization tasks: Stop, Connect to Virtual Machine, Manage Snapshots, Migrate to New Host, Save, Pause, and Power Off.

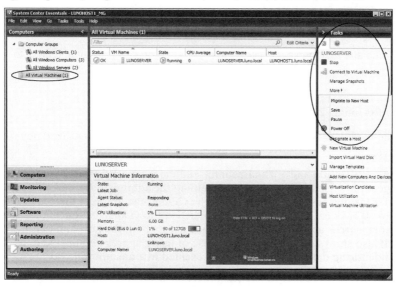

FIGURE 6.9 Relevant virtualization tasks such as Migrate, Save, Pause, and Power Off are presented as virtual machine tasks.

To the right of the Computers space in the task area are quick access links to the most useful virtualization reports—Host Utilization, Virtual Machine Utilization, and Virtualization Candidates. Figure 6.10 shows the Host Utilization report open on the Essentials 2010 desktop after clicking the inline reports link. The default report interval is 30 days but can be modified at run time. Metrics on the number of VMs running, processor, memory, disk, and network performance are presented in a single row of data. Below the metrics are two useful charts, as follows:

► CPU Usage by Virtual Machines compared with Total CPU Usage on the Host

► Memory Usage by Virtual Machines on the Host

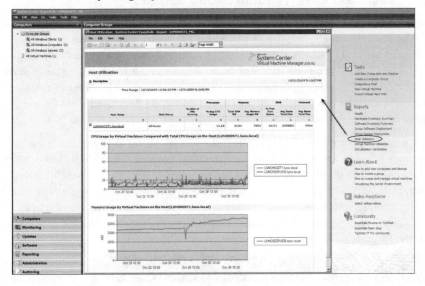

FIGURE 6.10 Rich and actionable virtualization reports are one click away and easy to read.

Design goals of Essentials 2010 include the following:

► Helping maximize limited IT resources by consolidating underutilized physical servers.

The Host Utilization and Virtualization Candidates reports directly contribute to the goal of consolidating servers by helping the administrator make informed decisions based on actual data. The CPU usage graph in the center of Figure 6.10 answers a simple—but often difficult to visualize—question: How are host resources actually being consumed across both the host and guest level? It also shows off the power and ease of using aggregated host and in-guest monitoring data synthesized and presented in a meaningful way.

► More rapidly provisioning new virtual machines.

Essentials 2010 shines at guiding the administrator through several relatively simple decisions that lead to deploying new virtualized computers. To enable repeatable on-demand VM generation in Virtual Machine Manager 2008 R2 (VMM, the full enterprise product that the virtualization features Essentials 2010 are an evolved subset of), you need to install a VMM library component, manually configure VM templates in the library, and manually create and configure the Virtual Network Switch(es) used by the templates.

Essentials 2010 hides this complexity by abstracting the user from the virtual switch component, and installing three ready-to-use VM templates. Figure 6.11 shows the templates named Basic Server, High-End Server, and Recommended Configuration. The pre-configured VM templates are at the administrator's fingertips without further configuration, and can be edited and added to.

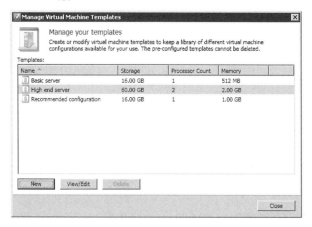

FIGURE 6.11 Essentials pre-configures three virtual machine templates.

After designating one or more virtualization hosts, the New Virtual Machine task is available in the Essentials 2010 Computers space. Accepting the default settings, only four clicks are needed to generate a new VM (excluding the keystrokes to enter the name of the new VM). Figure 6.12 shows the first page of the four-page wizard: Select Template.

Notice the drop-down box where High-End Server is selected; this clarifies how the pre-configured templates for new virtual machines are an effective accelerator to deploy new VMs. Here are the four clicks to deploy a new VM:

1. **Select Template**—Use one of the pre-created templates, optionally modifying the properties of the new VM, such as add more memory than the default in the selected template.

2. **Install Operating System**—Use a local DVD drive in the host computer or point to an ISO image file. There is also a useful option to boot from the network if you have deployed Windows Deployment Services (WDS) for OS install.

3. **Select a Host**—Hosts already designated appear to select from. Essentials 2010 supports Hyper-V and Virtual Server hosts.

4. **Virtual Machine Name**—You do have to type a unique computer name here.

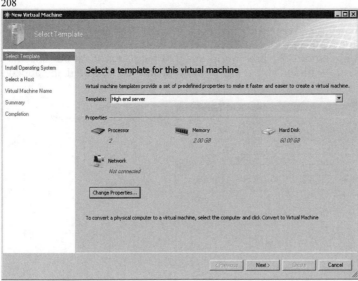

FIGURE 6.12 Using the New Virtual Machine wizard and the built-in virtual machine templates takes the guesswork out of provisioning new machines in Essentials 2010.

After your new virtual machine is deployed, Essentials discovers it at the next regularly scheduled automatic discovery, which is daily at midnight by default. Once an Essentials agent is deployed to the new VM automatically by the discovery process, you have full visibility of the guest and host health in the Essentials 2010 console and reports. Essentials 2010 delivers a simple yet complete virtualization deployment and management solution for the SMB space.

Other New Essentials 2010 Features

Essentials 2010 introduces several unique innovations beyond the virtualization features added to Essentials and the feature upgrades inherited from OpsMgr 2007 R2. These include a long sought-after ping monitor, some automation assistance with management pack identification and download, and some new and enhanced reports of particular use to the administrator in the SMB space.

Ping Monitor

A frequent feature request for both System Center Essentials 2007 and System Center Operations Manager 2007 has been a simple ping monitor. Purists may respond that you don't need a ping monitor with the agent-based monitoring the System Center products have, but that has not stopped the need to ping something! Essentials 2010 includes two kinds of ping monitors you can deploy or enable, as follows:

▶ For any computer or device, even computers running unsupported operating systems and devices that do not have Simple Network Management Protocol (SMNP) compatibility, the Add Monitoring wizard now includes the ping monitor as a type of monitoring you can create. Added devices appear in the Monitoring -> Ping Monitor -> Ping Monitor Checks State view.

► You can augment Essentials agent-based monitoring of computers by creating an override that enables a ping monitor in the availability branch of the computer's health explorer. Computers with a ping monitor enabled will include that monitor in the availability health monitor rollup of their computer object.

Figure 6.13 highlights those settings in the Administration space that are unique to Essentials (not present in an Operations Manager 2007 installation). Essentials 2007 and 2010 include an update and software management feature built on WSUS not available with OpsMgr. In addition, the Daily Health Report is an Essentials-only feature. The Daily Health Report in Essentials 2010 is the same as Essentials 2007, with the exception of one new feature added: a listing of computers in the domain that were discovered and added to management in the last 24 hours.

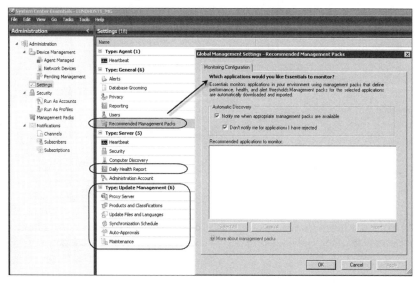

FIGURE 6.13 Settings in the Administration space that are unique to Essentials, focusing on the new automatic management pack discovery feature

Management Packs

A new System Center feature is highlighted in Figure 6.13, which is the Recommended Management Packs setting. During initial configuration of Essentials 2010 features in the Configure Essentials wizard, you are prompted to select the applications you want Essentials to monitor. If you select Automatic Discovery, Essentials will recommend importing management packs that apply to discovered applications and notify you when management packs are available for new software detected in your environment. You can also manually select which applications to monitor and change these settings at any time in the Essentials Administration space at the location shown in Figure 6.13.

Reporting

The Essentials reports are a collection of nine reports that draw data from the WSUS portion of Essentials. The Windows Update client gathers information about computer hardware in order to download drivers from Microsoft Update. Essentials leverages this data to provide reports on discovered hardware, seen in Figure 6.14. The Hardware Summary report details Computer Manufacturers, Computer Models, Operating Systems, BIOS Manufacturers, Physical Memory, Processor Names, Processor Architectures, Sound, Video, Network Card Manufacturers, and others.

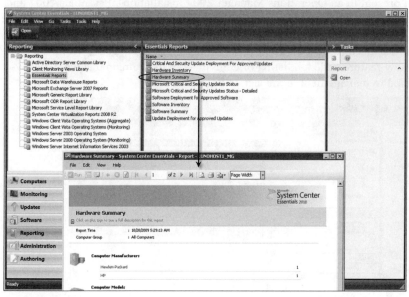

FIGURE 6.14 The Hardware Summary report is unique to Essentials; data comes from the Windows Server Updating Services (WSUS) database component of Essentials.

Three new reports for Essentials 2010 involve Microsoft Critical and Security Updates status. This is an overdue investment by Microsoft to improve the usability of the WSUS service, and Essentials 2010 users may be the first to benefit. It has always been problematic, with either Essentials 2007 or WSUS alone, to accurately and easily report on the patching compliance status of the network. Many organizations use a third-party product either for patching itself, or to assess WSUS patching discrepancies independently so that tickets to fix individual computers can be generated.

Figure 6.15 shows the detailed version of the updates status report. This is an all-new spreadsheet-style report format for the System Center family, featuring color-keyed columns and bar graphs that make it easy to identify update deployment problems. A giant enhancement over all previous WSUS reports involving update compliance is the ability to drill down in an update summary report to see the actual computer names reporting issues. In Figure 6.15, the yellow bar graph segment calls attention to an update in the Needed category. Expanding the plus icon next to the update name exposes details about the update and a line-item list of each computer with their individual status. You can see that the computer Hope needs this particular update.

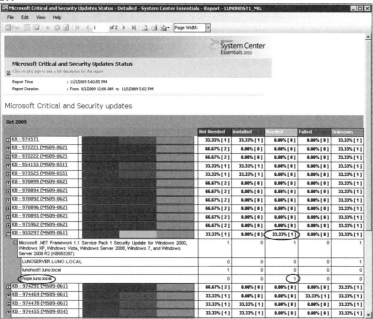

FIGURE 6.15 The Microsoft Critical and Security Updates Status report includes inline drill down to quickly see the names of computers missing particular updates.

Although no details are available yet, the next version of Essential Business Server (EBS) is in development, and Essentials 2010 will likely be the primary management component in EBS. In particular, the new virtualization and updates management features previewed in Essentials 2010 will be welcome and valuable additions to a future EBS suite.

NOTE: NEW FEATURES ADDED IN THE ESSENTIALS 2010 RELEASE CANDIDATE

Some additional functionality from VMM 2008 R2 is included with a later pre-release build of Essentials 2010. The most significant news is that Essentials 2010 will support Hyper-V Clusters and Live Migration. In addition, the Computers space in Essentials 2010 now exposes active PRO tips as well as the status of virtualization jobs completed and in progress.

Summary

This chapter explored the management aspects and Operations Manager integration scenarios of two shipping Microsoft server products for the small and medium business space: SBS 2008 and EBS 2008. Emphasizing simplicity and a small footprint, SBS 2008 includes its own lightweight management engine, and depends on emailed alerts and daily and weekly health summaries to keep the administrator informed of issues. SBS 2008's big sister, EBS 2008, is built around the Essentials 2007 application, which is pre-installed and optimized for managing the medium-sized network. A pre-release version of the next edition of Essentials was previewed that introduces seamless management of virtualized computers and eases the security update compliance job for administrators of small and medium-sized networks.

## CHAPTER 7

Operations Manager and Virtualization

Observe a paradox in the datacenter today—although virtualization is fast becoming the de-facto model for IT organizations, deploying virtualization management tools lags significantly behind. This chapter explains why closing the Virtual Machine (VM) management gap is vital for the industry. After discussing VM management using native and third-party management packs, the chapter focuses on Microsoft's preferred solution—System Center Virtual Machine Manager (VMM). The chapter steps through deploying VMM and integrating it with Operations Manager (OpsMgr), discusses using the System Center framework to manage new VMs, and concludes with a discussion on virtualizing the OpsMgr components themselves.

The Case for VM Management

There are almost "perfect storm" conditions in the atmosphere of virtualization management; consider the following statistics:

▶ Virtualization is rampant, with over 50% of new servers sold in 2008 destined for virtualization roles (IDC).

▶ Only 35% of IT shops in 2007 had deployed virtualization management solutions (ScienceLogic).

▶ Less than 45% of IT managers in 2008 felt that their companies were doing an effective job of virtualization management (Computer Associates).

Virtual computing is still in its infancy compared to other mainstream contemporary datacenter disciplines, such as backup and networking. These more mature Information Technology (IT) technologies have decades of best practices to fall back on, with dozens of management products and solutions available.

When everyone is virtualizing but with few tools or industry standards on best practices available, you get a wide variation in deploying and managing virtualization technologies. This can make it difficult for the IT manager to assess the health of his or her virtualized infrastructure, leading to inefficient use of personnel and equipment, and even to a decrease in application and service availability compared to pre-virtualization days.

Virtualization Challenges and Rewards

Old school mainframe engineers will tell you they were virtualizing computing loads decades ago, beginning in 1964 with the IBM System/360. So, although many of the issues discussed here are not "new," managing virtualization in the post-millennial Internet world requires rediscovering or developing new and evolved solutions.

Let's start with the good news about virtualization. As most system administrators have discovered, when VMs take the place of physical servers, almost magical things can happen:

▶ New servers can go from concept to production in a few hours or even minutes, contrasting with days or weeks or longer to provision physical servers.

▶ The cost to deploy and license a new VM can decrease ten-fold or more below the costs of physical servers, which is an overpowering and driving economic force.

▶ The overall IT engine of the enterprise is greatly accelerated, particularly for the lab and test environments that support enterprise application development.

It's a safe bet that the sharp trend away from a one physical server = one computer paradigm will continue. Considering these revolutionary gains in technological and business efficiency, let's examine the other side of the virtualization paradigm—the costs, risks, and added complexity when architecting a virtualized environment. Some of the risks to mitigate are more obvious, such as the all-your-eggs-in-one-basket situation, where many or all your critical servers are VMs on a single host.

Let's take a stab at quantifying the complexity factor when considering the importance of having an effective virtualization management solution. As a baseline, consider an HP ProLiant server. Using the HP Insight agents, Table 7.1 identifies the principal, discrete elements that require management, which are at least a dozen objects to manage just on the physical aspect of one server.

TABLE 7.1 Management Elements: Physical Server (in No Particular Order)

Physical Elements: Traditional Physical Server Includes These (About 12)			
Firmware	Hardware drivers	Cooling fans	Memory
Power supply	Processor(s)	Temperature	Storage
Network interface card(s)	UPS and/or generator status	System board including serial number	Hardware remote console (lights out)

Now look at an apples-to-apples comparison of the complexity in managing physical servers compared to virtual servers. The hypothesis is that going virtual increases overall management complexity significantly for a small number of VMs, decreasing with more VMs managed, with a break-even point at some (still) fairly low number of VMs.

This information is used to further justify virtualization projects, and ensure that those deployments are accompanied by a proper virtualization management solution.

The virtualization complexity baseline in Table 7.2 utilizes the main configuration settings of a Hyper-V host computer and guest VM as they appear in the Hyper-V management console.

TABLE 7.2 Management Elements: Virtualization (in No Particular Order)

Host Elements: One Set per Host (About Three)		
Virtualization drivers	VM storage location(s)	Virtual networks
Guest Elements: Each VM Includes These (About Six)		
Memory	Processor(s)	Storage
Network interface card(s)	VM integration services and drivers	VM start/stop action(s)

Counting the management elements, also known as configuration control items (CCIs), notice that about nine elements are added when you virtualize one server, for a total of about 21 CCIs for a single host with a single guest VM, versus about 12 CCIs for a single physical server. That's roughly a 75% increase in complexity to manage one virtualized server compared to a single, traditional physical server. The numbers get better quickly…add a second VM, and the ratio increments nicely to 27 CCIs (21 + 6), compared to the 24 CCIs (12 + 12) of two physical servers, or a much smaller complexity increase of just 12.5%. With the third VM, you pass a break-even point, and you can observe that a host with three VMs is about 8.3% less complex than with three physical servers (33 vs. 36 CCIs).

An important conclusion for virtualization architects is that there is increased risk with a larger number of hosts, each with a low number of VMs, compared to a decreasing risk with a smaller number of hosts, each running many VMs (but this makes each host exponentially more valuable). Deploying System Center tools like Operations Manager and Virtual Machine Manager mitigates risk in both deployment scenarios.

VM Management Standards: Cloud Computing Enabler

Virtualization is a prime enabler of cloud computing, making dynamic deployment of thousands of servers at cloud service provider datacenters possible for a fraction of the investment in money and time previously required to ramp up high-end capacities. Virtualization has contributed more to making IT agile and adaptive to changing business requirements than another other recent innovation.

Large enterprises can fully leverage virtualization's potential by creating their own cloud architectures that feature rapid response to changing conditions and are almost infinitely scalable. Inside a private corporate cloud of mainly virtualized computers, standardization on just one (or a very few) virtualization platforms is likely, as is deploying a virtualization management solution that supports that platform.

A small or mid-size company typically lacks the resources to build its own cloud, such as having multiple, well-connected, highly survivable datacenters. To compete with larger organizations, smaller shops need to leverage the cloud computing resources of one or more trusted service providers. This brings up one of the strongest impediments to wide-scale enjoyment of cloud computing benefits by organizations of all sizes: trust. The very livelihood of a small business is at stake when they offload critical business data processes to an outsourced partner.

Put yourself in the place of a small business owner considering moving an in-house application server to a virtual server in "the cloud." Your desires are to increase the survivability, connectivity, and scalability of your business, without relying on a dedicated, physical server. Your concerns include long-term viability of the service provider, privacy of your data, and the security and well-being of your application in the cloud.

Many legitimate concerns involving trust in the cloud can be addressed when service providers select the System Center suite to orchestrate their VM provisioning and management operations. Consider that trust and familiarity with the Microsoft Exchange product line are making for a smooth transition by many organizations to Exchange Online services, which you can implement in a granular fashion, such as archiving, anti-spam, and other options. For customers with virtualized infrastructures seeking to outsource some or all aspects of virtualization management—there is great appeal if those host and guest computers can easily "snap into" a System Center-based solution.

Allowing the customer to continue to use the virtualization platform that works for them (Microsoft's Hyper-V or VMware's ESX), the System Center virtualization management stack is a known quantity, with an extensive and trusted support and development community. Like Exchange Online services, hosted models of the different System Center components such as Operations Manager and Virtual Machine Manager logically follow as options for the customer to select according to the evolving needs of their organization. Such a framework enables customers to view their managed applications running both on in-house servers and on cloud-based datacenters through the same pane of glass (the OpsMgr console, Web console, and reporting components). The line between in-house and cloud begins to blur—with effective management tools, leveraged directly for the customer's best interests being a key enabler.

Using a System Center-based framework as a VM deployment, maintenance, and management solution is a valid business model for cloud computing service providers that are Microsoft partners. This can be a competitive edge over cloud service providers without such a broad VM management and support portfolio, and a bridge to future service offerings including cloud-based and virtualized storage and server components.

Managing VMs without VMM

Microsoft's centerpiece of their virtualization solution, Virtual Machine Manager 2008, is covered beginning in the "Installing VMM and Connecting It to OpsMgr" section. This discussion might help you decide whether, and to what extent, to deploy VMM alongside OpsMgr in your organization. There is no "one size fits all" solution. Even if you deploy VMM and integrate it with OpsMgr, you will probably use some of the capabilities of the non-VMM 2008 features discussed in the next sections.

Choosing Not to Deploy Virtual Machine Manager

With virtualization becoming highly pervasive, it would not be surprising to see future versions of OpsMgr (and System Center Essentials) more tightly integrated with VMM features. For now, you can choose to deploy VMM, or instead use only native connectors, add no-cost virtualization management packs from Microsoft, or purchase third-party management packs for non-Microsoft virtualization technologies. Although VMM adds many features, deploying VMM can have a significant cost. Here are some scenarios where you might consider not deploying VMM:

▶ You have a very small number of VMs, just one or two on a single host; in this case, VMM might be overkill.

▶ No plans to use any VMM-specific features, such as automatic VM image deployments, central VM libraries, or Physical-to-Virtual (P2V) migrations.

▶ After reviewing the features available without VMM, you determine that with using OpsMgr and native Microsoft management packs alone (or third-party management packs), you can manage your virtual infrastructure just fine.

If you don't use VMM, there are two principal management packs from Microsoft to consider, as follows:

▶ **Server Virtualization Management Pack**—This converted MOM 2005 management pack has been around for several years.

▶ **Windows Server Hyper-V Management Pack**—Microsoft released this native management pack in mid-2009.

Between these two management packs, you can monitor and manage Virtual Server 2005 Release 2 (R2) very well and have basic Hyper-V monitoring capabilities. Figure 7.1 displays the virtualization management packs; notice the view folders named Microsoft Windows Hyper-V 2008 (above) and Virtual Server (below).

FIGURE 7.1 The Virtual Server and Hyper-V monitoring view folders

Monitoring Virtual Server

For a number of years, the only virtualization software available from Microsoft was Virtual Server and Virtual PC. These no-cost, downloadable 32-bit virtualization solutions use the host operating system to integrate hardware resources for virtual machines. The last and still-current version of Virtual Server 2005 R2 is fully supported by VMM, and an appropriate platform in some situations. It is common to encounter Virtual Server in educational, training, development, testing, and lab environments. You may even find some business critical applications deployed on Virtual Server because it was available at the time, on short notice, and at low cost.

If you are responsible for maintaining infrastructures that include Virtual Server, Microsoft has a good management pack available. The Server Virtualization management pack for OpsMgr 2007 contains all functionality necessary to monitor Virtual Server 2005 R2. The management pack also supports the first version of VMM, which did not yet include Hyper-V support. Even though you do not intend to monitor legacy VMM versions, if you want to monitor Virtual Server with OpsMgr 2007, import the Server Virtualization Management Pack, and only use the portions applicable to Virtual Server.

Look again at Figure 7.1 to see how this management pack communicates a critical piece of information—the guest VMs running on each host. In this example, the Detail view shows VM Ambassador on host Quicksilver. To quickly see how powerful OpsMgr and virtualization are together, notice in Figure 7.2 that you have the ability to start and stop VMs from anywhere via the Web console. (These useful tasks are also available in the Operations console as well.)

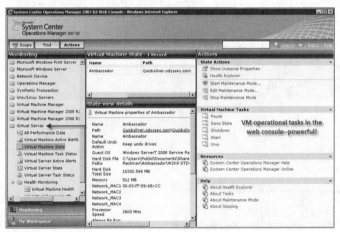

FIGURE 7.2 Perform VM operations via tasks in the Web console.

A number of reports come with the Server Virtualization management pack, including a Virtualization Candidates report. This full-featured management pack is almost like a "VMM lite" for the 32-bit Virtual Server product and a must-have for those environments still using Virtual Server.

Monitoring Windows Server Hyper-V

A commonly asked question is: "Do I need to deploy VMM to monitor Hyper-V with OpsMgr?" Until June 2009, the answer was yes—there was no native Hyper-V management pack available. An entire year after Hyper-V's release in June 2008 passed before Microsoft released the Windows Server Hyper-V management pack. This is a very basic management pack without any reports or tasks. A more appropriate question might be: "Are my monitoring needs for Hyper-V only 'basic?'"

The left pane of Figure 7.3 shows the four Hyper-V view folders created when importing the management pack. The Hyper-V management pack does a fine job of making clear what guest VMs are running on which host Hyper-V servers. The path name in Figure 7.3 (circled) shows that VM Armada.continent.com is running on host Tornado.odyssey.com. The guide for the management pack states that up to 20 guest VMs are supported by the management pack per host; if you run a high-volume Hyper-V environment, such as Windows Datacenter Server 2008 hosting over 20 guests, you would need to deploy VMM to assure monitoring of all VMs.

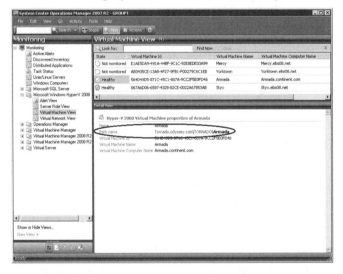

FIGURE 7.3 The Hyper-V management pack has four simple view folders that convey basic health and status information.

Although the functionality of the built-in management pack views is rudimentary, here are several positive management elements that can increase the uptime of your Hyper-V servers:

► Some monitors have automatic recoveries to restart the Virtual Machine Management service.

► Other monitors target Hyper-V-specific performance aspects such as the free space remaining on the logical disk that contains the virtual hard drive of a VM.

Of significance for OpsMgr management pack authors interested in building on the foundation of a native management pack are the classes added to the management group when importing the management pack. Figure 7.4 shows that the Hyper-V Server Role and Hyper-V Virtual Machine, as well as each VM subcomponent, are classes that can become the target of custom reports, views, rules, and monitors.

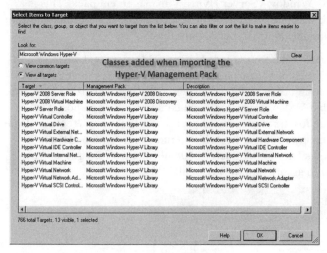

FIGURE 7.4 Microsoft Windows Hyper-V Server classes

Monitoring VMware ESX with OpsMgr

An industry-leading feature of VMM 2008 is the ability to manage both Hyper-V and ESX hosts in the same context and the same VMM console. (This feature of VMM requires you to also purchase, install, and configure the optional vCenter management software from VMware in advance.) What about those OpsMgr installations with ESX servers that do not have Hyper-V, and also may not have purchased or installed VMware vCenter?

In the ESX management scenario, well-established third-party management packs are available from Veeam, Jalasoft, and Bridgeways that do a great job of monitoring and managing VMware ESX with OpsMgr (Chapter 2, "Unix/Linux Management: Cross Platform Extensions," includes a discussion of the Bridgeways management pack). With some reduced functionality, you can monitor ESX from OpsMgr without deploying vCenter at all.

Many installations use the nWorks management pack for VMware from Veeam Software to monitor ESX (more information available at http://www.veeam.com/vmware-microsoft-esx-monitoring.html). Figure 7.5 exposes some of the extensive view folder hierarchy from this management pack. A management server in your management group runs additional services that directly poll the ESX hosts for their status, as well as sharing information with any vCenter installations.

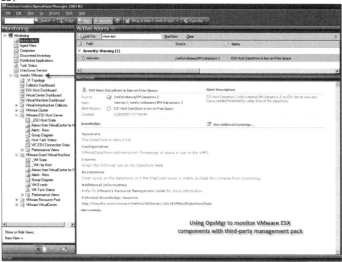

FIGURE 7.5 Viewing the details of an alert about free space on an ESX host volume

Deploying a third-party management pack to monitor your ESX hosts and guests is an easy way to integrate the health status monitoring of VMware resources in your organization. Figure 7.6 lists the useful tasks related to VMware guest VMs that nWorks makes available in the Operations console.

FIGURE 7.6 VM guest tasks available on ESX host

Installing VMM and Connecting It to OpsMgr

The whole is sometimes greater than the sum of the parts, and such is the case with System Center Virtual Machine Manager and System Center Operations Manager. Although these management products are independently installed, performing the integration steps outlined in this section results in a hybrid System Center management suite that increases the functionality of both products. Any administrator running only VMM or OpsMgr should consider installing the other product to enable this integration. New deployments of virtualization infrastructure should seriously consider integrating OpsMgr with VMM into their architecture as a first step, and then use System Center to deploy both the virtualization components and the VMs. This approach affords the possibility of deploying a virtualized infrastructure that is highly available, highly automated, and even self-regulating.

Before installing VMM components on your network, consider running the VMM Configuration Analyzer to pre-screen your target VMM server(s) and host(s). There is a link to download the VMM tool on the setup splash screen for VMM. Figure 7.7 displays the link, the tool, and the output.

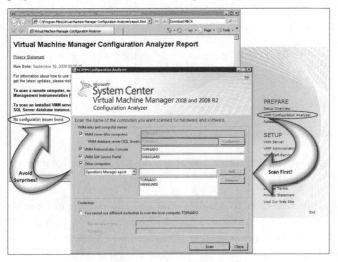

FIGURE 7.7 Scanning target computers for possible install issues with the VMM Configuration Analyzer.

Installing Virtual Machine Manager

Similar to OpsMgr, System Center Virtual Machine Manager 2008 is a modular product with a wide variety of installation options and topologies. Here are the basic VMM components:

► VMM server

► VMM Administrator console

► VMM self-service portal

► VMM agent

The VMM Server component uses a SQL Server database; to install VMM, you must have a pre-existing local or remote SQL Server 2005 or SQL Server 2008 instance, or select to have VMM Server setup install SQL Server 2005 Express Edition locally. Follow these basic steps to install VMM components:

1. **VMM Splash Screen**—From the desktop of your target VMM Server, run Setup.exe on the VMM source media and select the VMM Server action.

Figure 7.8 presents the VMM setup splash screen; notice the five setup actions listed on the right.

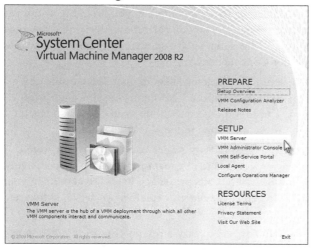

FIGURE 7.8 Setup actions available from the VMM setup splash screen—the cursor is selecting the main server setup action.

2. **VMM Database**—Select to install and use SQL Server Express 2005 on the local computer, or specify the local or remote SQL Server instance in which to create your VMM database.

    The default name for a VMM database instance is **MICROSOFTVMM** and the default database name is **VirtualManagerDB**. The VMM server database role is a light load and not demanding on the SQL Server.

3. **VMM Library**—Create a Library Share on local or networked storage of the VMM Server; the default share name is **MSSCVMMLibrary**.

    If you do not have enough local storage on the VMM server, it is easy to add other server shares and make other libraries available after initial setup. The library is where you store VM images and copies of setup media in the .ISO file format. This is a very handy feature of VMM.

4. **VMM TCP Ports**—Confirm communication settings for the new VMM server. Here are the default settings:

    ▶ **TCP 8100**—Communication between the VMM server and VMM Administrator console.

    ▶ **TCP 80**—Communication to agents on hosts and library shares (using the Windows Remote Management protocol, WinRM).

    ▶ **TCP 443**—File transfers to agents on hosts and library shares (via BITS/Background Intelligent Transfer Service file transfer protocol).

5. **Windows Automated Installation Kit**—If not already installed, VMM Server setup installs the Windows Automated Installation Kit (WAIK). You can

optionally use WAIK components such as the ImageX capture tool to customize and use the VM provisioning features of VMM.

6. **VMM Console**—When VMM server setup is complete, you probably also want to install the VMM Administrator console so you can administer VMM from the server's desktop. Return to the VMM setup splash screen in Figure 7.8; this time, select the VMM Administrator Console action.

7. **Add Hosts**—When console setup is complete, select to open the console and observe (in the Hosts -> All Hosts node of the VMM console) the status message: No hosts are managed. The first thing you will do is add hosts, so launch the Add Hosts wizard from the Actions pane in the VMM console.

   Select the default option to discover Windows server-based hosts in an Active Directory domain and provide credentials to connect to the host(s). Successively pressing the Next, Search and Search buttons presents a list of all servers in your domain, as seen in Figure 7.9, whether they have virtualization server software installed or not.

   Select to add all those servers you expect to play a role in your virtualization topology, including virtualization candidates and servers that will only be VMM library servers. Both the VMM agent and the Windows Remote Management (WinRM) service are installed on target hosts.

CAUTION: ADDING HOSTS CAN CAUSE SERVICE OUTAGE

If the selected hosts are Hyper-V candidates, and the Hyper-V role is installed automatically by VMM, those servers will actually shut down and boot back up several times, so do not perform this work during normal production hours.

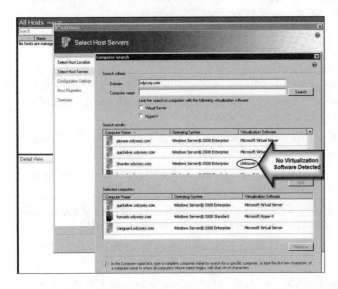

FIGURE 7.9 Selecting all the default Add host options lets you pick from all servers in your Active Directory.

8. **Check for Guests**—After successfully installing the VMM agent on your target hosts, VMM automatically discovers and displays (in the Virtual Machines pane of the VMM console) the VMs found running on the added hosts. No software or other configuration is required to discover guest VMs and add their information to the VMM database.

Figure 7.10 shows that two VMs (Ambassador and Armada) were found among the three hosts added in step 7 (Quicksilver, Tornado, and Vanguard). The lower detail pane shows health and status information on the selected VM (Ambassador), along with a remote desktop view.

9. **VMM Setup Complete**—You have now deployed all the core VMM components. Install other VMM options as desired, such as the Self-Service Portal. Then proceed to integrate VMM with OpsMgr using the steps that continue in the next section.

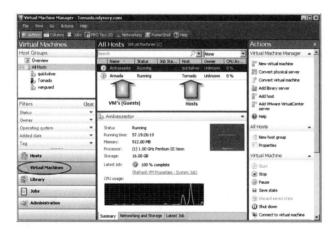

FIGURE 7.10 Viewing the guest virtual machines discovered on managed hosts in the VMM Administrator console

Integrating Operations Manager with VMM

The following steps are a bit of a ballet that integrates the OpsMgr and VMM products. This basic scenario assumes a full two-way trust relationship between all hosts and the VMM and OpsMgr instances: that Operations Manager 2007 Service Pack (SP) 1 or R2 is deployed and OpsMgr agents installed on all hosts and guests, as well as VMM 2008 R2. You also must previously import the SQL and Internet Information Server (IIS) management packs into the OpsMgr management group.

Each VMM server can only be associated with one OpsMgr management group. However, one OpsMgr management group can manage many VMM servers. Follow these basic steps to integrate OpsMgr with VMM:

1. **Install OpsMgr console on VMM server**—From the desktop of your VMM server, run SetupOM.exe on the OpsMgr source media and install just the Operations Manager Console component on the VMM server.

2. **Integrate the RMS with VMM**—From the desktop of the root management server (RMS) of the OpsMgr management group, run the Configure Operations Manager action from the VMM setup splash screen (once again, see Figure 7.8).

   Enter the name of the VMM server when prompted, and note that console to server communication uses TCP port 8100. The Configure Operations Manager action installs the VMM console and PowerShell VMM command shell on the RMS, imports the VMM management pack into the management group, and adds the VMM service account to the Administrator role in OpsMgr.

3. **Install the VMM console on management servers**—From the desktop of each additional management server in the management group, run Setup.exe from the VMM distribution media and select the VMM Administrator Console install action. Each management server needs the VMM console and specifically the PowerShell VMM command shell components installed locally.

4. **Add OpsMgr accounts to VMM security**—In the Administration view of the VMM console, click User Roles. Edit the properties of the Administrator user role and add the default OpsMgr action account for the RMS and each management server. If those servers are using Local System for their action account(s), add the computer account of the RMS (such as **HYDRA$**) and each management server to the VMM Administrator user role.

5. **Add VMM account to OpsMgr security**—The service account of the Virtual Machine Manager service running on the VMM server must be able to write to the OpsMgr database, so this account can require the same rights as the System Center Management Configuration service (named the OpsMgr SDK service in OpsMgr 2007 pre-R2). If using the Local System account, the computer account of the VMM server (TORNADO$, in this example) can be added to an appropriately privileged domain security group such as the OpsMgr Administrators domain security group, or manually added to the Administrators local security group of the OpsMgr operations database computer.

6. **Link VMM with OpsMgr**—Open the VMM Administrator console. At the Administration -> System Center -> Operations Manager Server setting, select the Modify action. Enter the name of the RMS and press OK.

   If you installed the optional (but recommended) Reporting component in your OpsMgr management group, you can also enable links to OpsMgr reports from the VMM console. At the Administration -> System Center -> Operations Manager Reporting URL, select the Modify button. Enable reporting, enter the URL to the reporting server in the OpsMgr management group (such as http://Quicksilver/ReportServer), and press OK.

7. **System center integration complete**—You have performed all the integration steps for both the OpsMgr and the VMM products. Advanced features such as Performance and Resource Optimization (PRO), described later in the "Performance and Resource Optimization" section, are ready to configure and use. An example of the product integration is the Reporting tab in the VMM console, which

does not appear unless the Operations Manager Reporting URL is correctly specified. Figure 7.11 demonstrates the Reporting feature of VMM with OpsMgr integration; information gathered by the OpsMgr agent about VM performance is accessed from the VMM console.

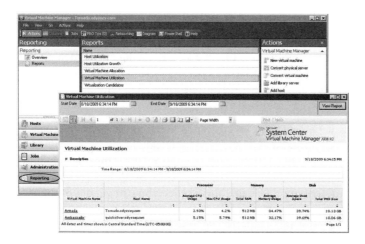

FIGURE 7.11 The Reporting component of VMM is enabled with OpsMgr integration.

NOTE: ESSENTIALS 2010 PREVIEWS NEW APPROACH TO VIRTUALIZATION MANAGEMENT FOR SYSTEM CENTER

To see where Microsoft may be headed in its approach to virtualization management with future versions of Operations Manager, refer to Chapter 6, "Management Solutions for Small and Midsize Business."

The VMM Management Pack

The System Center Virtual Machine Manager 2008 management pack monitors availability of all components of VMM 2008 and availability, health, and performance of all VMs and virtual machine hosts that VMM manages. The management pack is automatically imported when performing the OpsMgr/VMM integration steps covered in the previous section, "Installing VMM and Connecting It to OpsMgr;" you can also download it from the Operations Manager 2007 online catalog. Here are the ways the VMM management pack extends VMM:

▶ Comprehensive health monitoring of VMs

▶ Performance and resource optimization in VMM

▶ VMM reports

▶ Diagram views available from the VMM console

All rules in the VMM management pack are enabled by default except one—the VMM task failed alert. Here is the rule to enable in the Authoring node of the OpsMgr console to receive a warning alert each time a task fails in VMM:

```
Microsoft.SystemCenter.VirtualMachineManager.2008.Engine.TaskFailure
```

A helpful VMM/OpsMgr integration feature involving OpsMgr maintenance mode available after integrating the two products is that the VMM management pack automatically places VMs in maintenance mode when they are moved into the VMM library. This enables you to avoid alerts and notifications associated with the loss of OpsMgr agent heartbeat when a VM is stored.

By deploying the VMM management pack and using its views and reports, you can stay on top of your virtualized infrastructure—keep well informed, be in control, and optimize your assets. You will be able to track host to guest relationships, watch both for overburdened hosts and underpowered guest VMs, and fully account for the virtualization layer in your network topology. Use the intelligence you can get out of the management pack to tune your configurations to get maximum safe utilization out of your hosts. Here are four scenarios that demonstrate how to use features of the VMM management pack:

► **Compare performance of similar VM workloads on different hosts**—Open the OpsMgr console and navigate to Monitoring -> Virtual Machine Manager 2008 R2 -> Host Performance Data; then select the disk, network, processor, or memory counters of interest. Observe the chart populate with the data. To change the time scale of the chart, click Select Time Range from the Actions panel. Figure 7.12 illustrates this scenario.

Here both Quicksilver (a Virtual Server host) and Tornado (a Hyper-V host) are running VMs with the same memory and processor settings and the same workloads (each hosts one OpsMgr gateway server VM). The performance chart indicates Hyper-V is a more efficient hosting platform, using less than half the processor time of the Virtual Server host for virtualization processes.

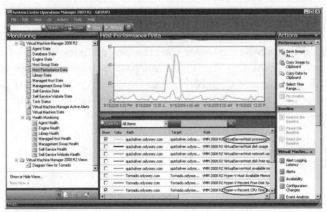

FIGURE 7.12 Comparing the CPU time of Hyper-V vs. a Virtual Server host processes for the same VM load

▶ **Account for the health of your entire virtualization infrastructure**—Open the OpsMgr console and navigate to Monitoring -> Virtual Machine Manager 2008 R2 Views -> Diagram View and observe the diagram generated from the VMM Server's health model. If one or more components are in a Critical (red) or Warning (yellow) state, press the Filter by Health button and select to show the critical path of the unhealthy condition(s).

Figure 7.13 is the expanded diagram view of the VMM server Tornado's health model. You can see that the health of the virtualization environment is represented by a roll-up of the health of the hosted VMs, the VMM library, and the VMM server and database. (If you installed the VMM Self-Service Portal, that component is also part of the health model.)

When you select objects in the diagram view, you will expose context-sensitive Action panels listing tasks appropriate to the object. As an example, selecting the VMM database object enables tasks such as Set Database Online and Open SQL Management Studio. Selecting a VM enables tasks such as Create Checkpoint and Shutdown.

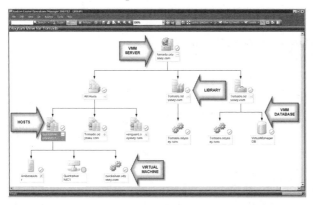

FIGURE 7.13 Exploring the health model of the VMM server thorough the diagram view

▶ **Access Historical Data for Trending Analysis**—Open the OpsMgr console and navigate to Reporting -> Microsoft Virtualization Reports. Observe the five reports provided with the VMM management pack, as follows:

  ▶ **Virtualization Candidates**—This report helps identify those physical computers that are good candidates for conversion to VMs. Use the Virtualization Candidates report to identify little-used servers and display average values for a set of common performance counters for processor, memory, and disk usage, along with hardware configurations, including processor speed, number of processors, and total RAM. You can limit the report to computers that meet specified CPU and RAM requirements, and you can sort the results by selected columns in the report.

  Figure 7.14 is the result of a Virtualization Candidates report run where the Average CPU Usage is less than 15%, indicating lightly used computers. The default time range is the last week of data. Set the Computer Group to All Windows Computers to report on all computers in your management group.

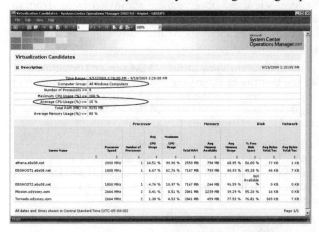

FIGURE 7.14 Identifying virtualization candidates from among all computers where average CPU usage is less than 15%

▶ **Virtual Machine Allocation**—The Virtual Machine Allocation report provides information you can use to calculate chargeback to cost centers for VMs. You can set up this report by Cost Center grouping to summarize CPU, memory, disk, and network usage for VMs within your cost centers. The cost center is a property of a VM, which can also be set on VM templates.

▶ **Virtual Machine Utilization**—This report provides information about resource utilization by your VMs. For a specified period, this report shows average usage and total or maximum values for VM processors, memory, and disk space. You can use this report to identify under-utilized or over-utilized VMs and determine whether any changes are necessary. (Figure 7.11 shows an example of this report.)

▶ **Host Utilization**—For the specified time period and host group, this report shows the number of VMs running on each host and the average usage and total or maximum values for host processors, memory, and disk space. Double-clicking a host in the list opens a Host Performance report with details about resource usage on the host.

▶ **Host Utilization Growth**—The Host Utilization Growth report shows the percentage of change in resource usage and the number of virtual machines running on selected hosts during a specified time period.

▶ **Perform VM Operations Remotely**—The virtual machine tasks that are available in the OpsMgr console, (such as Start, Stop, and Create Checkpoint) are also available in the Web console. Using a web browser, you can perform operations on managed VMs from anywhere on the Internet. Open the Operations Manager Web console and navigate to Virtual Machine Manager 2007 R2 -> Virtual Machine State.

The Results pane in the center displays a combined list of all VMs running on all your managed hosts: Hyper-V, Virtual Server, and ESX guests. Select a VM and observe the Virtual Machine Manager 2008 R2 Managed Virtual Machine Tasks panel in the Actions area on the right. Figure 7.15 is a partial view of the Web console highlighting this panel. From here, you can perform actions on the VMs. All actions are available for all guests, regardless of virtualization platform.

Virtual Machine State - 46 Records				Actions
State	**Name**	**Path**		**State Actions**
Critical	RMS1N2	Tornado.odyssey.com		Virtual Machine Manager 2008 R2 Managed Virtual Machine Tasks
Healthy	Ambassador	Tornado.odyssey.com		Create Checkpoint
Healthy	Armada	Tornado.odyssey.com		Pause
Healthy	301-B	Tornado.odyssey.com		Save State
Healthy	302	Tornado.odyssey.com		Shutdown
Healthy	303	Tornado.odyssey.com		Start
Healthy	309	Tornado.odyssey.com		Stop
Healthy	311	Tornado.odyssey.com		
Healthy	AS02	Tornado.odyssey.com		**Resources**
Healthy	AS03	Tornado.odyssey.com		
Healthy	AS04	Tornado.odyssey.com		**Help**

FIGURE 7.15 Execute remote tasks from the OpsMgr Web console against VMs running on any virtualization platform.

To provide an even deeper level of integration between the OpsMgr and VMM products, consider creating OpsMgr web views that nest the VMM Self-Service Portal for each of your managed VMM servers. Although you can stop, start, and perform basic VM operations over the web using just the OpsMgr Web console, the VMM Self-Service Portal includes additional functions such as Store VM and a thumbnail view of VM desktops, seen in Figure 7.16.

Ensure that the Uniform Resource Locator (URL) of the VMM portal you enter in the OpsMgr web view definition (such as https://vmmportal.odyssey.com) is resolvable by the DNS client of the users of the Web console.

FIGURE 7.16 The OpsMgr Web console with nested VMM Self-Service Portal in a web view

ESX vCenter Integration

The market leader in virtualization host platforms is VMware—in particular, the flag-ship ESX Server technology. Enjoying a lead of several years over Microsoft's compet-ing Hyper-V product, ESX is used by the majority of large enterprise datacenters. Many OpsMgr administrators will have ESX hosts on their networks that need to be managed, and VMM can combine management of VMware hosts and guests alongside Hyper-V and Virtual Server hosts and guests. Integration between OpsMgr and VMM brings visibility of the ESX topology into the OpsMgr consoles and reports, even though there is no direct connection at all between OpsMgr and the ESX environment.

OpsMgr (and VMM) have an indirect connection to ESX hosts that leverages the VMware VirtualCenter virtualization management product, also known as vCenter. The principal prerequisite to manage an ESX environment with System Center is that you must already be managing the ESX hosts with an existing vCenter Server. Simply point VMM to vCenter, and VMM uses vCenter as an intermediary to learn informa-tion and execute a number of tasks in the ESX environment. However, vCenter is an extra-cost optional product from VMware, and not all shops with ESX have purchased and deployed vCenter. Some obvious scenarios arise involving OpsMgr, vCenter, and VMM; see if your situation fits one of these:

▶ **Pure ESX shop; already have vCenter; don't have VMM**—Because you don't plan to have any virtualization hosts other than ESX, you have little to gain by adding VMM. You would be better served with a third-party man-agement pack for ESX such as nWorks, described in the "Monitoring VMware ESX with OpsMgr" section of this chapter, or Bridgeways, introduced in Chapter 2.

▶ **Mixed ESX/Hyper-V shop; already have vCenter; don't have VMM**—Consider acquiring VMM. Because you cannot manage your Hyper-V hosts with vCenter, but can manage ESX hosts alongside your Hyper-V hosts with VMM, this is a clear choice since you already have a vCenter investment.

▶ **Have some ESX; don't have vCenter yet**—Your choices would include pur-chasing vCenter and using that alone, possibly with a third-party OpsMgr management pack, which would be a valid choice if you had no plans to de-ploy Hyper-V hosts. If you have a small number of ESX hosts, some third-party ESX management packs, such as nWorks and Bridgeways, permit lim-ited management of ESX hosts even without vCenter (and this is the least-expensive option for an all-ESX shop with OpsMgr but without vCenter). If you have several ESX hosts as well as Hyper-V hosts, consider purchasing both vCenter and VMM server licenses for the most integrated management solution.

Adding a VMware Virtualization Manager

The following actions take place in the VMM console. You will need network access to the vCenter server, including domain credentials to log into the vCenter console. For full management of ESX hosts, you will also need a root-level user name and pass-word. Perform the following steps to bring ESX servers into management by VMM:

1. Navigate to Administration -> Virtualization Managers. In the Actions panel, click Add VMware VirtualCenter server.

2. Enter the Computer name or IP address of the VirtualCenter server; accept the default TCP/IP port of 443 unless you are using a non-standard port. In the Administrative account area, enter a domain username and password with administrative access to the VirtualCenter server.

3. Deselect the option to Communicate with VMware ESX server hosts in secure mode and press OK.

4. At the certificate import prompt, select to Import the VMware certificate. (To verify the identity of the VMware VirtualCenter server, VMM imports the server's security certificate into the local machine certificate store.)

5. Move to the Hosts -> All Hosts view and observe the VMware ESX host(s) that appears in the list. Any VMware datacenter or folder objects carry across as VMM host groups. VMware ESX hosts will first appear with an "OK (Limited)" status. In a limited management status, only some VMM functions are enabled.

6. To enable full management status on an ESX host, select the host in the Hosts view and click Properties from the Action panel. Enter the root user password for the particular ESX host and push the Retrieve button. The certificate and public key thumbprint fields should populate with some hex notations. Tick the box to Accept both the certificate and public key for this host and press OK. (See Figure 7.17 for an example of this step.)

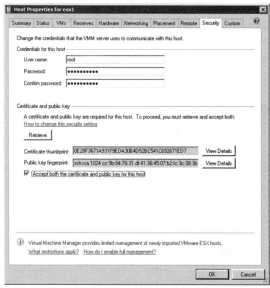

FIGURE 7.17 Specify individual ESX host root-level credentials, and import server certificates for full management of ESX hosts.

7. Check for Guest VMs in the Virtual Machines view. Select a VMware VM in the list of VMs and observe in the lower details area, on the Summary tab, that you

are prompted to install the VMware ActiveX control on the computer running the VMM console. This will enable the thumbnail view of the VM guest computer in the VMM console.

Managing ESX Hosts and Guest VMs

After performing the VMM/vCenter integration steps described in the previous section, you can automatically view the configuration and health status of the VMware environment in the OpsMgr console. There are no views or reports specific to ESX; rather, interaction with ESX hosts and guests occurs in the same context as Hyper-V and Virtual Server hosts and guests.

This paradigm of integrated management of heterogeneous virtualization technologies—at the virtualization management layer—is powerful and unique. Although differences between the virtualization stacks become apparent when performing operations, the OpsMgr console has parity between ESX, Hyper-V, and Virtual Server in presentation and features at the guest VM level, as well as in the host performance monitoring views and reports.

At the host management level, ESX hosts always appear as unmonitored computer objects, because ESX hosts essentially run a modified version of a Linux-based operating system. The cross platform monitoring features of OpsMgr 2007 R2 unfortunately do not natively support monitoring ESX hosts as computer objects.

Visibility of ESX hosts and their guests is excellent in the OpsMgr console; as an example, Figure 7.18 shows an alert at the ESX host level about a guest VM that is in trouble. You can easily see which VMM server (tornado) the ESX host (esx1) is associated with, and know where the VM (RMS1N2) is located. You can perform tasks against the VM, such as attempting to recover by starting the VM on the ESX host.

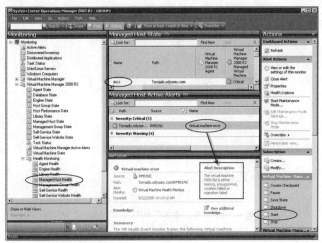

FIGURE 7.18 Learning of problems in the ESX environment by viewing an alert in the OpsMgr console

Key components enabled by the System Center integration between OpsMgr and VMM are topology diagrams and virtualization reports. The same diagram and reports are available from either the OpsMgr or VMM consoles. The diagram view is actually created as a distributed application (DA), and can be invoked in the OpsMgr console as the diagram view of the distributed application named for the VMM server, or by navigating to the Virtual Machine Manager 2008 R2 Views folder. There will be a separate diagram view for each VMM server associated with the OpsMgr management group.

Because all the managed VMware objects are already contained in a DA, it's a simple matter to create your own targeted DAs combining relevant objects from the automatically created VMM server topology view(s) and other management packs. As an example, you can diagram a server farm composed of both ESX VMs and Hyper-V VMs that accurately represents common dependencies such as shared storage, network devices, and even power and cooling systems. Like all OpsMgr diagrams, you can export to Visio for living documentation.

Figure 7.19 is the diagram view of a VMM server that includes an ESX host cluster. This figure extends the diagram view introduced in Figure 7.13, which presented three managed hosts in the All Hosts group (circled in Figure 7.19). Those three hosts were placed in a VMM host group named ODYSSEY Data Center, seen in the center right of Figure 7.19. In the upper left, notice the VMware virtualization manager object, which represents the vCenter server managed by this VMM server.

In the center left of Figure 7.19, at the same level as the VMM host group on the right, is a VMware datacenter object that appears in OpsMgr as a host group. Below the VMware host group is an object representing a VMware cluster (presented in the same manner as Hyper-V failover clusters). In the lower levels of the diagram, see Hyper-V guest VMs and ESX guest VMs, as well as ESX virtual networks and Hyper-V virtual switches, all presented in the same context. If you are managing both Hyper-V and ESX virtualization hosts, this approach may make a lot of sense.

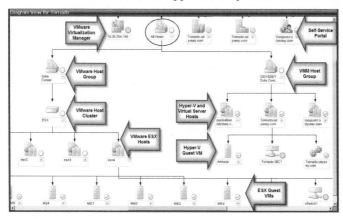

FIGURE 7.19 The single pane of glass: Unified presentation of ESX and Hyper-V components in a VMM server diagram view

OpsMgr does a great job at collecting and storing performance information, and then generating reports exposing that data. The VMM management pack leverages the ability to collect performance data on ESX hosts and report on host utilization. Figure 7.20 is the Host Utilization report of a three-node ESX host cluster running 38 VMs over a 24-hour period. The data in the report can help you identify ESX hosts that are unequally or inefficiently loaded, compared to other members of the cluster.

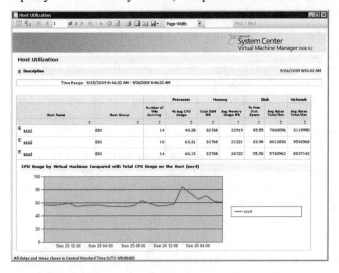

FIGURE 7.20 Get the most out of your hosts: a report view of ESX host utilization across members of an ESX host cluster.

Performance and Resource Optimization

Performance and Resource Optimization is an available feature of System Center when you integrate Operations Manager 2007 and Virtual Machine Manager 2008. PRO is new, native Microsoft technology that enables dynamic management of virtualized infrastructure. This is an attempt by Microsoft to foster an industry protocol for automatic issue resolution of events arising from virtual environments—an enabler of cloud computing with hints of artificial intelligence. PRO leverages the management pack infrastructure of OpsMgr and the virtualization abstraction model used by VMM to create a real-time analysis and decision-making tool. Optionally, you can place optimization recommendations (PRO tips) in a "full automatic" mode, creating cloud neural networks that operate faster than humans can and scale in seconds to changes in demand.

Enabling PRO Tips

Before enabling PRO tips, perform all applicable OpsMgr to VMM integration steps described in the "Integrating Operations Manager with VMM" section of this chapter. Once all two-way communication between OpsMgr and VMM is in place, you can enable PRO tips globally for all hosts and guests managed by the VMM server. Figure 7.21 shows where you find this setting and what it looks like when you select to receive Warning and Critical PRO tips but not to automatically implement them. You will not receive any PRO tips until you enable them here!

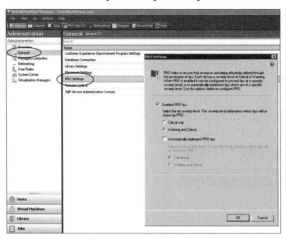

FIGURE 7.21 Enable PRO tips globally for all hosts and guest VMs managed by the VMM server.

After enabling PRO tips globally for the VMM server, you can granularly apply different PRO tip policies to each host group and cluster in the environment. The Properties page of each host group and cluster includes a PRO Settings page just like the global settings page seen in Figure 7.21. The default behavior is to inherit the PRO settings of the parent, but you can exempt groups and clusters from parent-relationship, global, or All Hosts group settings.

At the guest VM level, the PRO Settings page of each virtual machine includes a configuration that exempts the VM from host-level PRO tips. The default for a VM is the setting is not selected, which means that the VM will respond to host-level PRO tips, such as a failed fan in the host computer. You can granularly exempt VMs only from host-level actions, not from guest-level actions. If you enable PRO tips for a host, all VMs on that host will always respond to guest-level issues, such as memory exhaustion of a VM.

VMM Native CPU and Memory PRO Feature

VMM natively includes PRO features that focus on CPU utilization and available memory on hosts and VMs. Looking for low memory or high CPU conditions on hosts or guests, a VMM native PRO tip will offer to move VMs to more suitable hosts, to free resources on a host, or give additional resources to a guest. PRO tips apply universally to all host architectures including ESX.

If you select automatic implementation of PRO tips, expect that to happen. VMs will move using the Live Migration method between Hyper-V hosts if that method is available. The vMotion method is used between ESX hosts if the VM virtual hard drives exist in shared storage (such as Storage Area Networks, known as SANs) store. PRO tips use the same "five-star" rating system (to locate the best available host) that a VMM console user sees when migrating a host manually. The PRO tip will select the target host with the most stars.

If you enable notification only in the case of PRO tips, be aware that a PRO tip is waiting on a decision. PRO tips appear in the VMM and OpsMgr consoles, and you can implement them from both locations as well. Figure 7.22 shows the PRO tips window as it pops-up when the VMM console is running, whereas Figure 7.23 shows an alert view in the OpsMgr console examining the details of a PRO tip.

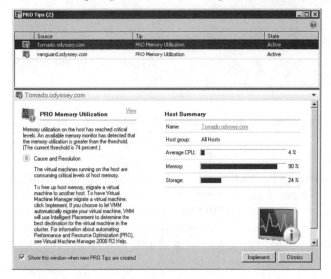

FIGURE 7.22 PRO tips as they pop up in the VMM console

If you hunt in the VMM interface for the default PRO thresholds, you will search in vain. The default thresholds are automatically determined by the VMM management pack in OpsMgr and do not appear in the VMM console. Here are the default PRO tip thresholds in the VMM management pack:

- **Host PRO tip thresholds**—In the original VMM 2008, the thresholds for CPU and memory in the host monitors are fixed at 90% of CPU capacity and 75% of memory capacity. In VMM 2008 R2, those thresholds are dynamic and determined by the host reserves that are in effect for each host.

- **Guest PRO tip thresholds**—For both versions of VMM, guest VM thresholds are fixed at 90% for either memory or CPU.

All threshold monitors are based on one-minute samples and will alert based on the average of three consecutive samples. To modify the alerting criteria or the thresholds for specific hosts or guests, create overrides to the appropriate PRO Hyper-V Host target in the Authoring node of the OpsMgr console.

FIGURE 7.23 A PRO tip seen as an alert in the OpsMgr console

Figure 7.24 makes clear the two default VMM host PRO-enabled threshold monitors for CPU and memory utilization in the left side of the Health Explorer of a managed host. This computer has an active PRO tip condition for memory utilization. On the right side, in the Additional Recovery Options section, Figure 7.24 shows you can implement the PRO tip also from here.

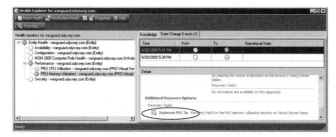

FIGURE 7.24 Implement a PRO tip from the Health Explorer.

PRO-Enabled Vendor Management Packs

To add additional PRO-enabled features to your management group, import third-party management packs from hardware and software vendors that are PRO-enabled. PRO provides an extensible framework to create management packs for virtualized applications or associated hardware. Vendors are expected to incorporate deep product and process awareness of their solutions in their PRO-enabled management packs. Using these pre-determined watch points and resolution steps, PRO can react dynamically to adverse situations and avoid poor system performance or worse. Here are some examples of third parties that have released PRO-enabled management packs:

▶ **Dell Servers**—The PRO-enabled Dell Management Pack ensures that host machines operate under normal power and temperature thresholds. Dell's VMM PRO Alert for temperature monitors the chassis temperature; should the monitor exceeds normal operations, the administrator can automatically trigger a quick migration from one host to another.

▶ **Emulex Host Bus Adapters (HBAs)**—Emulex's PRO-enabled management pack monitors I/O rates across the HBA relative to maximum available bandwidth. The PRO tip will notify customers to take corrective actions, to either move the VM to a different physical server or reduce the link speed.

▶ **Secure Vantage Security Auditing**—The Security Management PRO-enabled management pack mitigates risk and remediates policy violations across virtual environments. VMs can be restored to a last known good configuration or bring new systems online in response to key policy and configuration control violations.

Using VMM in DMZs and Untrusted Domains

For both OpsMgr and VMM, the default security mechanism between servers and agents is Kerberos, the Microsoft Active Directory (AD) security provider. Many networks include a Demilitarized Zone (DMZ), which is a less-trusted, intermediate network in between the local area network (LAN) and the Internet. (Another term for DMZ is *perimeter network*.) Usually computers in the DMZ have Internet-facing roles, such as web publishing and messaging edge. Computers in a DMZ are often not joined to a domain (known as *workgroup mode*), or the computers are in a separate perimeter network domain not trusted by the primary domain. In these scenarios, Kerberos is not available to authenticate agents and servers to one another.

OpsMgr and VMM Agent Alternate Security Modes

OpsMgr provides for installing and fully monitoring an OpsMgr agent on a computer in a perimeter network, regardless of domain membership or domain trust status. This alternative security method uses a central, mutually trusted certificate authority (CA) rather than an AD forest or explicit trust relationship. When OpsMgr components (such as management servers, gateway servers, and agents) are issued certificates from the same CA, they trust other OpsMgr components with certificates from that CA as if they were in a trusted domain environment. This is the primary method to manage computers with OpsMgr in service provider and leased datacenter models. Here is a high-level overview of the steps to enable OpsMgr monitoring with certificates:

1. Install a certificate authority and create a suitable computer identity certificate to be issued.

2. Import the CA certificate into the Trusted Root Certificate Authority certificate store of the host computer to be managed, as well as into the certificate stores of

the management servers and/or gateway servers the agent will communicate with.

3. Issue an individual certificate in the Fully Qualified Domain Name (FQDN) of each computer. The certificate must be exported to a .PFX file with the private key.

4. Install the OpsMgr management server, gateway server, or agent component. In the case of a gateway server, prepare the management group using the gateway approval tool.

5. Install the certificate on the computer using the MOMCertImport.exe utility. (Ensure that Domain Naming System [DNS] support is in place for the managed host to permit resolution of the name(s) of its respective management servers or gateways.)

6. For a manually installed agent, approve the pending action in the Administration node of the OpsMgr console.

VMM also uses Kerberos as its primary security mechanism, usually requiring a domain trust relationship with Windows hosts to manage them with VMM. However, VMM includes an alternate security method using certificates designed for DMZ and workgroup scenarios where there is no trust relationship between the managed host and the VMM server. Although the VMM security certificate method and the OpsMgr certificate mode use completely different techniques to accomplish the same goal, you can install both the OpsMgr and the VMM agents on a computer in their respective certificate-based modes. Here are the steps to manage a Windows virtualization host computer with VMM not in a trust relationship with the VMM server:

1. On the host to be managed, run Setup.exe from the VMM installation media and select to install Local Agent.

2. At the Security File Folder page of the setup application, enable This Host Is on a Perimeter Network. Enter a password in the Security file encryption key box and note the path where the security file will be exported.

3. At the Host Network Name page, select to use the local computer name or IP address for how VMM will contact the host. If you select computer name, the VMM server must have a hosts file to provide name resolution of the host.

4. Agent installation will proceed with a file named Securityfile created in the specified location. Physically copy the Securityfile file to a local or networked drive accessible to the VMM console you will use to add the host to VMM.

5. On the computer running the VMM console, in the Hosts view, select Add host from the Actions pane on the right.

6. Select to add a Windows-based host on a perimeter network.

7. On the Select Host Servers page, enter the computer name or IP address and the password (encryption key) you specified during the agent setup. If using the computer name, make a hosts file entry for the host in the perimeter network. Figure 7.25 illustrates this page of the Add Hosts wizard and discloses that the SecurityFile content is that of a digital certificate file.

8.   Accept the defaults at the remaining screens unless your specific configuration requires changing them. Press Add Hosts when complete.

After completing the Add Hosts wizard, hosts located in the perimeter, DMZ, or other un-trusted network appear in the All Hosts list in the VMM console, and discovered VMs appear in the Virtual Machines list, almost indistinguishable from hosts in trusted domain networks and ESX hosts from trusted vCenter servers. There are some differences in management features between hosts in perimeter networks and hosts that are Windows computers in a trusted domain—these are described in the next section, "VMM and OpsMgr Agent Architecture Differences."

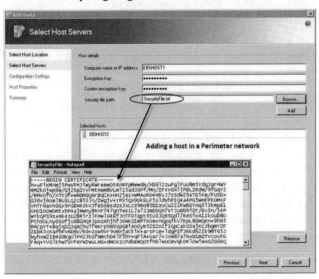

FIGURE 7.25 Each perimeter host has its own unique SecurityFile, produced as part of manual VMM Agent setup.

If you need to use the perimeter network mode to manage hosts (because those hosts do not have a trust relationship with your management domain), it is likely you will also use the OpsMgr method of certificate-based agent authentication rather than Kerberos authentication with a trusted Windows domain. This dual-agent technique, each with their own method of certificate-base authentication, provides a complete stand-off model of virtualization management that requires no domain trusts.

Figure 7.26 expands on the VMM topology view introduced in Figure 7.13 (with Virtual Server and Hyper-V hosts in a trusted domain) and extended with ESX hosts and VMs in Figure 7.19. Here, two hosts in a perimeter network model (Ebshost1 and Ebshost2) are added to a new VMM host group Customer EBS08. Using an OpsMgr gateway component on the remote network, an OpsMgr agent pushed to the guest VMs provides in-guest monitoring of the applications running in the VM. OpsMgr makes clear that the virtual machine Mercy contains the Windows computer Mercy.ebs08.net.

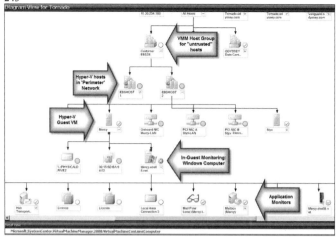

FIGURE 7.26 End-to-end monitoring of VM application workloads achieved even across trust and network boundaries.

VMM and OpsMgr Agent Architecture Differences

The OpsMgr agent is able to fully monitor and manage a remote host using the certificated-based model; there is no loss of function compared to monitoring a fully trusted agent. However, the VMM agent has some features that work only in Kerberos trust mode. In other words, when managing a host with VMM in certificate-based mode, you sacrifice these features:

▶ You cannot store VM images in VMM libraries not in the perimeter network (this requires you to place a VMM library in the perimeter network to use library features).

▶ You cannot migrate VMs from hosts not in the perimeter network.

▶ The thumbnail displays in the VMM console and VMM self-service portal are disabled (however, the Connect to VM and Remote Desktop tasks in the self-service portal work if you have name resolution and network routing from your web browser to the host in the perimeter network).

An important difference for network architects to remember between the OpsMgr and the VMM agents is the direction and nature of their communication paths. The OpsMgr agent on a managed host communicates outbound on port 5723, possibly to service provider OpsMgr gateways on the Internet. The VMM agent, rather, is polled by the VMM server on port 80, requiring inbound publishing of managed hosts to the VMM server.

The VMM and OpsMgr agents are independent of one another, and you can install one product's agent using the default Kerberos trust model and the other product's agent in the certificate-trust mode. This would be the indicated combination in a scenario where the VMM server is part of the local network and domain of the managed hosts, whereas the OpsMgr components are in a remote, untrusted domain:

► The VMM agent would be installed in Kerberos mode, enabling you to use all VMM features, not just the subset available in certificate mode. A best practice if possible is to locate VMM server(s) on the local network segments and in the domains where managed host computers are located.

► The OpsMgr agent would function in certificate mode with a remote service provider instance of OpsMgr, with no sacrifice in monitoring fidelity compared to Kerberos mode. This scenario applies equally when the OpsMgr agent reports to a local OpsMgr gateway server via Kerberos, and the gateway server reports to a remote service provider gateway server using the certificate-based trust model.

In addition to the ports and protocols used by the OpsMgr agent (principally outbound TCP 5723), consider the following ports and protocols listed in Table 7.3 used by the VMM agent and server components.

TABLE 7.3 VMM Ports and Protocols

Connection Type	Protocol	Default Port
VMM server to VMM agent on Windows Server–based host (control)	WinRM	80
VMM server to VMM agent on Windows Server–based host (data)	SMB	445
VMM server to remote Microsoft SQL Server database	TDS	1433
VMM server to P2V source agent	DCOM	135
VMM Administrator console to VMM server	WCF	8100
VMM Self-Service Portal web server to VMM server	WCF	8100
VMM Self-Service Portal to VMM self-service web server	HTTPS	443
VMM host-to-host file transfer	BITS	443
VMRC connection to Virtual Server host	VRMC	5900
VMConnect (RDP) to Hyper-V hosts	RDP	2179
Remote Desktop to virtual machines	RDP	3389
VMware Web Services communication	HTTPS	443
SFTP file transfer from VMWare ESX Server 3.0 and VMware ESX Server 3.5 hosts	SFTP	22
SFTP file transfer from VMM server to VMWare ESX Server 3i hosts	HTTPS	443

Virtualizing OpsMgr 2007 and VMM Components

When you architect a new OpsMgr or VMM deployment, or if considering extending an existing installation with additional components, the best solution may well feature some or all OpsMgr and VMM components running as guest virtual machines, hosted by your choice of virtualization technologies. Here are some potentially game-changing scenarios where virtualization enhances OpsMgr:

- ▶ Leveraging high-availability features of the host, such as Microsoft's Hyper-V failover clustering, to increase uptime of the guests, particularly those without redundant OpsMgr components; that is, OpsMgr components that are not themselves clustered.

- ▶ Dynamically responding to changing business needs by cloning, storing, and deploying management servers and gateways as virtual machines; rapidly swelling and shrinking management group capacity as needed.

- ▶ Achieving at little effort a credible disaster recovery (DR) plan for the OpsMgr environment; backup or "snapshot" copies of the Virtual Hard Disk (VHD) files of VMs that are OpsMgr components just need to be staged for recovery.

These virtualization-centric possibilities involving OpsMgr are in addition to the dramatic cost saving and economy of scale benefits empowered by virtualization itself, discussed earlier in "The Case for VM Management" section. OpsMgr customers substantially onboard with a virtualization platform will be compelled to install OpsMgr and VMM components in VMs to the greatest extent possible, devoting dedicated physical servers to OpsMgr and VMM only when necessary. Most OpsMgr and VMM components run fine as VMs with a few exceptions, as detailed in Table 7.4. High-volume OpsMgr 2007 management group deployments on both Hyper-V and VMware ESX are well known and present few issues, as long as all database and RMS roles are *not* virtualized.

TABLE 7.4 OpsMgr/VMM Virtualization Suitability

Component	OK as VM?	Notes
OpsMgr Databases (Operational, Data Warehouse, and Audit)	Generally no	Only virtualize OpsMgr databases in lab/test and with a very low number of managed computers.
VMM Server or Database	Generally yes (under 150 managed hosts)	OK as VM except with a high number of managed hosts.
OpsMgr Root Management Server (RMS)	Generally no	Memory and CPU intensive; not a good VM except in very small environments.
OpsMgr Additional Management Servers, Audit Collection Servers, and Gateway Servers	Yes	Subject to normal capacity limits of management, audit collection, and gateway servers.
VMM Self-Service Portal, VMM Library	Yes	Give libraries maximum network bandwidth.
OpsMgr Reporting Server	Generally yes	Except in very demanding reporting environments.
OpsMgr Web Console	Yes	Scale out with load-balanced web farm.

Summary

Because virtualization can save so much time and money, virtualized server workloads are found in most every datacenter and are rapidly becoming commonplace in networks of all sizes. This chapter clarified why having a management solution for virtualization components is vital for both smaller deployments, where risk is otherwise increased, and in scale-up scenarios, when individual virtualization hosts can assume very high-value roles. The chapter covered features of the native virtualization management packs and third-party approaches, and then focused on deploying Virtual Machine Manager. You can integrate VMM with Operations Manager to manage different virtualization technologies in a variety of heterogeneous networks. The chapter concluded with a discussion on best practices when virtualizing OpsMgr components.

CHAPTER 8

Management Pack Authoring

The primary goal of a management pack is to help Information Technology (IT) operations teams more effectively monitor the applications and services the organization relies on to conduct business. As organizations have come to expect IT to identify and resolve issues before the customer (internal or external) notices them, you will want to design your management packs with IT operations in mind.

A well-designed management pack (MP) supports this objective by providing actionable alert data to identify application performance and availability issues before these result in costly (and potentially embarrassing) outages. It provides alert and performance data in easily navigable views. Finally, a well-designed management pack meets this goal with the simplest design and lightest footprint on monitored systems. This chapter provides a blueprint of a successful management pack authoring process from start-to-finish, including the following:

▶ Management Pack Authoring Tools

▶ Designing and Building Your MP

▶ Best (and Worst) Practices for MP Design

▶ Building Custom Workflows

▶ Optimizing MP Performance (Minimizing the Monitoring Footprint)

▶ Testing and Troubleshooting

The chapter examines these concepts not only in theory but also in practice, demonstrating how to design, build, and instrument a management pack cognizant of IT operations and Microsoft best practices.

What's in a Management Pack?

Management packs contain the logic to discover, monitor, and manage applications using Operations Manager 2007. Here are the components of a management pack:

▶ **Classes and relationships**—These represent the application objects that are monitored and how they are connected. They represent the model of the application you are monitoring.

▶ **Discoveries**—This name is a bit of a misnomer, as it implies that you are searching for something that you don't know exists. Discoveries identify the agent components represented by classes.

▶ **Monitors**—Monitors measure the health of application components.

▶ **Tasks**—These are application commands either initiated by an operator or performed automatically in response to a detected problem.

▶ **Rules**—Rules collect information about the application. This can include performance data for trend reporting or events important to daily activities.

▶ **Views**—These present information collected by the management pack to operators, including event, alert, and performance data.

▶ **Knowledge**—Knowledge describes detailed information about detected problems, common causes, and potential resolutions. This may be the most important part of the management pack, as it is how knowledge of the application experts is communicated to the IT operations staff entrusted with daily administration.

▶ **Reports**—Use reports to consolidate historical data delivered from the data warehouse. This can deliver cost savings to the organization and assist in future planning by providing information on historical operation of the application and environment.

Before beginning the MP authoring process, let's discuss the tools you'll need for the task.

MP Authoring Tools

There are several tools you can use when authoring a management pack. These include the following:

▶ The Authoring console

▶ The Operations console

▶ An eXtensible Markup Language (XML) editor

▶ A script editor

The next sections describe these tools.

The Authoring Console

The Authoring console is the primary tool for authoring a management pack and the primary tool used in authoring concepts presented in this chapter. Operations Manager 2007 Release 2 (R2) significantly improves the Authoring console, and it provides the functionality to develop virtually every aspect of a management pack. However, even the most experienced management pack author may use one of the other tools available. Along with the Authoring console, the R2 Authoring Resource Kit should be considered required equipment. It contains tools vital in validating accuracy of your MP, as well as compliance with Microsoft best practices for MP authoring. You can download the R2 Authoring Resource Kit at
http://www.microsoft.com/downloads/details.aspx?FamilyID=9104af8b-ff87-45a1-81cd-b73e6f6b51f0&displaylang=en.

The Operations Console

The Operations console provides the ability to perform a subset of the authoring tasks available in the Authoring console. However, for novice MP authors, this console can be a valuable tool in the learning process. For example, if you cannot determine how to create a particular management pack element in the Authoring console, you can import the MP into a management group and continue the task in the Operations console; then export the MP and view the result in the Authoring console. Even as you gain experience in authoring MPs, you may find some tasks to be quicker and easier to complete using the Operations console. Many experienced MP authors will continue to use the Operations console for specific authoring tasks, and this is fine as long as you understand the limitations and side effects. These limitations include the following:

▶ Some operations are not possible, such as more object discoveries using VBScript or PowerShell.

▶ The Operations console automatically generates names for all management pack elements (discoveries, rules, monitors, and so on) and the resulting format does not conform to best practices, nor is it easy to understand.

When authoring in the Operations console, you will likely want to export your MP and update the XML names frequently to match your organization's MP naming conventions. You can do this easily by using the find-and-replace feature available in most XML editors. The "Naming Conventions" section discusses recommendations for MP naming.

An XML Editor

A management pack is an XML file, and in theory, you can edit it using Notepad. However, Notepad lacks the pretty formatting of a good XML editor that makes management pack XML easier to read. If you perform some of your MP authoring in the Operations console, an XML editor is necessary to clean up the XML to match your naming conventions.

You can spend hundreds of dollars on an XML editor, such as Altova's very popular XMLSpy (see http://www.altova.com/), but there are free editors that can meet the needs of most MP authors. Here are some examples:

▶ **MS XML Notepad 2007**—This free XML editor from Microsoft supports IntelliSense (Microsoft's implementation of auto complete), drag-and-drop between files, as well as XML file comparison (XML Diff, which highlights the differences between two XML files). You can download XML Notepad at http://www.microsoft.com/downloads/details.aspx?familyid=72d6aa49-787d-4118-ba5f-4f30fe913628&displaylang=en.

▶ **Notepad++**—This is an open-source multi-purpose editor that includes an XML plug-in providing format cleanup, making it a good tool for MP authoring. It is likely that most authors will find this more suitable for editing XML (especially for cut-and-paste operations) than XML Notepad. The disadvantage here is the lack of IntelliSense or XML Diff. Notepad++ is available at http://notepad-plus.sourceforge.net/uk/download.php.

TIP: VALIDATING THE MP XML

Many XML editors (including XML Notepad and Notepad++) will automatically verify the syntax of your management pack XML (called XSD validation) if you supply the management pack XML schema. The MP schema definition is contained in a file named *ManagementPackSchema.xsd*, located in the installation folder of the Authoring console (*%ProgramFiles%*\System Center MP Authoring Console 2007\MP Schema by default).

A Script Editor

You can use VBScript, JScript, and PowerShell in object discoveries, rules, monitors, and tasks in your management packs. Whether writing your own scripts from scratch or repurposing samples available on the Internet, it is very likely that you will need to work with scripts on multiple occasions. A number of script editors are available; including the following widely used editors:

▶ **Notepad++**—With the available PowerShell plug-in, Notepad++ (described in the previous section) can serve as a VBScript/JScript/PowerShell editor, in addition to serving as a XML editor, making it a great all-in-one tool.

▶ **PowerGUI**—PowerGUI is a good free PowerShell editor, but offers little support for other scripting languages. For additional information, see http://powergui.org/index.jspa.

Among commercially available script editors, you will find that PrimalScript 2009 Studio (http://www.primaltools.com) supports virtually every scripting language known to man (including VBScript, JScript, and PowerShell) and delivers advanced features including IntelliSense, versioning, and debugging functionality.

Scripting in OpsMgr 2007

Scripting is frequently an important part of the authoring process. You can write OpsMgr 2007 scripts in VBScript or JScript, and the agent runs the scripts. The agent launches a Cscript process for each script as it executes. This is exactly the same script engine used when running any VBScript on a Windows computer. OpsMgr uses the OpsMgr Scripting API (MOM.ScriptAPI) to submit data from the script back to the workflow in which the script is running. The API is used only to submit data to OpsMgr, not to obtain data from OpsMgr, which is often accomplished through the OpsMgr Software Development Kit (SDK). You can pass data to a script from a previous step in the workflow by using script parameters.

New in R2 are native modules to allow PowerShell scripts to be used for monitoring and discovery functions. However, the MP author must be very comfortable using the Authoring console (and ultimately XML), as neither the Operations nor Authoring consoles provide a wizard-driven GUI to create PowerShell-based discoveries, rules, or monitors. See the Operations Manager 2007 R2 Management Pack Module Reference at http://technet.microsoft.com/en-us/library/dd391800.aspx or http://msdn.microsoft.com/en-us/library/ee533840.aspx for additional information on these modules.

Preparing Your Development Workstation

You can write and test discovery and monitoring scripts outside a live management group. To prepare a development workstation for scripting, load the following:

▶ **An OpsMgr Agent**—This provides a local OpsMgr Event Log on your workstation so you can validate that events are being logged when expected.

▶ **A Script Editor**—Technically, you could use Windows Notepad, but it lacks the user-friendly color-coding, auto-correction, and IntelliSense features of a good script editor. See the "MP Authoring Tools" section for a discussion of authoring tools including script editors.

If you are new to OpsMgr scripting, you may find the scripting portion of this chapter to be more useful if you have a development workstation available to follow the examples.

NOTE: ABOUT THE SAMPLE SCRIPTS IN THIS CHAPTER

The authors have simplified the scripts in this chapter for demonstration purposes, removing error handling and some common debugging. Use the resources recommended in this chapter to learn about proper error handling and script debugging techniques for testing your OpsMgr scripts.

Types of Scripts in OpsMgr 2007 Management Packs

There are two categories of scripting in Operations Manager (OpsMgr)—Discovery and Monitoring. The next sections discuss the two types.

Discovery

Use a *discovery script* to discover the existence of an application, application components, or device. You can write a single discovery for multiple types of objects and multiple instances of an object type. The script will then submit the data to the management group, where the snapshot of discovered instances will be updated both on the agent in the OpsMgr health service cache and in the Operational database.

TIP: SUBMITTING DISCOVERY DATA IN A SCRIPT

Write your discovery script to submit discovery data on every execution, even if no instances of an object were discovered. If an application is uninstalled and the discovery script that discovered the instance does not submit data for a null result, OpsMgr will not know that the object no longer exists!

Monitoring

Use *monitoring scripts* to fulfill the requirements of a monitoring scenario where the off-the-shelf rules and monitors will not meet the need. You can use monitoring scripts for a variety of functions, including the following:

▶ **Identifying the Health State of an Object**—If you can determine whether a monitored object is healthy or unhealthy in a script, the object's health state can be represented in a Timed Script Two-State Monitor. For example, if an application folder growing larger than 1GB in size represents an application issue, you can monitor and detect this condition by using a script.

▶ **Logging an Event**—Scripts can be written to detect a condition and then log an event to the Operations Manager Event Log. One of the event-driven rules or monitors in OpsMgr could detect this event and raise an alert.

▶ **Collecting Performance Data**—If a Windows performance counter does not exist, a monitoring script can be used to collect and store the data in the Operational database and data warehouse as performance data. As an example, the monitoring script discussed in the "Create the Custom Data Source" section of this chapter collects the size of a folder in Windows so the data can be used to both trigger and alert when the folder becomes too large. You can also leverage the same folder size data collected by this script to provide data for graphs in a performance view and report.

ADDITIONAL RESOURCES FOR MONITORING SCRIPTS

Here are several tutorials explaining how to use monitoring scripts for the purposes mentioned in this section in far more detail than provided in this chapter. You may want to check out these resources after completing the examples in this chapter:

▶ **How to Create a Timed Script Two-State Monitor—**
http://www.systemcentercentral.com/Downloads/DownloadsDetails/tabid/
144/IndexID/7362/Default.aspx

▶ **How to Use a Monitoring Script to Collect Performance Data—**
http://www.systemcentercentral.com/Downloads/DownloadsDetails/tabid/
144/IndexID/7803/Default.aspx

Nuts and Bolts of the OpsMgr Scripting API

The OpsMgr Scripting API is comprised of a number of properties and methods used to collect, store, and submit data back to Operations Manager. A *property* defines the characteristics of an object. A *method* is a programming term used to describe the capabilities of an object. In the text that follows, you will see several basic examples of some of the capabilities of the OpsMgr Scripting API.

The top-level object in the OpsMgr Scripting API is MOMScriptAPI. Creating an instance of the MOMScriptAPI object in VBScript is quite simple. Simply type the following in a script editor on your development workstation and save the file with a .vbs extension:

```
Dim oAPI
Set oAPI = WScript.CreateObject("MOM.ScriptAPI")
```

Creating the MOMScriptAPI object (called *instantiating an instance* of the object) unlocks all the properties and methods of this object for use in a monitoring or discovery script. Table 8.1 lists a description of the methods available to the MOMScriptAPI.

TABLE 8.1 Methods of the MOMScriptAPI Object

Method	Description
CreateDiscoveryData	Creates a new discovery data object, which stores discovery data and submits the collected data back to the management group. This method is used in discovery scripts.
CreatePropertyBag	Creates a new property bag object, which will temporarily store discovery data as a collection of name-value pairs. A common use of this method is to store data used in a custom performance object.
CreateTypedPropertyBag	Creates a special property bag object, enabling you to specify the data type stored in the property bag.
LogScriptEvent	Writes a message to the Operations Manager Event Log. This is useful for logging events to trigger alerts, and in logging script failures to make troubleshooting easier.
Return	Submits discovery and monitoring data back to the management server and ends execution of the script.

Logging an Event

Knowing how to log an event to the OpsMgr Event Log is a necessity for anyone writing OpsMgr scripts. Logging an event can be useful for a variety of debugging, testing, and monitoring tasks. Fortunately, this is a simple task using the `LogScriptEvent` method.

Carrying forward the code from the previous section needed to create an instance of the MOMScriptAPI object, all you need to log an event is one additional line of code. An additional line beginning with a ', called a *comment*, is added to provide a description of what is performed in the script. In VBScript, the ' at the beginning of a line tells the scripting engine (Cscript) to ignore this line:

```
'This script creates an instance of MOMScriptAPI and Logs and Event to the →
OpsMgr Event Log
Dim oAPI
Set oAPI = WScript.CreateObject("MOM.ScriptAPI")

oAPI.LogScriptEvent "Test Event", 1000, 0, "This is my first test event with →
OpsMgr scripting!"
```

Save this file as test.vbs. To test your work, open a command prompt, change to the folder where you saved the script, and run the following command:

```
Cscript /nologo test.vbs
```

Now open the OpsMgr Event Log, and you should see the event displayed in Figure 8.1.

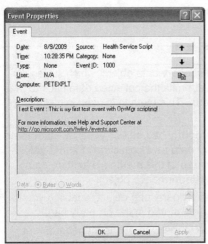

FIGURE 8.1 Event written by the test script

Using the /nologo switch with Cscript when testing your scripts; it suppresses the Microsoft copyright message normally echoed to the screen. This makes redirecting XML script output to a file rendering in a browser or XML editor easier, as you do not have to remove the extra text manually.

Scripting for Health Monitoring and Displaying Performance

As mentioned in the "Scripting in OpsMgr 2007" section, you can use a monitoring script to collect and return data to other modules in a workflow to use in a script-based monitor or display in performance views and reports. When data is collected in an OpsMgr script, it is stored in an object called a *property bag*.

The property bag object stores data in a collection of one or more name-value pairs. As an example, you could write a script that defines a folder name and folder size, and stores these values in a property bag object. If another script retrieves the name and size of the c:\windows\temp folder, which is 200KB in size, the property bag would contain the following name value pairs:

```
name, "temp"
size, 200
```

This can be demonstrated with relative ease. Carrying forward the code needed to create an instance of the MOMScriptAPI object, you need only a few lines of VBScript to perform the action described in this example. Comment lines explain the actions of the script. The following example uses the CreatePropertyBag method of the MOMScriptAPI object to create a property bag object (MOMPropertyBag):

```
'This script collects the name and size of a folder and stores the results
'in a property bag
'Declare variables
Dim objFSO, strFolder, strFolderSize, strDateModified
Dim Folder, FileColl, FileCount
Dim oAPI, oBag

'Create Objects
Set oAPI = WScript.CreateObject("MOM.ScriptAPI") 'MOMScriptAPI Object
Set oBag = oAPI.CreatePropertyBag() 'Create Property Bag
Set objFSO = CreateObject("Scripting.FileSystemObject") 'Create FileSystem Object

'Set name of the folder to retrieve
strFolder = "c:\windows\temp"

'Retrieve target folder
        Set Folder=objFSO.GetFolder(strFolder)
'Retrieve folder size (in bytes)
        strFolderSize = objFSO.GetFolder(strFolder).Size
```

```
'Add folder name & size (in kilobytes) to the Property Bag.
        oBag.AddValue "FolderSize", CDbl(Int(strFolderSize/1024))
        oBag.AddValue "FolderName", Folder.Name

'Close the Property Bag and submit
        oAPI.AddItem oBag

        oAPI.ReturnItems()
```

Save this file as test2.vbs. To test your work, open a command prompt, change to the folder where you saved the script, and run the following command:

```
Cscript /nologo test2.vbs
```

You should see data very similar to the following returned to the window in which you ran the script. This is the property bag object (in XML form) that would be passed to the next module in the workflow. Notice the folder size and name in the output:

```
<Collection><DataItem type="System.PropertyBagData"
time="2009-07-27T20:13:10.1332500-05:00" sourceHealthServiceId=
"F4BFD0E3-C4D2-C0D0-1896-EA760C886476"><Property Name="FolderSize"
VariantType="5">30858</Property><Property Name="FolderName"
VariantType="8">Temp</Property></DataItem></Collection>
```

When authoring a monitoring script that returns property bag data (a very common OpsMgr scripting scenario), a great way to verify that the script works before inserting it into a rule or monitor in a management pack is by testing from the command line, to verify the property bag is returned.

TIP: ADDITIONAL HELP WITH MONITORING SCRIPTS

You may want to check this detailed tutorial, which explains how to use a monitoring script and the property bag object to collect performance data step-by-step:

How to Use a Monitoring Script to Collect Performance Data—
http://www.systemcentercentral.com/Downloads/DownloadsDetails/tabid/144/Inde
xID/7803/Default.aspx

Using a Script in Discovery

Unlike monitoring scripts, you cannot create a discovery in the Operations console; use the Authoring console to create script-based object discoveries. Similar to monitoring scripts, you can often write and test discovery scripts on your development workstation. Even simple discovery scripts are a bit more complex than their monitoring counterparts as multiple objects, methods, and properties are involved.

The short sample discovery script used in the next example checks for the presence of a folder installed on computers running the application targeted for monitoring. The CreateDiscoveryData method of the MOMScriptAPI object is used to create a Discovery Data object (MOMDiscoveryData), which will contain the discovery data returned to the management group. The Discovery Data object has properties and methods of its own, as listed in Table 8.2.

TABLE 8.2 Methods of the Discovery Data Object

Method	Description
AddProperty	Adds a named value to the monitoring object.
AddInstance	Adds an item to the collection of discovery data.
CreateClassInstance	Creates a new monitoring class instance.
CreateRelationshipInstance	Creates a new relationship instance object.

The CreateClassInstance method of the Discovery Data object will be used to create a Class Instance object (MOMClassInstance). This represents a monitoring object—an instance of the discovered object class.

There are several other objects, methods, and properties involved, a complete discussion of which could go on for several pages:

```
'Declare variables
Dim SourceID, ManagedEntityId, TargetComputer
Dim oAPI, oDiscoveryData, oInst
Dim oArgs, oFSO

    'Create object to accept script arguments (parameters)
        Set oArgs = WScript.Arguments

        'Define the 3 arguments required by every discovery script
        SourceId = oArgs(0)
        ManagedEntityId = oArgs(1)
        TargetComputer = oArgs(2)

        Set oFSO = CreateObject("Scripting.FileSystemObject")

        Set oAPI = CreateObject("MOM.ScriptAPI")
        Set oDiscoveryData = oAPI.CreateDiscoveryData(0, SourceID, ManagedEntityId)

        'Check for the folder that indicates presence of the application we are →
discovering
        If (oFSO.FolderExists("c:\program files\ACME\POSBatchProcess\Processing")) →
Then

        'Create an instance of the class
                Set oInst = oDiscoveryData.CreateClassInstance("$MPElement[Name= →
'Unleashed.POSBatchProcess.Version1.POSJobProcessingServer']$")

        'Add properties of the class to the discovered instance
                Call oInst.AddProperty ("$MPElement[Name= →
'Windows!Microsoft.Windows.Computer']/PrincipalName$", TargetComputer)
```

```
            Call oInst.AddProperty("$MPElement[Name='System!System.Entity'] →
/DisplayName$", "POS Job Processing Server")
            call oDiscoveryData.AddInstance(oInst)
        End If


    'Submit the discovery data to the management group
    oAPI.Return(oDiscoveryData)
```

Save this file as test3.vbs. Testing discovery scripts is a bit more complex and less certain than monitoring scripts. Discovery scripts have three required parameters that are passed to the script as part of the workflow. Table 8.3 provides a description of discovery script parameters. For testing purposes, you need Globally Unique Identifiers (GUIDs) to represent the first two parameters. Any GUID you can find in the Operations console or using the Command Shell will suffice.

To test your work, open a command prompt, change to the folder where you saved the script, and run the following command:

```
Cscript /nologo test3.vbs {f37790e5-1cb5-cab0-62b9-ef69fe75543d} →
{f37790e5-1cb5-cab0-62b9-ef69fe75543d} server.contoso.msft
```

You should see data very similar to the following returned to the window in which you ran the script. This is the discovered class instance (in XML form) that would be passed to the management group and inserted into the Operational database. Notice the class name and properties in the output:

```
<DataItem type="System.DiscoveryData" time="2009-07-27T21:15:14.3676250-05:00"
sourceHealthServiceId="F4BFD0E3-C4D2-C0D0-1896-EA760C886476"><DiscoveryType>
0</DiscoveryType><DiscoverySourceType>0</DiscoverySourceType>
<DiscoverySourceObjectId>{F37790E5-1CB5-CAB0-62B9-EF69FE75543D}
</DiscoverySourceObjectId> <DiscoverySourceManagedEntity>
{F37790E5-1CB5-CAB0-62B9-EF69FE75543D}</DiscoverySourceManagedEntity>
<ClassIn-
stances><ClassInstanceTypeId="$MPElement[Name='Unleashed.POSBatchProcess.Version1.POS
JobProcessingServer']$">
<Settings><Setting><Name>$MPElement[Name='Windows!Microsoft.Windows.Computer']
/PrincipaName$</Name><Value>server.contoso.msft</Value></Setting><Setting><Name>
$MPElement[Name='System!System.Entity']/DisplayName$</Name>
<Value> POS Job Processing Server </Value></Setting></Settings></ClassInstance>
</ClassInstances></DataItem>
```

When authoring a discovery script, you will want to test from the command line to verify that discovery data is returned. This is a good start to verify that the script works before inserting it into an object discovery in a management pack. However, you will have to allow the discovery to run in a live (test) management group to ensure that the XPath contained in the script is accurate.

TABLE 8.3 Required Parameters for Discovery Scripts

Method	Description
`$MPElement$`	The workflow ID.
`$Target/Id$`	The base-managed entity ID for the object the workflow is running against.
Computer Principal Name (in XPath format)	For hosted class discovery only.

TIP: ADDITIONAL HELP WITH DISCOVERY SCRIPTS

The OpsMgr product team provides a detailed guide explaining how to create and use discovery scripts step-by-step. As you have seen, discovery scripts involve XPath (XML), so it is not for the faint of heart.

You can download the Discovery Scripting Guide from http://www.opsmanjam.com/OpsManJam%20Library/Management%20Packs/Scripting%20Guide%20for%20Discovery.zip.

Designing Your Management Pack

At this stage of the process, you are not building anything in any of your authoring tools, but rather developing the logical representation of your application. This ensures that you will have specific objects when you begin actual construction of the MP.

The MP design process consists of the following high-level steps:

- ► Identifying application components (classes)
- ► How the components are related (relationships)
- ► Defining the health model (monitoring and health rollup)
- ► Tips and best practices

Typically, each phase of developing a management pack is an iterative process, so don't expect everything to work the first time. It is also a group process, involving both the MP author(s) (you, in this case) and the subject matter experts for the application targeted by the MP you are developing. To describe the components of an application, how those components are related, and how to monitor their health requires in-depth knowledge of application architecture and function. This is true for all organizations engaging in MP authoring, even Microsoft! The MP authors of the Operations Manager team interact with the product team architects for the target application in all phases of the authoring process, with the intent of capturing their deep understanding of how the application functions and how to measure its health most effectively. Using whiteboard sessions and successive test cycles, you will frequently uncover new ideas of how to more effectively model and monitor your application. This is a normal and healthy part of the MP authoring process.

Identifying Application Components (Classes)

The first step in designing a management pack is designing the service model for your application (sometimes called the *façade*). This includes answering a number of questions, including the following:

▶ **What components in the application need to be described?**

These components will make up the first iteration of the object classes defined for the application.

▶ **What information should be collected? What properties of the class are of interest?**

As an example, if you are writing a management pack for an antivirus application, you may want to define properties on the classes to capture application version number or installation path.

▶ **Can more than one instance reside on a single server?**

If so, you will need to define a key property to identify the class uniquely. Examples of multi-instance components in an MP include SQL databases or IIS websites. In the case of a SQL database, the key property is the database name, which, along with the host server and SQL Server instance, uniquely identifies a given database on a particular server.

▶ **Is this application typically the only one hosted on the server, or just one of many?**

The answer to this question determines what abstract class your classes will be based on. This information will be useful when choosing a base class and defining class properties.

How the Components Are Related (Relationships)

The next step is to consider the types of relationships required between the application components. Here are the three types of relationships in a management pack:

▶ **Hosting**—The *hosting* relationship is the most specific relationship type in Operations Manager. It is a one-to-many relationship—one host hosts one or more instances (targets or hosted objects). In this type of relationship, the hosted object cannot exist without its host. You typically will use this to define relationships between components on the same health service.

An example of a hosting relationship is an instance of the Windows Server 2003 Operating System hosting multiple Windows services.

▶ **Containment**—The next most specific type of relationship in Operations Manager is the *containment* relationship. This is a many-to-many relationship in which one object "contains" one or more objects. However, in a containment relationship, the contained objects do not depend on the container for their existence.

An example of a containment relationship is an OpsMgr group containing objects, such as computers or databases. If a database is removed from a group, the database continues to exist.

▶ **Reference**—If one type of object uses or works with another, but does not host or contain the other, then the objects are considered to have a *reference* relationship.

As an example, two Microsoft SQL 2005 server databases participating in log shipping (one being the publisher and the other the subscriber) would have a reference relationship.

Defining the Health Model (Health Rollup)

The health model of an application is the logical representation of how the health of the application components affects one another. Do not automatically assume that the health of all child classes should be rolled up to their parent; think carefully about what the health of one application component means for another to accurately reflect the operating health of the target class.

As an example, just because a SQL Server database is offline does not mean that the SQL instance (SQL DB Engine) is unhealthy; therefore, the Microsoft SQL management pack does not roll up the health of the SQL database class to the SQL DB Engine that hosts the database.

Two elements are necessary to roll up health from one application component to another, as follows:

▶ **Relationship**—For the health of one object class to affect another, they must share a hosting or containment relationship.

▶ **Rollup Monitor**—A rollup monitor is used to reflect (or roll up) the health of one or more child application class instances to their host.

Here are the two types of rollup monitors:

▶ **Dependency Rollup Monitor**—Used to roll up health across object classes. As an example, in the Windows Operating System management packs, the collective health of monitored Windows services is reflected on the Windows Server Operating System object class using a dependency rollup monitor.

▶ **Aggregate Rollup Monitor**—Used to roll up the health of two or more like monitors. As an example, the Windows Core Services Rollup monitor is an Aggregate Rollup Monitor that rolls up the health of Windows Service Monitors to a single state of health. Aggregate Rollup Monitors are typically the target of Dependency Rollup Monitors.

The ultimate goal of the health model is to identify the symptoms of the error conditions that an application component may experience in the health state of that component. Creating an appropriate health model for your application ensures that component health state is appropriately reflected in the Operations console to the operator.

Design Best Practices

Here are some best design processes:

▶ **Create the simplest health model possible, containing only classes of interest for monitoring**—It is not the job of OpsMgr to perform inventory. Although possible through Operations Manager, hardware and software inventory are intended for System Center Configuration Manager (ConfigMgr) agents, which are architected for this purpose.

▶ **If you aren't going to treat classes differently, consider consolidating them**—As an example, if you have created four classes for various server roles, but discover and monitor them all in the same way, you may need only one class!

Design Worst Practices (AKA Good Stuff NOT to Do)

Here are some worst design processes:

▶ **Create, discover, and monitor classes that have more instances than you can effectively monitor and report on**—Typically, you do not want to create more than 50–100 instances per hosting parent. You could create a File class with an instance for every file on the Windows OS, but this would be impossible for your server operators to manage and will generate tremendous load on OpsMgr.

▶ **Create classes containing attributes that frequently change**—If the properties of a class change often, this may potentially generate an unacceptable load on the root management server (RMS). As an example, if you create an object class named File and discover every file in the c:\windows folder on every managed server, the load would almost certainly overwhelm the RMS. Every new instance of an object or change to an existing object instance represents change, which must be calculated and updated in the Operational database by the RMS.

▶ **Create object discoveries scheduled to run to frequently and/or at the same time as other discoveries**—Microsoft best practices suggest that object discoveries should not be scheduled to run more frequently than once an hour. See the sidebar "What is the Right Frequency for Discovery?" later in this chapter for additional detail.

Discovering Application Components

Discovery is the process of locating instances of classes defined in a management pack. Object discoveries are processes that identify objects on an Operations Manager agent that should be monitored by workflows in a management pack. These discoveries are scheduled to run on a periodic basis so that any changes, additions, or deletions to these components are discovered during the next scheduled execution of the discovery. Remember, an object will not be monitored until it is discovered.

The most common types of discoveries use the Registry, Windows Management Instrumentation (WMI), and scripts (VBScript, JScript, and PowerShell) to locate application components. It is important to remember that you do not need to discover all components of the application at once. Using layers of discovery (sometimes called *progressive discovery*) allows the MP author to minimize the impact of monitoring on managed systems. WMI queries and scripts (VBScript, JScript, or PowerShell) will have a more noticeable footprint on managed systems, and you will want to target them more narrowly.

The recommended strategy for discovering application components is to begin with a registry-based discovery targeted at a broad abstract class, such as Windows Computer or Windows Operating System (or Windows Server Computer or Windows Server Operating System if your application only runs on servers). This is your *root discovery* or *seed discovery*, an example of which is illustrated in Figure 8.2.

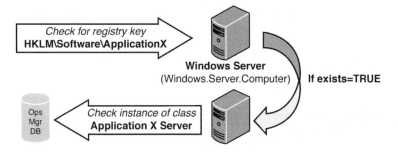

FIGURE 8.2 Root discovery sample

After the root discovery successfully discovers the presence of the target application using the Registry, for deeper discovery, you can target WMI or scripts to the application class, which in this case is the Point-of-Sale (POS) Batch Processing Application. This prevents deeper (and potentially more resource-intensive) discovery from running on computers not hosting an instance of the target application.

WHAT IS A WORKFLOW?

Workflow is a term you will find mentioned frequently in blogs and forums on OpsMgr, but seldom explained. A *workflow* is a group of modules that run in succession, passing data (known as *dataitems*) between them.

Here are the four types of modules in Operations Manager:

- ► Data Source
- ► Condition Detection
- ► Probe Action
- ► Write Action

These four types are the basis of over 300 modules available out of the box in Operations Manager 2007. Modules are the building blocks used to create every type of discovery, rule, monitor, and task in Operations Manager. You can use the

Authoring console to combine these modules types in unique ways to create your own custom workflows.

The "Modules: The Building Blocks of Workflows" section later in this chapter discusses module types and custom workflows.

Discovery Best Practices

Here are some best discovery practices:

► **Create a root (seed) application class that can be discovered through the registry**—This provides a more specific target class for more detailed WMI and script discoveries.

► **Target a registry discovery at the Operating System class first**—This allows search for the existence of the application across all servers without running WMI or script discoveries on every monitored system.

Discovery Worst Practices

Here are some worst discovery practices:

► **Run object discoveries too frequently**—Ask yourself how quickly the application must be discovered once installed on a system; the answer is generally not more than every few hours to daily.

► **Use WMI and script discoveries to discover root (seed) class**—Targeting these more resource-intensive discovery methods to broad operating system classes (representing all or a large percentage of OpsMgr agents) may ultimately result in OpsMgr workflows consuming unacceptable amounts of resources on monitored systems.

Now that you have defined a health model and service model for your application and discussed the optimal strategy for discovering these components, let's step through the process of turning these theories into reality in the Authoring console.

Building Your Management Pack

The next sections develop classes, relationships, discoveries, monitors, and other components for a sample application, the Point-of-Sale Batch Processing Application, using components and methods that apply to many applications in the real world. This may provide you with some source material to repurpose and expand on these examples for a number of custom monitoring scenarios you may encounter.

The Point-of-Sale Batch Processing Application

The Point-of-Sale (POS) Batch Processing Application processes job requests submitted to an application server from hand-held barcode scanners used by employees fulfilling orders and tracking product inventory in a distribution warehouse. The requests are submitted across a wireless network to a distribution server responsible for receiving and routing order requests. Figure 8.3 illustrates this application.

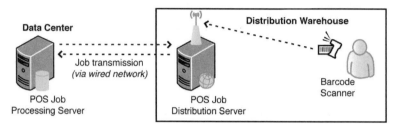

FIGURE 8.3 POS Batch Processing Application

Successive sections will step through an overview of the process and tasks for modeling the application and creating a management pack for the POS Batch Processing Application.

The application consists of the following two server roles:

▶ **POS Job Distribution Server**—The POS Job Distribution Server receives requests from wireless barcode scanners. It then formats and forwards job requests to the POS Job Processing Server for processing and order completion.

▶ **POS Job Processing Server**—The POS Job Processing Server receives the requests from the POS Distribution Server, updates inventory, and customer records. It then returns the completed order manifest to the distribution server, where warehouse personnel can retrieve and fulfill the order.

To simulate these application roles in your test environment, run the following scripts in the online content included for this chapter. You may install the roles on the same server or separate servers:

▶ **POS Job Distribution Server**—Run CreatePOSJobDistServer.ps1 on the target system.

▶ **POS Job Processing Server**—Run CreatePOSJobProcessServer.ps1 on the target system.

Naming Conventions

Operations Manager does not enforce a strict naming convention, although you can observe one in every management pack delivered by Microsoft. The naming convention resembles the dot naming convention (called a *namespace*) used in .NET programming languages.

Although Operations Manager does not enforce this, it is considered a best practice that all elements within a management pack use a common namespace.

The recommended syntax to use as the prefix for your management pack objects is as follows:

```
Vendor.ProductName.Version.
```

As an example, the namespace in the Windows 2003 Active Directory management pack is the following:

```
Microsoft.Windows.Server.AD.2003.
```

Not all properties of objects (whether a class, rule, monitor, and so on) are required to be unique. Technically, you could give multiple rules the same display name. However, this would only be confusing to operators and ultimately difficult to manage.

With that in mind, Microsoft recommends that all objects—such as rules, monitors, tasks, and images—use the namespace prefix you create for your management pack. This usage makes it easy for operators to find objects in the database through the Operations console and when using the Operations Manager Shell. Fortunately, the Authoring console makes using the same namespace prefix quite easy. You simply replace the "NewElement" shown in Figure 8.4 with the unique value for the object you are creating, whether it is a class, discovery, rule, monitor, and so on.

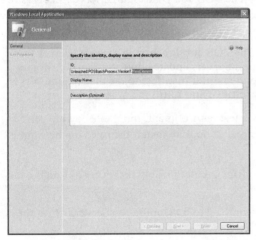

FIGURE 8.4 Namespace auto completion in the R2 Authoring console

The namespace for the POS Batch Processing Application will be the following:

```
Unleashed.POSBatchProcess.Version1
```

Classes and Relationships

One of the first things you will notice when creating a class type in the Authoring console is you are prompted to choose a *base class*. Your class will inherit all properties, monitoring definitions, and relationships defined for the base class, so these do not need to be defined again.

INHERITANCE AND SPECIALIZATION

Fundamental to creating classes and choosing base class is understanding the concepts of inheritance and specialization. The article "MP Creation ZEN using the R2 MP Authoring Console," available at http://www.systemcentercentral.com/Details/tabid/147/IndexID/24878/Default.aspx, provides a good explanation of how these work.

This raises the obvious question: "Which base class should be used?"

The answer is: *It depends*. More specifically, it depends on the type of application and the MP author's desired health model. Let's look at the base classes recommended by Microsoft and the advantages each brings to developing health and service models. Table 8.4 contains a list of the most commonly used base classes and the default behavior and inherent advantages of each.

TABLE 8.4 Common Base Classes

Class	Description
Microsoft.Windows. ComputerRole	An application that is a Windows-based server role (such as SQL Server, DNS Server, Exchange Server), and is often the only application installed on the server. This class is hosted by the Windows Computer class has automatic health rollup to the Windows Computer.
Microsoft.Windows. LocalApplication	A standalone application that is not a server role, and represents one of many applications installed on a server. This class is hosted by the Windows Computer class and does NOT have automatic health rollup to the Windows Computer.
Microsoft.Windows. Application. Component	An application component that is part of a local application or server role. There are no pre-defined relationships. The MP author must define the desired hosting relationship.
Microsoft.System Center.Instance Group *and* .ComputerGroup	These are groups used for logical grouping of similar components. Groups are unhosted singleton classes that will appear in group lists.
System.Service	Distributed application; used for health rollup of an application as a whole. Like groups, these are also unhosted singleton classes. Groups are unhosted singleton classes that will show up in group lists. These will appear in Distributed Application view.

As shown in Table 8.4, there are base classes that automatically provide health rollup to the hosting class and others that do not. When there are multiple instances of an application component to discover, the Windows Application Component class gives you the flexibility to define the desired hosting relationship.

Understanding these characteristics makes it easier to choose the appropriate base class for a given monitoring scenario.

NOTE: SINGLETON CLASS

A *singleton* class is a special type of class where there is only one instance of the class. The class is really the instance and, as such, needs no discovery. The root management server will always manage a singleton class. Groups in Operations Manager are singleton classes.

Service and Health Model in the POS Batch Processing Application

Figure 8.5 shows a diagram of the service model (classes and relationships) and health model (health rollup) of the fictional sample application discussed in this chapter. Let's look at how this diagram explains the model, and why the base classes shown were selected.

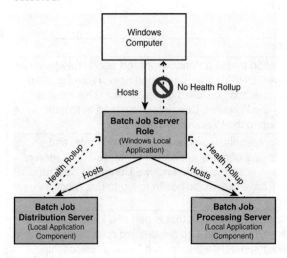

FIGURE 8.5 Service and health model for the POS Batch Processing Application

Using the questions in the "Designing Your Management Pack" section of this chapter as a guide, the following are the object classes defined for the application. For clarity, the rationale behind the base classes selected is also provided:

▶ **POS Batch Job Server Role**—The POS Batch Job Server Role is a server application, but not the primary or only role on a server. The application developed here used the Windows local application for the base class, so the author can define health rollup.

► **POS Job Distribution Server**—This is a specialized POS Batch Job Application Server Role not installed on every server. The base class for this role is *Local Application Component*. This allows the MP author to define the relationship to the appropriate local application.

► **POS Job Processing Server**—This is a specialized POS Batch Job Application Server Role not installed on every server. As with the POS Job Distribution Server class, the base class for this role is Local Application Component.

NOTE: DOES THE APPLICATION COMPONENT REQUIRE A CLASS?

It is not always appropriate to create a class for an application component. A class was not defined for barcode scanners, as warehouse personnel will power them on and off on-demand. The device displays an error code in the event of malfunction informing operator of corrective action. Because you cannot reliably discover and monitor these devices, no object class is necessary.

Using the R2 Authoring Console to Create Object Classes and Relationships

Now it is time to start defining object classes and relationships. Start by creating the management pack:

1. From the Start Menu, select Programs -> System Center Operations Manager R2 -> Authoring Console.

2. From the File menu, select New -> Empty Management Pack.

3. In the Management Pack Identity field, enter **Unleashed.POSBatchProcess.Version1** (shown in Figure 8.6) and click Next.

4. In the Display Name field, enter **Unleashed Point-of-Sale Batch Processing** and then click Create.

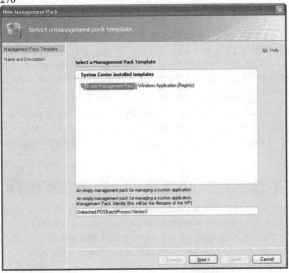

FIGURE 8.6 Adding the management pack identity

Creating the Object Classes and Relationships

The first class you will define is the POS Batch Job Server Role and its relationship to the Windows Server Operating System. Perform the following steps:

1. In the Authoring console, select the Service Model workspace and then the Classes node.

2. In the Object pane (top center) of the console, right-click and select New -> Windows Local Application. Notice that the namespace established for this MP is carried forward automatically.

3. Enter the following information, displayed in Figure 8.7:

    ▶ In the ID field, enter **Unleashed.POSBatchProcess.Version1. ApplicationRole**.

    ▶ In the Display Name field, enter **Unleashed POS Batch Process Version1 Application Role**. Click Next.

4. On the Key Properties screen, accept the defaults and click Finish.

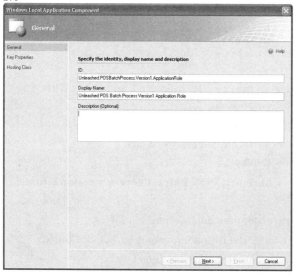

FIGURE 8.7 Completing the General screen

Next, create the object classes and relationships for the specific POS Batch Processing Application roles.

Start by performing the following steps to create the POS Job Distribution Server class and hosting relationship:

1. In the Authoring console, select the Service Model workspace and then the Classes node.

2. In the Object pane (top center) of the console, right-click and select New -> Windows Local Application Component.

3. On the General screen, enter the following and then click Next:

   ▶ **ID—Unleashed.POSBatchProcess.Version1. POSJobDistributionServer**

   ▶ **Display Name—Unleashed POS Batch Process Version1 Job Distribution Server**

4. Accept the defaults on the Key Properties screen and click Next.

5. On the Hosting Class screen, enter the following values and then click Finish:

   ▶ **Hosting Class**—Use the drop down to select Unleashed.POSBatchProcess.Version1.ApplicationRole.

   ▶ **Hosting Relationship ID—Unleashed.POSBatchProcess.Version1. AppRoleHostsPOSDistServer.**

   ▶ **Hosting Relationship Name—POS Batch Job Server Role Hosts POS Job Distribution Server.**

Now create the POS Job Processing Server class and hosting relationship. Perform the following steps:

1. In the Authoring console, select the Service Model workspace and then the Classes node.

2. In the Object pane (top center) of the console, right-click and select New -> Windows Local Application Component.

3. On the General screen, enter the following values, and then click Next:

   ▶ **ID—Unleashed.POSBatchProcess.Version1. POSJobProcessingServer**

   ▶ **Display Name—Unleashed POS Batch Process Version1 Job Processing Server**

4. On the Key Properties screen, accept the defaults and click Next.

5. On the Hosting Class screen, enter the following values and click Finish:

   ▶ **Hosting Class**—Use the drop down to select Unleashed.POSBatchProcess.Version1.ApplicationRole.

   ▶ **Hosting Relationship ID—Unleashed.POSBatchProcess.Version1. AppRoleHostsPOSProcessServer.**

   ▶ **Hosting Relationship Name—POS Batch Job Server Role Hosts POS Job Processing Server.**

Object Discoveries

You now have created the object classes and relationships in the service and health model described in Figure 8.5. Next, you will create the Object Discoveries to identify installed instances of these classes on agent-managed servers.

Here are the discovery methods for each object class and rationale:

▶ **POS Batch Job Server Role**—The POS Batch Job Server Role is a server application, but not the primary or only role on a server.

▶ **Discovery Method**—The discovery method can be discovered through the Windows Registry. All servers with the following registry key have one or more POS Batch Processing v1.0 application roles installed:

   ▶ **Key**—HKLM\Software\ACME\POSBatchProcess

   ▶ **Value**—Version = 1.0

▶ **POS Job Distribution Server**—This is a specialized POS Batch Job Server Role not installed on every server.

The role must be discovered separately using WMI. Here is the WMI query:

```
Select * from CIM_DataFile where
Name = "c:\\program files\\ACME\\POSBatchProcess\\POSJobDistConfig.ini"
```

▶ **POS Job Processing Server**—This is a specialized POS Batch Job Server Role not installed on every server.

You must discover the role separately using VBScript that checks for the presence of the folder *%ProgramFiles%*\ACME\POSBatchProcess\ Processing. The discovery script is included with the online content for this chapter.

TIP: BEST PRACTICES FOR DISCOVERY

The strategy described in this section follows Microsoft best practices for discovery, by initially discovering the presence of the application using a lightweight discovery method (Registry). You can then target deeper discovery to this object class, minimizing the number of systems on which deep (and more resource-intensive) discovery will be executed.

Now that you know the methods used to discover instances of each class, you will create the object discoveries that will identify instances of each class on agent-managed servers.

Perform the following steps to create the object discovery for the POS Batch Job Server Role class:

1. In the Authoring console, select the Health Model workspace and then the Discoveries node.

2. In the Object pane (top center) of the console, right-click and select New -> Registry (Filtered) to launch the Registry Discovery wizard.

3. On the General screen, enter the following values, as displayed in Figure 8.8, and then click Next:

   ► **Element ID—Unleashed.POSBatchProcess.Version1. DiscoverPOSAppRole**

   ► **Display Name—Unleashed POS Batch Process Job Server Role Discovery**

   ► **Target—Microsoft.Windows.Server.OperatingSystem**

   ► **Category—Discovery**

4. On the Schedule screen, set the Run every: interval to **1** Hour and click Next.

5. On the Computer screen, accept the default and click Next.

6. On the Specify the Registry Attribute to Be Collected screen, click the Add button.

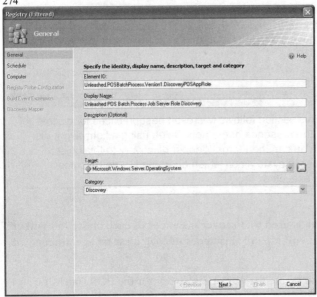

FIGURE 8.8 Specifying the identity, display name, description, target, and category

7. On the Edit Attribute Properties screen, enter the following values, click OK, and then Next:

   ► **Key or Value**—Value

   ► **Name**—**POSJobServer**

   ► **Path**—**HKLM\Software\ACME\POSBatchProcess\Version**

   ► **Attribute Type**—String

8. On the Build Event Expression screen, click Insert. In the Expression Builder interface, enter the following values displayed in Figure 8.9 and click Next:

   ► **Parameter Name**—Values/POSJOBServer

   ► **Operator**—Matches Wildcard

   ► **Value**—**1***

9. On the Discovery Mapper screen, use the Class ID drop down to select the Unleashed.POSBatchProcess.Version1.ApplicationRole.

10. In the Key Properties (required) text box, use the flyout tool to select (Host = Windows Computer), Windows Computer (Principal Name).

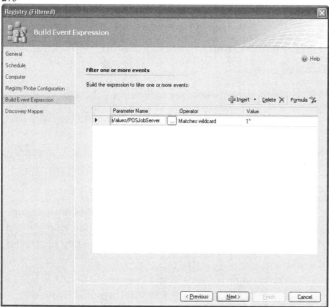

FIGURE 8.9 Building the expression for the event

WHAT IS THE RIGHT FREQUENCY FOR DISCOVERY?

When authoring object discoveries in a management pack, it can be challenging to determine the appropriate frequency for discovery. During testing, you would want to set the frequency more frequently—perhaps every 2 minutes. Production discoveries should run less often.

Microsoft recommends scheduling registry discoveries for 60 minutes at minimum. More resource-intensive WMI and script-based discoveries should only be run as often as required. Generally, you would schedule these to run once every 4 hours to as much as 24 hours. Determine how quickly you need to discover changes in application resources in your environment, and set the frequency accordingly with Microsoft guidelines in mind.

Perform the following steps to create the object discovery for the POS Job Distribution Server class:

1. In the Authoring console, select the Health Model workspace and then the Discoveries node.

2. In the Object pane (top center) of the console, right-click and select New -> WMI to launch the WMI Discovery wizard.

3. On the General screen, enter the following values and then click Next:

    ▶ **Element ID—Unleashed.POSBatchProcess.Version1. DiscoverPOSDistSvr**

▶ **Display Name—Unleashed POS Job Distribution Server Discovery**

▶ **Target—Unleashed POSBatchProcess.Version1.ApplicationRole**

▶ **Category**—Discovery

4. On the Configure WMI Settings screen, enter the following values and click Next:

    ▶ **WMI Namespace—root\cimv2**

    ▶ **Query**—Select * from CIM_DataFile where Name = "c:\\program files\\ACME\\POSBatchProcess\\ POSJobDistConfig.ini"

    ▶ **Query Interval—3600**

5. On the Discovery Mapper screen, enter the required key properties and any optional non-key properties. Non-key properties can always be added later should you find that one or more are required. Enter these values for the key properties and then click Finish:

    ▶ **Class ID**—Use the drop down provided to select Unleashed.POSBatchProcess.Version1.POSDistributionServer.

    ▶ **PrincipalName$**—Use the flyout tool to select (Host = Windows Computer), Windows Computer (Principal Name).

    ▶ **Non Key Properties**—(optional).

    ▶ **System.Entity\DisplayName**—POS Job Distribution Server ($Target/Host/Host/Property[Type="Windows!Microsoft. Windows.Computer"]/PrincipalName$).

Now, create the object discovery for the POS Job Processing Server class:

1. In the Authoring console, select the Health Model workspace and then the Discoveries node.

2. In the Object pane (top center) of the console, right-click and select New -> Script to launch the Script Discovery wizard.

3. On the General screen, enter the following values and click Next.

    ▶ **Element ID—Unleashed.POSBatchProcess.Version1. DiscoverPOSProcessSvr**

    ▶ **Display Name—Unleashed POS Job Processing Server Discovery**

    ▶ **Target—Unleashed.POSBatchProcess.Version1.ApplicationRole**

    ▶ **Category**—Discovery

4. On the Schedule screen, configure the schedule to run every 240 minutes and click Next.

5. On the Script screen, enter the following values:

    ▶ **File Name**—POSJobProcessDisc.vbs

    ▶ **Timeout—1** Minutes

6. Copy and paste the discovery script into the window provided. The discovery script is included in the download materials for this chapter.

7. Click the Parameters button, and enter the following parameters displayed in Figure 8.10, separated by spaces:

`$MPElement$`

`$Target/Id$`

`$Tar-`

`get/Host/Host/Property[Type="Windows!Microsoft.Windows.Computer"]/PrincipalName`

`$`

FIGURE 8.10 Discovery script and parameters

8. Click OK and then Finish to create the discovery for the POS Job Processing Server class.

CAUTION: CASE SENSITIVITY

Discovery script parameters (shown in Figure 8.10) are case sensitive!

Monitoring

Now it is time to create monitors to monitor the health of application components, as well as to implement the health model of the MP. As mentioned in Chapter 14, "Monitoring with Operations Manager 2007," in the predecessor to this book, *System Center Operations Manager 2007 Unleashed*, there are three types of monitors, discussed in the following sections.

Unit Monitors

Unit monitors, discussed in detail in Chapter 14 of *System Center Operations Manager 2007 Unleashed*, are those monitors implemented to identify the state of a monitored object and set the object's health state accordingly. It is beyond the scope of this chapter to create a complete set of unit monitors; however, creating at least one will be necessary to validate that health rollup is configured correctly. You will create a custom unit monitor in the "Advanced Authoring: Creating a Custom Workflow" section of this chapter.

Aggregate and Dependency Rollup Monitors

You implement dependency rollup monitors to allow health rollup to the hosting class (the Windows Server Operating System in this case).

Start by examining what is already in place. In the Authoring console, select the Health Model workspace -> Monitors node. By default, aggregate rollup monitors are created for each of the four health categories. However, notice in Figure 8.11 that no dependency rollup monitors exist.

This is expected, since the base classes selected were Windows Local Application and Local Application Component. As mentioned in Table 8.4, these classes do not have health rollup to their hosting class previously defined. It is up to the MP author to determine the appropriate health rollup strategy and implement dependency rollup monitors to meet the desired end.

As previously shown in Figure 8.5, the following health rollup is desired:

▶ POS Job Distribution Server health rolls up to POS Batch Job Server Role.

▶ POS Batch Job Processing Server health rolls up to POS Batch Job Server Role.

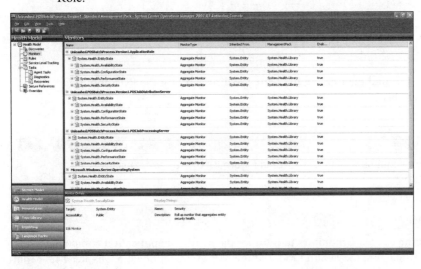

FIGURE 8.11 Aggregate rollup monitors are created by default.

Create Dependency Rollup Monitors to Implement Desired Health Rollup

The first monitor you will create is a dependency rollup monitor that will roll up the health of the POS Job Distribution Server class to the POS Batch Job Server Role. Here are the steps to create the dependency rollup monitor to roll up the health of the POS Job Distribution Server to the POS Batch Job Server Role:

1. In the Authoring console, select the Health Model -> Monitors.

2. In the Object pane (top center) of the console, right-click and select New -> Dependency Monitor.

3. In the Choose a Unique Identifier textbox, enter
Unleashed.POSBatchProcess.Version1.DistServerRollup and then click OK.

4. On the General tab of the dependency rollup monitor properties, enter the following values:

   ▶ **Name—Unleashed POS Batch Process Version1 Distribution Server Rollup**

   ▶ **Description—Rolls up health state of POS Job Distribution Server to POS Batch Job Server Role**

   ▶ **Target—Unleashed.POSBatchProcess.Version1.ApplicationRole**

   ▶ **Parent Monitor**—System.Health.EntityState

5. On the Monitor Dependency tab, select Entity Health under the POS Batch Process Distribution Server class, as shown in Figure 8.12.

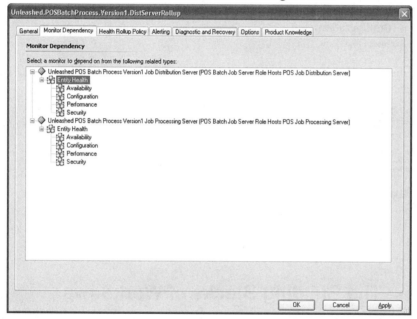

FIGURE 8.12 Setting an aggregate monitor to roll up to the hosting class

6. On the Health Rollup Policy tab, accept the default Health Rollup Policy of Worst state of any member.

7. The default values on all remaining tabs are acceptable, so click OK to finish.

   Note that you did not configure this monitor to generate an alert. Because the primary function of dependency rollup monitors is health rollup, you generally will not configure these monitors to generate alerts.

8. Repeat these steps to create a dependency rollup monitor to roll up the health of the POS Job Processing Server class to the POS Batch Job Server Role.

Product Knowledge

The Product Knowledge tab is present throughout the authoring process for rules and monitors, and is perhaps the most important tab in the entire process. This tab is designed as an area where MP authors can insert explanatory text to describe what the alert from a rule or monitor signifies, common causes, and common resolutions. To insert product knowledge into your management pack elements, click the Edit button to open a template for entering knowledge (in MS Word). This template is displayed in Figure 8.13, and requires Microsoft Word (preferably version 2003) and the Visual Studio Tools for Office Runtime.

Knowledge Article

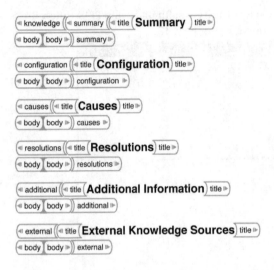

FIGURE 8.13 Inserting Product Knowledge

Modules: The Building Blocks of Workflows

Modules are the foundation of a management pack. Modules are classified as either native or composite:

► *Native modules* are written in native or managed code and must be installed on the agent computer.

► *Composite modules* are composed of one or more other modules. They allow other modules to be combined and specialized for specific functionality required for a given workflow. Composite modules are automatically deployed to the agent with the management pack.

There are over 300 modules in Operations Manager 2007. Microsoft documents approximately 35 of the most commonly used modules at http://msdn.microsoft.com/en-us/library/ee533840.aspx.

As an MP author, you may encounter a monitoring scenario you cannot address using the rules and monitors that come out of the box with OpsMgr. In these situations, you can create your own composite module(s) to create a custom workflow to meet your custom monitoring needs. Even if you can use an off-the-shelf monitor, there are situations where creating your own composite module would be more efficient from a performance perspective. For further discussion on scenarios warranting a custom workflow, see the "Advanced Authoring: Creating a Custom Workflow" section later in this chapter.

All modules (including composite modules you create) are composed of one or more of each of four types: data source, probe action, condition detection, or write action. The following sections explain each of these module types in more detail.

Data Source

The data source module is the module type used at the beginning of a workflow for initial data source collection and insertion into the workflow. As such, a data source has zero inputs and zero or one outputs. A data source may perform one of a variety of functions to collect this data, such as monitor an event log for a particular event, execute a script at a scheduled interval, or probe a Simple Network Management Protocol (SNMP)-enabled device for the value of an SNMP object identifier (OID).

Condition Detection

Condition detection modules can have one or multiple inputs, but only a single output. They perform one of three different functions, as follows:

- ▶ Filter data inputs to determine if they meet a defined criterion, such as a numeric threshold or text string match.

- ▶ Map input from data type to another. For example, mapping property bag input to performance data output.

- ▶ Consolidate multiple inputs into a single output.

Write Action

Write actions have only one input and may have zero or one output. It is the only module that is intended to change system state. Typical write actions include writing data to the Operational database, generating an alert, or running a script or command.

Probe Action

Probe actions have a single input and a single output. They are similar to data sources in that they retrieve a piece of data, but must be triggered by a data source to perform an action. A probe action would include actions that do not change the state of a monitored system. Here are some examples of probe actions:

▶ Running a command to retrieve a list of running processes on a system

▶ Displaying the IP configuration on a server

Workflow Summary

On their own, module types are not very exciting. However, when combined in unique ways to create custom workflows, the possibilities are virtually endless.

Figure 8.14 shows an example of a custom workflow. Let's review this custom workflow sample, which you will create in the remaining portion of this chapter. You may want to review this example again after you have actually created the workflow. Here are the processes depicted in Figure 8.14:

1. A data source module executes a VBScript every 60 seconds to gather the name and size of the *%windows%*\temp folder. The module then formats the data into a format suitable for use in a performance counter (with object, counter, instance, and value definitions as seen in a normal Windows performance counter).

2. The data collected by the data source is passed into the workflow as a piece of XML data (known as a dataitem).

3. The "monitor type" is a template that allows the MP author to define how the data will be processed. This enables the author to create multiple monitors using the data from the script without the need to manually insert the script into the unit monitor repeatedly.

4. The single data item is then passed to the following objects:

▶ A performance collection rule, which consumes the XML data and writes the performance data to the Operational database and the data warehouse.

▶ A two-state unit monitor that utilizes a condition detection module to compare folder size to the value contained in a user-customizable threshold. An alert is generated if the folder size exceeds the threshold.

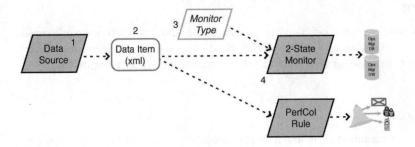

FIGURE 8.14 Example of a custom workflow

Advanced Authoring: Creating a Custom Workflow

The question that may come to mind when reading the heading of this section is: "Why do I need to create a custom workflow?" This is an excellent question, and it is important that MP authors understand that creating a custom workflow (a composite module) is sometimes advantageous, or even absolutely necessary. Situations where a custom workflow may be helpful or necessary include the following:

▶ **When no off-the-shelf rule, monitor, task, or discovery will perform the actions required in your monitoring scenario**—This is especially common when using scripts for discovery or monitoring.

▶ **When multiple overridable parameters are required**—When using the Operations console, it is not possible to create multiple overridable parameter fields. All parameters must be passed in a single Parameters parameter in space-separated format, which is not an easily interpreted presentation to system operators responsible for MP tuning.

▶ **When optimizing workflows for cook down**—*Cook down* is a process savvy MP authors leverage to reduce the number of executions of more resource-intensive workflows, such as scripts and WMI queries targeting multi-instanced components.

Cook down is a feature in Operations Manager in which a health service passes the output of a single discovery or monitoring script (generally contained in a data source module) to multiple workflows requiring data from the script. The System Center Management (HealthService) service is programmed to identify modules with the same configuration running in different workflows, and where possible, execute the script or other action only once, passing the output (the dataitem) to the like modules in the various workflows, as shown in Figure 8.15.

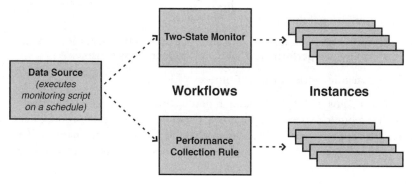

FIGURE 8.15 Cook down example for Point-of-Sale Batch Job Application

For cook down to work successfully in your custom modules, the following must be true:

▶ If using a script, it must contain all data needed for all workflows and all instances for best results.

▶ No overrides are created with conflicting workflow data.

▶ All workflows must have identical schedules in place, so all workflows using the output of the data source are prepared to accept it at the same time.

TIP: HOW TO VERIFY COOK DOWN IS WORKING

When authoring custom modules to take advantage of cook down, it is important to validate that the modules actually cook down successfully. To do so requires a bit of additional customization in the modules you create. How can you accomplish this?

When using a script in a composite module, you can add use the `LogScriptEvent` method from the OpsMgr Scripting API to log an event when the script starts and when the script ends. This logs an event to the Operations Manager Event Log on the target system where the workflow is executed. If cook down is not working, you will find more occurrences of these events, indicating that the script is executing multiple times at each scheduled execution rather than just once.

The POSFolderSizeCookDown.vbs script, included in the online content available for this chapter, illustrates an example of this method.

Step-by-Step: Creating a Custom Workflow with Cook Down

The next part of this chapter takes you through building a custom workflow that implements cook down. The workflow will execute a script that collects the name and size of a folder on a Windows computer. There are two places where the data collected by the script (in a single execution) is used, as follows:

▶ A two-state threshold monitor that checks that the folder size has not grown beyond a user-defined threshold.

▶ A performance collection rule used to store the data in the Operational database, for display in a performance view in the Operations console.

The structure of the custom workflow is as follows:

1. The workflow begins with a data source module containing two member modules. The first module (Microsoft.Windows.TimedScript.PropertyBagProvider) executes a VBScript at a scheduled interval. The script collects the name and size of the %*windows*%\temp folder on a target system and stores the data in a property bag.

2. The second module in the data source (Sytem.Performance.DataGenericMapper) will transform the property bag data to a format suitable for use in a performance view.

3. The data source then passes the collected data in XML format, known as a data item.

4. You will then create a monitor type, which allows easy reuse of the data collected by the script.

5. Next, you will create a custom unit monitor based on the monitor type created in step 4. The unit monitor will compare the size of the folder (in kilobytes) to a user-defined threshold.

6. Finally, you will create a performance collection rule to store this data in the Operational database for use in a performance view.

Set the same interval and sync time on both the rule and the monitor, which will allow the workflow to cook down, running the script only once for each scheduled interval. As mentioned earlier in the "How to Verify Cook Down is Working" sidebar, the sample VBScript is written to log an event every time the script is executed, and each time it completes successfully.

Now that you have defined the workflow you are about to create, you can build the workflow in the Authoring console.

Create the Custom Data Source

Perform the following steps to create the data source for the custom workflow in the POS Batch Job MP. You will begin by adding the module that will run the VBScript at a scheduled interval:

1. In the Authoring console, select Type Library -> Data Sources.

2. In the Object pane (top center) of the console, right-click and select New -> Composite Data Source.

3. In the Choose a Unique Identifier textbox, enter **Unleashed.POSBatchProcess. Version1.CustomDS** and click OK.

4. On the Data Source Properties General tab, in the Name field, enter **Unleashed R2 Examples Custom Data Source**.

5. On the Member Modules tab, click the Add button. In the Choose Module Type dialog, select the Microsoft.Windows.TimedScript.PropertyBagProvider.

6. In the Module ID field, enter **ScriptDS** and click OK.

7. On the ScriptDS dialog, enter the following values and then click OK:

   ▶ **IntervalSeconds—3600**

   ▶ **SyncTime**—Erase any default value (should be empty).

   ▶ **ScriptName—POSFolderSizeCookDown.vbs**

   ▶ **Arguments**—Erase any default value (should be empty).

   ▶ **ScriptBody**—Click the Edit button and paste the POSFolderSizeCookDown.vbs sample VBScript between the <ScriptBody>ScriptBody</ScriptBody> tags. Replace the *ScriptBody* value with the sample script.

   ▶ **TimeoutSeconds—30**

If you receive an error message when you click OK, you may need to wrap the script in CDATA tags. The CDATA (character data) tag indicates to the parser to interpret the VBScript as only character data, not XML markup. Simply add the following between the <ScriptBody> tags:

```
<ScriptBody><![CDATA[ Paste script HERE! ]]></ScriptBody>
```

Next, add the module to the data source that will reformat the property bag data as performance data. Perform the following steps:

1. While still on the Member Modules tab, click the Add button again. In the Choose Module Type dialog, select System.Performance.DataGenericMapper.

2. In the Module ID field, enter **PerfMapper** and click OK.

3. On the PerfMapper Properties screen, click in each field and use the flyout to select Promote in each field, resulting in the following values; then click OK:

   ▶ **ObjectName**—$Config/ObjectName$

   ▶ **CounterName**—$Config/CounterName$

   ▶ **InstanceName**—$Config/InstanceName$

   ▶ **ValueName**—$Config/Value$

4. While still on the Member Modules tab, set the NextModule value as follows:

   ▶ **ScriptDS**—PerfMapper

   ▶ **PerfMapper**—Module Output

5. On the Configuration Schema tab, change the Type field to the right of Value from string to Double.

6. On the Overridable Parameters tab, accept the defaults.

7. On the Data Types tab, use the drop down to set the data type to System.Performance.Data.

8. On the Options tab, accept the default values and click OK.

Create the Monitor Type

Here are the steps to create the monitor type:

1. In the Authoring console, select the Type Library workspace and then the Monitor Types node.

2. In the Object pane (top center) of the console, right-click and select New -> Composite Monitor Type.

3. In the Choose a Unique Identifier textbox, enter **Unleashed.POSBatchProcess. Version1.TwoStateMT** and click OK.

4. On the General tab of Monitor Type Properties, in the Name field, enter **Unleashed POS Batch Process Version1 Two State Monitor Type**.

5. On the States tab, select the radio button labeled 2 State Monitor Type and enter the following values:

    ► **ID of state 1—GOOD**

    ► **ID of state 2—BAD**

6. On the Member Modules tab, click the Add button and select the data source you created—Unleashed.POSBatchProcess.Version1.CustomDS.

7. In the Module ID field, enter **DS** and click OK.

8. On the DS screen, use the flyout to select Promote in each field, resulting in the following values; then click OK:

    ► **ObjectName**—$Config/ObjectName$

    ► **CounterName**—$Config/CounterName$

    ► **InstanceName**—$Config/InstanceName$

    ► **ValueName**—$Config/Value$

9. While still on the Member Modules tab, click the Add button again. Select the Condition Detection module System.ExpressionFilter.

10. In the Module ID field, enter **FilterTooBig** and click OK.

11. On the FilterTooBig screen, click the Configure button. This brings up the Expression Builder interface.

12. Click the Insert button, enter the following values, and then click OK:

    ► **Parameter Name**—Value

    ► **Operator**—Greater than or equal to

    ► **Value—10000**

    This effectively defines a default threshold of 10,000 bytes as the file size threshold that will trigger an unhealthy state for the monitor.

13. Before you click OK again, change the @Type fields from String to Double by typing **Double** in the space provided. Failure to change the String to Double results in data type conversion errors when importing the MP into a management group. Figure 8.16 shows these settings.

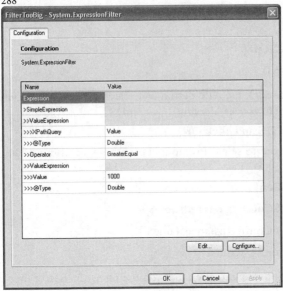

FIGURE 8.16 Expression filter configuration in the monitor type

14. On the Member Modules tab, click the Add button one last time. Select the Condition Detection module System.ExpressionFilter.

15. In the Module ID field, enter **FilterUnderLimit** and click OK.

16. On the FilterUnderLimit screen, click the Configure button. This brings up the Expression Builder interface.

17. Click the Insert button, enter the following values, and then click OK:

  ▶ **Parameter Name—Value**

  ▶ **Operator—Less than**

  ▶ **Value—10000**

18. Before clicking OK again, change the @Type fields from String to Double.

19. On the Regular tab, select the GOOD State. In the window, select the checkboxes next to DS and FilterUnderLimit. Set the Next Module values as follows.

  ▶ **DS**—FilterUnderLimit

  ▶ **FilterUnderLimit**—Monitor State Output

20. Now, select the BAD State; in the window, select the checkboxes next to DS and FilterTooBig. Set the Next Module values as follows:

  ▶ **DS**—FilterTooBig

  ▶ **FilterUnderLimit**—Monitor State Output

21. On the On Demand tab, accept the defaults.

22. On the Configuration Schema tab, use the Add button to add the values shown in Table 8.5.

TABLE 8.5 Values on the Configuration Schema Tab in MonitorType

Name	Type	Required
ObjectName	String	Yes
CounterName	String	Yes
InstanceName	String	Yes
Value	Double	Yes

Before you leave this tab, set the Type column for Value to Double.

23. On both the Overridable Parameters and Options tabs, accept the default values. Click OK to complete configuring the monitor type.

Create the Custom Unit Monitor

Perform the following steps to create the custom unit monitor:

1. In the Authoring console, select the Health Model workspace and then the Monitors node.

2. Right-click in the Object pane, and from the content menu, select New -> Custom Unit Monitor.

3. In the Choose a Unique Identifier textbox, enter **Unleashed.POSBatchProcess.Version1.TwoStateCustom**, and then click OK.

4. On the General tab of the Monitor Type properties, enter or select the following values:

   ▶ **Name—Unleashed POS Batch Process Version1 Folder Size Monitor**

   ▶ **Target**—Unleashed.POSBatchProcess.Version1. POSJobDistributionServer

   ▶ **Parent Monitor**—System.Health.PerformanceState

5. On the Configuration tab, click the Browse for a type hyperlink.

6. From the list provided, select Unleashed.POSBatchProcess.Version1. TwoStateMT and click OK.

7. On the Configuration tab, enter the following values:

   ▶ **ObjectName—Folder Size (Custom).**

   ▶ **CounterName**—Using the flyout provided, select (Unleashed POS Version1 Application Role) -> (Host=Windows Server Operating System) -> (Host=Windows Computer) -> NetBIOS Computer Name (Windows Computer). This will insert the appropriate XPath variable for the NetBIOS Computer Name of the host system running the workflow.

   ▶ **InstanceName**—Enter **$Data/Property[@Name='FolderName']$.**

   ▶ **Value**—Enter **$Data/Property[@Name='FolderSize']$.**

8. On the Health tab, set the Health State values for each monitor condition:

▶ **GOOD**—Operational State GOOD, Health State Healthy

▶ **BAD**—Operational State BAD, Health State Critical

9.   On the Alerting tab, configure the following alert settings:

▶ Select the Generate alerts for this monitor checkbox.

▶ **Generate an alert**—When the monitor is in a critical health state.

▶ Select the Automatically resolve the alert checkbox.

▶ **Alert Name—Unleashed POS Batch Process Version1 Folder Size Monitor.**

▶ **Alert Description—Please see the alert context for details.**

You can customize the alert description by typing in static text, as well as using XML (XPath) variable to insert dynamic values, such as the value of a performance counter at the time the alert was raised. For a detailed list of XPath syntax for inserting dynamic values into alert descriptions, see the OpsMgr XML Cheat Sheet at http://www.systemcentercentral.com/Downloads/DownloadsDetails/tabid/144/IndexID/7369/Default.aspx.

10.   On the Diagnostic and Recovery tab, accept the default values.

11.   On the Options tab, uncheck the Remotable check box, as this monitor cannot be executed by a management server against a remote computer.

12.   Click OK on the Product Knowledge tab to complete monitor configuration.

Create the Performance Collection Rule

Here are the steps to create the performance collection rule:

1.   In the Authoring console, select the Health Model workspace and then the Rules node.

2.   Right-click in the Object pane, and from the content menu, select New > Custom Rule.

3.   In the Choose a Unique Identifier textbox, enter **Unleashed.POSBatchProcess.Version1.CustomPerf** and then click OK.

4.   On the General tab of the Monitor Type properties, enter or select the following values:

▶ **Name—Unleashed POS Batch Process Version1 Custom Performance Collection**

▶ **Target—Unleashed.POSBatchProcess.Version1. POSJobDistributionServer**

5.   On the Modules tab, click the Create button to the right of the Data Sources window.

6.   On the Choose modules type screen, select the Unleashed.POSBatchProcess. Version1.CustomDS module.

7.   In the Module ID box, enter **CustomPerfDS**.

Now, add a Write Action module to publish the custom performance data to the OperationsManager database. Perform the following steps:

1.   While still on the Modules tab, click the Create button to the right of the Actions window.

2.   On the Choose modules type screen, select Microsoft.SystemCenter.CollectPerformanceData.

3.   In the Module ID box, enter **CustomPerfDB**.

4.   Highlight CustomPerfDS and click Edit. Enter the following values and click OK:

    ▶ **ObjectName—Folder Size (Custom)**

    ▶ **CounterName**—Using the flyout provided, select (Unleashed POS Version1 Application Role) -> (Host=Windows Server Operating System) -> (Host=Windows Computer) -> NetBIOS Computer Name (Windows Computer). This inserts the appropriate XPath variable for the NetBIOS Computer Name of the host system running the workflow.

    ▶ **InstanceName—$Data/Property[@Name='FolderName']$**

    ▶ **Value—$Data/Property[@Name='FolderSize']$**

Add a Write Action module to publish the custom performance data to the Data Warehouse:

1.   Click the Create button to the right of the Actions window again.

2.   On the Choose modules type screen, select Microsoft.SystemCenter.DataWarehouse.PublishPerformanceData.

3.   In the Module ID box, enter **PublishDWPerf**.

4.   Accept the defaults on the Product Knowledge tab. On the Options tab, set the Category to PerformanceCollection (displayed in Figure 8.17), and click OK to finish.

If you fail to set the appropriate category for the performance collection rule, you will not see the rule in the list of rules available for insertion into a performance view.

FIGURE 8.17 Performance rule category

Create a Performance View

Views are the primary means of presenting health state, alert, event, and performance data to operators, and as such, deserve some time and attention to ensure that data is easily accessible to operators interacting with your MP in the Authoring console.

However, when creating a performance view, you will first need to create a folder to store the views you create, which will appear in the monitoring space. Unlike MPs created in the Operations console, MPs created in the Authoring console do not automatically have a folder structure.

Create a Root Folder for Views

Start by creating a root folder for views. Perform the following steps:

1. In the Authoring console, select the Presentation workspace -> Folders/Folder Items.

2. In the Object pane, expand the Microsoft.SystemCenter.ViewFolder.Root -> Microsoft.SystemCenter.Monitoring.ViewFolder.Root.

3. Right-click Microsoft.SystemCenter.Monitoring.ViewFolder.Root. Now select New -> Folder, as shown in Figure 8.18.

4. In the Choose a Unique Identifier textbox, enter **Unleashed.POSBatchProcess. Version1.POSBatchRootFolder** and then click OK.

5. On the General tab of Unleashed.POSBatchProcess.Version1. POSBatchRootFolder folder properties, enter the following value in the Name field—**Unleashed POS Batch Processing**. This friendly name will be displayed

by the folder for this MP in the folder tree presented in the Monitoring node of the Operations console.

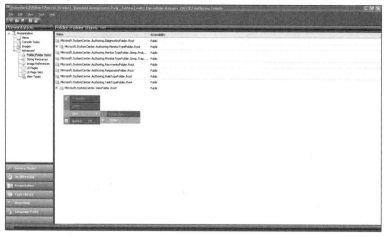

FIGURE 8.18 Creating a views folder for POS Batch Processing MP

6. On the Folder tab, verify that the only item selected is Microsoft.SystemCenter. Monitoring.ViewFolder.Root, as displayed in Figure 8.19. Note that selections here determine where the folder will appear in the folder tree presented in the Monitoring node.

FIGURE 8.19 Verifying the parent folder for the POS Batch Processing MP views folder

Create a Performance View for the Performance Collection Rule

Now you will create a performance view, which will display the performance data collected by the performance collection rule previously created in the "Create the Performance Collection Rule" section of this chapter. This is moderately difficult, as the Authoring console does not provide a friendly interface for selecting the target performance collection rule. Perform the following steps:

1. In the Authoring console, select the Presentation workspace and then the Views node.

2. Locate and right-click on the Unleashed.POSBatchProcess.Version1. POSBatchRootFolder folder, and select New -> Performance View.

3. On the General screen, enter the following values and then click Finish to create the performance view:

> ▶ **Element ID—Unleashed.POSBatchProcess.Version1. POSDistSvrPerfView**

> ▶ **Display Name—POS Job Distribution Server Folder Size**

> ▶ **Target—Unleashed.POSBatchProcess.Version1. POSJobDistributionServer**

> ▶ **Category—PerformanceCollection**

The target must match the target of the performance collection rule that collects the data that will be presented. The category must be Performance Collection.

4. Right-click the performance view you just created and select Properties.

On the Configuration tab, click the Edit button. Copy and paste the following XML (PerfView.xml in the online content for this chapter) over the existing content in the Notepad document. The value between the quotes in the "Name=" string in the XML below should be the ID of the performance collection rule created in the "Create the Performance Collection Rule" section:

```
<Configuration xmlns:p1="http://www.w3.org/2001/XMLSchema-instance">
  <Criteria>
    <RuleList>

<Rule>$MPElement[Name="Unleashed.POSBatchProcess.Version1.CustomPerf"]$</Rule>
    </RuleList>
  </Criteria>
  <Presentation>
    <SortedColumnIndex>0</SortedColumnIndex>
    <SortOrder>0</SortOrder>
    <StartTime>2009-07-14T17:46:37.0721904-04:00</StartTime>
    <EndTime>2009-07-15T17:46:37.0721904-04:00</EndTime>
    <DynamicTimeTicks>864000000000</DynamicTimeTicks>
    <IsDynamic>true</IsDynamic>
    <Is3DMode>false</Is3DMode>
    <ShowAlerts>false</ShowAlerts>
    <ShowMaintenanceMode>false</ShowMaintenanceMode>
    <BaselineMode>false</BaselineMode>
```

```
<ShowPointLabels>false</ShowPointLabels>
<EnableSmartLabels>true</EnableSmartLabels>
<RightAngleAxes>false</RightAngleAxes>
<ClusterSeries>false</ClusterSeries>
<Title></Title>
<TitleFont>Microsoft Sans Serif,12,Regular</TitleFont>
<ChartFont>Microsoft Sans Serif,8.25,Regular</ChartFont>
<ShowBands>false</ShowBands>
<BandColor>-1579033</BandColor>
<ChartType>Line</ChartType>
<Depth>100</Depth>
<GapDepth>100</GapDepth>
<Perspective>10</Perspective>
<GraphXRotation>0</GraphXRotation>
<GraphYRotation>0</GraphYRotation>
<XLabelAngle>0</XLabelAngle>
<LabelColor>-16777216</LabelColor>
<LabelFont>Microsoft Sans Serif,8.25,Regular</LabelFont>
<XAxisVisible>True</XAxisVisible>
<XShowMajorGridlines>false</XShowMajorGridlines>
<XShowMinorGridlines>false</XShowMinorGridlines>
<ShowInterlaceStrips>false</ShowInterlaceStrips>
<XInterlaceColor>16777215</XInterlaceColor>
<XShowSideMargin>true</XShowSideMargin>
<XAxisFont>Microsoft Sans Serif,8.25,Regular</XAxisFont>
<AutoAxis>true</AutoAxis>
<AxisMax>100</AxisMax>
<AxisMin>0</AxisMin>
<YAxisVisible>True</YAxisVisible>
<YShowMajorGridlines>true</YShowMajorGridlines>
<YShowMinorGridlines>false</YShowMinorGridlines>
<YShowInterlaceStrips>false</YShowInterlaceStrips>
<YShowSideMargin>true</YShowSideMargin>
<YAxisFont>Microsoft Sans Serif,8.25,Regular</YAxisFont>
<BackgroundColor1>-1</BackgroundColor1>
<BackgroundColor2>-1</BackgroundColor2>
<GradientType>None</GradientType>
<Series></Series>
</Presentation>
<Target></Target>
</Configuration>
```

5. On the Folder tab, verify that the only folder selected is the Unleashed. POSBatchProcess.Version1.POSBatchRootFolder you created in the "Create a Root Folder for Views" section of this chapter.

Best Practices for Views

Here are some best practices when creating views:

▶ **Create views for only the most commonly accessed data in the top-level folder**—This will generally include a state view (and possibly a diagram view) for each of the top-level classes. In the Point-of-Sale Batch Processing Application, this would translate to state views for the POS Job Distribution Server and POS Job Processing Server classes.

▶ **Create an alert view for alerts generated by the application**—Be sure to filter on resolution state on the view so only *active alerts* are presented.

▶ **Create subfolders to house views for less-important views for individual application components**—In the Point-of-Sale Batch Processing Application, this could mean that event views and less frequently used performance views are created in subfolders.

When creating your own management packs, consult application subject matter experts (SMEs) for advice on which data is most relevant for troubleshooting, and how to access the functional state of the application.

Worst Practices for Views

Here are some worst practices when creating views:

▶ **Creating top-level views for every class in the MP**—Usually only a subset of classes is of primary interest. Limit top-level views to only the most frequently referenced classes for ease of use.

▶ **Creating views with too much information**—How much is too much is subjective, but remember that more information rendered in a single view means a greater load on the Operational database. Filter views to display only a reasonable amount of information. Again, this is a subjective decision as to what is appropriate—for alert views, this may be 1 or 2 days. For performance views, this may be 1 to 8 hours.

Error in the direction of showing a bit less history than operators may require. They can always personalize their view settings in the Operations console!

Verifying Cook Down

How you can verify cook down depends on the type of modules used in the data source that collects and inserts data into the workflow. When using a script in the data source, as in this example, you can verify cook down quite easily by modifying the script to log an event to the Operations Manager Event Log each time the script executes. You can do this easily with the LogScriptEvent method.

If you see only one event on each scheduled interval, cook down is working. If you see multiple events (indicating multiple script executions) at each scheduled interval, cook down is failing. For detailed information on how to add event logging to your monitoring scripts, open the sample script included with the online content for this chapter, POSFolderSizeCookDown.vbs, and search on the string **Cook Down Check**.

Here's how to verify cook down in the POS Batch Processing management pack:

1. Import the script into your test management group. To verify that an agent received the MP, look for event ID 1201 in the Operations Manager Event Log. The name of the MP received will be mentioned in the event description. This event will be followed by an event 1210, which indicates that MPs have been loaded by the agent.

2. On the sample POS Job Distribution Server, verify that the agent received the MP.

3. Watch the Operations Manager event log for events 1002 and 1003, displayed in Figures 8.20 and 8.21, which indicate that the POSFolderSizeCookDown.vbs script in the custom data source is executing.

If cook down is working, only one occurrence of each event should be logged at each scheduled interval.

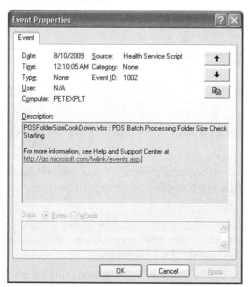

FIGURE 8.20 Cook down check "script starting" event

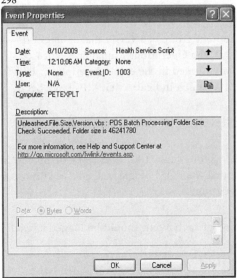

FIGURE 8.21 Cook down check "script completed" event

Troubleshooting Cook Down

If cook down is not working as expected, check for some common culprits that prevent successful cook down, as follows:

► **Missing Data in Script**—If a workflow requires a piece of data not included in the script, cook down will fail. This is often due to a change in the overridable parameters of the script.

► **Schedule Differences**—If the workflows that could possibly consume the output of the single workflow do not run at the same interval, they will require separate script executions to provide the required data input.

In the example shown in the "Create the Performance Collection Rule" section of this chapter, it is possible that the performance collection rule could run at a longer interval that is a multiple. For example, if the data source is configured to execute every 5 minutes, the performance collection rule could run every 10, 15,... minutes without breaking cook down.

► **Overridable Parameters**—Beware of overridable parameters if cook down is of critical importance. It is conceivable that the data item passed from the data source into multiple workflows cooks down as expected in testing, but then at some point fails to do so. If overridable parameters are provided that allow operators to change the execution schedule or data returned by the script, cook down can be broken after implementation in a production environment.

If your monitoring scenario involves script-based data sources and many instances of a target class (such as a large number of web sites), cook down may be critical to scalability. 10, 20, or even more simultaneous executions may result in unacceptable resource utilization. If this describes your monitoring scenario, think carefully about which parameters are configured as overridable.

Create an Overridable Parameter

Overridable parameters add flexibility to your MP components by allowing operators to modify the behavior of a rule, monitor, discovery, or other MP components to suit a specific environment. With cook down verified, you will add an overridable parameter so operators can modify the folder size threshold that generates the alert in the unit monitor in created earlier in the "Create a Unit Monitor" section.

The steps in this section will modify the schema of the monitor type on which the folder size unit monitor is based. You must first delete the folder size unit monitor before adding an overridable parameter to the monitor type. Begin by defining Threshold as an overridable parameter on the monitor type. Perform the following steps:

1. Delete the unit monitor created in the "Create the Custom Unit Monitor" earlier in this chapter.

2. In the Authoring console, select the Type Library workspace and then the Monitor Types node.

3. Locate and right-click on the Unleashed.POSBatchProcess.Version1. TwoStateMT monitor type and select Properties.

4. Select the Configuration Schema tab and click the Add button.

5. In the Please Enter the Requested Value box, enter **Threshold** (Figure 8.22).

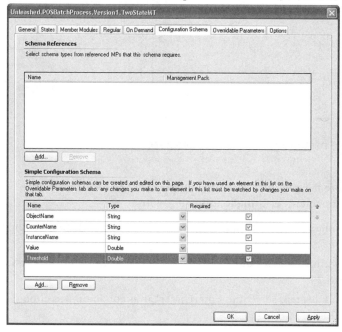

FIGURE 8.22 Creating an overridable parameter (in monitor type properties)

6. In the Type column next to Threshold, set the value to Double.

7. Next, select the Overridable Parameters tab. Click the Add button, and from the context menu, select Threshold.

8. In the Choose a Unique Identifier box, enter **Threshold**.

9. In the Add Parameters dialog, enter the following values, displayed in Figure 8.23:

    ▶ **Type**—Using the flyout provided, select $Config/Threshold$.

    ▶ **Configuration Element**—Using the drop down provided, select Double.

FIGURE 8.23 Overridable parameters (monitor type properties)

Now you need to configure the condition detection modules to use the value set through the Threshold parameter. Perform the following steps:

1. On the Member Modules tab, select the FilterTooBig condition detection module and select Edit.

2. Change the Value setting from a static number to **XPath: $Config/Threshold$**, as shown in Figure 8.24.

3. On the Member Modules tab, select the FilterUnderLimit condition detection module and select Edit.

FIGURE 8.24 Configuring monitor type properties for an overridable parameter

4. As with the other condition detection module, change the Value setting from a static number to the following: **XPath: $Config/Threshold$**.

5. The monitor type update is complete. Recreate the folder size unit monitor you deleted using the steps in the "Create the Custom Unit Monitor" section.

Verify That the Overridable Parameter Is Functional

Perform the following steps to verify that the overridable parameter is functional:

1. Import the Unleashed.POSBatchProcess.Version1 MP into a test management group.

2. Select the Authoring workspace. Use the Change Scope option to scope the view to the Unleashed POS Batch Process Version1 Job Distribution Server class.

3. Expand the class view -> Entity Health -> Performance to locate the folder size monitor, displayed in Figure 8.25.

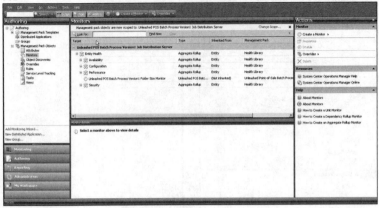

FIGURE 8.25 Custom folder size monitor

4. Right-click the folder monitor and select Overrides -> Override the Monitor -> For all objects of class. In the list of overridable parameters, you should now see Threshold, as displayed in Figure 8.26.

5. Override the Threshold value to something below the current size of the %*windows*%\temp folder (the folder watched by this monitor). If the folder is very small, copy some files to it to push its size above the threshold. You should see an alert shortly.

6. Using the Discovered Inventory View in the Monitoring workspace, target the Unleashed POS Batch Process Version1 Job Distribution Server class.

7. Select the instance of the class and launch Health Explorer. Verify that the monitor is now in an error state.

8. Remove the override created in step 6. Verify the monitor returns to a healthy state.

FIGURE 8.26 Overridable parameters (custom folder size monitor)

Reports

Beginning with the R2 release of the Authoring console, you can create a linked report using the Authoring console user interface (UI). This requires inserting an XML parameter block, which defines the target. Also new with R2 is the capability to limit the list of objects in the Object Picker in the report header by using the new filter option. This allows authors to define a filter to limit objects returned to a particular object class. As an example, in a report on SQL Server 2005 database size, you can use the filter option to return only SQL 2005 databases when the operator clicks the Add Object button.

To complete this successfully, you first need to add a reference to the management pack containing the reports in the Microsoft Generic Report library. These are the reports commonly referenced in linked reports. Perform the following steps:

1. Select File -> Management Pack Properties.

2. On the References tab, click the Add Reference button.

3. In the Add Management Pack Reference window, browse to the \Reporting subfolder of the OpsMgr installation folder (%*Programfiles*%\System Center Operations Manager 2007\Reporting by default).

4. Select the Microsoft.SystemCenter.DataWarehouse.Report.Performance.mp, select Open, and then click OK to add the reference.

In this section, you will create a linked performance report to display the folder size of the c:\windows\temp directory being monitoring on the POS Batch Process Version1 Job Distribution Server class.

Perform the following steps to insert the parameter block into the management pack:

1. In the Authoring console, select Reporting -> Linked Report.

2. In the Object pane (top center) of the console, right-click and select New -> New Linked Report.

3. In the Choose a Unique Identifier textbox, enter **Unleashed.POSBatchProcess. Version1.LinkedPerfReport** (see Figure 8.27) and then click OK.

4. On the General tab, enter the following values:

> ► **Id—Unleashed.POSBatchProcess.Version1.LinkedPerfReport**

> ► **Name—POS Folder Size Linked Report - Performance**

> ► **Base**—Microsoft.SystemCenter.DataWarehouse.Report.Performance

> ► **Target**—Unleashed.POSBatchProcess.Version1. POSJobDistributionServer

FIGURE 8.27 Setting name, base report, and target class for linked report

5. On the Parameters tab, click the Edit in external editor button. This will open a Notepad document with a random name.

6. Paste the report parameter block provided in the Report_Parameterblock.xml file in the online content for this chapter. Select File -> Save to save the changes to the management pack.

7.   On the Options tab, under Visibility, select True. If you want to reference the report from another management pack, you also need to set Accessibility = Public.

For details on how to modify the parameter block XML for a linked report, see the OpsMgr Reporting Authoring Guide at http://technet.microsoft.com/en-us/opsmgr/bb498235.aspx.

You now have created the framework of a management pack for the POS Batch Process Application. Although the application is a fictional example, the planning and implementation tasks demonstrated are very similar to what you would use when modeling a real server application.

Tips for a Successful MP Authoring Experience

Here's what you will want to remember when authoring a management pack for your production applications:

- ► **Start on paper**—Sketch the service model and health model for the application before you do any work in the Authoring console.

- ► **Enlist the help of application architects**—For in-house applications, the application developers who wrote the application are your best resource when modeling the application. You cannot create effective service and health models for an application if you do not understand how it is put together and how it functions.

- ► **Enlist the help of IT operations**—Who better than the staff responsible for managing the application on a daily basis to explain the common issues and how to resolve them? IT operations staffs are frequently a great resource when determining the common issues for which proactive monitoring is necessary.

- ► **Remember that MP authoring is an iterative process**—Do not expect to get the model just right on the first try. Multiple iterations of the health and service models, as well as the monitoring and presentation logic, are a healthy and normal part of the process.

Summary

This chapter introduced the management pack authoring process, incorporating a variety of discovery and monitoring techniques. It discussed the OpsMgr Scripting API and utilizing it to support creating, testing, and troubleshooting custom workflows. You were also introduced to advanced authoring techniques for building efficient custom workflows. The chapter provided best practices at each step of the process to ensure that you are armed with the knowledge needed to design and build basic management packs for your custom monitoring scenarios in the real world.

For detailed guidance on management pack authoring topics, the authors recommend the Microsoft Management Pack University webcast series at http://74.52.12.162/~microsft/conference_agenda.php?cid=19.

Unleashing Operations Manager 2007

This chapter takes a deep dive into Operations Manager (OpsMgr) 2007, examining expert topics not previously discussed in depth in the predecessor to this book, *System Center Operations Manager 2007 Unleashed* (Sams, 2008). Topics covered include using OpsMgr in distributed environments, high availability, business continuity, the new Visio add-in for OpsMgr, advanced use of Audit Collection Services (ACS), network monitoring with distributed applications, and targeting. Presented by subject matter experts in each area, this chapter presents information from some of the best minds on OpsMgr 2007.

Distributed Environments

The first part of the chapter examines designing and implementing OpsMgr 2007 in a distributed environment. A distributed environment presents its own challenges in setting up a management and monitoring infrastructure. This is an environment existing in more than a single geographic location. As an example, a large, multi-national company maintaining offices in London and New York has a distributed environment. An environment is considered *distributed* if users are accessing OpsMgr or if OpsMgr agents are reporting and forwarding data from a remote location. The next sections examine configuring management servers and gateways in distributed environments and the process of deploying and managing agents in such complex infrastructures. Also discussed is accessing the Operations console and reporting from remote locations.

Explaining Distributed Environments

This section discusses using OpsMgr in a distributed environment—whether this is an initial deployment into a distributed environment or scaling out an existing OpsMgr environment to cover a geographically remote site. Figure 9.1 shows an example of a typical distributed environment.

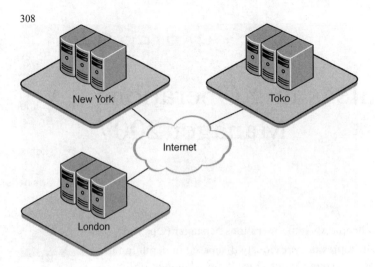

FIGURE 9.1 A typical distributed environment

When planning an OpsMgr deployment, take particular care to select the most appropriate site to host the majority of the OpsMgr infrastructure. Yes, that is correct…the majority of the OpsMgr infrastructure is almost always hosted in a single site. As you know, OpsMgr without the ACS component consists of two databases, a root management server (RMS), a number of management servers and gateways, plus an optional dedicated web console and reporting server. The location of these components in relation to each other is critical to ensure that your OpsMgr infrastructure functions correctly and performs well. There are several simple rules to remember when planning a distributed OpsMgr environment. These include the following:

▶ Physical location of servers

▶ Primary user location

▶ Supporting multiple time zones (following the sun)

Physical Location of Servers
The consideration in a distributed OpsMgr implementation is the location of the majority of the systems you will be managing. This generally is where you deploy the majority of your OpsMgr environment, and should be the first thing you consider during planning. Here's why:

▶ You can usually assume that if the majority of your servers are in a single datacenter or location, it will be easier to provision additional hardware in that location, minimizing deployment and configuration costs.

▶ Storage Area Network (SAN) equipment for hosting large and heavily utilized OpsMgr databases is often found in datacenters.

▶ From an agent point of view, it makes far more sense to host the majority of the OpsMgr infrastructure close to the majority of intended agents. This is discussed in the "Distributing Management Servers and Gateways" section.

Primary User Location

Consider where your primary users of OpsMgr are located. Although technology such as Terminal Services and Citrix allow access to the Operations console from anywhere, these technologies have some inherent issues, explained in the "Terminal Services Access Issues" section. It also makes logical sense to host the OpsMgr environment close to where your primary users (and hopefully administrators) are.

Following the Sun

Following the sun refers to spanning international time zones. If your business has a sizeable presence in several locations spanning international time zones, you need to plan management and maintenance to ensure coverage of working hours in all relevant time zones—that is, following the sun. Plan adequately to support the OpsMgr infrastructure and monitored environment during all hours users may be accessing the servers. Depending on the time zones spanned and hours of operation of your servers, you may need to provide 24-hour server support from one or multiple locations; in this case, consider access to the OpsMgr environment for users supporting OpsMgr from a site other than where the OpsMgr servers are located. This access can lead to primary user location issues, investigated in the "Remote Operations" section of this chapter.

Distributing Management Servers and Gateways

OpsMgr is designed to monitor enterprise-size environments consisting of several thousand servers. However, as the environment becomes larger and more complex, there are factors to consider and steps to take to maximize the effectiveness of OpsMgr and minimize issues in these large and complex environments. This section looks at several of these factors, to help you avoid some of the pitfalls of deploying OpsMgr into a large and complex infrastructure. However, note that while this section will provide valuable information, you should never undertake a significant deployment of OpsMgr without assistance of an expert.

Companies maintaining multiple offices typically have a number of long-distance wide area network (WAN) links. In some cases, these organizations require multiple OpsMgr management groups to monitor their environment, although they often favor a single pane of glass. As using connected management groups significantly reduces the depth of the monitoring data one can display in a single console, the discussion in this chapter primarily considers a single management group scenario.

Typically, when monitoring servers in a number of locations, you simply add additional OpsMgr management servers to the remote locations to monitor local servers in that site. However, when these remote sites are located at the end of a long-distance WAN link, deploying management servers may not work as expected and can significantly reduce management group performance, resulting in alert delays and data loss. The following sections explain why.

The authors consider a long-distance WAN link to be either a link that spans continents or links that experience greater than expected latency, although it should be noted that a latency of less than 100ms is desired.

Management Servers and Long-Distance WAN Links

In a traditional OpsMgr deployment, agents report to management servers that update the OpsMgr database and synchronize with the RMS. However, this approach is not viable when facing data transmission over long-distance WAN links. To understand this, look at how a management server transfers data to and from the database. A traditional management server uses a simple SQL OLEDB connection to connect the database. The connection works (in simple terms) as listed here, and Figure 9.2 shows several of the steps graphically:

1. Request to establish connection sent from management server to database server.

2. Request received by database server and request for credentials sent to management server.

3. Credentials sent from management server to database server.

4. Credentials verified.

5. Connection established.

6. Data transmitted.

7. Connection terminated. (The common term for this is "torn down," meaning that no part of the connection is left intact.)

This type of connection is appropriate when a management server is on the same local network to the database server, but not when transferring data over long-distance WAN links. This is due not to technology, but to physics. The physics of "Speed of Light" refers to the speed at which data is able to travel across a fibre link. The traffic associated with the SQL connection (see Figure 9.2) shows that the connection is very active or "chatty." This is acceptable over a good, high-speed local area network (LAN) link, but when transferring data this way over a long-distance WAN link, each step of the process is affected by latency caused by speed of light delay. Table 9.1 shows how speed of light can affect the latency of a connection across a long-distance WAN link.

The latency figure does include latency caused by signal boosting and data conversion from Ethernet (electrical) signal to fiber (optical) signal. With this in mind, it would be reasonable to assume that the total latency for the Hong Kong—New York link would be greater than 200ms when considering these factors.

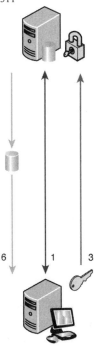

6   1   3

FIGURE 9.2 Management server communications with the database server

TABLE 9.1 Illustrating Data Transfer Across Long-Distance WAN Links

Source—Destination	Distance (approx.)	Roundtrip Latency (approx.)[1]
Hong Kong—New York	16,500km	165ms
London—New York	5,500km	55ms

[1]*Latency across fiber is calculated as follows (approximated):*
The distance from Hong Kong to New York is 16,500km.
*The speed of light in vacuum is 300 * 10^6 m/s.*
The speed of light in fiber is roughly 66% of the speed of light in vacuum.
*The speed of light in fiber is 300 * 10^6 m/s * 0.66 = 200 * 10^6 m/s.*
*The one-way delay from Hong Kong to New York is 16,500 km / (200 * 10^6 m/s) = 82.5ms.*
The round-trip delay is 165ms.

Additional latency on the connection can manifest as severe delays in updating alert and health service data, and even cause loss of agent data if the cache fills up and overwritten. You can address this by using the Gateway Server role in place of management servers in remote locations. Gateway servers service agents the same way as a management server but differ in the way they forward that data to the database:

▶ Unlike management servers, gateways do not directly connect to the database. Instead, they forward (proxy) data to another management server for transmission to the database.

▶ Differing from the very active OLEDB connection used by management servers, gateways establish a Transmission Control Protocol (TCP) connection with the assigned management server, maintaining this connection in an open state until the connection fails with an error or the management server is no longer available.

▶ Data sent from the gateway server is consolidated, resulting in an estimated 20–30% reduction of total data sent to the database compared to individual agents reporting directly to a management server across the WAN link.

Given these characteristics, the gateway offers a much more efficient method of monitoring large numbers of agents at the end of a long-distance WAN link.

Using Gateways Across WAN Links or to Monitor Large Numbers of Agents

Having established the advantages of using a gateway server to monitor agents across a long-distance WAN link, let's look at the impacts of making such a decision.

There are many factors to consider when using a gateway for any purpose other than monitoring agents in a DMZ. Typically, when you monitor DMZs, the number of machines monitored is relatively small compared to the bulk of the corporate network. For that reason, Microsoft engineered gateways to monitor fewer agents. Prior to OpsMgr 2007 Service Pack 1 (SP 1), gateway servers supported a maximum of 200 agents, making them unsuitable for any other purpose than monitoring DMZs and small untrusted networks. However, with SP 1 and now Release 2 (R2), gateways have been tested to 1,500 agents with R2, and depending on the hardware configuration and WAN link specifics, could theoretically support many more than this. Although management servers can support up to 3,000 servers with R2, gateways are a welcome alternative in complex, distributed environments.

Remember that the gateway forwards its data to a management server for relaying to the database. This means you need to plan for additional management servers to act as proxies for the gateway servers. These additional management servers should be dedicated to hosting gateways and not host agents, due to how gateways function.

Here's why: In terms of priority, a management server does not distinguish between a traditional agent and a gateway server it is hosting. This means data from a gateway is assigned the same level of priority as that from a standard agent. That may seem reasonable on the surface, but if 100 agents report to the gateway, each agent is afforded only 1/100 of the standard priority otherwise afforded to an agent. If the management server hosting the gateway also has 100 agents of its own, each receiving 1/100 of the total priority, the agents reporting to the gateway will ultimately only receive 1/100 of that 1/100 slice of priority, or in more understandable terms, 1/10,000 of the priority. Figure 9.3 shows this priority assignment.

The authors and Microsoft recommend assigning a dedicated management server with no traditional agents reporting to it (even in a failover scenario), for the sole purpose of collecting data from your gateway server(s).

When planning for failover, consider the number of gateways reporting to a management server; plan for failover, and ensure you do not failover gateway servers to a management server already hosting a large number of gateways. This means you typically will want to host no more than 3–4 gateways per management server during normal operation, and control failover such that no more than six report to a single management server at any time. Although Microsoft has not documented a maximum number of management servers and gateways for a management group, the maximum tested and validated number is 10 management servers. There is no limit on gateways, but the maximum the authors have experimented with is 16 per management group.

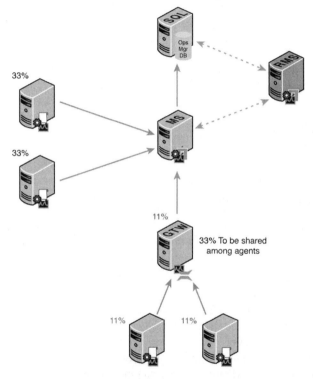

FIGURE 9.3 Priority assignment of gateways

When a single management server hosts multiple gateways, consider that for supportability purposes, you must not exceed the maximum number of 3,000 total agents reporting to the management server. That means if you have three gateways reporting to a management server, each with 1,100 agents, this exceeds the supported limit of agents reporting to a management server, as that management server will have 3,300 agents reporting to it.

It is also important to spread agents equally across multiple gateway servers that are reporting to a single management server. Once again, this is due to how the management server prioritizes data from the gateway servers. The gateway behavior displayed in Figure 9.3 shows how this works.

Finally, when planning to use gateway servers this way, ensure that the management server hardware is sufficiently powerful to handle the excess load. When planning for the RMS and management servers, RAM is critical followed by CPU and finally disk I/O (which is largely unimportant). Gateways, however, cache far more data to disk than management servers do, so the order of importance of resources shifts. In the case of gateways, disk I/O is the priority, followed directly by RAM and then CPU. For this reason, gateways used in this configuration do not make the best candidates for virtualization, as disk I/O is often the first resource to suffer when virtualizing. (Although, as virtualization technology improves, this will become less of a concern.)

Agent Deployment and Management

After planning the location of your databases, management servers, and gateways, you need to consider how to deploy agents. This will come down to the size of your environment:

▶ Small environments generally use the Operations console for agent deployment.

▶ For large and complex environments, Active Directory (AD) integration is a much better option.

When building a resilient infrastructure in OpsMgr and when using gateway servers to host machines across long-distance WAN links, it is critical that you manage agent failover to ensure if a management server fails, the agents are distributed relatively equally across all remaining servers. This is difficult to accomplish on a large scale without using AD integration.

Active Directory integration enables you to assign agents to a management group and retrieve management server information directly from Active Directory. This is convenient for large enterprises, which typically do not deploy agents using the Operations console but will use a software delivery mechanism such as System Center Configuration Manager (ConfigMgr). By itself, however, this does not provide a strong enough reason to use AD integration. What really adds weight to implementing this is the difficulty in managing agent failover without AD integration. AD integration is the only reliable and manageable method available in OpsMgr to facilitate which management servers or gateways host which agents.

How Active Directory Integration Works

AD integration creates a custom container in the directory, populating it with auto-created groups pertaining to the different management servers. The agents identify these groups by using Service Connection Points (SCPs), and the groups are automatically populated by OpsMgr based on an expression specified in the Administration node of the Operations console. Enabling AD integration does not require a schema update, which should make the AD team happy!

This section does not look at the method for configuring AD integration, but at ensuring that you can accurately control agent failover effectively using AD integration. After enabling AD integration, you need to configure the agent assignment queries in the Operations console. This populates the necessary SCP data into AD that the agents will query at startup. To configure the assignment queries, perform the following steps:

1. Open the Operations console, and in the Administration node, navigate to Device Management -> Management Servers.

2. Right-click on the appropriate management server (the one for which you want to create a query) and select Properties. Figure 9.4 shows this screen.

FIGURE 9.4 Management Server Properties

3. Click Add to create a new AD (LDAP) query.

   Specific information for creating a query is in the predecessor to this book, *System Center Operations Manager 2007 Unleashed*, in Chapter 9, "Discovering and Deploying Agents."

A standard query may use machine names to define the results. However, this may not be granular enough in a large number of cases. It is far more useful to query a custom group for members. A custom group lets you add machines to the group that will be correctly assigned to the proper management servers. To query a group, use the following AD query in place of the technique discussed in *System Center Operations Manager 2007 Unleashed*:

```
(&(sAMAccountType=805306369)(memberOf=cn=groupx,ou=Groups,dc=ODYSSEY,dc=COM))
```

You can automatically populate the custom group in AD from a SQL database using the SCPopulate.js script, found in the OpsMgr 2007 Resource Kit located at http://technet.microsoft.com/en-us/opsmgr/bb625978.aspx. This technique is particularly useful, as many organizations use asset management systems that list all servers in use. You can feed the SCPopulate script the results of a SQL query with a list of computer names, adding those names automatically to your custom group (assuming the computer object exists in the directory). Here is an example of the command-line syntax used to run the script:

```
SGPopulate.js Thunder InventoryDB "SELECT ServerName FROM Servers WHERE ServiceLevel
= 3" ADOpsMgrGrp01
```

To ensure the SQL query works, run the query in SQL Query Analyzer, and verify the output is similar to that listed next. Of course, the specific output depends on how you configured your source database and which servers exist within that database:

```
PANTHEON
PIONEER

TORNADO
```

After you populate your computer groups and configure the AD assignment queries in the Operations console, OpsMgr automatically populates AD with the necessary objects (assuming the AD Assignment Account Run As Profile is configured with the necessary access rights). Figure 9.5 is an example of the objects created. All that remains is deploying the OpsMgr agents to those machines you will monitor.

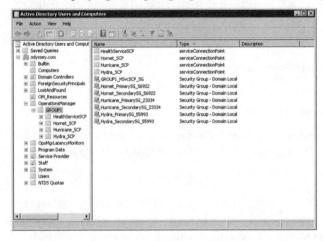

FIGURE 9.5 AD auto-created groups

Using AD integration, you do not deploy the agents from the Operations console—this assigns them a management server rather than configuring them for AD integration. You must install the agents manually using some other method. A common approach is deploying the agent with ConfigMgr 2007 or a similar application. (A companion book in this series, *System Center Configuration Manager 2007 Unleashed*, discusses the steps to deploy the OpsMgr agent.) Verify that the command-line parameters are specified properly to enable AD integration to be correctly enabled and configured. Here are the required command-line parameters:

```
%WinDir%\System32\msiexec.exe /i \\<path\folder>\momagent.msi /qn
USE_SETTINGS_FROM_AD=1 USE_MANUALLY_SPECIFIED_SETTINGS=0
```

Ongoing Agent Management

After deploying the agents and enabling AD integration, there will be ongoing agent maintenance. Examples include applying hotfixes, and reassigning the primary and/or secondary management server an agent reports to keep the number of agents reporting to a single management server balanced across your management group.

Remote Operations

Another concern with distributed environments is accessing the monitoring environment. Most distributed environments require users in remote geographical locations to access OpsMgr, who be located in a completely different physical location across a long-distance link. However, the Operations console works best over a high-speed LAN, as it transfers a large amount of data between the client and the RMS. The next sections look at several methods to provide access to the Operations console and reporting in distributed environments, and discuss potential issues in accessing the console from remote locations. Also discussed is using the Web console rather than the thick client (full console).

Terminal Services

The OpsMgr console was not designed for use across a WAN link. It transfers a significant amount of data between the client and RMS during normal use and slows down considerably when communicating over anything less than a high-speed LAN connection. This means that running the thick client on a computer in a location remote to the RMS will not offer the best user experience!

This is where Terminal Services (TS) comes in. As this is not a book about Terminal Services, this chapter does not cover the technology in any depth. Terminal Services is a component of the Microsoft Windows Server platform that enables users to access applications and data on a remote computer across LAN and WAN links. It can present a full desktop or an application stored on the terminal server to a user in a remote location. The data presentation takes place in a protected memory space so each user's session is dedicated and accessible only to that individual. Figure 9.6 shows the architecture of TS in a more succinct manner, and Table 9.2 describes the components. For additional information, see http://technet.microsoft.com/en-us/library/cc755399(WS.10).aspx.

TABLE 9.2 Terminal Services Components

Component	Description
CSRSS.exe	The Client-Server Runtime Subsystem is the process and thread manager for all logon sessions.
RdpDD.sys	Captures the Windows user interface and translates it into a form readily converted by RDPWD into the RDP protocol.

RdpWD.sys	Unwraps the multi-channel data and then transfers it to the appropriate session.
SMSS.exe	Session Manager creates and manages all sessions.
Termsrv.exe	Manages client connections and initiates creation and shutdown of connection contexts.
Termdd.sys	RDP protocol; listens for RDP client connections on a TCP port.
Tdtcp.sys	Packages the RDP protocol onto the underlying network protocol, TCP/IP.
Wlnotify.dll	Runs in session's WinLogon process to create processes in the user session.
Win32k.sys	Manages Windows GUI environment by taking mouse and keyboard inputs and sending them to the appropriate application.
WinLogon.exe	This system service handles user logons and logoffs and processes the special Windows key combination Ctrl-Alt-Delete. WinLogon is responsible for starting the Windows shell (usually Windows Explorer).

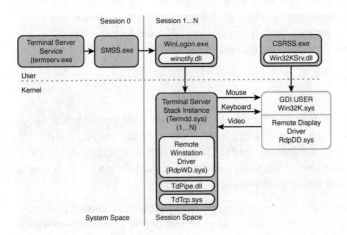

FIGURE 9.6 Terminal Services architecture

Microsoft fully supports using the Operations console in a TS environment; you can install it on a terminal server located on the same LAN as the RMS for fast data access. Users may then log into the terminal server remotely and access the console. This offers the best of both worlds—users are not only able to gain the same or similar experience as if their machine was on the same LAN as the RMS, but the console itself will respond much better since *it is* on the same LAN as the RMS.

Terminal Services by itself is a very acceptable and effective way of distributing the console but suffers some limitations, one being the difficulty of sharing the console seamlessly. Using standard TS, users often must log into the server first and then open the console, which adds administrative overhead and perplexes those users unfamiliar with TS. This is where Citrix can help.

Citrix Presentation Server/XenApp

Through the years, the Citrix XenApp application (as currently known) has existed under various names, from "MetaFrame" through "Presentation Server" and now "XenApp." Through improvements and new features, the core function of the product is unchanged—it lets you maximize investment in Terminal Services technology.

XenApp functions similarly to TS and uses the same underlying technology. However, XenApp provides some very nice features that enhance your ability to give users access to remote applications and data. The primary features that assist with access to the Operations console are seamless application presentation and high availability, as follows:

▶ **High Availability**—Citrix lets you *publish* (the name given to applications presented through XenApp) to multiple XenApp servers, configuring the clients to access a virtual address that routes to one of these physical servers. In the event of a server failure, users are generally unaware of any problem (except perhaps their console briefly disconnects while another server takes over the session). This capability inherently makes the solution more scalable and allows for more simultaneous connections, although Microsoft does not recommend more than 50 consoles connected to the RMS at any one time.

▶ **Seamless Application Presentation**—Perhaps XenApp's most prominent feature is seamless integration. This means that you can publish an application through Citrix and have a shortcut appear on a user's desktop or Start menu. When the user clicks the icon, the application launches, seemingly on the local machine, but actually running on the Citrix server. However, as far as the user is concerned, the application is running from that desktop. This capability provides similar functionality to Terminal Services, with the added bonus of significantly improving and simplifying the user experience.

Terminal Services Access Issues

While Terminal Services and Citrix provide a great method to run the Operations Console from a remote location, using these technologies introduces some inherent issues. The most prevalent of these issues concerns console tasks. OpsMgr has two forms of tasks—agent-based tasks and console tasks:

▶ *Agent-based tasks* do not cause any issues; regardless of where they are initiated from, they filter down to an agent's primary management server, and then to the agent where the task is run locally. Results are passed back the same way—through the agent's primary management server, and then displayed in the Operations console. An example of an agent-based task would be ipconfig, which you cannot execute remotely and therefore runs on the agent.

▶ *Console tasks* are a different story, as these are initiated and run within the console. An example of a console task is the Microsoft Management Console (MMC) Computer Management application, which is loaded on the local machine and connects remotely to the target machine. This may not initially appear to be an issue when using TS, as the RMS and the console are both on the same LAN. However, consider this scenario:

You are monitoring machines in both London and Los Angeles (LA). Your OpsMgr environment is located in LA, with monitored servers in both LA and

London. Your user accesses OpsMgr via Citrix in London. The admin wants to stop a service on a server located in London (about 20 feet from where he is sitting), so he runs the Computer Management task from OpsMgr. As a console task, the task is executed from the console…in Los Angeles, targeted at a server on the other side of the world in London! Computer Management also runs better on a high-speed LAN connection; hence, it can be expected to run exceptionally slowly across the WAN link.

Running more intensive snap-ins such as Exchange System Manager only intensifies the problem. Unfortunately, there is no easy way around this issue if your environment is configured as described here, other than training and setting expectations.

TIP: RUNNING REMOTE TASKS

It is important to educate your users that when running tasks such as launching Computer Management from a remote location, they should expect slow performance and time delays; this typically cannot be avoided.

Web Console

When remotely accessing your management environment, it is often better to utilize the other effective method of connecting to an OpsMgr management group—the Web console. The Web console historically offered a very low level of functionality and was only a useful glance at open alerts. Even through OpsMgr 2007 SP 1, the Web console lacked some fundamental features to make it a powerful tool. With R2, Microsoft provides a real alternative to the thick client by adding much-needed functionality in the form of the Health Explorer to the Web console. In addition, beginning with SP 1, the Web console can run console and agent-based tasks.

High Availability

You will typically see distributed OpsMgr environments in large enterprises where the business relies heavily on its Information Technology (IT) infrastructure, and use of High Availability (HA) technologies is prevalent. A *highly available infrastructure* is one able to tolerate a failure or disaster. A failure can range from a hardware fault on an individual server to a major environmental event affecting all or a large portion of the IT estate. In addition to considering HA, it is critical to plan for the worst-case scenario, which is where Business Continuity (BC) comes in. The "Business Continuity" section of this chapter discusses BC in more detail.

Inherently, OpsMgr offers some degree of high-availability support, although for some aspects of the product, HA is supported by other Microsoft technologies such as Cluster Services and SQL Server. To consider an infrastructure as "highly available," it should be able to withstand at least a single software or hardware failure anywhere without a noticeable loss of service. For OpsMgr, this equates to planning for failure of a management server, gateway, the RMS, the databases, and, in some cases, the Web console. Ideally, a highly available solution could tolerate multiple failures across different components of the product; but there is a limit to how available an infrastructure can be, and the nature of the failure ultimately affects how the product reacts. Although you cannot mitigate some failures by high availability, it is best to plan for the worst-case scenario wherever possible.

Clustering the OpsMgr Components

By design, the RMS and Operational database represent single points of failure for OpsMgr. OpsMgr itself does not provide a native method to deal with a failure of these components; if either is unavailable, the OpsMgr architecture is effectively dead in the water until you recover that component. For large deployments, failure of the data warehouse will have a noticeable and adverse effect on the performance of the management group and should be considered a single point of failure as well. To keep your management group operational, the authors recommend that you take advantage of supporting Microsoft technologies to facilitate high availability. The most prevalent technology here is Microsoft Cluster Services, although it is possible (if unsupported) to use alternative clustering solutions.

Clusters function by presenting a "virtual" server to users while actually hosting the data on two or more physical servers. These servers share the storage media on which the clustered application data is located. If one server fails, another server assumes responsibility and continues servicing user requests. Figure 9.7 diagrams this architecture. Two main types of cluster configurations exist, discussed in the next sections. There are additional types, but these are ultimately based on the two main types, typically with more physical servers (nodes).

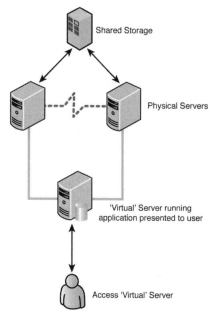

Shared Storage

Physical Servers

'Virtual' Server running
application presented to user

Access 'Virtual' Server

FIGURE 9.7 Cluster architecture

Active-Passive Cluster

In an Active-Passive cluster, one node hosts the application and the other sits idle. If the active server fails, the application fails over and the passive node becomes the active node.

Active-Active

In an Active-Active cluster configuration, both nodes host an application simultaneously. In the event one server fails, the application it was hosting will fail over and the other node will now host both its own application and the failed over one.

Recommendations

The authors recommend Active-Passive clustering in an OpsMgr environment. For reference, the supported cluster configurations for the OpsMgr components are listed on TechNet at http://technet.microsoft.com/en-us/library/bb309428.aspx.

For the databases, you can cluster SQL Server such that if one node fails, the database "fails over" to the available node and continues to service the management group. You can also cluster the RMS role. Clustering the RMS tends to be very reliable, though a little complex and awkward to install and configure.

> **NOTE: SQL CLUSTERING INSTRUCTIONS**
>
> As SQL clustering is covered in detail in the predecessor to this book, *System Center Operations Manager 2007 Unleashed*, and various locations on the Internet and other publications, it is not discussed in detail here. A good example of a SQL clustering configuration document is http://msdn.microsoft.com/en-us/library/ms179530.aspx.

Microsoft does not support OpsMgr management servers and gateways in a cluster configuration, primarily because the application itself is designed to tolerate failures of these components. Agents can failover to an available management server or gateway if there is a server failure, and gateways can automatically fail over to alternate hosting management servers in the event the server they are connected to fails.

As an alternative to clustering the RMS, you can promote another management server to be the RMS when there is a failure. Because the RMS should not host agents, you should provision a dedicated a management server to act as a backup RMS, also without agents reporting to it. More information is available in the "Root Management Server High Availability" section.

When promoting the backup RMS to the RMS role, follow all the usual steps. For detailed steps on promoting a management server to the RMS, see Chapter 12, "Backup and Recovery," of *System Center Operations Manager 2007 Unleashed*, or the TechNet article at http://technet.microsoft.com/en-us/library/cc540401.aspx.

NOTE: THE BACKUP RMS IS NOT AN EXPLICIT OPSMGR ROLE

The backup RMS is not an existing role within OpsMgr. It is merely a descriptive name the authors have given to a management server whose sole purpose is to be online so that it may be promoted to an RMS in the event that the RMS fails and cannot be quickly and easily recovered.

Root Management Server High Availability

As discussed in the "Clustering the OpsMgr Components" section, the primary supported method for RMS high availability is Microsoft clustering. The two currently supported cluster configurations are standard Active-Passive and an Active-Active-Passive configuration where the RMS and SQL databases exist on the same cluster, albeit on different nodes. Because of the extra node, the two components should never need to exist on the same physical node, but each node should still be able to physically support both SQL and the RMS role in the event of a major failure.

NOTE: RMS AND MAJORITY NODE SET CLUSTERS

A root management server cannot be configured to run on a Majority Node Set (MNS) cluster configuration. The RMS requires shared disks for the storage of the Health Service State for the RMS services. This information needs to be available to the other node when the cluster fails over. When using ManagementServer-ConfigTool, it will not let you proceed if you cannot point to a shared storage path.

The RMS role in OpsMgr is not strictly cluster-aware. The RMS is supported on a cluster, but the installation routine is not designed specifically to install onto a cluster and requires significant manual configuration. If the entire cluster fails and must be restored, re-promoting the cluster to an RMS is tricky (and not possible until SP 1). Configuring the RMS in this manner consists of four main steps, as follows:

- ▶ Installing OpsMgr
- ▶ Creating cluster resources
- ▶ Restoring the RMS key onto the second node
- ▶ Configuring the RMS cluster

The first three steps are relatively straightforward and well documented. Install the management server component on the first node of the cluster, and then install the management server component on the second node.

To configure the cluster, perform the following steps:

1. Manually create the following cluster resources in a new cluster resource group:

    - ▶ Physical Disk
    - ▶ IP Address
    - ▶ Network Name

▶ Generic Service (Health Service/System Center Management Service)

▶ Generic Service (Config Service/System Center Management Configuration Service)

▶ Generic Service (SDK/System Center Data Access Service)

2. Back up the RMS key from the first node (which is now the RMS) and restore it to the second node.

3. Use ManagementServerConfigTool.exe, located on the OpsMgr installation media, to configure the two cluster nodes to host the RMS role. In addition, the tool configures the location of the cache files to the shared disk and sets the RMS name as the name of the cluster virtual server.

Note that you must do all of this *prior to* starting the OpsMgr services. This is well documented in the OpsMgr high-availability guide on TechNet at http://technet.microsoft.com/en-us/library/dd789024.aspx and therefore not covered in detail here.

USING SETSPN WITH MANAGEMENTSERVERCONFIG

If you did not run ManagementServerConfigTool using the account running the cluster service, you must manually run the SetSPN utility to set the Health Service SPN on the cluster virtual server. Use the RunAs command to execute the SetSPN utility, specifying the same account the cluster service is running under:

```
runas /user:<domain>\<username> "SetSPN.exe -A
MSOMHSvc/<VirtualManagementServerFQDN> <VirtualManagementServerNetbios>"
```

Here's what you need to do when running SetSPN:

▶ Specify the MSOMHSvc SPN as the server name of the virtual server.

▶ Register the SDK service SPN against the service account running the SDK (System Center Data Access) service.

▶ If this is an RMS cluster, you must register the two nodes rather than the virtual server.

Here is an example of the command-line syntax incorporating two nodes:

```
runas /user:<domain>\<username> "SetSPN.exe -A MSOMSdkSvc/<Node1FQDN>
<Node1Netbios>"
runas /user:<domain>\<username> "SetSPN.exe -A MSOMSdkSvc/<Node2FQDN>
<Node2Netbios>"
```

Additional information is available at Walter Chomak's blog at http://wchomak.spaces.live.com/blog/cns!F56EFE25599555EC!824.entry?dir=Next&ph=F56EFE25599555EC!973 and Chapter 10, "Complex Configurations," of *System Center Operations Manager 2007 Unleashed*.

In addition to ensuring that the RMS is available in the event of a failure, you will want to prepare for a worst-case scenario. Using a cluster supports a degree of failure but is not failsafe. As an example, if the shared storage ceases to function, the cluster may also be severely affected. Therefore, it is highly recommended that you provision a backup RMS, as discussed in the "Recommendations" section. Technically, a backup RMS is not an OpsMgr role; it is simply a management server without agents reporting to it, whose sole purpose is to be promoted to an RMS if the primary RMS or RMS cluster fails. The backup RMS should have the RMS key restored to it in advance (as the key rarely, if ever, changes). Do not configure any agents to report to the backup RMS; should it become the RMS, you do not want to have to reassign agents to another management server. Clearly, not all organizations will budget (or have capacity) for an additional server that effectively does very little the majority of the time. With that in mind, here are several options to maximize the server acting as the backup RMS:

▶ The server does not solely have to act as a backup RMS. This section mentioned that you should not connect agents to this machine, but you can certainly use this server to host the Web console or the reporting website. Both these roles are relatively lightweight and should not significantly affect the server if it is running as an RMS—and when it is a backup RMS, it will be utilized rather than sitting idle.

▶ In all but the largest of environments, the backup RMS can usually be a virtual machine (VM). If there is a failure, other servers and services will likely be affected, so any degradation of performance encountered by running the RMS role temporarily on a VM should be of limited concern.

Finally, backups are critical to ensure that you can recover from a major disaster. The "Business Continuity" section looks at backup and recovery in more detail.

Advanced Cluster Configurations

The assumption is that your cluster configuration is fairly standard: two nodes sitting close to one another with shared storage in between them. However, some environments may have a more advanced cluster configuration. In this case, advanced means you may be using multi-node clusters, geographically remote (geo) clusters, or not using Microsoft Clustering technologies at all, and instead opting for Veritas or some other third-party vendor. In these cases, supportability may be an issue, and the authors cannot guarantee that your configuration will meet the minimum-supported requirements, but nonetheless, advanced cluster configurations do exist and therefore warrant some discussion.

Advanced and Third-Party Clustering

In the authors' experience, the most commonly seen advanced clustering configurations are third-party cluster solutions, with the most common being Veritas Storage Foundation (now Symantec, but referred to as Veritas, as this is the more recognized name of the technology). Veritas clustering (Storage Foundation) is an alternative clustering technology to Microsoft's Cluster Services. In large-scale OpsMgr deployments, the authors have come across Veritas clusters hosting the OpsMgr SQL databases and even the RMS. As every environment is different and the OpsMgr components are not strictly supported on a Veritas cluster (particularly the RMS), specific instructions are not offered here. However, here is some advice:

► Ensure that you are running the most recent version of Storage Foundation and that all firmware and drivers are current.

► The RMS role requires some additional configuration to enable it to function, namely for the cluster virtual server name to be correctly registered in Active Directory and to have a valid AD computer account. Although this is straight-forward with MSCS, it does require some specific configuration when using Veritas clustering. The exact location of the settings to apply will vary, based on the particular version of Veritas clustering.

Multi-node clusters are generally unsupported with OpsMgr. The one exception is maintaining an Active-Active-Passive cluster with SQL Server and the RMS roles on different physical nodes at all times. SQL Server also supports creating a multi-node cluster to host databases, although this is currently unsupported for OpsMgr, as the product team has not validated the configuration.

Geo Clustering

Geo-clustering is not a new concept, although it is now appearing more often in large enterprises. A geo-cluster is effectively the same as a regular two- (or multi-) node cluster, except each node is located in a geographically remote location from each other; one in Manhattan and one in Brooklyn, for example. This technology typically takes advantage of the latest advancements in hardware utilizing SAN replication and switch trunking:

► SAN replication synchronizes data between two SANs, keeping the data on both systems current. If one SAN fails, the other can immediately assume re-sponsibility for the cluster connections keeping the system online.

► Switch trunking allows a switch VLAN to stretch across two (or more) switches located remotely to one another; this means that for the cluster heart-beat, data can be transmitted as if the machines were plugged into the same physical switch or hub.

Geo-clustering requires a large hardware investment and significant bandwidth be-tween sites in large environments, but if resources are available, you can configure the system using MSCS such that the system functions and responds as if the nodes of the cluster are located close to each other; providing very fast failovers and minimal issues. Although this configuration was previously unsupported, the Microsoft OpsMgr prod-uct team announced in May 2009 that they now consider geo-clusters to be a supported configuration—providing the cluster itself adheres to Microsoft's guidelines on both standard and geo clustering. More information can be found on the OpsMgr supported configurations page at http://technet.microsoft.com/en-us/library/bb309428.aspx.

Clustering Alternatives

As discussed in the "Clustering the OpsMgr Components" section, clustering is the recommended method to provide high availability for the OpsMgr databases and RMS.

However, there are several other options if clustering is not an option due to hardware, software, or skill limitations.

RMS Redundancy Alternatives

You can use a backup RMS to add an additional level of redundancy to a clustered RMS, and when clustering the RMS is not possible, use the backup RMS as the primary method of providing high availability. Keep in mind that promoting a dedicated management server to an RMS is, for the most part, a manual process. You can script the process, but that involves custom development and is beyond the scope of this chapter.

SQL High Availability

Providing high availability to the SQL databases in the absence of clustering is possible in two ways—SQL log shipping or database mirroring:

▶ SQL log shipping is the process of creating a second instance of SQL (usually on separate physical hardware) containing a copy of the OpsMgr databases. Logs are periodically transferred (or "shipped") to the backup server and replayed against the copy databases, providing a relatively up-to-date copy of the data in the event the primary database server fails.

▶ Database mirroring is available in SQL 2005 SP 1 and above. Database mirroring achieves the same result as log shipping but is managed fully by SQL Server. Mirroring also provides an up-to-date "synched" copy of the database as opposed to a copy updated on a schedule, which therefore may be somewhat out of date.

The "SQL Log Shipping and Database Mirroring" section discusses these technologies in more detail.

On the surface, database mirroring seems the obvious choice. However, as this is not fully tested by the OpsMgr product team, it is currently unsupported. Log shipping, although less functional, is fully supported.

Before deciding on either approach, realize that the database copies will be hosted on physically unique SQL systems with different computer names and possibly different SQL instance names. This means that if you have to invoke disaster recovery and utilize the backup database, you must make registry changes to each management server and update OpsMgr databases to reflect the new database server name. However, you can script this process or simplify it by using SQL aliases.

Business Continuity

The "High Availability" sections of this chapter looked at configuring OpsMgr for high availability. The next sections take the high-availability story one step further by exploring the options available to ensure that following a disaster you can recover OpsMgr—first to enable you to regain visibility into your environment, and ultimately to help you troubleshoot and resolve issues arising from the disaster.

Business Continuity is concerned with how to minimize the impact of a disaster and the processes and technology to ensure that your business can recover quickly and with minimal data loss. IT forms the backbone of many businesses, with the vast majority of company data existing solely in digital format and replacing traditional files and folders. For many companies, if this data were lost, they would simply cease to function. This makes it important to construct a reliable business continuity plan. OpsMgr not only requires consideration in this plan but also can help execute it by providing much needed visibility into the affects of any disaster, helping you prioritize your disaster recovery plan and ensure service resumes quickly.

Backup and Recovery

The first and simplest form of Business Continuity is backup and recovery. This process ensures your data is copied to alternative media (preferably away from the server it exists on) and that it can be copied back if the original copy is lost or damaged. OpsMgr is no different from any other application in that it needs to be backed up. However, OpsMgr does not offer any automatic backup solution out of the box, so you need to ensure all components of the product are backed up and that you have a process to restore them in the event of a failure. There are a number of OpsMgr components requiring backup; this is discussed in Chapter 12, "Backup and Recovery," of *System Center Operations Manager 2007 Unleashed*. The main components requiring backup are the operational database, the reporting data warehouse, and the RMS encryption key.

Backing Up the Operational Database and Reporting Data Warehouse

The OpsMgr databases are hosted in SQL Server, and it is recommended you use the SQL Server backup utility to back up the databases to disk, at which point you can copy the flat files to a remote disk or to tape.

> **TIP: THIRD-PARTY SQL AGENTS**
>
> Some backup solutions provide their own backup agents for SQL Server, but for supportability reasons both the authors and Microsoft recommend using the built-in SQL Server backup utility.

It is also highly recommended that you back up the SQL Server system databases (Master and MSDB). See Chapter 12 of *System Center Operations Manager 2007 Unleashed* for the specific processes to back up the databases.

> **NOTE: THE TEMPDB DATABASE**
>
> TempDB is a system database but cannot be backed up—it is strictly used as a temporary store of data and recreated each time SQL Server starts.

Master

Back up the Master database file as often as necessary. Here is a list of events that update the Master database and therefore require performing a new backup:

► Creating or deleting a user database. (If a user database grows automatically to accommodate new data, Master is not affected.)

► Adding or removing files and filegroups.

► Adding logins or other operations that are related to login security. (Database security operations, such as adding a user to a database, do not affect Master.)

► Changing server-wide or database configuration options.

► Creating or removing logical backup devices.

► Configuring the server for distributed queries and remote procedure calls (RPCs), such as adding linked servers or remote logins.

Backing up the Master database ensures you can restore the database server in the event of a failure.

MSDB

The MSDB database is used by the SQL Server Agent for scheduling alerts and jobs and by other features such as Service Broker and Database mail. Treat this database as a user database and back it up nightly utilizing a full database backup.

Reporting Databases

SQL Reporting Services and therefore the Reporting component of OpsMgr use the ReportServer and ReportServerTempDB databases. You should treat these as user databases and back them up nightly utilizing a full backup.

Database Recovery

In the event of an Operations Manager database corruption or database server failure, you may need to recover the database from backup. Providing the database was backed up to a .bak file (as the authors and Microsoft recommend), restoring the database is straightforward.

The following procedure will restore the Operations Manager database (this procedure is appropriate to the OperationsManager and OperationsManagerDW databases).

First, ensure that the .bak file(s) are copied from tape to a local disk or a network share before following the steps below. This discussion assumes that the .bak file(s) were copied to *C:\temp* and SQL Server 2008 is used to host the databases:

1.   Stop the System Center Data Access service on the RMS.

2.   Log into the SQL Server system, using an account with rights to restore an SQL database.

3.   From the Start menu, click Programs -> Microsoft SQL Server 2008 -> SQL Server Management Studio.

4.   When prompted, verify that the SQL instance is correct and click Connect.

5.   Expand Databases in the left-hand pane.

6.   Right-click Databases; then select Restore Database....

7.   Type the name of the database (or select an existing database if replacing it).

8.   Select Restore From Device and click the ... button.

9.   Select backup media as File and click Add.

10.   Browse to the location of the .bak file—in this case, C:\temp\<*database*>.bak.

11.   Click OK three times.

12.   Restart the System Center Data Access service on the RMS.

To ensure a restore is possible if required, back up the server using the Windows backup engine or a suitable third-party backup solution, such as System Center Data Protection Manager (DPM). The authors recommend backing up the items listed in Table 9.3 on the database server to ensure that you can restore the server from backup in the event of a failure.

TABLE 9.3 Objects Requiring Backup on the Database Server

Server	Object Type	Object
OpsMgr Database Server	System Databases (Using SQL Agent)	Master, Model, Msdb
	User Databases (Using SQL Agent)	OperationsManager
	Database Transaction Logs (Using SQL Agent)	OperationsManager
	Files (Using backup software)	*.bak *.trn
	System State (Using backup software)	System State Data
Data Warehouse Database Server	System Databases (Using SQL Agent)	Master, Model, Msdb,
	User Databases (Using SQL Agent)	OperationsManagerDW, ReportServer, ReportServerTempDB
	Database Transaction Logs (Using SQL Agent)	OperationsManagerDW
Reporting Server	Files (Using backup software)	*.bak *.trn
	System State (Using backup software)	System State Data
	OpsMgr Files	%*ProgramFiles*%\System Center Operations Manager\
	Website Files	%*inetpub*%
	SQL RS Data	%*Program Files*%\Microsoft SQL Server

IIS Metabase (assuming you have configured the backup in the IIS management console)	%*Windir*%\System32\inetsrv\MetaBack

The RMS Encryption Key

The RMS is responsible for securing all Run As account and Operations Manager account data in the Operational database. This data is encrypted with a secure key created during setup of the RMS. In addition to backing up the files on the RMS, you must also back up this key.

If you rebuild the RMS or move the role to a different server, you must re-import the RMS encryption key, so back up this key to file and to disk and/or tape. The RMS key is typically stored locally on the RMS cluster nodes and backed up to tape or copied to a network share with a backup process in place. Because this file is not updated, you can easily maintain multiple copies for redundancy. Chapter 12 of *System Center Operations Manager 2007 Unleashed* discusses the process to back up the RMS key.

Recovering the RMS from a Failure

If the RMS cluster suffers a catastrophic failure, you may need to move the RMS role temporarily to an available management server to enable the management group to continue functioning while you recover the cluster. There should only be a single RMS at any one time, so after recovering the cluster, do not bring the RMS role online before removing it from the management server temporarily hosting it. See Chapter 12 of *System Center Operations Manager 2007 Unleashed* for the procedure to promote an existing management server to a RMS in a disaster recovery scenario.

Running two RMS servers simultaneously (that is, having the System Center Data Access and System Center Management Configuration services enabled and running on two servers at the same time) can seriously damage an OpsMgr infrastructure. It is critical to ensure that when promoting a management server to an RMS, if the old RMS is still running, the services are stopped and disabled.

NOTE: AD INTEGRATION RECONFIGURATION

If you utilize AD integration and move the RMS role, you must again execute MOMADAdmin (used to enable Active Directory Integration in OpsMgr by creating the necessary objects in Active Directory). This is because the objects in AD reference the RMS server, which has changed. Once the original RMS is back online, run the MOMADAdmin.exe tool one final time to reconfigure the AD objects to reference the original RMS.

SQL Log Shipping and Database Mirroring

Although SQL backups are critical to ensure that you can recover in the event of a failure, they have limitations. The most significant is that backups typically run on a schedule (even when doing regular transaction log backups if the database uses the Full Recovery model), meaning that the data created between backups will be lost during a restore. If your data is critical enough that a loss is unacceptable, Microsoft provides several additional technologies you can utilize to further reduce the risk of data loss in the event of a major disaster—SQL Log Shipping and SQL Database Mirroring. Both log shipping and database mirroring work similarly in that they transfer the delta changes from the primary database to a copy stored elsewhere (preferably offsite).

Log Shipping

Log shipping, introduced in the "SQL High Availability" section, is the more mature of the two technologies but not as functional as the newer database mirroring technology.

Database Mirroring

Database mirroring works similar to log shipping but is more real-time. Using SQL log shipping, data is shipped on a schedule; with database mirroring, data transfer can be configured in one of two ways—synchronous and asynchronous:

- ► In asynchronous mode, data is transferred from the primary to the secondary database but no error checking is performed (unless utilizing a witness server).

- ► When using synchronous mode, data is not committed to the primary database until a successful write is confirmed on the backup database. This method ensures a reliable backup copy but can have a negative impact on the performance of the primary database.

It is important to note that database mirroring only supports copying data to a single database, whereas log shipping can copy transaction logs to multiple servers. You can use log shipping and database mirroring in conjunction with one another to utilize the best of both technologies. Additional information is available at
http://msdn.microsoft.com/en-us/library/ms187016.aspx.
Information on configuring database mirroring is available at
http://msdn.microsoft.com/en-us/library/ms188712.aspx.

Visio Add-In for OpsMgr 2007

The Visio Add-In for OpsMgr 2007, released in mid 2009, provides the ability to map out a diagram in Microsoft Visio using standard Visio icons and connect the diagram to OpsMgr to view the state from OpsMgr within the Visio diagram. Figure 9.8 shows an example of a diagram created using the Visio Add-In.

This tool provides the ability to expand upon the distributed application designer within OpsMgr, enabling you to draw maps and diagrams that more accurately represent your environment and display the live state from OpsMgr directly in the diagram. This is particularly useful for displaying on big screens and presenting to management.

Here are the features included in the Add-In (see http://technet.microsoft.com/en-us/library/ee342533.aspx for additional information):

▶ Distributed applications exported from OpsMgr 2007 R2 as Visio documents automatically show live health state information on the exported objects when opened in Visio.

▶ Easily create new Visio documents and link shapes to any managed object (computer, database, website, perspective, and so on) to show the current health state.

▶ Automatically link entire existing Visio documents to the computer and network devices managed by Operations Manager by matching computer names or IP addresses.

▶ Automatically refresh health states in Visio documents. Use this option along with Visio's full-screen view to create dashboard views suitable for use as a summary display in a datacenter control room.

▶ Predefined data graphics enable you to toggle from Operations Manager health icons to shape color for health state.

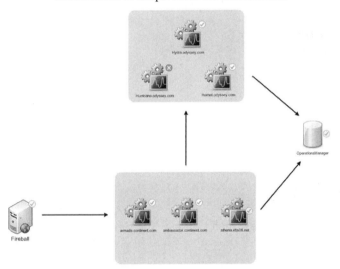

FIGURE 9.8 A diagram created with the Visio Add-In for OpsMgr 2007

If you are familiar with Visio, you'll find it easy to use the Add-In. Download the Add-In from the Visio Toolbox at http://go.microsoft.com/fwlink/?LinkId=159727. Installation information is available at http://technet.microsoft.com/en-us/library/ee355210.aspx. Perform the following steps to create a basic diagram:

1. Install the Add-In itself; this requires installing Visio 2007 somewhere. (The authors recommend a desktop machine.) You will also need to install the Visual Studio Tools for Office 3.0 Runtime, available at http://www.microsoft.com/downloads/details.aspx?FamilyId=54EB3A5A-0E52-40F9-A2D1-EECD7A092DCB&displaylang=en.

2. With Visio and the Runtime installed, the add-in is simple to install with no options to specify during the installation. When first loading Visio after installing the Add-In, you are presented with the dialog in Figure 9.9. Click Install.

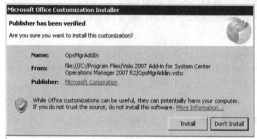

FIGURE 9.9 Visio Add-In Installer dialog

3. Create a new network diagram. The first step is connecting Visio to OpsMgr. From the new menu that appears, select Configure Data Source to bring up the screen shown in Figure 9.10.

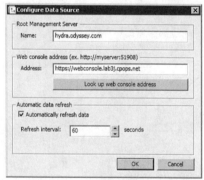

FIGURE 9.10 The Configure Data Source screen

4. Here is the information to configure on the screen displayed in Figure 9.10:

   ▶ **Root Management Server Name**—This is the Fully Qualified Domain Name (FQDN) of the RMS. Figure 9.10 shows **HYDRA.ODYSSEY.COM** specified.

   ▶ **Web console address**—The easiest way to find the Web console address is by clicking the Look Up Web Console Address button.

   ▶ **Automatically refresh data**—Choose whether the diagram will automatically update. If you plan to use the diagram to visualize the live status of your environment, check this option and specify a reasonable refresh interval. The example in Figure 9.10 shows an interval of every 60 seconds.

With the data source configured and the add-in linked to OpsMgr, more menu items become available, shown in Figure 9.11. To begin creating a basic diagram, start by inserting shapes. This example creates the view of the OpsMgr architecture displayed in Figure 9.8.

FIGURE 9.11 Additional menu options

5. Select Insert Shape from the Operations Manager menu displayed in Figure 9.11. This brings up Figure 9.12, where you will choose Other Class as the class object in the drop-down box. Search for **Root Management Server** from the subsequent dialog and select the Hydra.Odyssey.com RMS instance. Click Insert. The Hydra shape is added to the diagram and a small status icon appears in the top-right corner, indicating this object's state is being pulled from OpsMgr. Repeat the procedure, this time adding the management servers (When you select Other Class, search for **Management Server**.)

FIGURE 9.12 The Insert Shape menu

Figure 9.13 shows the management servers added, with a generic server shape to the left of the management servers and RMS. The bottom pane in the Visio window displayed in Figure 9.13 shows several links were created with the objects in OpsMgr. It is possible to link existing Visio objects to OpsMgr in addition to creating new shapes using the OpsMgr add-in. Let's create a link for the genetic server icon.

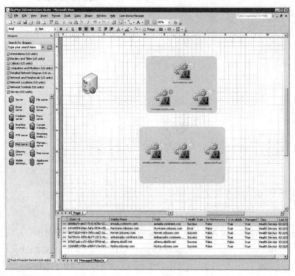

FIGURE 9.13 The diagram including a generic server shape

6. Before you can link the shape, you must add something in the shape properties to identify it in OpsMgr. There are various ways to do this—in this case, add the name of the server to the shape data; this is the Network Name data item. Right-click the shape and select Shape – Shape Data. In the dialog, enter the machine's FQDN in the Network Name field as shown in Figure 9.14 and click OK.

7. After adding the shape data, select the generic shape and click the Automatically Link option from the Operations Manager menu. This starts a wizard to link the shape automatically:

▶ On the first screen, choose the Selected Shapes option and click Next.

▶ On the next screen, choose the Network Name option from the drop-down on the left and match it to display name on the right. Click Next.

▶ If you are successful, the Windows Computer object of the server appears in the following screen, shown in Figure 9.15.

8. Click Next and then Finish, completing the linking. Observe the status icon appearing on the top right of the shape, verifying the shape is linked. It is also possible to manually link, but automatic linking is often easier.

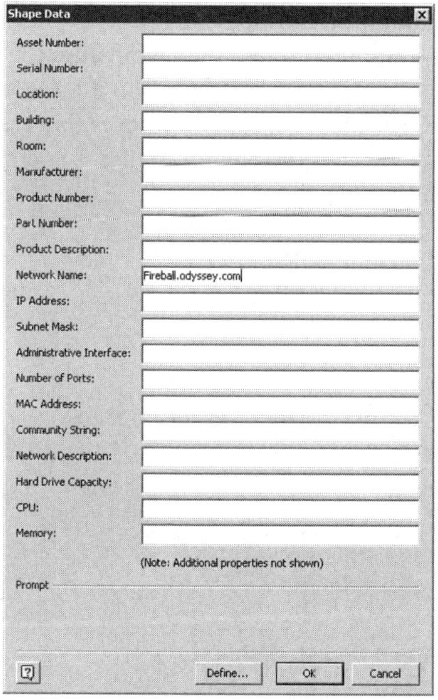

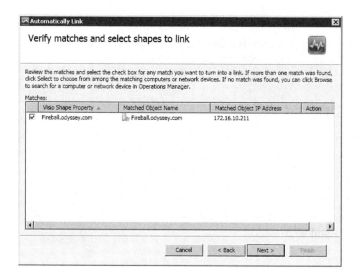

FIGURE 9.14 Enter the FQDN to add shape data.

FIGURE 9.15 Server found when linking the shape

Once you know the basics, you can embellish the diagram as much or as little as you choose. This example added several linking arrows and rearranged the layout slightly from Figure 9.8, but you can add additional shapes, containers, and even clip art. Once the diagram is completed, not only does it link to OpsMgr for display purposes, but (as shown in Figure 9.16) right-clicking a shape lets you access the Health Explorer and Alerts View in the Web console directly from the Visio diagram!

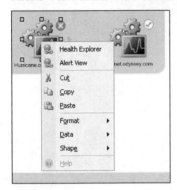

FIGURE 9.16 Accessing the Health Explorer from the completed shape

Although the Visio Add-In provides more diagramming functionality to OpsMgr and enables creating custom diagrams, a third-party product is available that extends this capability even further. LiveMaps from Savision provides the ability to create custom maps you can integrate into the OpsMgr console. You can configure these diagrams with nested relationships enabling drill through from one report to another. More information on Savision LiveMaps is available at http://www.savision.com.

Beyond the Basics of ACS

The Audit Collection Service component of Operations Manager 2007 enables users to centrally collect and report on Windows security logs for audit and regulatory compliance requirements. While Chapter 15, "Monitoring Audit Collection Services" of *System Center Operations Manager 2007 Unleashed* discusses the core architecture and planning concepts of ACS, this discussion takes an in-depth look at what's new in OpsMgr 2007 R2, how users can further optimize ACS, and the wealth of community resources for administrators and engineers.

ACS in OpsMgr 2007 R2

The release of OpsMgr 2007 R2 provides several significant updates. This includes the following:

▶ A rollup of all ACS hotfixes

▶ SQL Server 2008 support

▶ Updated event schema and `adtAdmin` command

▶ Consolidated Windows Server 2003 and 2008 audit reporting

While seemingly a short list, these updates provide significantly greater auditing capabilities and a more reliable ACS infrastructure.

With the rollup of ACS hotfixes, users have more reliable audit database indexing and grooming enforcement as well as enhanced processing of security event globally unique identifiers (GUIDs). Here are the Microsoft knowledge base articles providing details on these enhancements:

▶ http://support.microsoft.com/kb/949969/

▶ http://support.microsoft.com/kb/954948/

▶ http://support.microsoft.com/kb/954329/

Complementing the hotfix rollup, Microsoft updated the ACS eventschema.xml, which normalizes events before they are inserted into the Audit database. Although all security events are collected by ACS, these schema updates provide full support for processing new Vista SP 1 and Windows Server 2008 SP 1 security events (such as Network Access Protection [NAP] quarantine events), and the new Cross Platform auditing events within ACS, enabling additional audit reporting and more robust usage.

Another important infrastructure update is the new command switches for the adtAdmin cmdlet used to administer ACS. These include get and set functionality for partition retention, partition switch offset and interval, converting to local time, and index maintenance. Previously one had to edit these configurations directly in the dtConfig table, a method that was prone to error. Now those attributes are exposed and can be administered via adtAdmin.

The next major improvement found with the OpsMgr 2007 R2 update for ACS is official support for SQL Server 2008. This provides vast improvements in overall SQL performance, resource usage and governance, and advanced data auditing, which can be written to the local security event log. For a full list of what's new in SQL Server 2008, see http://www.microsoft.com/sqlserver/2008/en/us/whats-new.aspx.

Finally, Microsoft revamped the out-of-box audit reports to improve performance and include consolidated auditing across Windows Server 2000, 2003, and 2008. Those with mixed environments or already fully migrated over to Windows Server 2008 can run the same audit reports previously available, along with some new additions across all your Windows devices.

NOTE: WINDOWS SERVER 2008 EVENT PROCESSING

Windows Server 2008 introduces security event subcategories that unfortunately ACS does not process correctly, resulting in null values inserted into the Category field in the Audit database. Additionally some security events do not include the user Security IDs (SIDs) or the SID may not always be captured on high-volume events, which could affect filter reliability, some audit reports, and alerting that rely on those values' consistency.

ACS Noise Filtering

Out of the box, ACS is configured to collect all security events. One of the most important administrative activities to perform—after an ACS installation and routinely afterwards—is to filter noise events from being inserted into the Audit database. Noise events are usually considered anything unnecessary that is not required for audit collection or reporting. Removing noise reduces the overall event volume collected by ACS, which directly relates to ACS load, storage needs, and reporting performance. ACS noise filters are managed at each local collector by the adtAdmin command with the /getquery or /setquery switch, as discussed in Chapter 15 of *System Center Opera System Center Operations Manager 2007 Unleashed*. Here are several key considerations about ACS noise filtering to keep in mind:

▶ The default query out-of-box is SELECT * FROM AdtsEvent, which allows all events to be inserted into the Audit database. You will want to modify this to support audit requirements and minimize event load by removing unnecessary events.

▶ The query syntax is Windows Management Instrumentation (WMI) Query Language (WQL), not SQL, which has some minor syntactical differences. In particular, WQL does not support advanced string manipulations such as querying null values. For detailed Microsoft guidance on WQL, visit http://msdn2.microsoft.com/en-us/library/aa394606(VS.85).aspx.

▶ Noise filter length and complexity can affect query performance and event processing via the collector. You will want to write noise filters to exclude the noisiest events first, optimizing processing at the collector. You can assess noise by evaluating the event load on the collector prior to enabling filters.

▶ Filters can be tested by running a WQL query that represents the filter expression, but does not include the NOT statement, against the ACS WMI stream.

Noise filtering is a bottom-up approach, starting with the domain and local audit policies, then objects (if auditing Directory Services or Object Access), then specific Events IDs, and finally specific use case scenarios such as a successful logon by a domain service account. Figure 9.17 illustrates this approach to noise filtering.

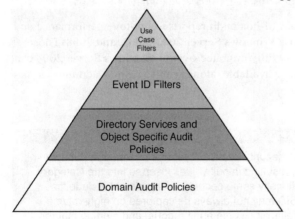

FIGURE 9.17 ACS noise-filtering approach

Note that for Windows Server 2000 and 2003, audit policies are enabled at the category level, whereas in Windows Server 2008, users can enable policies at the subcategory. This is especially useful when planning your audit policies in consideration of noise filtering requirements. Chapter 15 of *System Center Operations Manager 2007 Unleashed* discusses audit policy planning. You can also find a list of recommended audit policies and security guidelines in the Microsoft Windows Server 2008 Security Compliance Management Toolkit available at http://technet.microsoft.com/en-us/library/cc514539.aspx.

Keeping in mind noise filter planning always starts with assessing those domain and object audit policies in use or required, you will need to plan your event and use case noise filters. This is best achieved using a lab or live environment that generates the relevant security events that might require filtering. For additional information, examples, and guidance on ACS noise filtering, see the "Community Resources" section of this chapter

ACS Access Hardening

Given the role of ACS and the data it collects, you may need to lock down the environment and secure the infrastructure components. You can harden ACS on forwarders, collectors, audit databases, and reporting servers. Whether you will need to employ these types of measures to secure your environment depends on security requirements, risk concerns, and your specific business needs. Figure 9.18 illustrates a generic ACS architecture in association with potential vulnerabilities that could be further protected, and Table 9.4 lists ACS component vulnerabilities and mitigation options.

TABLE 9.4 ACS Component Vulnerabilities and Mitigation Options

Item	Vulnerability	Mitigation
1	Forwarder service can be stopped or reconfigured to undesired state.	Apply domain policy to start service automatically; auto-restart service on failure; apply restrictive permissions and/or service level auditing.
2	Collector service can be stopped, and noise filters manipulated.	Apply domain policy to start service automatically; auto-restart service on failure; apply restrictive permissions and/or service-level auditing.
3	Collector to database communications is unencrypted.	Apply TLS/SSL to communications channel.
4	Audit database is governed via SQL security.	Lockdown SQL Server; enable audit policies to track privileged activity.
5	Reporting via OpsMgr opens all reports to all users using console.	Lockdown reports in OpsMgr using Software Development Kit (SDK).
6	Archived files should be secured and monitored for any use other than authorized accounts.	Restrict access to archive directory; implement File/Folder auditing policies where files are stored.

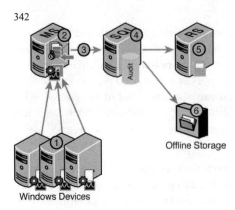

Offline Storage

Windows Devices

FIGURE 9.18 ACS access hardening

Although this chapter cannot cover every scenario in detail, it documents the following two tasks:

▶ Hardening the ACS services

▶ Locking down audit report access via the OpsMgr console

The following steps outline how to apply a domain group policy to the ACS forwarder service that automatically starts the service, auto-restarts the service on failure, defines user access, and enables auditing of failure actions. You can use this as a model to build a custom group policy object (GPO) specifically for your environment and audit requirements. The full HTML report of this GPO is with the online content accompanying this book:

1. Open the Group Policy Management Console, select a domain, right-click, and select Create a GPO in this domain, and link it here.

2. Enter a name for the GPO, such as **Lockdown ACS Forwarder Service**.

3. Select the new GPO. Under Security Filtering, remove authenticated users and add the Domain Computers or applicable computer group.

4. Right-click the new GPO and select Edit.

5. Go to Computer Configuration ->Policies -> Windows Settings -> Security Settings -> System Services.

6. Select Operations Manager Audit Forwarding Service, right-click and select Properties.

7. Select Define this Policy.

8. Under Select service startup mode, select Automatic.

9. Click the Edit Security button.

10. Choose the users or groups with access to this service. Keep in mind the default service account for ACS forwarders is the Network Service account.

11. Click the Advanced button to configure specific rights to service and auditing policies.

12. Close the open windows by clicking OK to accept your changes.

13. Now, go to Computer Configuration -> Preferences -> Control Panel Settings -> Services.

14. Right-click Services and select New -> Service.

15. Find AdtAgent as the service; configure recovery and startup modes as desired.

16. Click OK to save your settings.

When using a single report server for both OpsMgr and ACS reporting, members of the Operations Manager Reporting Operators role have global access to all reports, meaning anyone in the default OpsMgr reporting group is able to run ACS audit reports. If you desire integrated reporting in OpsMgr with greater separation of duties, you can use PowerShell to create a new role to partition access between the OpsMgr and ACS reports.

The following example walks through the basic steps of locking down audit reports as demonstrated in the ACS Master Class session ACS Access Hardening (see the "Community Resources" section for more information on the ACS Master Class Series). The PowerShell scripts referenced in this example are included in the online content accompanying this book:

1. On the root management server, create a new reporting role using the CreateRepRole.PS1 PowerShell sample script. The default name of this role is Security Auditors Reporting Role.

2. On the RMS, get a list of user roles and GUIDs using the PowerShell sample script ListRole.PS1. You will need the GUID for Operations Manager Reporting Operators and the new reporting role created in step 1.

3. On the OpsMgr reporting server, open SQL Server Reporting Services (SRS) via a web browser by going to http://localhost/Reports, browse to the targeted audit reporting folder, select the target folder, click the Properties tab, and then click the Security option on the left-hand menu to edit user and group access.

   ▶ Remove the GUID associated with the Operations Manager Reporting Operators role.

   ▶ Add a new role assignment to the folder with the GUID associated with the OpsMgr role created in step 1 that has Browser, My Reports, and the Report Builder SRS roles associated with this account.

4. Assign users to the new role.

TIP: REFRESHING CONSOLE AND UPDATING NEW GROUP

Active users will need to close and reopen the OpsMgr console for the new role assignments to take effect. Users not in the new Security Auditors Reporting Role will not be able run or see the reports in the console.

Using the preceding guidance, you should be able to harden the ACS forwarder service and lock down audit reporting access quickly and per requirements. Whether or not you need to harden the ACS infrastructure, lock down components, or implement more auditing will depend on your specific environment, ACS configuration, security risks, and business requirements. For more information on locking down ACS and hardening the infrastructure components, refer to the Operations Manager 2007 Security Guide available at http://technet.microsoft.com/en-us/library/bb821997.aspx and the community resources listed later in this chapter.

Auditing SQL Server 2008

One of the greatest features in SQL Server 2008 Enterprise Edition from an auditor's perspective is the ability to define granular data audit policies to track everything from database authentication activity and administrative activities on servers to specific access auditing for databases and record-level activity. In addition to being able to log these events natively, users can also opt to write these events to the local server's Security log, which ACS can then use for centralized audit collection and reporting. Microsoft has a great whitepaper discussing these new auditing capabilities available at http://msdn.microsoft.com/en-us/library/dd392015.aspx.

Even though the process to enable SQL Server 2008 auditing is fairly simple, it should be planned per audit requirements with a database administrator (DBA) and only enabled as required. When planning SQL Server 2008 auditing in the ACS environment, it is important to reassess existing capacity and performance on the collector and ACS database in relation to the new event loads being collected. Auditing SQL Server 2008 can be very verbose and generate high volumes of events per server. The new event load from SQL Server auditing will be primarily dependent on the audit policies and specifications applied in association with applicable activity on the server.

When writing these events to the Windows security log, you will find the following properties consistent within each event:

▶ The event source will be the database/instance name (default of MSSQLSERVER$AUDIT).

▶ The event ID is always 33205.

▶ The original timestamp, action ID, and event strings are written to the event details.

The following steps show how to create a new audit policy that logs all authentication failures and permission changes to the local Audit database. This assumes that users have already validated the local policies to ensure audit Object Access success/failure is enabled, and the user right Generate Security Events is assigned to the SQL Server service account. It is also highly recommended that you plan the audit policies and specification with a DBA to define appropriate audit policies. For more guidance and step-by-step instructions on understanding SQL Server audit, see Microsoft MSDN books online, at http://msdn.microsoft.com/en-us/library/cc280386.aspx.

1. Under the Security Folder, right-click the Audits folder; then select New Audit:

▶ Define the audit name, such as *<ServerName>* **Security Log Audit**.

▶ For Audit Destination, select the Security log. Click OK.

2. Under the Security Folder, right-click Server Audit Specifications folder; then select New Audit Server Specification:

▶ Define name, such as *<ServerName>* **Server Auditing**.

▶ For Audit, associate with new Audit Policy created in step 1.

▶ Select audit policies desired for the server and click OK.

3. Optionally, configure specifications for database and record-level auditing. Expand the target database, open the security folder, and repeat step 2.

4. Enable new policies by right-clicking objects created in steps 2 and 3 and selecting Enable.

NOTE: SQL SERVER 2008 SECURITY LOG AUDITING PREREQUISITES

To confirm audit policy and user rights prerequisites, see Microsoft's article on how to write server audit events to the Security log at http://msdn.microsoft.com/en-us/library/cc645889.aspx.

After enabling audit policies and specifications, defined activity is audited, written to the local Security log, and collected by ACS. The events provide a granular audit trail of the SQL Server database, administrator, and user activity, thereby helping to enforce security controls, improve investigative capabilities, and mitigate potential risks.

Here is a sample showing a SQL Server 2008 audit event as written to the Windows Security log. This event represents a user creating a new database where the details identify who made the change, when, and the type of change made:

```
Log Name:      Security
Source:        MSSQLSERVER$AUDIT
Date:          8/12/2009 2:24:23 PM
Event ID:      33205
Task Category: (3)
Level:         Information
Keywords:      Classic,Audit Success
User:          ODYSSEY\SQL_Service_OM
Computer:      Thunder.odyssey.com
Description:
Audit event: event_time:2009-08-12 19:24:23.3606735
sequence_number:1
action_id:CR
succeeded:true
permission_bitmask:0
is_column_permission:false
session_id:89
server_principal_id:2
database_principal_id:1
```

```
target_server_principal_id:0
target_database_principal_id:0
object_id:6
class_type:DB
session_server_principal_name:ODYSSEY\JBeckett
server_principal_name:ODYSSEY\JBeckett
server_principal_sid:0105000000000051500000054f41c76e5d5201d3812ee997d040000
database_principal_name:dbo
target_server_principal_name:
target_server_principal_sid:
target_database_principal_name:
server_instance_name:THUNDER
database_name:master
schema_name:
object_name:AuditTest
statement:CREATE DATABASE [AuditTest] ON  PRIMARY
( NAME = N'AuditTest', FILENAME = N'C:\Program Files\Microsoft SQL
Server\MSSQL10.MSSQLSERVER\MSSQL\DATA\AuditTest.mdf' , SIZE = 2048KB , FILEGROWTH =
1024KB )
LOG ON ( NAME = N'AuditTest_log', FILENAME = N'C:\Program Files\Microsoft SQL
Server\MSSQL10.MSSQLSERVER\MSSQL\DATA\AuditTest_log.ldf' , SIZE = 7168KB , FILEGROWTH
= 10%)
additional_information:
```

Once ACS collects the SQL Server security events, you can start to leverage the data for alerting and reporting. Given all events use the same ID, you will need to use the event details for defining new alerts and reports. As shown in the sample event log output, the new events contain a wealth of information users can leverage for auditing.

NOTE: SQL SERVER 2008 AUDITING NUANCES

Unfortunately, unlike a normal Windows Security event where each unique attribute is defined as a new string, all the event details shown in the SQL Server event written to the security log are actually concatenated into a single string. This limits how the data can be used in ACS. Given the volume of information in a single event string, the data will be truncated and dropped by ACS, usually after the server_principal_sid property as highlighted in the sample audit event. Users looking for a more robust integration of SQL Server events can look at the new cross-platform capabilities discussed in the next section.

The native auditing capabilities of SQL Server 2008 include significantly more capabilities out-of-box, which you can integrate with an existing ACS infrastructure and use for enterprise and regulatory auditing. Not only can you collect this data with ACS, you can build alerting for key controls or access violation scenarios in addition to customized reporting. With the right skills, you could even integrate the data with some of the Windows audit reports to have centralized logon failure and account management reporting! Imagine being able to run a query to find all activity in Active Directory, on local systems, and within SQL Server for a specific user—this is powerful and now very achievable. If you are leveraging SQL Server 2008 today or planning to in the future, you now know some of the auditing possibilities using ACS and can further extend your auditing capabilities.

Auditing Cross Platform

Microsoft added support post-OpsMgr 2007 R2, in December 2009, for the cross-platform providers to write events to a local security log via a new Security Event Log (SEL) write action module. This enables you to collect security events from essentially any OpsMgr provider and write them to a Windows Security log for ACS to collect. This feature not only enables event collection; it also provides customized parsing of the event messages to extract key attributes and strings for improved reporting and analytics within ACS. Using this feature, you can natively collect Unix, Linux, network and environmental devices, applications, and other security events via ACS for centralized audit collection and reporting.

Figure 9.19 illustrates the high-level concept of how cross-platform events are transformed into a Windows Security event.

Cross Platform
Security Events

Event Transformation

Windows Security
Event Generated

Events

Transform   WinSec
Event

Provides event specific transformation
and parsing of message strings

FIGURE 9.19 Transforming cross-platform events into a Windows Security event

This feature supports collecting events from the following platforms at time of release:

- ► Red Hat Enterprise 4, 5
- ► Novell SLES 9, 10
- ► Solaris 9, 10
- ► HPUX 11iv2, 11iv3
- ► AIX 5.3, 6.1

For the most current list of System Center Operations Manager supported configurations, see http://technet.microsoft.com/en-us/library/bb309428.aspx.

Each major platform supported by Cross Platform now includes an updated management pack that has base providers with data sources for Syslog, su log, and audit, including collection and alerting rules for key security events that should be audited. This enables OpsMgr 2007 R2 users to have cross-platform auditing of activities such as

successful and failed logons, privilege use activity, account activity, security violations, and more within a single audit repository. Complementing the canned providers
and event collection is a series of reports to assess access violations, user logon activity, administrator activity for su and sudo, account management changes such as new
and deleted users, and forensics to investigate all events for a specific computer or
event ID.

You will find the OpsMgr 2007 R2 eventschema.xml has already been updated to include the new source, CrossPlatformSecurity (which is also added to the dtSource table), six new events ranging from 27001 through 27006, and generic string attributes
for Primary User, Client User, System Service, Sub System, Session Name, and Process ID. Table 9.5 summarizes the new generic event IDs available in the event schema.

TABLE 9.5 New Generic Event IDs with the R2 release

Event ID	Name
27001	General Event, can be used generically for any new security event type
27002	Successful Login
27003	Failed Login
27004	Account Added
27005	Account Deleted
27006	Super User Activity

Including the new events, this feature will also let you parse the event message strings
to extract key values. Most events will include a source event ID, severity, machine,
and timestamp, along with an event message string composed of friendly text in-lined
with details from the event like user names, source IP address, protocol, process ID,
and so on. Having the ability to extract this information enables users to optimize the
data for analysis and correlation within ACS and reporting.

Security events can now be collected via OpsMgr providers including Syslog, su logs,
and standard event logs to provide consolidated audit collection across the enterprise
with ACS. Users can get Windows security, SQL Server 2008, and Cross Platform OS
auditing out of the box. You can also customize new providers for additional sources
such as network and environmental devices, applications, and custom logs. Essentially
any event exposed by Operations Manager can now be collected, processed, and integrated with ACS—providing a central auditing solution that supports today's enterprise audit requirements.

Secure Site Log Replay

Some secured environments may have a single server or several servers sitting in isola-
tion or "black site" environments with audit requirements that must be supported, but
given size or resource constraints, these may not warrant additional infrastructure for
dedicated auditing. In these situations, you can create a new dedicated ACS collector
and database environment to replay log files for analysis and audit reporting. Although
this method of audit requires human intervention given the isolated systems, it gives

you the capability to centrally load, audit, and archive the log data from these systems into an ACS audit database.

TIP: ONLY RUN LOG REPLAY ON ISOLATED COLLECTOR

Log replay should only be performed against security log files and never on an active collector. Replaying log files to an active collector could be considered tampering with the ACS collection stream and audit database integrity.

Several actions are necessary to prepare and implement ACS log replay. The following steps outline how you could approach this implementation:

1. Configure local audit policy to store local security log as required.

2. Implement process to copy data on regular basis to secure moveable storage like USB drives.

3. Transfer data from moveable storage to secured permanent media and local system that replays log files.

4. Replay log files into isolated ACS environment for audit reporting and analysis by running the `adtagent -x -f<`*filename.evt*`>` command on a Windows Server with an ACS Forwarder installed but not running. The following command would load a file named TestLog.evt into the Audit database: `adtagent -x -fC:\TestLog.evt`.

On successful connection, the collector generates a 4628 event identifying the account that initiated the command, which is mapped to the AgentMachine value in the Audit database. You will also find an entry in the dtMachine table for each unique account that has connected to a collector via this method. The source machine where the log originated from is mapped to the Event Machine value, and the rest of the event details are processed like a normal security event.

Although you can run the log replay feature against any Windows .EVT or .EVTX file, the ACS event schema only normalizes Windows Server security events. If you try to replay log files other than the security log, the event header and strings are not mapped as expected and ACS drops all data after the first 21 strings in the event. If you are looking to integrate other security events and logs, you may want to consider the new auditing for Cross Platform feature discussed in the "Auditing Cross Platform" section.

Community Resources

While *System Center Operations Manager 2007 Unleashed* and Microsoft resources provide the foundation of knowledge users need to successfully plan, deploy, and manage ACS environments, there are a wealth of community resources available providing everything from extended planning guidance and utilities to how-to documents, training videos, and more. The following list summarizes several key community resources available when this chapter was written:

► The ACS Master Class Series provides over five hours of free expert training led by OpsMgr MVPs. The series covers everything ACS engineers and administrators need to know about planning, deploying, managing, supporting, and troubleshooting ACS along with advanced topics like disaster recovery and failover, access hardening, noise filtering, and much more. The series is available at http://www.securevantage.com/ACSTraining.aspx.

► The ACS Resource Kit offers a wealth of field-hardened documents, utilities, and accelerators for planning and managing ACS environments, including the ACS Noise Filter Guide, an audit database load analysis workbook, a list of all Windows Server 2003 and 2008 security events, a script to groom by age and event ID, create event scripts, and other material. Download the resource kit from http://www.securevantage.com/Products/ACSResourceKit.aspx.

► The ACS Wiki on System Center Central (www.systemcentercentral.com) is a growing repository of anything and everything relating to the Audit Collection Service. You will also find all community ACS downloads referenced on the wiki, including a script for enabling forwarders in bulk using PowerShell, an event count script, a database and disk-sizing calculator, and additional expert user guidance. The wiki is at http://www.systemcentercentral.com/ACS.

Network Monitoring Using Distributed Applications

Chapter 19, "Managing a Distributed Environment," of *System Center Operations Manager 2007 Unleashed* discusses getting started with distributed applications. Chapter 18 of that book, "Using Synthetic Transactions," goes through the steps of creating and using a TCP port monitor. This discussion goes a step further, by giving a practical example of using TCP port monitors, distributed applications, the Multi-Host Ping management pack, and Savision's Live Maps product to monitor network links.

Monitoring Redundant LAN Links

Assume you have a geographically distributed environment that uses redundant WAN links to provide connectivity between locations, and you want to monitor these links with OpsMgr. Specifically, you want to know if a remote location is up or down, and be alerted which specific links go offline. You can use TCP port monitors by themselves to provide rudimentary network monitoring (up/down, and response time). However, this gets more complex when you have redundant links and want alerts if you lose the link to the remote location and a critical alert occurs, or if you lose all connectivity to the remote location. This situation is one where using distributed applications can be extremely useful.

Using the Distributed Application Designer

To provide redundancy if a single watcher node fails, configure two different watcher nodes for each network link you are monitoring using a TCP port monitor monitoring the IP address of the router or switch on port 22. Use the distributed application designer to model this network configuration, as displayed in Figure 9.20. The distributed application consists of a top-level Network Link pointing toward the items it is dependent upon (the Primary Network Link and the Backup Network Link). Each link is watched by two different watcher nodes, so if an issue occurs with a single watcher node, it does not cause the distributed application to go red.

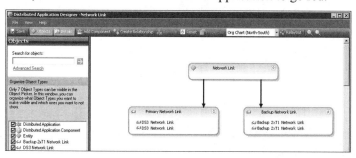

FIGURE 9.20 Modeling the network configuration in the distributed application designer

Configure the two links to provide a warning alert if both watcher nodes report an error. Use the Rollup Algorithm of Best Health State so that if a single watcher node experiences an issue, this would not be enough to indicate that the network link is down. Figure 9.21 shows this configuration.

Next, highlight the Network Link box shown in Figure 9.20. Use the Rollup Algorithm of Best Health State to configure the top level of the distributed application to provide a critical alert if both the network links are experiencing issues. You could design this to roll up if either link is down, but the focus here is the functionality of the remote site and not the availability of the network links. If you lose a link and can still reach the remote site, this does not affect the ability to continue to monitor servers in the remote location. This is displayed in Figure 9.22.

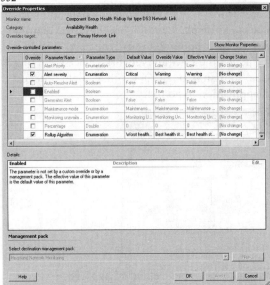

FIGURE 9.21 Configure rollup and alert severity.

FIGURE 9.22 The top level of the application provides a critical alert.

Now bring Savision's tool into this equation. OpsMgr can provide a view of the health of a distributed application and a diagram view of the distributed application, but it lacks a user interface with the capability to represent the network topology graphically. To provide a high-level overview of the state of the entire network, use Savision Live

Maps (www.savision.com) to show the map for locations, including the network link between Austin and Denver, displayed in Figure 9.23. This map displays the status of the servers at each location, and shows how you can add a network link to this view.

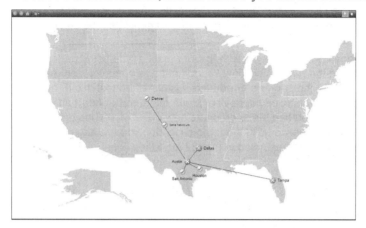

FIGURE 9.23 Showing the Denver network links using Live Maps

Using Live Map, you can highlight the Denver Network Link. Right-click and open the diagram view in the OpsMgr console, which zooms the view from the United States into a view showing the distributed application for the Austin to Denver network link. Figure 9.24 shows the Topology view for the Denver Network Link. This shows both the Network Link Distributed Application at the top, the Backup and Primary links below, and at the bottom displays the watcher nodes for each link.

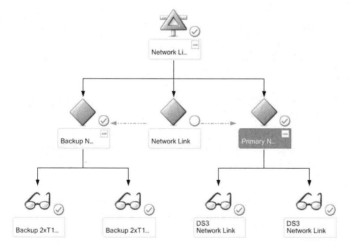

FIGURE 9.24 The diagram view for the Network Link Distributed Application using TCP Port monitoring

The TCP Port monitor is only one of several options for monitoring network links. There are also third-party management packs, SNMP monitoring, and other options. See http://cameronfuller.spaces.live.com/blog/cns!A231E4EB0417CB76!1012.entry for a good review of available options.

Another free option to monitor network devices that easily integrates with a distributed application is the Multi-Host Ping management pack (available for download from www.systemcentercentral.com). This management pack provides a simple way to add ping type monitoring for devices with an IP address, such as routers or switches. For this application, let's add the Multi-Host Ping management pack and configure it to ping the IP address for the backup network link. This provides another method to monitor the backup network link that can be added to the distributed application. Perform the following steps:

1. Open the existing distributed application with the distributed application designer.

2. Change the components allowed for the backup network link by right-clicking it and choosing Properties.

3. Choose the ping target and ping watcher options, as shown in Figure 9.25, so you can add the ping-related components to the backup network link component.

4. Next, add the ping watchers to the Backup Network Link, as shown in Figure 9.26. These can be added by opening the Ping Watcher section, right-clicking on the object and choosing the Add To option, and then choosing the Backup Network Link.

   The example in Figure 9.26 shows two watcher nodes (OMGWP01V and OMGWP02V) added to monitor the Backup Network Link.

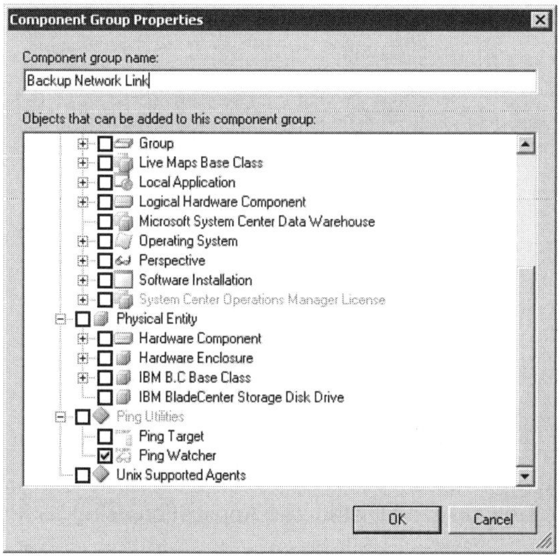

Component Group Properties

Component group name:

Backup Network Link

Objects that can be added to this component group:

- ⊞ ☐ 🖳 Group
- ⊞ ☐ 🖳 Live Maps Base Class
- ⊞ ☐ 🖳 Local Application
- ⊞ ☐ 🖳 Logical Hardware Component
- ☐ 🖳 Microsoft System Center Data Warehouse
- ⊞ ☐ 🖳 Operating System
- ⊞ ☐ 🖳 Perspective
- ⊞ ☐ 🖳 Software Installation
- ⊞ ☐ 🖳 System Center Operations Manager License
- ⊟ ☐ 🖳 Physical Entity
  - ⊞ ☐ 🖳 Hardware Component
  - ⊞ ☐ 🖳 Hardware Enclosure
  - ⊞ ☐ 🖳 IBM B.C Base Class
  - ☐ 🖳 IBM BladeCenter Storage Disk Drive
- ⊟ ☐ 🖳 Ping Utilities
  - ☐ 🖳 Ping Target
  - ☑ 🖳 Ping Watcher
- ☐ 🖳 Unix Supported Agents

[OK]   [Cancel]

FIGURE 9.25 Adding ping components to the Network Link Distributed Application

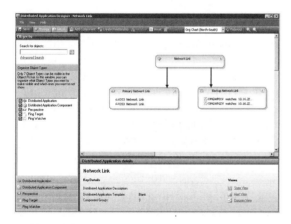

FIGURE 9.26 Modeling the network configuration in the distributed application designer with TCP Port and ping components

This monitor can provide seamless integration even into the existing Denver Network Link. Figure 9.27 shows the updated network link topology view, which now includes a primary link monitored with a TCP port monitor and a backup link that is monitored with a ping monitor. You could use a third-party network monitoring solution or SNMP monitoring to monitor these network links. The method of monitoring is not as important as the overall understanding of how you can integrate them into a single distributed application that shows the overall functionality of the network.

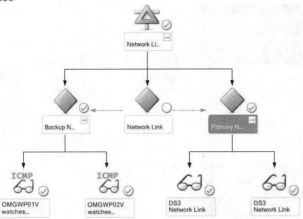

FIGURE 9.27 The diagram view for the Network Link Distributed Application using both TCP Ports and the Multi-Host Ping MP

Targeting

Proper targeting is a vital but often misunderstood part of OpsMgr 2007. Improperly targeting can lead, at best, to an overloaded management group, and at worst, to completely unmanageable monitoring. To discuss targeting, it is useful to define what it is, how it is used, and why it is pivotal to successful monitoring. *Targeting* is the practice of identifying the proper objects that should receive monitoring, and delivering monitoring in a focused way to only those objects. As you work in the OpsMgr console, the terms used may seem confusing. Some areas use the term "target." Elsewhere the console lists "classes" or "objects." These refer to the same thing, and you can use them interchangeably. This discussion will generally use the term *target*.

Given that targeting is key to delivering monitoring correctly, it is critical to understand targeting and the concepts behind it. Although targeting may initially seem straightforward, having an incomplete or inaccurate understanding has tripped up many an OpsMgr administrator. This is particularly true for those who previously used Microsoft Operations Manager (MOM) 2005 and are familiar with the targeting options available with that product. While it is tempting to attempt MOM 2005 style targeting in OpsMgr 2007, and operating with MOM 2005 concepts can work in OpsMgr, the two products are completely different. Using MOM 2005 style targeting has limited success, and can quickly become unmanageable.

Objects in OpsMgr 2007

Targeting in OpsMgr 2007 is object based, meaning it is object-oriented—a term familiar to most programmers. Understanding object-oriented programming concepts means you understand how targeting works in OpsMgr 2007. *Object-oriented programming* is the practice of defining an object that should have operations applied to it.

When defining objects, you want the initial definition of an object to be as generic as possible. As you define subsequent "types" of these generic objects, details will fall into place about these more specific objects. The building analogy presented in the MP Authoring Guide is a perfect example describing this approach of defining objects— and this approach exactly defines how OpsMgr defines objects. (For the MP Authoring Guide, search for **MP Authoring Guide R2** at http://www.microsoft.com/downloads, or see the OpsMgr R2 documentation at http://www.microsoft.com/downloads/details.aspx?displaylang=en&FamilyID=19bd0e b5-7ca0-41be-8c0f-2d95fe7ec636.) Think of it this way: Once you define an object (see the "Using the Authoring Console to Create a Target" section), it becomes a potential target for monitoring. In the truest definition, objects are targets—but they must be defined before you can use them to deliver monitoring.

The *entity* is the most generic type of object in OpsMgr 2007. It is used by the system itself; you should never see this object used as a target for any user-defined monitoring. Next in line is the *logical entity*, which is not that different from an entity. From there, you might derive the *computer role* object. This object "inherits" from the entity and logical entity objects, receiving all the properties associated with them, and then adds properties specific to an object of *type computer role*. Notice that the type of computer role is not defined yet; that is a further derivation of the computer role, and ultimately of the entity and logical entity objects.

A further derivation of the computer role object might define a Windows or Unix computer role object. From the Windows computer role object, you might have a child object defining an application running on the Windows computer, ultimately leading to an object describing the type of application—such as Exchange or SQL Server. Rather than continuing to describe object inheritance models, the graphic in Figure 9.28 presents a way to visualize this scenario and understand that specific objects are derived from objects that are more generic and inherit from parent objects.

This discussion of derivation and inheritance begins to describe another concept crucial to understanding OpsMgr 2007 objects; this is the relationship existing between them. Relationships are discussed in Chapter 8, "Management Pack Authoring," and are equally important to understand.

Targeting becomes more understandable as a concept once you start visualizing the link up between objects. OpsMgr 2007 has monitoring delivered to an object—not a computer. Although with MOM 2005, computers were the center of the monitoring world, now the object replaces the computer. This approach enables you to deliver focused monitoring to only the objects of interest. Rather than needing to know which server hosts an application such as SQL Server, just target the monitoring you want to the SQL object (target), and OpsMgr delivers it correctly. To deliver monitoring to the computer, it is also an object (which is why you can target using the MOM 2005 approach although it isn't scalable).

FIGURE 9.28 Object relationships in OpsMgr

What You Can Target

The objects of targeting in OpsMgr 2007 are typically monitors and rules, but also include discoveries, tasks, overrides, and reports. When building these types of items, you must supply a target against which the item will operate. Figures 9.29 and 9.30 show examples where the user interface (UI) asks you to specify a target:

▶ Figure 9.29 displays a new monitor being created, showing the requirement to add a target, along with a sample listing of available targets displayed when you click on Select.

▶ Figure 9.30 shows an existing discovery with the target already in place.

Once a target is selected, it cannot be changed through the user interface—so ensure that you understand your targeting strategy before creating many monitoring objects! While in various areas of the UI, you may see references to an object or class, it boils down to needing to supply a proper target. This leads to the question: "Which target should you use?" Figure 9.29 lists some available targets, although the target needed for a specific scenario may not be in the list! The next section explores these particulars.

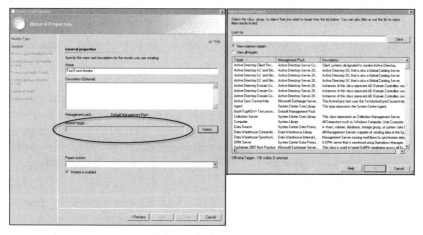

FIGURE 9.29 Creating a monitor and being asked to provide a target

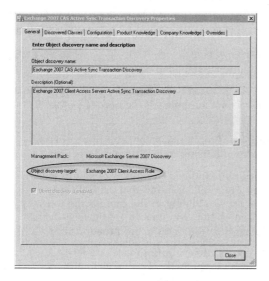

FIGURE 9.30 A discovery with an identified target

Targeting—Existing Targets

Targets are used to deliver monitoring in as focused a way as possible. As it is easiest to illustrate targeting with an example, this discussion will consider a requirement to monitor a fictional application, called BackITupNOW!. This application will be installed on all SQL Server systems, although it is not specifically associated with or dependent upon SQL Server. There is no existing management pack for BackITup-

NOW!, but it is necessary to monitor this application. Based on this scenario, what options are available to deliver monitoring to systems hosting this application? Here are several questions to ask when deciding on a target:

▶ Is an existing target suitable for the needed purpose?

▶ Is the chosen target specific enough to focus delivery of rules and monitors?

▶ Does the target chosen fit into and work with the overall OpsMgr health structure?

If existing targets are available and appropriate, you can bypass the discovery step when building monitoring (covered in the "Using the Authoring Console to Create a Target" section of this chapter). Figure 9.29 showed a list of available targets available by default that you could view when building monitoring. This list of available targets can grow quite large as you import additional management packs, and it can be confusing initially to sort out which is best to use. Let's see how this works by evaluating several targets—Windows Computer and SQL Server.

▶ **Windows Computer**—This object is often a first choice for targeting, particularly for those familiar with MOM 2005 where the computer itself was the focus of monitoring. The reasoning is since applications of interest run on Windows Computer, targeting this object will deliver required monitoring where needed. Although this logic initially makes sense, evaluating those three questions shows flaws in the reasoning. Examine the questions to see if using the Windows Computer object is appropriate as a target to deliver monitoring for BackITupNOW!:

   ▶ Is an existing target suitable for the needed purpose?

   The Windows Computer object already exists and contains the objects you want to monitor, but it is not suitable for the needed purpose. Here's why:

   Targets are really definitions of monitoring scope. Targets (classes) describe requirements for membership in a particular target class.

   The membership described by Windows Computer object in the Discovered Inventory node in Figure 9.31 shows that using Windows Computer object as the target would deliver the monitoring to every system that is a Windows computer, whether or not those systems host the BackITupNOW! application. This is too broad in scope.

   When choosing a target, you are determining the scope where the monitoring will operate. If the scope includes objects that do not apply, you will cause noise or potentially errors on systems without the application installed that you are trying to monitor.

   ▶ Is the chosen target specific enough to focus delivery of rules and monitors?

   Based on Figure 9.31, the answer is negative. However, there is a way to target Windows Computer, as this is an existing target that includes the necessary scope: After targeting it, override the monitor to disable it by default, and then add overrides to enable it just for those systems with BackITupNOW! installed.

This works in terms of limiting where monitoring is delivered, but adds a significant amount of effort to disable all the monitoring and create overrides for each monitoring component to activate monitoring for the systems of interest, introducing extra administrative effort to maintain the overrides as systems install/uninstall the application. Alternatively, you could use a group when introducing overrides, but even that would require maintenance. Although this approach is workable, it potentially is more effort and adds confusion to force a monitoring strategy that violates how OpsMgr was designed. The third question provides some additional information why this is not a desired option.

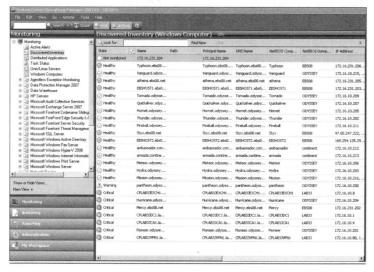

FIGURE 9.31 Objects defined by the Windows Computer target

► Does the chosen target fit into the overall health structure built by the OpsMgr relationship model?

Although you can build out a solution where you can target Windows Computer and limit the monitoring scope, there is no way to get around the problems this will cause related to the health model. Monitors operate in a very specific way, detecting a problem condition and changing the health state from green (OK) to yellow (warning) to red (critical) and back again. While a detailed discussion of the health model in OpsMgr is beyond the scope of this chapter, suffice it to say when a monitor changes state to either warning or critical, this state is generally reflected on the target object itself.

If you choose Windows Computer as your target for monitors designed to detect problems in BackITupNOW!, the overall state of the Windows Computer object changes from health to unhealthy when problems are detected. You could say this is not a problem and just cosmetic. This is true in a sense, as monitoring will work. However, building monitoring in this way violates the fundamental design principles for the OpsMgr health structure. The health structure is designed to be able to tell the overall health of an object at a glance according to defined rules. Although BackITupNOW! might have a problem, that doesn't mean the Windows Computer as a whole is having problems! Choosing to target BackITupNOW! monitoring to Windows Computer will make it appear that the Windows Computer is affected. Remember that the general principle in OpsMgr is *monitoring should be delivered in as focused a manner as possible*.

▶ **SQL Server**—Having determined that using Windows Computer isn't optimal, look again at the BackITupNOW! application. You know this application needs to be monitored in a focused way and it is only installed on SQL Server systems. The list of targets shown in Figure 9.29 shows a target available for SQL Server specifically, imported as part of the SQL management pack. Look at those three questions again to determine if this is a good solution:

   ▶ Is an existing target suitable for the needed purpose?

   The SQL Server target already exists and seems suitable for the intended purpose.

   ▶ Is the chosen target specific enough to focus delivery of rules and monitors?

   The BackITupNOW! application is only installed on SQL Server systems, and the monitoring scope needs to be kept specific to just servers hosting BackITupNOW!. Using SQL Server as the target satisfies this question.

   ▶ Does the chosen target fit into the overall health structure built by the OpsMgr relationship model?

   As mentioned in the discussion on using Windows Computer as a target, the health structure is intended to describe at a glance the overall health of the monitoring object. Although the BackITupNOW! application is specifically installed on just SQL Server systems, there is no specific requirement for SQL Server to be installed.

   This means that BackITupNOW! and SQL Server aren't actually related; it's coincidental they are installed together here. Targeting SQL Server to monitor BackITupNOW! means any problem detected in BackITupNOW! will affect the health of SQL Server, as that is your chosen target. This is incorrect; it gives a false reading that SQL Server is having problems when it likely is not. Therefore, while the first two questions pass, the third question shows that using SQL Server as the monitoring target is an incorrect choice.

When Existing Targets Are Appropriate

An assumption of this discussion is that BackITupNOW! is a unique application that requires targeting and does not have an existing management pack. Such situations lend themselves to custom target creation, as discussed in the "Using the Authoring Console to Create a Target" section. The previous section demonstrated why using the existing targets of Windows Computer and SQL Server (and most likely any existing target) is inappropriate to monitor this particular application. When can you use an existing target? Remember the three questions first presented in the "Targeting— Existing Targets" section—if you can answer yes to all three affirmatively, you have a candidate to use with an existing target.

As an example, say you need to monitor SQL Server. You start by loading the SQL Server management pack into a test management group to evaluate the monitoring it provides. During your evaluation, you notice that several specific monitoring scenarios you need are not covered by the management pack. To address this, you create supplemental monitoring (additional rules and/or monitors) and store them in a custom management pack. As you build out your monitoring, you choose various SQL Server targets loaded with the SQL management pack to use with your supplemental monitoring. If you run this scenario through the three questions, you likely will find that the answer to all three questions is affirmative:

▶ A target already exists—it is introduced by the SQL management pack.

▶ Because the supplemental monitoring is specific to SQL Server and you are using existing targets, the delivery scope for this monitoring is limited.

▶ As your supplemental monitoring is specific to SQL Server, it is likely OK for a problem picked up by the supplemental monitoring to affect the health state of the SQL Server objects.

Now consider whether it is ever reasonable to target the Windows Computer object. Consider a scenario where you need to introduce supplemental monitoring specific to the computer system itself running a Windows operating system (OS). You may or many not need to apply this monitoring to every Windows computer, depending on the object created. Look at the three questions, and you will again find you can answer all three affirmatively, although you might struggle a bit with the scope question.

For monitoring objects that don't need to be applied to every Windows computer but need to affect the health state of Windows computers they are monitoring, build the monitoring object disabled and create an override to activate it for just the Windows computers requiring monitoring. You can create this override for specific Windows computers or groups of Windows computers. Note that using overrides in this manner may or may not result in a dynamic detection of those systems to apply the override. Dynamic solutions are always preferred, but not always possible. Before asking why an override scenario is acceptable here but not with BackITupNOW!, remember BackITupNOW! monitors a specific application—using a Windows computer target would affect health state reporting adversely. In this latest example, the monitoring *is* looking for problems that would affect the health state of the Windows Computer object; this makes the scenario workable.

TIP: A BETTER OPTION THAN TARGETING WINDOWS COMPUTER

The "Targeting—Existing Targets" section discussed targeting the Windows Computer object. This object targets systems running any version of a Windows OS, from Windows XP to Windows Server 2008 and everything in between. Given that one of the targeting goals is to deliver monitoring to as focused an audience as possible, there are targets more specific than Windows Computer and further derivations of the Windows Computer target. The Windows Server and Windows Client targets break down systems as to server or workstation, and more specific forms of these targets explicitly identify a system by OS version. Using a more focused target is usually more appropriate than Windows Computer.

The "Targeting—Existing Targets" section introduced using groups for overrides. MOM 2005 targeted all monitoring objects to computer groups. Computer groups also exist in OpsMgr 2007; can you create groups to hold just the membership you want, based on attributes? The next section explores using groups for targeting.

Targeting with Groups

Native OpsMgr groups are *instance groups*, meaning that the group contains a listing of instances. These instances may be computer objects, or the membership may be another object type (target) altogether, such as a disk drive object or SQL database object.

Computer groups exist only when a converted MOM 2005 management pack is imported into OpsMgr 2007. In the early days of the product, virtually every management pack available was a converted management pack, but now most core management packs are native.

As groups (whether instance groups or computer groups) contain computer or other objects, can you target them? Figure 9.32 shows many computer groups in the list of targets. If you create your own, is it available in a list? You can certainly build groups of computers or other objects. You can filter group membership in any number of ways, including building an attribute (see Figure 9.33) to pick out specific objects of interest based on either a registry key or an entry in WMI. However, once you create this group, it may or may not show up in the list of targets, although computer groups from imported management packs appear and are selectable. Here's why.

Assume any group you create is visible and selectable in the list of targets. If you select the group as the target, it will not result in focused targeting that satisfies the three questions. Remember that OpsMgr is built on the idea of objects, and everything you see in the system in terms of targets ultimately is an object. By nature, objects describe a particular item and thus can be thought of as owned by the object they describe. Groups are also objects, serve a specific purpose, and are owned by a specific system—the RMS, in this case. This means if you can choose a group as a target, your monitoring will be delivered—but only to the system associated with your group object (the RMS). Although your group lists other objects, the RMS owns them, so the group is owned by and associated with the RMS.

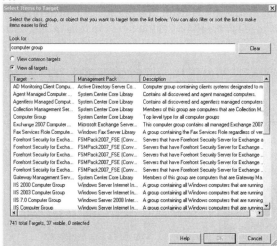

FIGURE 9.32 Computer groups in the list of targets

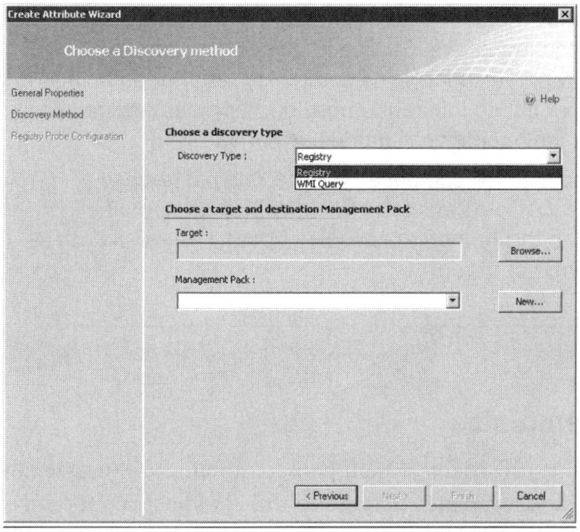

FIGURE 9.33 Building an attribute

BackITupNOW! does not have appropriate existing targets. In this case, properly targeting monitoring requires building your own custom targets that uniquely describe the application. In general, existing targets are workable primarily to extend monitoring for an existing management pack. If you have a unique application requiring monitoring that does not have a management pack, you must create the custom targets necessary to deliver that monitoring. Even if a management pack is available for a given application, it may not provide all of the targets necessary.

Creating a target has two parts—defining the target itself and populating the target through discovery. The next sections discuss the tools available to create a target.

CUSTOM AUTHORING

Discussing creating new targets or creating supplemental or target specific monitoring introduces the topic of management pack authoring. OpsMgr 2007 lets you use the Operations console for authoring, although some aspects require the Authoring console. Opinions vary as to which console to use. Here are several things to understand:

▶ Limit authoring with the Operations console in a production environment, such as to introduce overrides. Every change made in the Operations console causes updates to go to the affected clients, which can lead to unwanted churn.

▶ Authoring rules and monitors in the Operations console is perfectly acceptable in a test environment. When complete, you can import the management pack into production with far less impact to the management group.

▶ When authoring in the Operations console, all created objects are written to the management pack eXtended Markup Language (XML) and referenced by system-generated identifiers. Should you need to read management pack XML, this randomization adds complexity. Authoring in the Authoring console does not cause this randomization, representing the authored components by their configured names.

▶ The R2 Authoring console is more complete than the original release and there is very little this console cannot handle. For this reason alone, you will want to get used to the Authoring console; it doesn't even need a connection to a management group.

Using Management Pack Templates

Accessible only in the Operations console, management pack templates will create new targets. A number of management pack templates may be useful for specific monitoring, shown in Figure 9.34. This example will use the Process Monitoring template, new with R2. Perform the following steps to add a monitor to determine if the BackITup-NOW! process is running:

1. Right-click on Management Pack Templates -> Add Monitoring Wizard -> Process Monitoring, and select Next.

2. Provide a name for the monitor of **BackITupNOW! Test process monitor**; store it in a custom management pack as shown in Figure 9.35, and click Next.

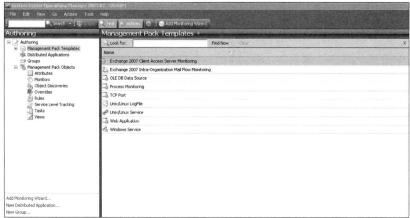

FIGURE 9.34 Available management pack templates

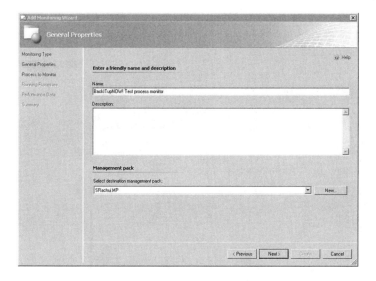

FIGURE 9.35 Provide a name for the monitor

3. Select the option to Monitor whether and how a process is running (for processes you want) and specify the process name of **notepad.exe** for the test (since BackITupNOW! is fictional). Now choose a target group of Windows Server 2003 Computer Group, as shown in Figure 9.36.

4. Take the defaults on the running processes and performance data pages and select Create. Now look at the list of targets and see a new one listed—the BackITupNOW! Test process monitor. If you review the objects associated with this target in discovered inventory, you will see a list as displayed in Figure 9.37.

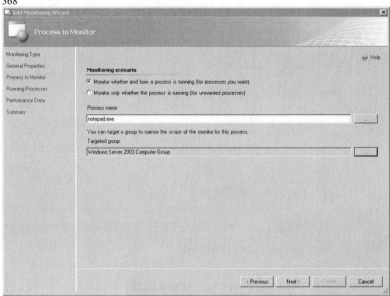

FIGURE 9.36 Specify the process to monitor.

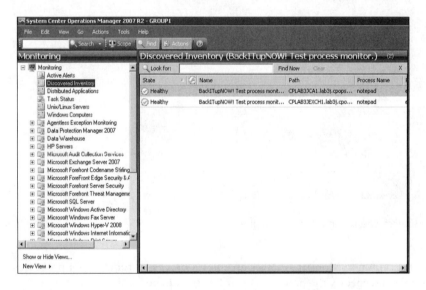

FIGURE 9.37 Resulting membership of new process monitor class

With the new target created, how do you know the criteria to cause objects to be associated with it? When you built the process monitor, you specified the group you wanted to use to scope this monitoring (Windows Server 2003 Computer Group, in Figure 9.36). The membership of this group becomes the membership of the target. The result is a target with the intended membership—the wizard just pulls it from a group, although the group is not used for targeting. Navigate to Authoring -> Management Pack Objects -> Monitors in the OpsMgr console; scope your view to the BackITupNOW! target, and you will see that the wizard created five monitors, each targeted to the BackITupNOW! target, not a group. This is shown in Figures 9.38 and 9.39.

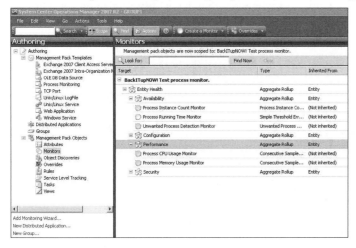

FIGURE 9.38 A list of monitors targeted to the BackITupNOW! target

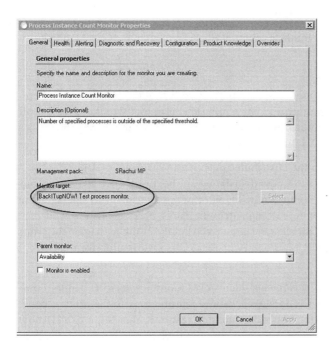

FIGURE 9.39 The Process Instance Count Monitor has a target of the BackITupNOW! Test process monitor.

There are two issues here:

- ▶ You didn't have any control over the creation of the target.

- ▶ The wizard creates monitors and rules that you may or may not want. In this case, there are five monitors when you may have only needed one or two.

In addition to the five monitors, the wizard created several rules, shown in Figure 9.40. You may or may not actually need these rules. You will find the other management pack templates function similarly. This extra monitoring likely will not be a problem, but for large management groups or hardware already performing at its limits, you will want to keep the management group operating as efficiently as possible; which means avoiding introducing unnecessary monitoring and complexity.

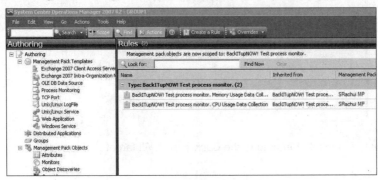

FIGURE 9.40 Rules created by the Management Pack Templates Process Monitoring wizard

An additional issue with the Process Monitoring wizard is that the class (target) it creates plugs into the OpsMgr structure and has a relationship directly to the Local Application class. You can see this by reviewing the class structure of the management group through the Distributed Application Designer.

In the Operations console, open the Distributed Application Designer (Authoring -> Distributed Applications -> Create a new distributed application). Give it a name, and instead of selecting a template, create a new blank drawing and specify a management pack to save it in (other than the default management pack). Next, select the Add Component icon to get a list of all classes (targets) currently in the management group and their relation to other targets. Figure 9.41 displays this information for the BackITupNOW! process monitor.

From a monitoring perspective, this means the process monitor was intended to monitor for a process specific to BackITupNOW!; should a problem with the process causes the application to show unhealthy, you won't get that result. Rather, Figure 9.41 shows that a problem with the BackITupNOW! application will be in relationship to the general process class and ultimately the local application class. This means any rollup of health built will not be centered on the BackITupNOW! application, but on the generic process class.

FIGURE 9.41 BackITupNOW! listed as a target in the management group

Because you want to build targets you have control over, use the Authoring console. The examples in this discussion will use the R2 Authoring console.

Using the Authoring Console to Create a Target

The Authoring console lets you create a new class (target) to describe the application you want to monitor. Creating a new class (target) is a two-step process—create the class, then create a discovery, which is the process used to populate the class with the proper objects.

There are many ways to create a discovery to populate a class, but you typically accomplish the discovery using one of three methods, as follows:

► Registry-based

► WMI-based

► Script-based

It is easy to default to using a registry-based method for discovery, and this is a workable approach. When choosing the discovery method, remember that ensuring that the discovery is dynamic is critical for the discovery to be successful. Building a discovery that relies on human effort, such as manually adding a registry key that the discovery will find, can lead to incorrect discovery results and monitoring. The next sections step through examples using the Authoring console to build each type of discovery.

Discussing the operation of the Authoring console is beyond the scope of this chapter, which covers only those sections relevant to building classes and discoveries. For a detailed understanding of the Authoring console, see http://technet.microsoft.com/en-us/opsmgr/bb498235.aspx.

Registry Discovery

The Authoring console does not appear to be particularly useful when initially launched. To begin the process of creating a class and discovery, first create a management pack. Perform the following steps:

1. Select File -> New, which initiates a wizard to create a management pack. Select whether to create an empty management pack or one based on a class populated with a registry discovery.

    If you are new to authoring, it is easy (and common) to choose to build with the registry option instead of the blank management pack. Here you will instead choose Empty Management Pack and manually build the components needed.

Working through the wizard to build a registry-based class/discovery can achieve the same results as building the discovery manually. The differences are the wizard presents different defaults in terms of discovery frequency and does not result in a discovered type being populated. If a discovered type is not populated, the discovery will not be visible in the Operations console when you import the management pack.

2. Click Empty Management Pack; give the management pack the name of **BackITupNOW! Discovery and Monitoring**, and select Next. This is shown in Figure 9.42.

3. On the next screen (see Figure 9.43), enter the name of the management pack as it should appear in the OpsMgr console, and click Create.

    Steps 2 and 3 illustrate an important concept for building management pack elements. An item, such as a class or discovery, is described by an internal ID but also has a display name visible to the user in the OpsMgr UI.

4. With the base management pack in place, it is time to build a class. Select the service model section of the Authoring console, select Classes, and in the middle section of the console, right-click and select New -> Windows Application.

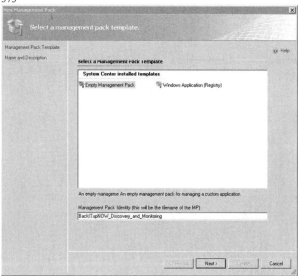

FIGURE 9.42 Select a template and specify the name of the management pack.

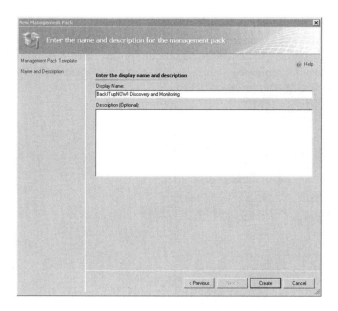

FIGURE 9.43 The name to be displayed in the OpsMgr UI

In the resulting screen, choose an ID for the class you are creating, the display name that will be visible in the OpsMgr console for the class, and an optional description. Note that you cannot change the ID after creating it without deleting the class or manually editing the management pack XML. Figure 9.44 shows the management pack ID. Click Next.

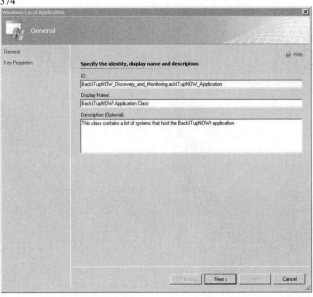

FIGURE 9.44 The identify, display name, and description

5.   On the next screen, specify a key property as shown in Figure 9.45 and click Finish. A key property is one that is guaranteed to be unique for the class. Key properties can be useful but are not required.

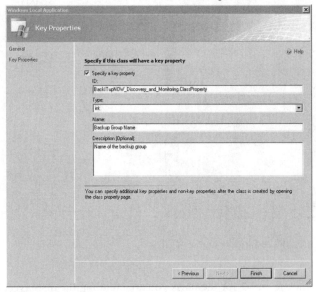

FIGURE 9.45 Specify a key property

6. Reviewing the classes node, you will see a class is created. Right-click on the class; then select Properties to see a screen similar to Figure 9.46.

On Figure 9.46, notice the ID, Name, and Description of the new class—just as you created in the wizard. Also notice the base class of LocalApplication, which is what you chose when you began to build the class.

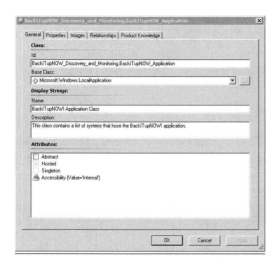

FIGURE 9.46 The class created in the Authoring console

Perhaps the most critical choice to make when building a new class is the base class to use. The base class determines where in the overall class hierarchy the new class is created, and has significant impact on the performance of the management group. There are generally five base classes considered to be appropriate choices. Table 9.6 lists the five options and describes when each is appropriate.

TABLE 9.6 Base Classes and When to Use Them

Base Class Name	When to Use
Microsoft.Windows.ComputerRole	For applications that are operating on dedicated systems, this would be a good first choice.
Microsoft.Windows.LocalApplication	Choose this option for applications that run on a system alongside other applications.
System.Service or System.ComputerRole	Use this option when fine control over hosting relationships and health rollup are important.
Perspective	Use this to drive a rollup across multiple distributed elements of the application.

In addition to base class, you must configure the attributes of the new class. Classes are either hosted (default) or non-hosted. In the vast majority of cases, the hosted attribute will be set—meaning the new class is hosted by a parent class and receives all the attributes of the parent class. There are two other class types besides the hosted class, as follows:

- ▶ **Abstract class**—This class exists purely for the purpose of inheritance and will never have any instances

- ▶ **Singleton class**—A singleton means only one instance of the class will ever exist. A good example of the singleton class is an OpsMgr Instance Group.

These two classes are beyond the scope of this chapter. For additional information, refer to http://technet.microsoft.com/en-us/library/dd362552.aspx. Chapter 8 also discusses the singleton class.

You can choose whether the class you are creating is to be treated as a public class, meaning other classes can inherit from it, or an internal class. An internal class cannot be further derived. As an example, to build an abstract class into a management pack that others can use to further extend what you provide, your class must be defined as public and your management pack must be sealed. Unsealed management packs cannot be referenced! To ensure that none of your classes are available for others to use, set them as internal. Note that the internal setting doesn't just apply to classes—setting an object to internal means that it can never be accessed outside of the management pack.

Clicking the Properties tab of the class displays a screen similar to Figure 9.47. The properties listed are those displayed when viewing the class in the OpsMgr console. This is the screen where you build out the properties describing your class.

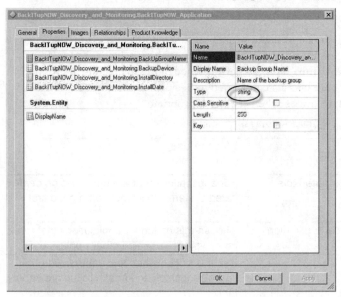

FIGURE 9.47 Properties for the class you created

CAUTION: MATCHING PROPERTY TYPES

The property type reflected in the class definition must match the type defined in the discovery. If the property type in the class is a string, the corresponding type returned by the discovery must be a string. If this is not the case, errors will be seen during discovery on the RMS.

Avoid properties with values that frequently change. The properties are populated when the initial discovery runs. If the values change after initial discovery, OpsMgr updates the discovery properties again. If they change often, OpsMgr may potentially update the discovery properties each discovery cycle, causing churn that can affect performance.

To add additional properties, right-click and then select to Add the property. Note that all properties defined specifically for this class will show up as attributes of the new class. Any inherited properties are shown, along with the class where they are defined. As an example, Figure 9.47 shows that DisplayName is inherited from System.Entity.

The Product Knowledge tab enables you to provide detailed information as to the purpose and use of the new class you created, provided the environment is properly set up (Microsoft Word installed) to allow editing in this field. The Images and Relationships tabs are beyond the scope of this chapter, and do not require editing for this discussion.

Now that you have built the class, it is time to build the discovery to populate the class. Perform the following steps:

1. Select the health model section of the Authoring console and click on Discoveries. In the middle section, right-click and select New -> Registry (filtered) to bring up the first screen of the wizard.

2. Fill in the information as shown in Figure 9.48, being cognizant of the following points:

   ► Similar to a class, you cannot easily change the element ID of a discovery once it is saved, so name the discovery appropriately. Only the display name is visible in the Operations console, not the element ID.

   ► You can change the display name at any time in the Authoring console.

   ► You will need to choose a target for this discovery. Choose a target that is as focused as possible and does not include objects not potentially needed.

   Click Next to continue the wizard.

TARGETING A DISCOVERY

Targeting a discovery is different from targeting a rule or monitor. With a rule or monitor, there already is a class (target) containing a set of objects where you want to focus monitoring. Discoveries, by nature, need to target a broader audience than rules or monitors; they are attempting to find systems that host the components you are trying to monitor.

This means that although it is generally unsuitable to use the Windows Computer object to deliver rules and monitors, it can be quite appropriate to use the Windows Computer object to deliver discoveries.

You will want to use the Windows Computer object for a discovery of components that may be running on both workstation and server systems. If you know your components of interest are only installed on server systems, choose the more specific server computer target; if you know your components are only on Windows 2008 servers, choose that target for the discovery (which requires including appropriate management packs as references in the Authoring console so the more specific classes would be available). The goal is to be as focused in your targeting as you can be, whether with rules and monitors or discoveries.

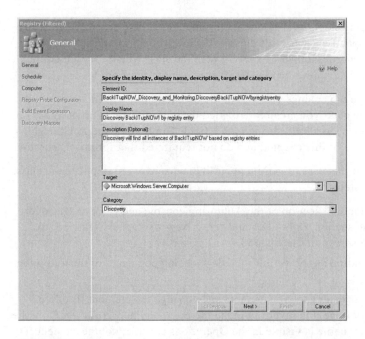

FIGURE 9.48 Specify the identity, display name, description, target, and category.

3.   The next screen asks you to define the schedule for the discovery. If you used the wizard when you built the management pack, the default schedule would be 15 seconds, but the default is 1 hour when created manually. Regardless, running a discovery every 15 seconds or even every hour is not appropriate. There generally is no reason to run a discovery more often than every 12–24 hours.

An often-heard argument is that when you install the management pack, you want discovery to start right away. That is understandable—and when a management pack is installed, discoveries attempt to run right away. From there, however, you don't need them to run excessively, which is why you decrease the frequency.

Choose to run the discovery once every 24 hours (see Figure 9.49) and click Next.

TIP: SPECIFYING THE LENGTH OF DISCOVERY INTERVAL

When testing, it is very appropriate to choose a very short discovery interval; when you move the management pack to production, be sure to reduce the frequency. In addition, make good use of the discovered inventory node in the monitoring section of the OpsMgr console. This view will show you the total membership of your class as discovered by OpsMgr and will confirm the discoveries that have been built are working!

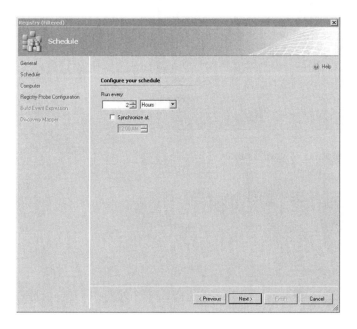

FIGURE 9.49 Specify the discovery schedule.

4. The next screen asks you to define the computer's name that will be discovered, shown in Figure 9.50. Accept the default and click Next.

5. Here is where you configure the registry key(s) you will use for the discovery. Click the Add button and fill in the information specific to the registry key of interest. In this instance, you are looking for a registry key, but it could just as easily be a value. Here it appears you are configuring the specific registry information to define which registry key to look at to find systems that should populate the class, which would make sense based on the fact that is how attribute discoveries work. Actually, all you are doing is telling OpsMgr where to look, not how. This becomes clearer on the following screen of the wizard. Figures 9.51 and 9.52 show the registry information to use. Multiple registry discoveries are necessary, as there are multiple discovery properties to be populated.

Click Next to proceed with the wizard.

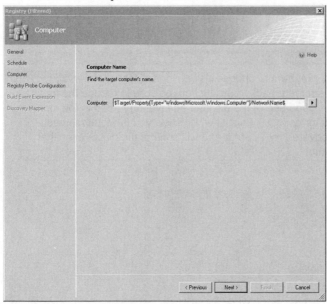

FIGURE 9.50 Define the target computer's name.

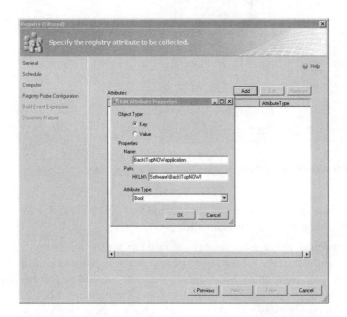

FIGURE 9.51 Enter the registry key properties.

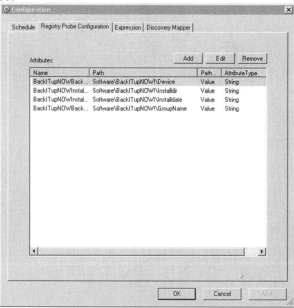

FIGURE 9.52 Additional registry configuration

6. The next screen asks for an expression to use when evaluating the registry key you entered, which is how you tell OpsMgr to evaluate that registry information. This particular example looks for the registry key to be present and related information, but you could just as easily look for the registry key to be absent or any of the values to be in specific formats or missing, whatever helps to identify an object properly. Figure 9.53 displays the selected filters.

7. The following screen is the discovery mapper. Particulars regarding the discovery mapper are beyond the scope of this chapter, but it will "map" the various values defined in the class and discovery together, as shown in Figure 9.54. Click Finish to save the discovery.

Right-click on Properties to edit any of the values just entered (except the discovery element ID). With the wizard complete, the discovery is ready. Save the management pack (incrementing the version each time you save the management pack) and import it into your management group.

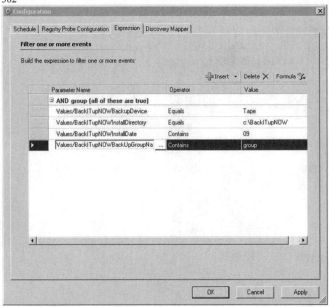

FIGURE 9.53 Specify the information to be evaluated for the registry key.

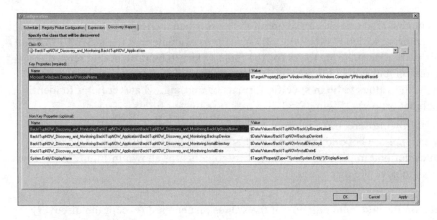

FIGURE 9.54 Mapping the values with the discovery mapper

After importing the management pack into the management group, you can explore it in the Operations console to ensure the import was successful and the discovery is working as expected. The first stop is at Authoring -> Management Pack Objects -> Object Discoveries. Here you will scope the display to the new class added by the management pack. Figure 9.55 shows there now are two BackITupNOW! classes that are selected: the one created with the Process Monitoring template, and the one just created in the Authoring console.

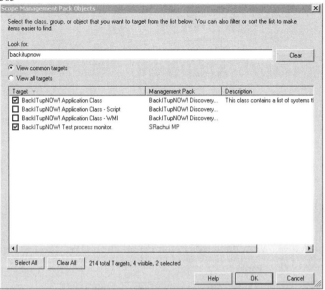

FIGURE 9.55 The BackITupNOW! Classes

With these classes selected, Figure 9.56 shows the discovery created in the Authoring console displayed under Object Discoveries. Because the management pack is not yet sealed, you can edit all the properties of the discovery (although without the nice user interface the Authoring console provides) with any overrides created saved in the base management pack. This is not generally a good idea, so for production systems, it is best to seal your management packs.

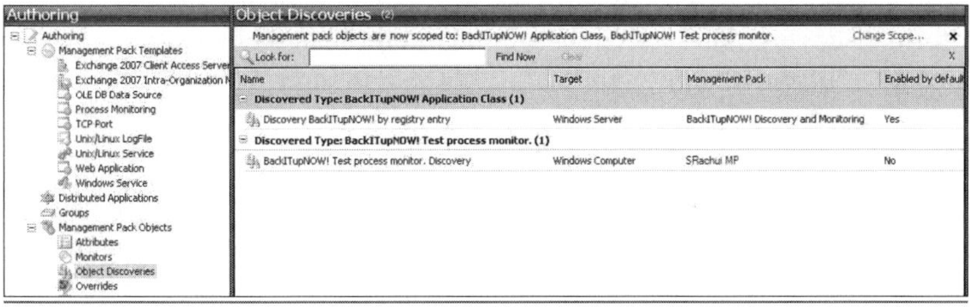

FIGURE 9.56 The discovery created in the Authoring console displayed under Object Discoveries

The class is displayed on the target list and the object discovery is available. To verify the class is populated, the authors created several registry keys on the Vanguard server, shown in Figure 9.57. (Because BackITupNOW! is a fictional application, the registry keys were created manually. In practice, these keys and values should be dynamic based on whether the application of interest is present or not.)

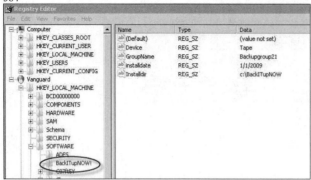

FIGURE 9.57 Registry keys created to verify the class is populated

Looking at the discovered inventory view focused on the BackITupNOW! class shows the class membership, displayed in Figure 9.58.

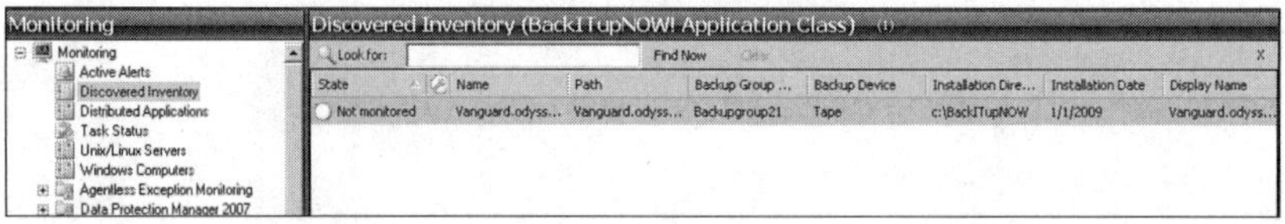

FIGURE 9.58 Discovered inventory on Vanguard

With the class populated, you can use it for targeting rules and monitors as needed. However, this is just one way you can discover items and populate classes. The "WMI Discovery" and "Scripts Discovery" sections will demonstrate the use of WMI and scripts to perform discovery. These sections will be briefer than the registry discussion and omit duplicative information, presenting just the salient information.

WMI Discovery

After what you learned about registry-based discovery, WMI discoveries become quite easy. Let's say you need a new class and a new discovery. Create the class, and then select Discoveries. Right-click in the middle area as in the "Registry Discovery" section of this chapter, but select the option to configure a WMI-based discovery. Figure 9.59 shows the configuration screen specific to WMI discovery. Because there is no BackITupNOW! WMI class (this is a fictional application), use the win32_ operatingsystem class, specifically looking for Windows 2008 systems. By default, the frequency for the discovery is 900 seconds. Figure 9.59 shows this changed to a more reasonable frequency of 86400 seconds (24 hours). The query in Figure 9.59 is an example only and will need to be changed to be more specific if used for a real discovery.

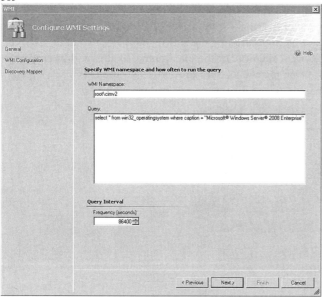

FIGURE 9.59 Configure WMI Settings

After configuring the settings, save the management pack and import it into the management group. Now look at the new class you created in Discovered Inventory, and confirm it is populated as expected. This is shown in Figure 9.60.

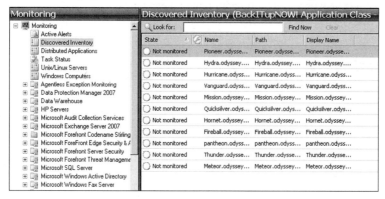

FIGURE 9.60 The class displaying in Discovered Inventory

Script Discovery

If registry or WMI-based discovery is not workable, script-based discovery almost certainly will be. Create a class to be populated by the script and then create the discovery. Figure 9.61 shows the new class. Take note of the class name, as this will be important when constructing the script. Also, notice the two properties for the class (see Figure 9.62) that you will need to handle in the discovery.

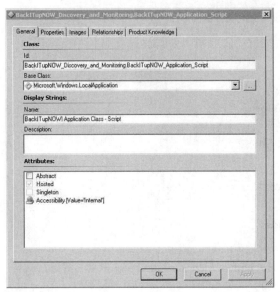

FIGURE 9.61 The new class used with the script-based discovery

FIGURE 9.62 The properties for the new class

From here, you need to create the discovery. Navigate to the Health Model section and click on the Discoveries node. In the middle area, right-click on an open area and select New -> Script. There are three steps to this wizard, as follows:

▶ Configuring the name of the discovery

▶ Configuring the schedule for how often the discovery should run

▶ Configuring the script that will do the work of the discovery

Figure 9.63 shows the script configuration.

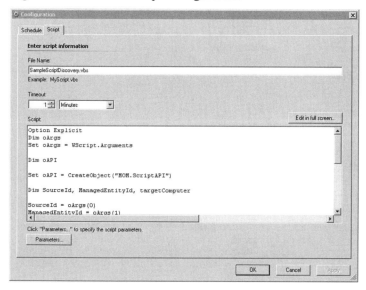

FIGURE 9.63 Configuring the script

The two key elements are the parameters passed to the script and the script itself:

▶ There are three parameters passed to every discovery script—SourceID, ManagedEntityID, and TargetComputer name. These values are represented by variables in OpsMgr, so pass these three variables to the script in the Parameters block as shown in Figure 9.64. You can use extra parameters as needed, but you must have these three.

▶ The script for this discovery is SampleScriptDiscovery.vbs. This extremely simple script runs and checks for the presence of a flagfolder on the specified systems. If the script finds that folder, it will discover the system along with values for DisplayType, DisplayResolution and PrincipalName, which are the properties defined for the class. In this example, the values given are static but in practice most likely would be supplied as a variable. The script follows with appropriate comments added:

```
Option Explicit
Dim oArgs
Set oArgs = WScript.Arguments

Dim oAPI

'Instantiate an instance of the MOM Scripting object
Set oAPI = CreateObject("MOM.ScriptAPI")

'Declare the variables that will hold the parameters being passed into the script
Dim SourceId, ManagedEntityId, targetComputer

'Read the parameter values from the command line
SourceId = oArgs(0)
ManagedEntityId = oArgs(1)
targetComputer = oArgs(2)

Dim oFSO, oDiscoveryData, oInst

'Instantiate an instance the discovery data object
Set oDiscoveryData = oAPI.CreateDiscoveryData(0, SourceId, ManagedEntityId)

Set oFSO = CreateObject("Scripting.FileSystemObject")

'Check for the flag folder and if it exists, populate an instance of discovery data.
Note here the MPElement names highlighted in italics and that these match the spe-
cific class we defined for this example or match well-known classes, in this case
Microsoft.Windows.Computer. If this section does not match up to the class defini-
tion, errors will be displayed during validation.
If (oFSO.FolderExists("C:\FlagFolder")) Then
        Set oInst = oDiscovery-
Data.CreateClassInstance("$MPElement[Name='BackITupNOW_Discovery_and_Monitoring.BackI
TupNOW_Application_Script']$")
        Call
oInst.AddProperty("$MPElement[Name='Windows!Microsoft.Windows.Computer']/PrincipalNam
e$", targetComputer)
        Call
oInst.AddProperty("$MPElement[Name='BackITupNOW_Discovery_and_Monitoring.BackITupNOW_
Application_Script']/DisplayType$", "Flat Panel")
        Call
oInst.AddProperty("$MPElement[Name='BackITupNOW_Discovery_and_Monitoring.BackITupNOW_
Application_Script']/DisplayResolution$", "1024x768")

'Once the discovery data is obtained it needs to be submitted
        Call oDiscoveryData.AddInstance(oInst)
        Call oAPI.Return(oDiscoveryData)
End If
```

FIGURE 9.64 Script parameters

Save the management pack and import it to your management group. Allow the discovery to run, and you will find the one system in the management group (see Figure 9.65) where the folder was created that is the subject of the discovery—flagfolder.

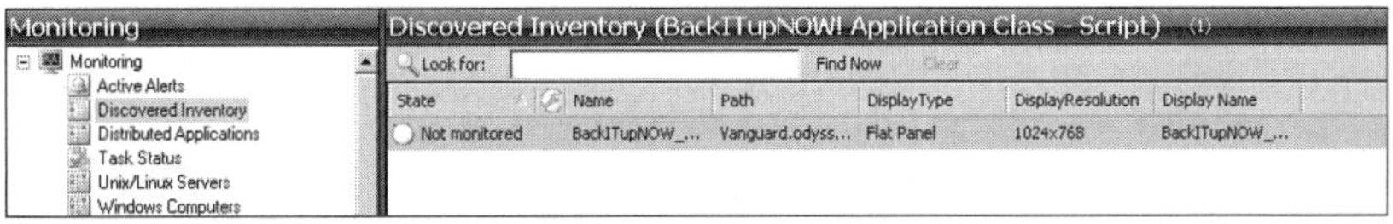

FIGURE 9.65 Discovered inventory displaying in the Operations console

Summary

This chapter looked at configuring OpsMgr in complex and distributed environments. It discussed configuring OpsMgr for high availability, looking in detail at clustering and alternatives; it discussed business continuity with OpsMgr, covering backup and recovery of the key OpsMgr components and advanced methods for configuring SQL Server database business continuity using log shipping and database mirroring. The chapter covered what's new with ACS in OpsMgr 2007 R2, how to approach noise filtering to reduce event loads and remove unwanted data from collection, how to harden and lockdown the ACS infrastructure, enabling and collecting security events from SQL Server 2008, auditing Cross Platform security events, log replay, and the wealth of community resources available for users. With the new capabilities of ACS in OpsMgr 2007 R2 and the extended auditing sources now readily available, users can truly extend and optimize ACS to be a cross-platform enterprise security auditing solution.

While *System Center Operations Manager 2007 Unleashed* discussed using the distributed application designer, this chapter went a step further. Using the TCP Port monitors and Distributed Applications tools built into OpsMgr, coupled with third-party tools such as Savision Live Maps and the System Center Central Multi-Host Ping management pack, you can model redundant networking connectivity between locations and provide alerts on both the loss of a single link and complete connectivity loss between locations.

Finally, proper targeting is fundamental to the proper function of OpsMgr, and there are many options available. Remember that targeting of monitoring objects should be as focused as possible, and target classes are useful to determine the health of the monitored objects. If a class doesn't exist, create it with the Authoring console.

APPENDIX A

OpsMgr R2 by Example

The core functionality of Operations Manager (OpsMgr) is provided via management packs. Although there is solid documentation for each management pack, there are benefits to having a high-level overview of how to implement and tune the management pack (MP). This appendix is a compilation of "OpsMgr by Example" articles, also published on the OpsMgr blog at http://ops-mgr.spaces.live.com. These discuss steps taken to implement the management pack, and include examples of alerts and tuning steps used in various environments. The intent is to provide a 5,000-foot/meter perspective, as well as show the details for a particular type of tuning performed in a sample deployment. Several of these management packs have tuning steps specific to OpsMgr 2007 Release 2 (R2), which are included as notes within this appendix. Many of these also include ideas for how the management packs could evolve going forward.

For new "by Example" information and updates to existing articles, be sure to check http://ops-mgr.spaces.live.com. The blog will continue to have postings adding to the "by Example" series.

Active Directory MP

The Active Directory management pack is available as a single download that contains different libraries to monitor Active Directory 2000, 2003, and 2008 domain controllers. You can also find this article online at http://tinyurl.com/ActiveDirectoryMP-ByExample.

How to Install the Active Directory MP

Perform the following steps to install the ADMP:

1. Download the Active Directory management pack from the Management Pack Catalog at the following URL:

http://pinpoint.microsoft.com/en-US/systemcenter/managementpackcatalog. The Active Directory Management Pack Guide is included in the download and labeled "OM2007_MP_AD2008.doc." Beginning with the R2 release of Operations Manager, you can download management packs directly using the OpsMgr user interface (UI). It is suggested that you actually download from the website and install it yourself so that you can have a copy of the Management Pack Guide available during installation. If you already have a copy of the Management Pack Guide, use the OpsMgr UI functionality to download and install the management pack.

TIP: ACCESSING THE MANAGEMENT PACK GUIDES ONLINE

The Management Pack Guides are available online at http://technet.microsoft.com/en-us/library/cc540358.aspx if you would prefer to use the OpsMgr user interface to import your management packs. In addition, Stefan Stranger has a blog entry describing how to provide direct access to the Management Pack Guides from the OpsMgr Console, available at http://blogs.technet.com/stefan_stranger/archive/2009/09/10/direct-access-to-the-mp-guides-and-mp-catalog-from-the-ops-console.aspx.

---

2. Read the Management Pack Guide—cover to cover. This document spells out in detail some important pieces of information you will need to know.

3. Import the AD management pack (using the Operations console or PowerShell).

4. Deploy the OpsMgr agent to all domain controllers (DCs). The agent must be deployed to all DCs. Agentless configurations will NOT work for the ADMP.

5. Get a list of all domain controllers from the Operations console. In the Authoring space, navigate to Authoring -> Groups -> AD Domain Controller Group (Windows 2008 Server). Right-click on the group(s) and select View Group Members.

6. Enable Agent Proxy configuration on all domain controllers identified from the groups. This is in the Administration node, under Administration -> Device Management -> Agent Managed. Right-click each domain controller, select Properties, click the Security tab, and then check the box labeled Allow this agent to act as a proxy and discover managed objects on other computers. Perform this action for every domain controller, even if you add the DC after your initial configuration of OpsMgr. For a simple method to bulk-add the proxy setting, see the article on enabling agent proxy for all computers hosting an instance of a specific object at http://blogs.technet.com/jonathanalmquist/archive/2009/09/22/enable-agent-proxy-for-a-class-classproxyenabler.aspx. (Thanks to Ziemek Boroski for his comment at http://ops-mgr.spaces.live.com on this.)

7. Configure the Replication account in the Operations console, under Administration -> Security. (Full details are in the AD MP Guide.) Do this for every domain controller, even if you add the DC after initially configuring OpsMgr.

CHANGES TO THE RUN AS ACCOUNTS IN R2

The new Run As Accounts in OpsMgr R2 for the Active Directory management pack have changed by adding the ability to define where you can target a Run As Account to. The simplest (and most insecure) approach is to use the All targeted options, but this causes the Run As Accounts to be deployed everywhere (including to remote forests where you should not attempt to use the account). The recommended approach is to create a Run As Account for the AD MP Account Run As Profile that specifies the domain controller's computer objects as their target. This is shown in Figure A.1.

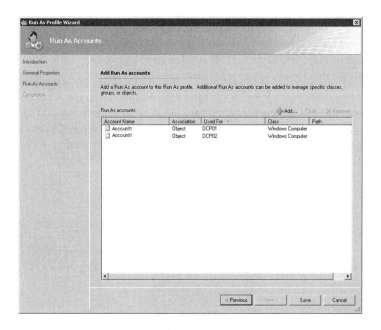

FIGURE A.1 Targeting the AD MP Account Run As Profile to specific domain controllers

8. Validate the existence of the OpsMgrLatencyMonitors container (previously named the MOMLatencyMonitors container). Within this container, there should be sub-folders for each DC, using the name of each domain controller. If the container does not exist, it is often due to insufficient permissions. (See information configuring the Replication account within the AD MP Guide for details.)

9. Open the Operations console. Go to the Monitoring node and navigate to Monitoring -> Microsoft Windows Active Directory -> Topology Views and validate functionality. (You may have to set the scope to the AD Domain Controllers Group to get these views to populate.)

10. Check to make sure Active Directory shows up under Monitoring -> Distributed Applications as a distributed application that is in the Healthy, Warning, or Critical state. If it is in the "Not Monitored" state, check for domain controllers that are not installed or are in a "gray" state.

11. Create a MicrosoftWindowsActiveDirectory_Overrides management pack to contain any overrides required for the MP. (Hey, if it's not created now, you'll never remember to create it, and you will end up using the default MP; that's not good—see http://cameronfuller.spaces.live.com/blog/cns!A231E4EB0417CB76!1152.entry or *System Center Operations Manager 2007 Unleashed* for details.)

12. The Active Directory Helper Object (oomads) needs to be installed on each domain controller OpsMgr will monitor. This file (OOMADs.msi) is available on the OpsMgr R2 installation media in the HelperObjects folder, under the subfolder for the appropriate version of the operating system (amd64, i386, or ia64).

Deploying the Active Directory 2008 management pack was relatively painless. After importing the management pack, the domain controllers showed no significant impact on processors. The Active Directory Topology Root appeared as a distributed application and showed a health state of green. The Active Directory diagram view also worked as expected.

Tuning/Alerts to Look for in the Active Directory MP

The following alerts were encountered and resolved while tuning the various Active Directory management packs (listed in alphabetical order by alert name):

▶ **Alert: (none)**

Issue: The SysVol for Windows 2008 portion of the management pack for Active Directory Server 2008 (Monitoring) identified an alert as part of the DFS Service Health alert monitor for one of the domain controllers in our environment. No additional knowledge was available.

Resolution: It was determined that the technician had uninstalled the Exchange 2007 tools from the domain controller at the time these alerts activated. These alerts had not recurred since that time. The alerts were closed to monitor to see if it will reoccur.

▶ **Alert: A problem has been detected with the trust relationship between two domains.**

Issue: A server in a location (site 1) lost communication with domain controllers that existed in a second location (site 2). This critical alert did NOT autoresolve. This was detected by the alert rule: "A problem has been detected with the trust relationship between the two domains." As part of troubleshooting, verify that the Last Modified date occurred during the outage (add this column to the display by personalizing the view on the Active Alerts to include the field) and the Repeat Count was not incrementing.

Resolution: Use the Active Directory Domain Controller Server 2008 Computer Role Task of Enumerate Trusts to validate that all trusts were working after site connectivity was re-established. Then log into the domain controller reporting the error and use the Active Directory Domains and Trusts Microsoft Management Console (MMC) snap-in to validate each of the trusts. Close the alert manually.

▶ **Alert: A problem has been detected with the trust relationship between two domains.**

Issue: This alert is occurring from domain controllers who cannot communicate with the domain controller in the trusted domain to validate this trust.

Resolution: These domain controllers do not require validation of the trust from these remote locations. Disable these alerts for the domain controllers not needing to validate the trust that were unable to reach the domain controllers that they trusted due to routing restrictions.

▶ **Alert: A problem was detected with the trust relationship between two domains.**

Issue: The domain controllers could not connect to the domain controller in the other domain. This was due to a routing issue between the specific domain controllers and the domain controller in the remote domain. Remote sites were connected via VPN and could not route to that subnet.

Resolution: Provided routing from the domain controllers to the domain controller in the other domain.

▶ **Alert: A problem has been detected with the trust relationship between two domains.**

Additional Alert: A problem with the inter-domain trusts has been detected.

Issue: This alert is occurring from domain controllers who cannot communicate with the domain controller in the trusted domain to validate this trust.

Resolution: Tested first with the NETDOM command (override with parameters to do a dsquery /domain: /verify dc) for the local domain (success) and then for the remote domain reporting the failure (failed; cannot contact the remote domain). Then perform an nltest; first for the local domain (success) and then the remote domain reporting the failure (ERROR_NO_LOGON_SERVERS). Next, ran a DCDIAG on the server and a NETDIAG. Failures on the server for both NETDOM and NLTEST queries. Ran the enumerate trusts task on the system, but it fails on the remote domain as well (AD_Enumerate_Trusts.vbs). DNS was inconsistent in the environment (used nslookup with different servers to validate that the results of the lookup to the remote domain name were not consistent). Made DNS consistent and flushed DNS on the server experiencing the alerts. The critical-level alert resolved itself and closed the other one.

▶ **Alert: A problem has been detected with the trust relationship between two domains.**

Additional Alert: A problem with the inter-domain trusts has been detected.

Issue: Specific domain controllers were reporting the alert as an issue to verify the trust between two forests in the environment.

Resolution: The DC in question did not have a zone to provide name resolution to the other forest. Added the zone to the domain controller's DNS.

▶ **Alert: A problem has been detected with the trust relationship between two domains.**

Issue: This occurs when a domain controller has been removed from the environment, and does not represent an issue if the alert description contains the information that it cleaned up the naming context.

Resolution: You can close alerts of this type, as they will occur on each domain controller in the environment that sees the piece of the replication that is no longer relevant.

▶ **Alert: A problem with the inter-domain trusts has been detected.**

Issue: A server in a location (site 1) lost communication with domain controllers in a second location (site 2). This critical alert did NOT auto-resolve. This was detected by the AD Trust Monitoring monitor, which runs every 5 minutes using the AD Monitor Trusts script. It was verified that the Last Modified date occurred during the outage (add this column to the display by personalizing the view on the Active Alerts to include the field) and the Repeat Count was not incrementing.

Resolution: Use the Active Directory Domain Controller Server 2008 Computer Role Task of Enumerate Trusts to validate all trusts are working after reestablishing site connectivity. Next, log into the domain controller reporting the error and use the Active Directory Domains and Trusts UI to validate each of the trusts. This alert should auto-resolve when the trust relationships are working, but that functionality does not appear to work. Closed alert manually.

▶ **Alert: A replication island has been detected. Replication will not occur across the enterprise.**

Issue: In sites and services, DC1 replicated with DC2 but DC2 did not replicate with DC1.

Resolution: DC1 was only referencing itself for DNS as 127.0.0.1, with no DNS to the remote DC on the TCP port properties. Rebooted DC2 after the change since DNS could not connect to itself on DC2.

The root cause of this alert was an issue with RPC between the two domain controllers. RPC in the environment is coded to a specific port, and this port change had not been made to the second domain controller.

▶ **Alert: Account Changes Report Available.**

Issue: Informational alert, which can be accessed in the AD SAM account changes report (available on the right under Active Directory Domain reports).

Resolution: No resolution required. Checked the AD SAM Account Changes report (available on the right under Active Directory Domain reports) to see the changes that were available.

▶ **Alert: Active Directory cannot perform an authenticated RPC call to another DC because the SPN for the destination DC is not registered on the KDC.**

Issue: One domain controller was offline during the time period, a second domain controller was promoted, the FSMO roles were moved, and then the process was rolled back due to technical issues. This was caused by replication issues in the environment. The domain controller had been dcpromoed back out and back in and resulted in old records in ADSIEdit that were invalid. This was part of the ForestDNSZones,DC=_msdcs.abcco.com records.

Resolution: Added SPN information manually to server to get around errors.

▶ **Alert: AD cannot allocate memory.**

Issue: The domain controller has 4GB of memory but when logged into, there were more than 6GB of memory in use. Attempted to stop programs that appeared to be causing this (large numbers of cmds and nslookup tasks that failed), but this did not end up freeing the memory.

Resolution: Per the product knowledge, rebooted the server and verified that the memory had returned to more reasonable numbers (less than 1GB in use). Closed the alert, but tracking this to see if it recurs on this server.

▶ **Alert: AD Client-Side Script-Based Test Failed to Complete.**

Issue: AD Replication Partner Op Master Consistency: The script "AD Replication Partner Op Master Consistency" could not create object "McActiveDir.ActiveDirectory." This is an unexpected error. The error returned was "ActiveX component can't create object" (0x1AD).

Resolution: In MOM 2005, this was resolved by changing the Action account. In OpsMgr 2007, this alert occurred in a different domain than the one with the OpsMgr root management server (RMS). To resolve this, create a Run As Account for the domain (DMZ) and assign the Run As Account to the AD domain controllers in the DMZ domain.

▶ **Alert: AD Client-Side Script-Based Test Failed to Complete.**

Issue: Alert is generated by the AD Replication Partner Op Master Consistency monitor. The system reporting the error was generating an error of event ID 45 in the Operations Manager Log from the source of Health Service Script.

This event is occurring on an hourly basis (12:57, 1:58, and so on):

AD Replication Partner Op Master Consistency: The script "AD Replication Partner Op Master Consistency" failed to execute the following LDAP query: '<LDAP://servername.odyssey.com/CN=Configuration,DC=ODYSSEY,DC=COM>;(&(objectClass=crossRefContainer)(fSMORoleOwner=*));fSMORoleOwner;Subtree'.

The error returned was "Table does not exist" (0x80040E37).

This alert is linked to "Could not determine the FSMO role holder" alerts that are occurring.

Resolution: Believe this was related to misconfigurations of the anti-virus settings on the domain controllers in the environment.

▶ **Alert: AD Domain Performance Health Degraded.**

Issue: More than 60% of the DCs contained in this AD domain report a performance health problem.

Resolution: This alert indicates that there are alerts that are occurring in more than 60% of the domain controllers in a domain. This alert does not require an action for itself but does require analysis to determine what is causing the domain controllers to be in a degraded state.

▶ **Alert: AD Op Master is inconsistent.**

Issue: Tested using the AD Replication Partner Op Master Consistency alert monitor, which runs every minute, to verify the incoming replication partners for the domain controller show the same operations masters. Also used the REPADMIN Replsum task in the Active Directory MP.

Resolution: The REPADMIN Replsum command validated that replication was functioning correctly (had to override the "Support Tools Install Dir" on Windows 2008 to %*windir*%\system32 to make the task work correctly). The override was used when the task was actually run. It's not created as an override in the OpsMgr console or in the Authoring node, but rather when the task is executed. The link between the domain controllers has been running close to fully saturated. The alert auto-resolved once the network utilization slowed down.

▶ **Alert: AD Op Master is inconsistent.**

Issue: Active Directory Operations Master role is found to be in a transitional state.

Resolution: Message generated when an AD Operations Master role is moved from one server to another and can be safely ignored.

▶ **Alert: AD Op Master is inconsistent.**

Issue: Tested using the AD Replication Partner Op Master Consistency alert monitor, which runs every minute, to verify the incoming replication partners for the domain controller show the same operations masters. Also used REPADMIN Replsum task in the Active Directory MP.

Resolution: Additional information on alert available at Marcus Oh's blog, http://marcusoh.blogspot.com/2009/07/understanding-ad-op-master-is.html.

▶ **Alert: AD Replication is occurring slowly.**

Issue: Same as identified in alert: AD Replication is slower than the configured threshold. This rule does not provide the ability to override the default configuration of 15 minutes. The AD environment is not configured with the default of 15 minutes so these rules do not apply because they are still replicating within a successful timeframe.

Resolution: Disabled this rule (AD Replication is occurring slowly) for group AD Domain Controller Group (Windows 2003 Server). You could also do this for individual servers if there were a limited number of these where the AD Replication was not configured with default replication times of 15 minutes. Closed the alerts.

▶ **Alert: AD Replication is occurring slowly.**

Issue: Occurred on a domain controller that had been having issues replicating for a period of time.

Resolution: Rebooted the domain controller; this alert was generated after the reboot. The script is scheduled to run every 900 seconds (15 minutes). Used REPADMIN Replsum command to validate replication was functioning correctly (had to override the "Support Tools Install Dir" on Windows 2008 to *%windir%*\system32). No errors found on the REPADMIN Replsum command. Waited the 15 minutes to verify that the domain controller was not continuing to experience the issue, and closed the alert.

▶ **Alert: AD Replication is slower than the configured threshold.**

Issue: Intersite Expected Max Latency (min) default 15; Intrasite Expected Max Latency (min) default 5.

Issue: This alert also occurs if connectivity is lost between sites for a long enough period of time.

Resolution: If alert is not current and not repeating, and if replication is occurring and REPADMIN Replsum task comes up clean, this alert can be noted (to see if there is a consistent day of week or time it occurs at) and closed. Added a diagnostic to the AD Replication Monitoring monitor, for the critical state, taking the information from the REPADMIN Replsum task that provided (You must have the admin utilities installed on the DC for this to work.):

```
REPADMIN.EXE
%ProgramFiles%\Support Tools\ /replsum 1200
```

Created the diagnostic to run automatically using:
Program: REPADMIN.EXE
Working Directory: *%ProgramFiles%*\Support Tools
Parameters: /replsum
Options available included changing the replication topology to replicate every 15 minutes or configuring overrides. To resolve, tried creating a custom group for the servers in the location (see the "Creating Computer Groups based on AD Site" posting at http://Cameronfuller.spaces.live.com for additional information) and created an override for the new group changing the Intersite Expected Max Latency to 120 (so it would be double the configuration in AD Sites and Services). Performed this configuration for each remote location that did not have a 15-minute replication interval. You could also do this for all domain controllers, using the domain controller computer group(s). This did not function as expected, but is used as an example for how overrides can be creatively configured (in this case, based upon sites)!

▶ **Alert: AD Replication Monitoring—Access denied.**

Issue: This occurred on one domain controller; there also was an alert stating that it failed to create the OpsMgrLatencyMonitors container. Validated the container by logging into the domain controller, opening up AD Users and Computers, View -> Advanced Features, and verifying that the container (and the two existing domain controllers as sub-containers) exists.

Resolution: Already resolved, as MSAA had permissions necessary to create this container. Validated that MOMLatencyMonitors container existed, and it included sub-folders matching the name of each domain controller. (If the container doesn't exist, it is often due to insufficient permissions; see configuring the replication account within the AD MP Guide for configuration information.)

▶ **Alert: AD Replication Monitoring—Access denied.**

Issue: This occurred on several domain controllers when OpsMgrLatency-Monitors container was removed. Validated the container by logging into the domain controller, opening up AD Users and Computers, View -> Advanced Features, and verifying that the container (and the two existing domain controllers as sub-containers) exists.

Resolution: Already resolved, as MSAA had required necessary to create this container. Validated OpsMgrLatencyMonitors container existed and it included sub-folders matching the name of each domain controller. (If container doesn't exist, it is often due to insufficient permissions; see configuring the replication account within the AD MP Guide for configuration information.)

▶ **Alert: AD Replication Monitoring—Time skew detected.**

Issue: Caused by domain controllers running on virtual servers that were synchronizing with the host operating system while the host operating system was not time synchronized.

Resolution: Fixed the actual time on the domain controllers and configured Guest operating system in virtual server to not synchronize with Host operating system. This was accomplished by shutting down the Guest operating system, configuring the Virtual Machine Addition Properties, under additional features uncheck Host Time Synchronization, and restarting the Guest operating system.

▶ **Alert: AD Site Availability Health Degraded.**

Issue: Caused by another alert that is affecting the DCs availability. Check the status of AD as a distributed application to determine what alert is affecting AD availability.

Resolution: Investigated alert causing the DC availability issue, which in this case was the Logical Disk Free Space is Low alert. Another example of this was a domain controller with a second power supply not plugged in and was alerting via the HP management pack.

▶ **Alert: AD Site Performance Health Degraded.**

Issue: More than 60% of the DCs contained in this AD site report a performance health problem.

Resolution: This alert indicates that there are alerts that are occurring in more than 60% of the domain controllers in a site. This alert does not require an action for itself but requires analysis to determine what is causing the domain controllers to be in a degraded state.

▶ **Alert: Could not determine the FSMO role holder.**

Issue: Each domain controller in the environment reported the error when trying to determine the Schema Op Master on the various domain controllers. The rule generating this was "Could not determine the FSMO role holder."

Resolution: Used NETDOM Query FSMO task (changing the Support Tools installation folder to %*windir*%\system32) to validate the FSMO role holders on each domain controller.

▶ **Alert: Could not determine the FSMO role holder.**

Additional Alert: AD Client-Side Script-Based Test Failed to Complete.

Additional Alert: AD Op Master is inconsistent.

Issue: These three alerts are DNS related. In one situation, there was a bad DNS record on one of the top-level DNS servers. One could ping the NetBIOS name, but not the FQDN. (It was a DC in another domain within the forest.) In the second instance, there was a bad IP address in the HOST file. Once all DNS resolution was resolved, the alerts auto cleared.

The alerts have also come in and then auto resolve on their own. This happened when someone rebooted a DC in another domain and that server was the only DC for that domain.

A good link to investigate DNS issues is http://www.windowsnetworking.com/articles_tutorials/Using-NSLOOKUP-DNS-Server-diagnosis.html.

Resolution: Resolving DNS issues in the environment.

Submitted By: CK on the ops-mgr.spaces.live.com website.

▶ **Alert: DC has failed to synchronize its naming context with replication partners.**

Issue: One of the domain controllers went to a grayed-out status.

The server having the issues reported the "DC has failed to synchronize its naming context with replication partners" issue and "A problem has been detected with the trust relationship between two domains" and "AD Replication is occurring slowly" and "Script-Based Test Failed to Complete" (for multiple AD-related scripts).

Other domain controllers reported "Could not determine the FSMO role holder" and "AD Client-Side Script-Based Test Failed to Complete."

Events also occurred on the client system (21006 OpsMgr Connector, 20057 OpsMgr Connector, and 21001 OpsMgr Connector).

Resolution: Installed the Telnet client feature to test connectivity to the management server. Telnet connectivity failed from this system but not from others. Restarted OpsMgr Health service, but it had no effect on the gray status. After rebooting the system, the status went back to non-gray.

▶ **Alert: DC has failed to synchronize its naming context with replication partners.**

Issue: A server in a location (site 1) lost communication with domain controllers that existed in a second location (site 2). The rule generating this alert is "DC has failed to synchronize naming context with its replication partner."

Resolution: Alerts occurred when connectivity was lost between the sites. These alerts had a Repeat Count of 0. Used the REPADMIN Replsum command to validate replication was functioning correctly (had to override the "Support Tools Install Dir" on Windows 2008 to %*windir*%\system32 to make the task work correctly). Closed the alerts manually.

▶ **Alert: DC is both a Global Catalog and the Infrastructure Update master.**

Issue: The domain controller was both a global catalog and the infrastructure master. This configuration is acceptable as long as all domain controllers are GCs, but it results in additional replication traffic for the additional domain.

Resolution: Options available would be to override this and disable it on the server but this does not resolve the issue in most situations. In this case, with all DCs being GCs and the additional domain a small child domain with only minor amounts of information, the recommended approach is to create the override.

If this is not the case, the preferred approach to take is to deploy an additional domain controller that is NOT a global catalog server and run the infrastructure update master on that server. You can deploy this new domain controller on either physical or virtual configurations depending upon the client requirements. Further detail on this condition is available in the Microsoft article at http://support.microsoft.com/default.aspx/kb/251095.

▶ **Alert: KCC cannot compute a replication path.**

Issue: KCC detected problems on multiple domain controllers

Resolution: Connectivity was lost from the central site to a remote site for several hours. The remote site was down due to a power outage. Errors were logged every 15 minutes from when it was down until when the site was back online. This also occurred when a domain controller was shut off but still existed from the perspective of Active Directory. This can also occur when the site topology is set to automatically generate the site links, but the network is configured so that some sites cannot see other sites (as an example, in a configuration with a hub in Dallas and sites in Frisco and Plano, where both sites can see Dallas but cannot see each other).

▶ **Alert: One or more domain controllers may not be replicating.**

Issue: The AD MP will report replication issues across all DCs if only one was down (and thus not able to replicate its monitor objects).

Resolution: Get all domain controllers monitored by OpsMgr. Validate replication in the environment.

▶ **Alert: Overall Essential Services state.**

Issue: The Overall Essential Services state monitor portion of the Active Directory Domain Controller Server 2008 Computer role identified an alert. No additional knowledge was available.

Resolution: Speaking with the technician, it was determined he had uninstalled the Exchange 2007 tools from the domain controller at the time these alerts activated. These alerts had not recurred since then. Closed the alerts to monitor if it will reoccur.

▶ **Alert: Performance Module could not find a performance counter.**

Issue: In PerfDataSource, could not resolve counter DirectoryServices and KDC AS Requests; Module will be unloaded.

Resolution: Created a Run As Account and configured the AD MP account (Administration -> Security -> Run As Profiles) for each of the two servers in the domain reporting errors.

▶ **Alert: Replication is not occurring—All replication partners have failed to synchronize.**

Issue: The alert description is the key on this alert. All replication partners are now replicating successfully.

Resolution: Alert description of "AD Replication Monitoring: All replication partners are now replicating successfully" is a success condition and does not require any intervention other than closing the alert.

▶ **Alert: Script-Based Test Failed to Complete.**

Issue: AD Lost And Found Object Count: The script "AD Lost And Found Object Count" failed to create object "McActiveDir.ActiveDirectory." This is an unexpected error. The error returned was "ActiveX component can't create object" (0x1AD).

Resolution: Configured the AD MP Account (Administration -> Security -> Run As Profiles) for each of the two servers in the domain reporting errors.

▶ **Alert: Script-Based Test Failed to Complete.**

Issue: AD Database and Log: The script "AD Database and Log" failed to create object "McActiveDir.ActiveDirectory." The error returned was "ActiveX component can't create object" (0x1AD).

Resolution: Configured the AD MP Account (Administration -> Security -> Run As Profiles) for each of the two servers in the domain reporting errors.

▶ **Alert: Script-Based Test Failed to Complete.**

Issue: AD Database and Log: The script "AD Database and Log" failed to create object "McActiveDir.ActiveDirectory." The error returned was "ActiveX component can't create object" (0x1AD).

Resolution: Installed OOMADS from OpsMgr 2007 R2 installation media. The OOMADs.msi file is included within the HelperObjects folder on the media within the appropriate version of the operating system (amd64, i386, or ia64).

▶ **Alert: Script-Based Test Failed to Complete.**

A problem has been detected with the trust relationship between two domains.

Issue: The server was a domain controller that was exhibiting a variety of different errors, including the following:

AD Monitor Trusts: The trusts between this domain (ABC.COM) and the following domain(s) are in an error state: xyz.com (inbound), the error is "There are currently no logon servers available to service the logon request" (0x51F).

AD Replication Partner Count: The script "AD Replication Partner Count" failed to bind to "LDAP://DC01.ABC.COM/CN=DC01,CN=Servers,CN=Plano,CN=Sites,CN=Configuration,DC=ABC,DC=COM." The error returned was "Object variable not set" (0x5B).

1153 of these in 4 days + 1 hour (1:17:28 pm)—failing every 5 minutes.

AD Lost And Found Object Count: Script "AD Lost And Found Object Count" was unable to bind to the lost and found container.

1152 of these in 4 days + 1 hour (1:17:28 pm)—every 5 minutes failing.

AD Database and Log: The script "AD Database and Log" encountered an error while trying to get the object "LDAP://DC01.ABC.COM/RootDSE." The error returned was "The server is not operational" (0x8007203A).

388 of these in 4 days + 2 hours (1:17:44 pm).

AD Replication Monitoring: encountered a runtime error. Failed to bind to "LDAP://DC01.ABC.COM/RootDSE." The error returned was "The server is not operational" (0x8007203A).

799 of these in 4 days + 2 hours (1:17:44 pm).

Resolution: Logged into server, attempted to open Active Directory Domains and Trusts and received message: "The configuration information describing this enterprise is not available. The server is not operational." Debugging, rebooting the server. After reboot the issue opening Active Directory Domains and Trusts no longer occurred. Closed the alerts generated to see if recur.

▶ **Alert: Script-Based Test Failed to Complete.**

Issue: AD Database and Log: The script AD Database and Log failed to create object McActiveDir.ActiveDirectory. The error returned was: "ActiveX component cannot create object (0×1AD)."

Resolution: Uninstalled OOMADS using Add/Remove programs, Active Directory Management Pack Helper Object (the original version was .05MB in size), and re-installed the 64-bit equivalent (AMD64 in this case). To do this, copy the MSI locally to the system to install it; after installation, it showed .07MB in size in Add/Remove programs.

▶ **Alert: Session setup failed because no trust account exists: Script "AD Validate Server Trust Event."**

Issue: Specific computer accounts were identified multiple times as not containing a trust account.

Resolution: This is caused either by systems that believe that they are part of the domain but no longer are, or often by systems that are being imaged. Resolution is either to drop and rejoin the system to the domain or to close the alert if the system is no longer online. These alerts are not actionable. Decreased the severity of these alerts from critical to informational via an override.

▶ **Alert: Some replication partners have failed to synchronize.**

Issue: A domain controller was offline and unable to be synchronized with.

Resolution: Bring the domain controller back online.

▶ **Alert: The AD Last Bind latency is above the configured threshold.**

Issue: One domain controller had consistently high AD last bind latency. Logon to the system showed it as extremely unresponsive.

Used the suggested tasks from product knowledge to validate that the bind was not going slowly and no high CPU processes were identified on the system. The view available in product knowledge pointed to a large spike in the time required for the LDAP query (checking Active Directory Last Bind counter). The spike occurred during a very heavy processor utilization on one of the domain controllers. This monitor checks every 5 minutes. Alert auto-resolved itself after the LDAP query was responding in an acceptable timeframe.

Resolution: Attempts to debug the issue were inconclusive and extremely difficult due to performance issue with the system. Rebooted domain controller, it came back online, and AD Last Bind Latency returned to normal values.

► **Alert: The AD Machine Account Authentication Failures Report has data available.**

Issue: The alert was raised on both domain controllers in the same physical location. The alert description contains the name of the computer account that is failing to authenticate. Have seen multiple examples of this alert where sometimes it is an actionable alert and sometimes it is not.

In one case, there was a server where the computer account had been removed from the domain. This was a fully actionable situation where the computer had to be re-added to the domain to resolve the issue. Then the alert was closed because this alert is generated by a rule so it does not auto-resolve.

In another situation, the computer account was for a workstation that was consistently unable to communicate with the domain controllers as it was connected remotely to another network via VPN.

Resolution: Disjoin from domain (no to reboot), rejoin the domain and reboot the system that is having the issue. These alerts are not actionable. Decreased the severity of these alerts from critical to informational via an override.

► **Alert: The Domain Changes report has data available.**

Issue: No issue—this was an informational message, generated when the PDC emulator role was moved between domain controllers in the environment.

Resolution: No actions required; this message is provided for situations where the PDC emulator role was moved unexpectedly.

► **Alert: The Domain Controller has been started.**

Issue: Notification that a domain controller was started, sent as an information message generated by an alert rule. (Because it is a rule, and not a monitor, it does not auto-resolve.) This is a good alert to keep because it provides a simple way to see when a domain controller is rebooted and when it is back online. Prior to this message, an information message should appear that the domain controller has stopped.

Resolution: Manually close the alert as the domain controller reboot was expected.

► **Alert: The Domain Controller has been stopped.**

Issue: Notification that a domain controller was stopped, sent as an information message, which is generated by an alert rule. (Since it is a rule, and not a monitor, it does not auto-resolve.) This is a good alert to keep because it provides a simple way to see what domain controllers have rebooted to identify situations where domain controllers are unexpectedly rebooted. A follow-up information message appears when the domain controller restarts successfully.

Resolution: Manually closed the alert as the domain controller reboot was expected.

▶ **Alert: The Op Master Domain Naming Master Last Bind latency is above the configured threshold.**

Issue: A large number of alerts are generated at > 5 seconds for warning and > 15 seconds for error.

Resolution: Per http://technet.microsoft.com/en-us/library/cc749936.aspx, the effective thresholds should be changed to warning at > 15 seconds and error at > 30 seconds. Created an override for all types of Active Directory Domain Controller Server 2008 Computer role to change Threshold Error Sec to 30 and Threshold Warning (sec) to 15 and stored it in the ActiveDirectory2008_ Overrides management pack.

▶ **Alert: The Op Master PDC Last Bind latency is above the configured threshold.**

Issue: Bind from the domain controller identified in the alert to the PDC emulator is slower than 5 seconds for a warning and slower than 15 seconds for an error. This occurred in a remote site connecting to a central site with the PDC emulator role.

Resolution: The alert appears to be due to slowness in the link between the two locations, or a condition where one of the two servers identified may have been overloaded. In this particular case, it was caused by a domain controller overloaded due to insufficient hardware, which had to be decommissioned.

▶ **Alert: The logical drive holding the AD Database is low on free space.**

Issue: Low disk space on the drive with the Active Directory database.

Resolution: The domain controller was a Windows 2008 virtual, which had a 20GB C drive assigned to it. This drive was increased to 30GB.

▶ **Alert: The logical drive holding the AD Logfile is low on free space.**

Issue: Low disk space on the drive with the Active Directory logfiles.

Resolution: The domain controller was a Windows 2008 virtual, which had a 20GB C drive assigned to it. This drive was increased to 30GB.

▶ **Alert: The Op Master Domain Naming Master Last Bind latency is above the configured threshold.**

Issue: A large number of alerts are generated at > 5 seconds for warning and > 15 seconds for error.

Resolution: Per http://technet.microsoft.com/en-us/library/cc749936.aspx, the effective thresholds should be changed to warning at > 15 seconds and error at > 30 seconds. Create an override for all types of Active Directory Domain Controller Server 2008 Computer role to change Threshold Error Sec to 30 and Threshold Warning (sec) to 15 and store it in the ActiveDirectory2008_ Overrides management pack.

▶ **Alert: The Op Master Schema Master Last Bind latency is above the configured threshold.**

Issue: A large number of alerts are generated at > 5 seconds for warning and > 15 seconds for error.

Resolution: Per http://technet.microsoft.com/en-us/library/cc749936.aspx, change the effective thresholds to warning at > 15 seconds and error at > 30 seconds. To resolve this alert, create an override for all types of Active Directory Domain Controller Server 2008 Computer role to change Threshold Error Sec to 30 and Threshold Warning (sec) to 15 and store it in the ActiveDirectory2008_Overrides management pack.

▶ **Alert: This domain controller has been promoted to PDC.**

Issue: No issue—this was an informational message. The message was generated when the PDC emulator role was moved between domain controllers.

Resolution: No actions required; this message is provided for situations where the PDC emulator role was moved unexpectedly.

During testing, there was a period of time where network connectivity was lost to a site with one of the domain controllers. The result was a flurry of alerts:

Critical Alerts:

A problem with the inter-domain trusts has been detected.

DNS 2008 Server External Addresses Resolution Alert.

OleDB: Results Error.

Warnings:

A problem has been detected with the trust relationship between two domains.

AD Client-Side Script-Based Test Failed to Complete (multiple).

Could not determine the FSMO role holder (multiple).

DC has failed to synchronize its naming context with replication partners (multiple).

Issue: Loss of network connectivity between one site and another; both had domain controllers.

Resolution: Once network connectivity was re-established, resolved all issues identified above.

Active Directory Management Pack Evolution

Three items would appear to be logical to enhance in future versions of the Active Directory management pack. These items are as follows:

▶ **Alert: A problem with the inter-domain trusts has been detected.**

Does not auto-resolve when the issue is resolved. A warning event ID of 83 from the source of "Health Service Script" creates the critical situation, but no alerts appear that indicate that a successful trust test was accomplished, so this alert always stays in a critical state.

▶ **Alert: AD Op Master is inconsistent.**

This alert is too sensitive. If it recurs two or three times, it is relevant, or it should be tested every 5 minutes instead of every 1 minute.

▶ The Repadmin, Repadmin Replsum, and Repadmin snap-shot should have the correct default path for Windows Server 2008 systems.

The path should be *%windir%*\system32.

Exchange 2007 MP

Version 6.0.62623.0 of the Exchange Server management pack requires Operations Manager 2007 R2 and is specifically for the Exchange 2007 product. This article is available online at http://tinyurl.com/Exchange-ByExample.

How to Install the Exchange 2007 MP

Perform the following steps to install the Exchange 2007 MP:

1. Download the Exchange Server 2007 management pack (URL). The Exchange Server 2007 Management Pack Guide is included in the download and labeled "OM2007_MP_EX2007_R2.doc."

2. Read the Management Pack Guide—it's just over 100 pages, so all the configurations are not discussed here. This is a complicated management pack, and the document spells some important pieces of information you will need to know, including how to enable discovery, as well as optional configurations available for the Exchange 2007 management pack. Marnix Wolf also has a good write-up on this, available at http://thoughtsonopsmgr.blogspot.com/2009/07/quick-guide-to-get-native-exchange-2007.html.

3. Import the Exchange Server 2007 management pack (using either the Operations console or PowerShell). If you have Exchange clusters, add the cluster management pack before adding the Exchange Server 2007 management pack.

4. Deploy the OpsMgr agent to all Exchange Servers. The agent must be deployed to all DCs. Agentless configurations will NOT work for this management pack.

5. Enable Agent Proxy configuration on all Exchange Servers identified from the groups. This is in the Administration node, under Administration -> Device Management -> Agent Managed. Right-click each Exchange 2007 server, select Properties, click the Security tab, and then check the box labeled "Allow this agent to act as a proxy and discover managed objects on other computers." Perform this action for every Exchange 2007 server, even if you add a server after your initial configuration of OpsMgr.

6. Check to make sure Exchange 2007 Service shows up under Monitoring -> Distributed Applications as a distributed application that is in the Healthy, Warning, or Critical state. If it is in the "Not Monitored" state, check for Exchange servers that are not installed or in a "gray" state.

7. Windows PowerShell and the Operations console need to be installed on the RMS. If not already installed, do so at this time.

8. The Exchange 2007 management pack is designed to not automatically discover any Exchange 2007 Server roles, so you can phase in monitoring. See the Management Pack Guide for details on how to enable discoveries.

9. Create an Exchange2007_Overrides management pack to contain any overrides required for the MP.

Exchange MP Tuning/Alerts to Look for

The following alerts were encountered and resolved while tuning the Exchange 2007 management pack (listed alphabetically by alert name):

▶ **Alert: Exchange 2007 ExBPA Generate Alert Rule.**

Issue: Application log size should be increased to 40MB.

Resolution: Logged into each system, opened the event viewer and changed the properties of the application log to 40960, and closed the alerts because they were generated by a rule not a monitor.

Determined the default domain policy was set to 12160. To change this, implemented a new group policy linked to the Exchange servers OU to set the application log file size to 40960. See http://technet.microsoft.com/en-us/library/cc778402(WS.10).aspx for details on how to configure this policy.

▶ **Alert: Exchange 2007 ExBPA Generate Alert Rule.**

Issue: There are multiple different alerts generated based upon the ExBPA. In this case, the issue was that the Exchange fatal information on the server is not set to automatically send to Microsoft for analysis.

Resolution: Because this particular environment does not allow these servers to have Internet connectivity, the rule had to be disabled. To do so, open the Operations console and navigate to Authoring -> Management Pack Objects -> Rules; look for Exchange 2007 Best Practice and sort by the rule name of Crash **u**pload **l**ogging **is** **d**isabled. Overwrote this rule to disable it for all Exchange 2007 servers and then closed the alert.

▶ **Alert: RPC latency is above the threshold.**

Issue: One Exchange server in the environment was reporting this frequently and automatically closing itself as part of the IS RPC Latency Monitor alert monitor. Per product knowledge, these commonly occur due to issues communicating with the Active Directory service or due to disk bottlenecks. This specific server is experiencing high disk queue lengths on the C drive and both storage group drives.

Resolution: This server cannot be upgraded and is scheduled for replacement with new mailbox servers. In the interim, configured an override for this object of class: Exchange IS Service, and set the new threshold to 100 from the default value of 50 to minimize the number of alerts on this issue on this server. The override value will vary depending upon what the actual daily average is for the particular server, which can be determined by right-clicking on the alert, opening the performance view, and seeing the RPC Averaged Latency counter over a period of time.

▶ **Alert: Exchange 2007 Test Local Mail Flow Alert.**

Issue: An Exchange 2007 mailbox server was failing when attempting to perform a local mail flow test. Logged into server and reviewed event logs but found no relevant information. Opened Exchange Management Shell, ran "test-mailflow" command. Received message "No mailbox databases were found on SERVERNAME to perform the operation. Check if the user has permission to read the Exchange configuration from Active Directory." This server does not have any user mailboxes (scheduled for decommissioning).

Resolution: Created an override to disable this alert and reset the health for this through the Exchange 2007 distributed application.

SQL Server MP

The SQL Server management pack is available as a single download that contains different libraries to monitor SQL 2000, 2005, and 2008 database servers. This article is available online at http://tinyurl.com/SQLMP-ByExample.

How to Install the SQL Server MP

Perform the following steps to install the SQL Server MP:

1. Download the SQL Server management pack from the Management Pack Catalog at http://pinpoint.microsoft.com/en-US/systemcenter/managementpackcatalog. The SQL Server Management Pack Guide is included in the download and named "OM2007_MP_SQLSrvr.doc."

2. Read the Management Pack Guide—cover to cover. This document spells out in detail some important pieces of information you will need to know.

3. Import the SQL Server management pack with the Operations console or PowerShell. Also import the appropriate version of the Windows Server management pack (Windows 2000, 2003, or 2008). The Windows Server management packs monitor various aspects of the OS that influence the performance of those computers running SQL Server! This includes disk capacity, disk performance, memory utilization, network adapter utilization, and processor performance.

4. Running the SQL Server Studio and SQL Profiler tasks from the OpsMgr console requires you install the associated software on all OpsMgr computers where these tasks will execute, or you will receive an error message "the system cannot find the file specified." Installing the Management Studio and Profiler are not required unless you want to run those tasks.

5. If your environment includes clustered SQL Servers, enable Agent Proxy configuration on all members of the SQL Server cluster. This is in the Administration node, under Administration -> Device Management -> Agent Managed. Right-click each SQL Server in the cluster, select Properties, click the Security tab, and then check the box labeled Allow this agent to act as a proxy and discover managed objects on other computers.

6. Create a SQLServer_Overrides management pack to contain any overrides required for the MP.

The SQL Server MP supports agentless monitoring with the exception of tasks that start and stop SQL Server services and SQL Server mail. The management pack installs two Run As Profiles:

► SQL Server Discovery account

► SQL Server Monitoring account

By default, the management pack uses the default action account.

SQL MP Optional Configuration

The SQL Server MP does not automatically discover all object types. Go to the Authoring pane of the Operations console to enable discovering additional components. Components not discovered include the following:

► SQL Server 2008 Distributor

► SQL Server 2005 Distributor

► SQL Server 2008 Publisher

► SQL Server 2005 Publisher

► SQL Server 2008 Subscriber

► SQL Server 2005 Subscriber

► SQL Server 2008 Subscription

► SQL Server 2005 Subscription

► SQL Server 2008 Agent Job

► SQL Server 2005 Agent Job

► SQL Server 2000 Agent Job

► SQL Server 2008 DB File Group

► SQL Server 2005 DB File Group

► SQL Server 2008 DB File

► SQL Server 2005 DB File

What this means is you will not receive alerts for these objects failing since they are not even discovered objects! For example, if you have scheduled SQL backups using the SQL Agent and the job fails, OpsMgr won't tell you about it. If an agent job failed in MOM 2005, the SQL MP generated an alert. So, these behaviors are not necessarily the same between MOM 2005 and OpsMgr 2007. You can use overrides to change the settings for automatic discovery to enable these object types. Be sure to change your settings in an unsealed MP other than the Default management pack (preferably the SQLServer_Overrides management pack).

SQL MP Tuning/Alerts to Look for

The following alerts were encountered and resolved while tuning the various SQL Server management packs (listed alphabetically by alert name):

► **Alert: A SQL job failed to complete successfully.**

Issue: A variety of scripts were failing on the system; however, these were on a development server.

Resolution: Created an override to disable this alert on the development server experiencing the issues, as there was no action required to address these on the development environment. Closed the alerts.

► **Alert: A SQL job failed to complete successfully.**

Issue: A variety of scripts were failing on the system, but the scripts were on a server with a database that had been decommissioned.

Resolution: These jobs were not required; accessed the SQL Server and disabled each of the jobs that were failing. Closed the alerts.

► **Alert: A SQL job failed to complete successfully.**

Issue: There are close to 100 of the systems in an environment with only about five servers generating the alerts.

Resolution: Created an override to set these to low-priority informational instead of warnings as no action was taken when they occurred.

► **Alert: Auto Close Flag.**

Issue: The auto close flag for database MSCUPTDB in SQL instance MSSQL SERVER on computer 123.abc.com is not set according to best practice.

Resolution: As this is a standard Microsoft application (patch management for SMS and Configuration Manager) and a default configuration, created an override to exclude this database.

► **Alert: Auto Close Flag.**

Issue: The auto close flag was set on a database used for anti-virus. This was an MSDE database upgraded to a full SQL Server installation. Changed the setting on the database to auto close false. The auto close setting is discussed at http://msdn.microsoft.com/en-us/library/ms190249.aspx. Per this article: "True for all databases when using SQL Server 2000 Desktop Engine or SQL Server Express, and False for all other editions, regardless of operating system."

Resolution: Changed the setting on the database to auto close equals false.

► **Alert: Auto Shrink Flag.**

Issue: The auto shrink flag for database (DBNAME) in SQL instance MSSQL SERVER on computer 123.abc.com is not set according to best practice.

Resolution: This was found on a series of standard Microsoft applications including SUSDB, WSUS, and MSCUPTDB. Additional databases found with the Auto Shrink Flag: Backup Exec, ItAssist, SOE, DSPre, XRXDBDiscovery (Xerox), and XRXDBCWW (Xerox). Options available include contacting the vendor to see if this flag can be changed (and changing the flag if it can) or to create an override to exclude this database from monitoring this configuration.

► **Alert: Cannot start SQL Server Service Broker on Database.**

Issue: This occurred when a large number of management packs and reports were being imported into the management environment. A total of three events were created in the application log (9697), each occurring about 2 minutes after the prior one.

Resolution: Validated it had stopped occurring and tracked back to a period of time when the OpsMgr environment was under significant strain.

► **Alert: Could not allocate space for object in database because the filegroup is full.**

Issue: The database could not extend because the filegroup was full. Logged into server and verified that there was free disk space and the filegroup was set to auto-grow. Attempted to manually extend the database, which failed because it was running in MSDE and restricted in size to 4096 MB. (See http://databases.aspfaq.com/database/what-are-the-limitations-of-msde.html for limits on MSDE.)

Resolution: Moved the database from MSDE to a full version of SQL Server and then expanded the database.

► **Alert: Percentage Change in DB % Used Space.**

Issue: This was on the ReportServerTempDB database.

Resolution: This was on the ReportServerTempDB database, which is very small to begin with (6MB). Major percentage changes occur as part of this being a temp table. Threshold ranges are between 25% and 45% (low value of threshold = 25, high value of threshold = 45). Created an override for this specific database due to its size (6MB in size). Threshold1 = 45 (this is the growth size, increased from 25). Threshold2 = 55 (this is the shrink size; left it this way). Increased due to the size of this database as the percentage figures become out of whack with a database of this size.

► **Alert: Service Check Data Source Module Failed Execution.**

Issue: Error getting state of service, error 0x8007007b. Documented in the SQL Management Pack Guide:

"If the SQL Full Text Search service is not installed on computers running SQL Server 2005 that are being monitored, disable the monitor."

Resolution:

For two systems that were running MSDE, configured an override to disable the alert.

For another system, the service had been set to manual. Configured the service to run automatically and started the service.

For another system, the primary instance had this service but the additional instance installed on it did not. Configured an override to disable the alert.

Finally, one system had the service running for a second instance but not for the first instance. Configured an override to disable the alert.

▶ **Alert: Service Check Probe Module Failed Execution.**

Issue: Error getting state of service; error 0x8007007b for workflow name Microsoft.SQLServer.2008.DBEngine.FullTextServiceMonitor. Documented in the SQL Management Pack Guide:

"If the SQL Full Text Search service is not installed on computers running SQL Server 2005 that are being monitored, disable the monitor."

Resolution:

For two systems that were running MSDE, configured an override to disable the alert.

For another system, the service had been set to manual. Configured the service to run automatically and started the service.

For another system, the primary instance had this service but the additional instance installed on it did not. Configured an override to disable the alert.

Finally one system had the service running for a second instance but not for the first instance. Configured an override to disable the alert.

▶ **Alert: Service Pack Compliance—MSSQLSERVER (SQL 2005 DB Engine) Warning.**

Issue: The database server was running SQL 2005 Service Pack (SP) 2, which is acceptable for the ACS database server. (SQL 2005 SP 2 has been approved for all OpsMgr database components per threads on the newsgroups.)

Resolution: Created override (for specific object of type SQL Engine DB) to allow this configuration for this server/set the enabled parameter to False for this server. Reset the health for this health monitor on this server, refreshed, and the state updated to green from yellow.

▶ **Alert: Service Pack Compliance.**

Issue: This particular SQL server was SQL Server 2005 with SP 2. OpsMgr identified this as non-compliant because the rule was checking for SP 1. Verified version of SQL through the query: SELECT @@Version, which returned the following:

```
Microsoft SQL Server 2005 - 9.00.1399.06 (Intel X86)
Oct 14 2005 00:33:37
Copyright (c) 1988-2005 Microsoft Corporation
Standard Edition on Windows NT 5.2 (Build 3790: Service Pack 2)
```

This issue occurred using version 6.0.6278.8 of the SQL management pack. There was a new version of the management pack available (6.0.6460.0). Downloaded and installed new version of the management pack, and closed alert. This did not resolve the issue.

Created an override to set the "Good Value" from 1 to 2 in the Service Pack Compliance monitor and stored it in the MicrosoftSQLServer_Overrides management pack created for the SQL MP. Closed alert, but this did not resolve the issue because the MP was actually identifying the error condition, but the OpsMgr administrator was incorrectly interpreting it.

http://support.microsoft.com/kb/321185 provides clarification as to what was seen here. The SQL install itself was RTM without SP 1 installed.

Resolution: Installed SQL 2005 SP 2 and closed the alert.

▶ **Alert: The SQL Server Service Broker or Database Mirroring transport is disabled or not configured.**

Issue: On the alert context, you will see that the description for eventid 9666 says, "The Database Mirroring protocol transport is disabled or not configured." What is interesting is that the same event ID (9666) means two different things: The Service Broker protocol transport is disabled or not configured, or The Database Mirroring protocol transport is disabled or not configured. The only way to tell which situation is occurring is on the alert context tab for the alert.

Resolution: The database mirroring protocol error reported is only relevant if database mirroring will be used on the server. If mirroring is not going to be used, the alert should be disabled. To do so, create an override to disable the alert for the specific server reporting the alert (assuming that it doesn't require database mirroring) and store it in a custom management pack (MicrosoftSQLServer_Overrides). Manually closed the alert.

SQL Server Management Pack Evolution

Microsoft wrote the SQL Server 2008 management pack to have functional parity with the SQL Server 2005 management pack. Other than SQL Job monitoring, the MP focuses primarily on the condition of SQL Server and its services, rather than what is built on top of those installed objects and how they are configured and running.

It would be nice if future versions could incorporate monitoring SQL Server 2008 policy management and the database tuning advisor. SQL 2008 also incorporates a resource governor, which puts constraint on the various SQL components. An updated management pack should be aware of the constraints the governor puts on the components such that thresholds become relative to what has been set, rather than what the overall system is otherwise capable of doing.

SQL Server 2008's Performance Studio and Performance Data Collection components have functionality at a depth beyond the current SQL MP. Incorporating this requires a transition from the high-level monitoring provided by the MP to the lower-level tracing and reporting provided by SQL Server itself. Optimally, a new SQL MP would defer to the performance data collector, with tasks, diagnostics, and such to make that happen. There also would probably need to be some discovery and diagramming work added to the MP to show relationships between those components running collections and the warehouse where the results are stored.

Windows Server MP

The Windows Server management pack is available as a single download that contains different libraries to monitor Windows Server 2000, 2003, and 2008. This article is available online at http://tinyurl.com/WindowsServerMP-ByExample.

How to Install the Windows Server MP

Perform the followings steps to install the management pack:

1. Download the Windows Server Operating System management pack from the Management Pack Catalog. The Windows Server Operating System MP Guide is included in the download as "OM2007_MP_WinSerBas.doc."

2. Read the Management Pack Guide—for things such as how to activate monitoring for physical disks and disk partitions.

3. Import the Windows Server Operating System management pack (using either the Operations console or PowerShell).

4. Create a WindowsServer_Overrides management pack to contain any overrides required for the MP.

Windows Server MP Tuning/Alerts to Look for

The following alerts were encountered and resolved while tuning the various Windows Server management packs (listed alphabetically by alert name):

▶ **Alert: Disk transfer (reads and writes) latency is too high.**

Issue: This monitor checks for high values on the performance counter every 60 seconds over a 5-minute timeframe.

Resolution: Determined spikes were occurring on a specific drive on the system. The drive needs to be either replaced with a higher-speed drive, or some uses of this drive should be moved to another physical drive.

▶ **Alert: Event log is full.**

Issue: Alert generated by the Windows Server 2003 management pack from the Event Log File is Full alert rule. The alert description contains information about which event log is full. (In this case, it was the PowerShell log file.)

Resolution: Logged into server and verified that log size was set to a maximum of 512KB and to override events older than 7 days. Re-configured to increase the size to 2048KB and to overwrite events as needed. Closed alert.

▶ **Alert: Logical Disk Free Space is Low.**

Issue: Low disk space on the drive identified in the alert.

Resolution: Can either free up disk space on drive or configure an override to change the monitoring configurations for the drive. You can configure overrides for the system drives or non-system drives. In this case, there is a C drive, D drive, and Q drive. The Q drive was critical, and free space could not be made available on the drive. The only options available without modifying the script (not viable in sealed management packs) are to set an override for non-system drives and set it to a level where the Q drive is no longer critical. This means that the levels for the D drive on that system will not fire until it hits the new critical levels. The other option is to acknowledge the alert and not resolve it for now. The script performing this check is called FreeSpace.vbs and automatically distributed into a temporary directory located under %*ProgramFiles*%\System Center Operations Manager 2007\Health Service State.

▶ **Alert: Network Interface failed.**

Issue: Network interface on a system was no longer online.

Resolution: The system in question had been accidentally unplugged from the network. Closed alert after the network interface was online. `

▶ **Alert: The device has a bad block.**

Issue: Bad block on the drive on the system.

Resolution: Ran chkdsk /F to scan for bad blocks that required a reboot due to the bad block being identified on the boot partition.

▶ **Alert: The event log file is full. New event instances will be discarded.**

Issue: The event log was set to override events older than 7 days.

Resolution: Increased event log size from 512KB to 2048KB, and set to overwrite events as needed.

▶ **Alert: The service terminated unexpectedly.**

Issue: The service identified in the alert failed.

Resolution: Verified server can be pinged using the tasks on the right side of the console, and using Computer Management task, verified that service was in a started state. Closed alert after placing information in company knowledge to track this for a pattern to see what is causing the service to fail. In one case, the service was actually down; used the Computer Management task to restart the service.

▶ **Alert: The share configuration was invalid. The share is unavailable.**

Issue: The share within the alert was a user share on a system.

Resolution: Determined that user still existed in Active Directory (AD Users and computers; validated that user name was the same). Recreated user folder per product knowledge. If user no longer existed, would have removed the share using the net share /delete option presented in the product knowledge.

▶ **Alert: Too many requests for performance counter data have timed out.**

Issue: In this environment, only seems to occur with Windows 2000 systems running Diskeeper. Diskeeper started just after 9 PM; then there is an alert just after 10:15 PM (perflib event ID 1015 in application log for PerfDisk performance data counter), and Diskeeper completes running just after event is logged.

Resolution: Disabled alert for the specific servers that are Windows 2000 running Diskeeper. Stored override in MicrosoftWindowsServer_Overrides management pack kept for overrides on the various Operating System-related management packs. If there were a large enough number of systems, would recommend instead upgrading the version of Diskeeper (or operating systems).

▶ **Alert: Total CPU Utilization Percentage is too high.**

Issue: Most likely, the processor on the system is over-utilized and indicating a bottleneck condition. Common potential causes for this include the following:

> ▶ Misconfigured anti-virus can cause high processor utilization if files that should be excluded from scanning are not (such as Exchange databases, logs, and the \bin folder).

> ▶ Hardware failure is another possibility to consider and research through the hardware vendor.

> ▶ A hung process may be consuming resources to the exclusion of all others.

> ▶ A large portion of time, the system actually is bottlenecked. This can be verified by checking the processor performance counters gathered by OpsMgr to determine if there is a consistent bottleneck. You can also check this by logging on the system and using task manager to determine what is using CPU cycles. Most likely, it is a process running on the system that is using too much processing.

A great Microsoft discussion on processor bottlenecks is available at http://technet.microsoft.com/en-us/library/aa995907.aspx.

Resolution: Add more processing resources (faster processors, additional processors), replace the system with stronger processor(s), split load through network load balancing, or move off programs/services creating load on the system. Until you can address the processing bottleneck, determine from trending the performance counters what an acceptable level is for this particular system, then set an override so that alerts will be generated only if the system goes beyond the identified levels.

▶ **Alert: Total Percentage Interrupt Time is too high.**

Issue: Most likely, the processor on the system is currently over-utilized and indicating a bottleneck condition. Common potential causes for this include the following:

> ▶ Misconfigured anti-virus can cause high processor utilization if files that should be excluded from scanning are not (such as for Exchange databases, logs, and the \bin folder).

> ▶ Hardware failure is another possibility to consider and research through the hardware vendor.

> ▶ A hung process may be consuming resources to the exclusion of all others.

> ▶ Often the system actually is bottlenecked. You can verify this by checking the processor performance counters gathered by OpsMgr to

determine if there is a consistent bottleneck. You can also check this by logging on the system and using the Task Manager to determine what is using CPU cycles. Most likely, it is a process running on the system that is using too much processing.

See http://technet.microsoft.com/en-us/library/aa995907.aspx for a discussion on processor bottlenecks.

Resolution: Add more processing resources (faster processors, additional processors), replace the system with stronger processor(s), split the load through network load balancing, or move off programs/services creating load to the system. Until you can address the processing bottleneck, determine from the trending of the performance counters what an acceptable level is for this particular system and set an override so that alerts will be generated only if the system goes beyond the levels identified.

▶ **Alert: Windows Event 2008—Unable to read an event log.**

Issue: The application log file had corrupted in one instance and the server application log in another instance.

Resolution: Verified the server was not in some way restricting access to the log file. Used Computer Management task to fix the corrupt event log by right-clicking on the event log and choosing option to Clear all Events, and then re-opening the event log that had been corrupt. Additional details may be required to resolve this, as there are some situations where the event log will clear but will not allow new events to be written into the event log after it is cleared. If this situation occurs, information on how to address the situation is available at http://forums.techarena.in/windows-server-help/1100969.htm.

Windows Server Management Pack Evolution

Overall, the Windows Server management pack provides a very strong set of functionality for Windows operating systems. Of use would be creating additional diagnostics and recoveries such as one to run the disk cleanup utility on low disk space situations, and one to report where drive space is used on a disk running low on disk space.

Operations Manager MP

The Operations Manager R2 management pack is automatically installed when you install System Center Operations Manager. This article is available online at http://tinyurl.com/OperationsManagerMP-ByExample.

How to Install the Operations Manager MP

Perform the following steps to install the Operations Manager MP:

1. Download the Operations Manager Management Pack Guide from the OpsMgr R2 Product Documentation site at http://technet.microsoft.com/en-

us/opsmgr/bb498235.aspx; named "Operations Manager 2007 R2 Management Pack Guide.doc."

2.   Read the Management Pack Guide as this covers items such as how to enable recovery for Health Service Heartbeats and creating Run As Accounts.

3.   Create an OperationsManager_Overrides management pack to contain any overrides required for the MP.

Operations Manager MP Tuning/Alerts to Look for

The following alerts were encountered and resolved while tuning the Operations Manager management pack (listed in alphabetical order by alert name):

▶   **Alert**: **AD Agent Assignment: Admins User Role needs at least one domain account.**

   Issue: AD-integrated agent deployment was not functional. The OpsMgr service was installed and running on the agent but would not show up in the pending management folder.

   Resolution: Per product knowledge, "Add the security group, which was provided as parameter to MOMADAdmin.exe to the Operations Manager Administrators User Role." In the OpsMgr console -> Administration -> Security -> User Roles -> Operations Manager Administrators, added the group specified when using the MomADAdmin.exe program to configure AD integration. Closed alert; re-started services on the server where AD agent assignment was failing (no change).

   Restarted the three services (in SP 1, these were OpsMgr Config Service, OpsMgr Health service, and OpsMgr SDK Service; in R2, they are System Center Data Access, System Center Management, and System Center Management Configuration) and agent appeared in the OpsMgr console -> Administration -> Device Management -> Pending Management as expected.

▶   **Alert: Agent proxying needs to be enabled for a health service to submit discovery data about other computers.**

   Issue: Agent specified in alert description does not have agent proxy enabled.

   Resolution: Found name of the system within the alert description field (dc.abcco.com), copied server name and opened the Administration node -> Device Management -> Agent Managed, and filtered on the name of the server (pasted in). Right-click the server; go to Properties -> Security tab. Check the Allow this agent to act as a proxy and discover managed objects on other computers checkbox. This is an alert rule, so will not auto-close; manually closed the alert on the monitoring section of the OpsMgr console.

▶   **Alert: Backward Compatibility Script Error.**

   Issue: MOM Backward Compatibility Service State Monitoring Script line 71.

Resolution: This is a bug in Windows Management Instrumentation (WMI). The Black-Berry MDS Connection Service has a very long ImagePath registry entry. When the health service script runs Select DisplayName, State, Name, StartMode, StartName FROM Win32_Service, a null is returned for StartName because the buffer allocated for the results is too small and the call fails; this can be verified using wbemtest. Connect to the root\cimv2 namespace and run the following query:

Select DisplayName, State, Name, StartMode, StartName FROM Win32_Service

In the results, scroll down to BlackBerry MDS Connection Service and double-click on the row to view the details; you will see in Properties that the StartName is null.

The problem is described at http://groups.google.co.uk/group/microsoft.public.win32.programmer.wmi/browse_thread/thread/4cef045b79c1b5cb/1ee2b09a1fa130ab?lnk=st&q=win32_service.startname+is+null&rnum=1&hl=en#1ee2b09a1fa130ab. Tried to obtain the fix mentioned, but Microsoft Support said that the bug ID did not exist.

The workaround is to change the path so it uses the short (8.3) folder names, as follows:

Original Key:

"C:\Program Files\Research In Motion\BlackBerry Enterprise Server\MDS\bin\bmds.exe" -s jvmpath="C:\Program Files\Java\jre1.5.0_11\bin\client\jvm.dll" -XX:+DisableExplicitGC -Xss64K -Xmx768M -Xms128M classpathdir="C:\Program Files\Research In Motion\BlackBerry Enterprise Server\MDS\classpath" wrkdir="C:\Program Files\Research In Motion\BlackBerry Enterprise Server\MDS\Servers\BES1" webserverdir="C:\Program Files\Research In Motion\BlackBerry Enterprise Server\MDS\webserver" -rbes "BES1_MDS-CS_1"

New Key:

"C:\PROGRA~1\RESEAR~1\BLACKB~1\MDS\bin\bmds.exe" -s jvmpath="C:\Program Files\Java\jre1.5.0_11\bin\client\jvm.dll" -XX:+DisableExplicitGC -Xss64K -Xmx768M -Xms128M classpathdir="C:\PROGRA~1\RESEAR~1\BLACKB~1\MDS\CLASSP~1" wrkdir="C:\PROGRA~1\RESEAR~1\BLACKB~1\MDS\Servers\BES1" webserverdir="C:\PROGRA~1\RESEAR~1\BLACKB~1\MDS\WEBSER~1" -rbes "BES1_MDS-CS_1"

Restart the service and rerun the query in WBEMTest; with the shorter path, the server now returns the correct username.

It would be preferable if the problem was fixed properly, but the workaround does not seem to cause any adverse effects.

UPDATE: This was found this on another system with a different type of service. The start name was null, and the service would not start when tried to start it. Used sc delete to remove service and rebooted the system, and it worked like a champ.

► **Alert: Check the application's security policy.**

Issue: Two management servers were added into an environment configured with AD integration. This alert occurred on both systems when RMS's OpsMgr Health Service was restarted.

Resolution: Gave the same access rights to the new management servers as was given to the RMS by adding the computer accounts to the MOMAD-SecurityGroup created as part of the process to configure AD integration in OpsMgr. After doing this, verified by checking in Active Directory Users and Computers (View -> Advanced Features) and validating in the Operations-Manager container under the name of the management group that the additional management servers had records defined.

▶ **Alert: Connection Timeout.**

Issue: On a TCP Port monitor, two alerts are generated when the system cannot be communicated with. The first is a Connection Timeout, and the second is a *<servername>* Group Roll-Up Monitor. The server in question was being monitored via a TCP Port monitor to provide up/down through monitoring the RDP port (3389).

Resolution: The system in question was offline and needed to be brought back online, so the monitor functioned as expected.

▶ **Alert: Failed Agent Push/Repair—Remote Agent Management operation failed.**

Issue: Failed attempting to push the agent to the system.

Resolution: Logged into the system and manually installed the agent.

▶ **Alert: Data Warehouse configuration synchronization process failed to write data.**

Issue: After importing a large number of management pack files, the data warehouse began reporting issues. The Health Explorer listed event number 31552 that the data filed to store in the data warehouse due to a SQLException Timeout expired.

Resolution: On the data warehouse server, used sp_updatestats to update the OperationsManagerDW database per notes in the newsgroups from Vitaly Filimonov. The alerts automatically closed after this action was performed.

▶ **Alert: Data Warehouse failed to deploy reports for a management pack to SQL Reporting Services Server.**

Issue: The DNS management pack can cause issues resulting in event ID 26319 from the OpsMgr SDK service. (The R2 service name is System Center Data Access.)

Resolution: Add the account designated as the Data Reader account to the group designated as Operations Manager Administrators during setup. (This group is added to the Operations Manager Administrators role.) This issue only exists with the DNS management pack (version 6.0.5000.0) and no other management packs.

▶ **Alert: Data Warehouse failed to request a list of management packs from SQL RS server.**

Issue: The data warehouse reporting server was being rebooted.

Resolution: Once the reporting server was back online, the alert auto-resolved.

▶ **Alert: Data Warehouse managed object type synchronization process failed to write data.**

Issue: After importing a large number of management pack files, the data warehouse began reporting issues. The Health Explorer listed event number 31554 on the workflow Microsoft.SystemCenter.DataWarehouse. Synchronization.TypedManagedEntity.

Resolution: On data warehouse server, used sp_updatestats to update the OperationsManagerDW database per notes in the newsgroups from Vitaly Filimonov. The alerts automatically closed after this action was performed.

▶ **Alert: Failed to Check for Password Expiration on Run As Account.**

Issue: Operations Manager is unable to monitor Run As Accounts for account and password expiration for the server specified.

Resolution: There was an error on the account (Administration -> Security -> Run As Profiles). In this case, the domain name had a typo on it.

▶ **Alert: Failed to send notification using server/device.**

Issue: Issues providing notification via instant messaging.

Resolution: The Instant Messaging (IM) configuration defaulted to port 5060, but the IM server was configured to use port 5061. Tested connectivity from OpsMgr server to LCS server with telnet <*servername*> and it answered on the telnet. Configured Run As Account for Notification account for OpsMgr server using the same account specified in the Notification settings. Tried logging on LCS using the account configured as the instant messaging and sent a test IM message.

▶ **Alert: Failed to send notification.**

Issue: Notification in OpsMgr was configured for a single SMTP server. When this server was offline, these alerts occurred (logically).

Resolution: Defined additional SMTP servers to provide failover in case of loss of primary SMTP server system. Used Alert Forwarding MP to validate connectivity to each SMTP server (discussed at http://cameronfuller.spaces.live.com/blog/cns!A231E4EB0417CB76!1737.entry).

▶ **Alert: Failed to send notification using server/device.**

Issue: Email was being sent to a remote email environment and communication was lost between the environments.

Resolution: When communication between the environments was restored, notification began to function again. Closed alert, which did not recur after communication was re-established.

▶ **Alert: Failed to send notification using server/device.**

Issue: Notification in OpsMgr was configured for a single SMTP server. When this server was offline, these alerts occurred (logically).

Resolution: Defined additional SMTP servers to provide failover in case of loss of primary SMTP server system. Used the Alert Forwarding MP to validate connectivity to each SMTP server (discussed at http://cameronfuller.spaces.live.com/blog/cns!A231E4EB0417CB76!1737.entry).

▶ **Alert: Failed to send notification using server/device.**

Issue: Blocked on Exchange 2007; see http://msexchangeteam.com/archive/2006/12/28/432013.aspx. The box that was being pointed to did not respond on port 25 because the system was a mailbox server, not a client access server. Notification failed later due to security issues from an anonymous connection (the default configuration).

Resolution: Re-configured OpsMgr to use the client access server that did respond on port 25. Configured notification to use Windows Integrated authentication. Configured a Run As Account and configured Run As Profile for the Notification account for the management server to use the account that was created.

▶ **Alert: Failed to send notification using server/device.**

Issue: RMS lost communication with the various SMTP servers defined. Once the network communication was back online, could send notifications.

Resolution: Lowered priority of this alert to warning, as the alert "Failed to send notification" occurs when not all SMTP servers can be communicated with.

▶ **Alert: Health service heartbeat failure.**

Issue: The OpsMgr health service on the agent was stopped. Another potential cause is if the OpsMgr health service on the agent was running but unable to communicate with the OpsMgr management server.

Resolution: Restarted OpsMgr agent with Computer Management through the Actions pane. For the unable to communicate issue, the server was running a security application that restricted network traffic and blocked the network traffic from the server to the OpsMgr management server via port 5723.

▶ **Alert: OleDB: Results Error.**

Issue: Network communication between the RMS and the Operations Manager database was interrupted. The alert rule that generates this critical alert is the OleDbProbe: Results error.

A good discussion on these types of alerts is available at http://blogs.technet.com/jonathanalmquist/archive/2008/07/29/oledb-results-error.aspx.

Resolution: In this case, once network connectivity was re-established between RMS and OpsMgr database, the alert was no longer relevant and was manually closed. Created an override to disable this alert for the RMS that was reporting these occasionally per the link listed in the issue section of this alert.

▶ **Alert: Ops DB Free Space Low.**

Issue: The Operations database for OpsMgr 2007 has less than 40% free space available.

Resolution: The OperationsManager database was not large enough to provide 7-day (default) retention for the number of agents monitored. Increased size of database using SQL Server Management Studio. (Install it on the system running the OpsMgr console for ease of use.) Connect to the server running the OpsMgr Operational database (shown in the alert), open the server/databases, right-click on OperationsManager database (default name), and click Properties. Click on the Files tab, change the MOM_DATA size to the new size, and click OK. You can validate the change in size occurred by going back to the properties of the database. The alert will resolve itself in Operations Manager in approximately 15 minutes if enough free space is available, as this monitor is defined to a 900-second frequency.

▶ **Alert: Recipient address is not valid.**

Issue: Recipient address is not valid for notification. Email was sent to remote email environment and communication was lost between the environments.

Resolution: When communication between the environments was restored, notification began functioning again. Closed the alert, as it did not recur once communication was re-established.

▶ **Alert: Root Management Server Unavailable.**

Issue: Alert occurring, but OpsMgr Health Service was running on the RMS server. The alert description said "The root management server (Health Service) is running but has reported limited functionality soon after (date/time)." The specific reason code is 49 and description is "The health manager has detected that entity state collection has stalled." This happened immediately after installing the reporting server into the OpsMgr environment.

Resolution: Restarted OpsMgr Health Service on RMS and the alert closed.

▶ **Alert: Root Management Server Unavailable.**

Issue: The following alert randomly recurs on an RMS with no related alerts and with no apparent cause:

The root management server (Health Service) has stopped heartbeating soon after (date and time). This adversely affects all availability calculation for the entire management group.

Resolution: If the alert truly had no discernable root causes, the Root Health Service Watcher should be tweaked to allow for a greater variance in the heart-beating interval by adding a DWORD value named Minutes-ToWaitBeforeAlerting to the following registry key and setting it to 5:

HKEY_LOCAL_MACHINE\Software\Microsoft\Microsoft Operations Manager\3.0\SDK Service\RHS Watcher

Restart the Health, SDK, and Config services on RMS after this change.

Submitted By: Jason Sandys

▶ **Alert: Root Management Server Unavailable.**

Issue: Saw issues with most of the distributed applications changing to a grey state seemingly for no reason. After a little digging, it was determined that the RMS server itself was actually in a grey state. To resolve, tried things that have worked in the past like reviewing the Operations Manager logs on the RMS, restarting services on the RMS, rebooting the RMS, and even went so far as rebooting pretty much all OpsMgr related servers just to be thorough. Still grey. Verified that database connectivity was functional, there was plenty of free space in the Operations Manager database, yet found no indications of the root cause. Just grey, grey, and more grey.

Resolution: This may not be supported, but at least it enabled bringing back up the Operations Manager environment. Stopped each of the three services on the RMS, renamed *%programfiles%*\system center operations manager 2007\health service state\health service store\ to another file name, and then restarted the services. This re-created the health service store folder and rebuilt the files within it. This situation has been seen in this environment twice in less than a year.

► **Alert: Run As Logon Type Check Failed.**

Issue: The Run As Account failed to log on interactively. The Run As Account needs to have the logon interactively right.

Resolution: Gave logon on interactively rights to the user created for Run As Account—in this case, through providing administrator access to the system in question.

► **Alert: Run As Successful Logon Check Failed.**

Issue: Domain controllers for the domain where the SQL Reporting Services server existed were offline.

Resolution: Brought back online the domain controllers for the domain and the alert auto-resolved itself.

► **Alert: Run As Successful Logon Check Failed.**

Issue: One or more Run As Accounts failed to log on. The account may be disabled or has an expired password.

Resolution: Gave logon on interactively rights to user created for the Run As Account—in this case, by providing administrator access to the system in question.

► **Alert: Script or Executable Failed to run.**

Issue: Scripts not running on agentless managed system that is a NAS, not an actual server. This occurs on both CPU utilization and memory utilization.

Resolution: The only option on this if the NAS was going to be monitored agentless was to disable the alert for the RMS.

► **Alert: Script or Executable Failed to run.**

Issue: Lots of "script or executable failed to run" errors on the same system all failing at the same time—in this case, about a half-dozen or more would all fail with a 21402 (timeout).

Resolution: WMI was non-functional on the system (stuck at 100% utilization for one processor). Stopped WMI service; when that failed, killed the process and re-started the WMI service.

► **Alert: Script or Executable Failed to run.**

Issue: Script failure for Nslookuptest.js. Reporting for tests to Microsoft.com, localhost IP address, and the fully qualified name of the server all failed at the same date and time.

Resolution: Noted the alert and the date/time to see if a root cause could be tracked back. Reviewed event logs on the system to track back potential issues, but none found. Reviewed performance counters gathered by OpsMgr, but no bottlenecks identified during that timeframe. Closed alerts.

▶ **Alert: Script or Executable Failed to run.**

Issue: The process exited with 0 Command executed: C:\Windows\system32\cscript.exe /nologo IsHostingMSCS.vbs.

Resolution: Occurred immediately after deploying agent to a new server. From the newsgroups, this can occur when discovery has not yet finished (written by Rob Kuehfus). Closed alert to see if it would recur on this system.

▶ **Alert: Script or Executable failed to start.**

Issue: Paging file is too small.

Resolution: Needed to add memory to the system.

DNS MP

The Windows DNS Server management pack is available as a single download containing different libraries to monitor Windows DNS on Windows 2000, 2003, and 2008 systems. This article is available online at http://tinyurl.com/DNSMP-ByExample.

How to Install the DNS MP

Perform the following steps to install the DNS MP:

1. Download the Windows Server DNS management pack from the Management Pack Catalog. The Windows Server DNS Management Pack Guide is included in the download and labeled "OM2007_MP_DNS2008_2003.doc."

2. Read the Management Pack Guide for topics such as configuring the URL for external DNS monitoring, configuring the global zone resolution monitor, and configuring the forwarder availability monitor.

3. Import the Windows Server DNS management pack (using either the Operations console or PowerShell).

4. Enable Agent Proxy configuration on all domain controllers identified from the groups. This is in the Administration node, under Administration -> Device Management -> Agent Managed. Right-click each domain controller, select Properties, click the Security tab, and then check the box labeled "Allow this agent to act as a proxy and discover managed objects on other computers." Perform this action for every DNS server, even if is added after initially configuring OpsMgr.

5. Create a DNSServer_Overrides management pack to contain any overrides required for the MP.

Agentless monitoring is not supported by the Windows Server DNS management pack.

DNS MP Tuning/Alerts to Look for

The following alerts were encountered and resolved while tuning the Windows Server DNS management pack (listed in alphabetical order by alert name):

▶ **Alert: Core Service File Writing.**

Issue: Alert created when adding a new reverse zone.

Resolution: This error will occur once after adding new reverse zone. Logged into the servers reporting the error and verified that the new zone was created and populated correctly. It can be closed out, and is not an issue unless it recurs.

▶ **Alert: Core Service Zone Transfer Error.**

Issue: Alert created when adding a new reverse zone.

Resolution: This error will occur once after adding the new reverse. Logged into the servers reporting the error and verified that the new zone was created and populated correctly. It can be closed out, and is not an issue unless it recurs.

▶ **Alert: DNS 2003 AD DS Load Alert.**

Issue: Error caused by converting a zone from secondary to an AD-integrated zone. This occurred only once on the server as the conversion occurred.

Resolution: Closed the alert.

▶ **Alert: DNS 2003 Configure Authoritative Servers Alert.**

Issue: A secondary zone defined on a server had two different systems from which it was configured to request zone transfers. One of these two systems did not allow zone transfers and was failing and causing this error.

Resolution: Allow zone transfers on the primary DNS server that was not configured to allow zone transfers.

▶ **Alert: DNS 2003 Configure Authoritative Servers Alert.**

Issue: Alert generated by a system with a secondary copy of the DNS zone. DNS had just been restarted on the server indicated in the alert as having refused the zone transfer.

Resolution: Closed the alert, as this is an expected condition when the DNS zone is down on the server configured to allow zone replication.

▶ **Alert: An exception was thrown while processing GetRelationshipTypes-ByCriteria for session ID.**

Issue: Check if you have installed DNS MP in RTM version.

Resolution: Upgrade to DNS MP for 2000/2003/2008 (6.0.6278.27).

Submitted By: ziembor

▶ **Alert: DNS 2003 Correct Master Server Problem Alert.**

Issue: An event of 6527 occurred in DNS event log, indicating that the zone had expired before it could obtain a successful zone transfer or update, and the zone was shut down.

Resolution: Logged into server and reviewed event logs, found an event number 3150 that the same zone had since had a new version of it written. Used nslookup to verify that the server was able to provide resolution for the zone that was listed as shut down. Closed alert because the monitor did not have an event defined to move it to a healthy state.

▶ **Alert: DNS 2003 delete zone copy alert.**

Issue: abc.xyz.com zone was previously loaded from a directory partition MicrosoftDNS, but another copy was found in the DomainDnsZones. The server will ignore the new copy of the zone. In this case, there was an inconsistency for this zone on the General tab for the DNS zone. Some were configured with the second option (To all DNS servers in the Active Directory domain abc.com), and some were configured for the third option (To all domain controllers in the Active Directory domain abc.com). These are caused by DNS events of 4515 in the DNS event log. Details on this issue are available at http://support.microsoft.com/kb/867464.

Resolution: Convert current Active Directory-integrated zone to a standard primary zone and back up the file. Delete the AD-integrated zone and allow the deletion to replicate. After change has replicated, convert the standard primary zone into an Active Directory-integrated zone.

Another option is using ADSIEdit to remove the partition stored in the MicrosoftDNS section.

Performed the first option above and then closed the alerts; restarted DNS services on the server that was reporting the warnings to verify they did not reappear.

▶ **Alert: DNS 2003 Resolution Time Alert.**

Issue: Large numbers of alerts are generated that indicate issues with performing a test of a query to the 127.0.0.1 system. Based on seeing the performance counters on these items (highlight the alert, right-click and choose Performance View, and select the DNS Server object -> Counter Response Time), these are alerting at values over 5 (which were overridden from the default value of 1) very frequently, which is the default threshold in this version of the management pack (6.0.6480.0). The implication is this value is 5 seconds, but during testing have not seen a single nslookup query that took more than a second. From the All DNS Performance View (Monitoring -> Microsoft Windows DNS Server -> Performance -> All DNS Performance Data), it is apparent that for this environment, 90% of the resolutions occur in less than a value of 20.

Resolution: Changed alert threshold to 20 seconds. See Kevin Holman's blog for additional details at http://blogs.technet.com/kevinholman/archive/2009/02/24/dns-mp-noisy-resolution-time-alerts-and-how-to-deal-with-them.aspx

▶ **Alert: DNS 2003 Server External Addresses Resolution Alert.**

Issue: The rule performs a DNS query of type "NS" (as provided in the Query Type parameter), which means the query is to search for the name servers of the domain provided in the Host parameter. The problem here is that the domain name provided is "www.microsoft.com." Because this is a host name rather than a domain, the query returns a referral rather than a list of DNS servers, resulting in the alert referenced previously.

Resolution: You can fix the error in one of two ways (pick one—not both):

▶ Set Host parameter to "microsoft.com" (without the quotes). Then the query returns a list of DNS servers for the microsoft.com domain.

OR

▶ Set the Query Type parameter to "A" and then the query returns the IP address(es) for www.microsoft.com.

▶ **Alert: DNS 2008 Correct the Configuration File Alert.**

Issue: Removal of the cache.dns file was taking place as part of the process to remove the root hints for this server.

Resolution: Closed alerts, since this was an expected situation as part of the process to remove the root hints for the DNS server.

▶ **Alert: DNS 2008 Correct Master Server Problem Alert.**

Issue: The alert context screen provided additional information in the description field that specified that the zone (zonename) expired before it could obtain a successful zone transfer or update from a master server acting as its source for the zone. The zone has been shut down. This came from an event ID of 6527. This occurred on an Active Directory-integrated stub zone.

Resolution: Logged into the server reporting the problem and verified that the zone did exist and was populated with what appears to be valid information. This was caused by removal of a DNS zone from the master server that was defined for the zone. While investigating this, found there was a single master server defined for the zone. Added a second master server to provide additional redundancy to avoid issues with communicating with a single master server.

▶ **Alert: DNS 2008 Forwarder Availability Alert.**

Issue: DNS forwarders for the systems existed in another physical location, and network connectivity was lost between the locations. This is identified by the DNS 2008 forwarder availability monitor, which executes every 900 seconds (15 minutes).

Resolution: Specified a DNS forwarder in the same site as the system reporting the forwarder availability alert. Another time this occurred; saw the alert and re-tested the forwarder configuration, but it was no longer erroring out. After 15 minutes, OpsMgr automatically closed the alert.

▶ **Alert: DNS 2008 Forwarder Availability Alert.**

Issue: The DNS server was configured to conditionally forward resolutions to other DNS servers in other forests. However, the remote server was unable to be connected to via UDP port 53, so this alert was occurring.

Resolution: Worked with the firewall team to open UDP port 53 from the DNS server to the DNS server receiving the forward zone lookups.

▶ **Alert: DNS 2008 Monitor Zone Resolution Alert.**

Issue: The specific reverse lookup zone creating the alert had been deleted.

Resolution: Manually closed the alerts.

▶ **Alert: DNS 2008 free memory or other system resources alert.**

Issue: Removal of the cache.dns file taking place as part of the process to remove the root hints for this server.

Resolution: Closed the alerts, as this was an expected situation as part of the process to remove the root hints for the DNS server.

▶ **Alert: DNS 2008 free memory or other system resources alert.**

Issue: This error occurred along with a large number of other Active Directory and DNS-related alerts. This one, however, was key to identifying the core issue that was occurring. After logging into the system, verified the server was unable to see its own file shares, including \\localhost and \\<*ip address*>. The alert description field said "The DNS server could not bind a Transmission Control Protocol (TCP) socket to address 0.0.0.0. The event data is the error code. An IP address of 0.0.0.0 can indicate a valid "any address" configuration in which all configured IP addresses on the computer are available for use. Rebooting the server with this issue would temporarily resolve the issue. Restart the DNS server or reboot the computer."

Resolution: Tracked this down eventually to Microsoft hotfix #961775, which is required for multiple processor systems running Windows Server 2008 (or Vista/Windows 7) with anti-virus software installed.

▶ **Alert: DNS 2008 Monitor Zone Resolution Alert.**

Issue: Occurs for some Active Directory-integrated stub zones or DNS zones hosted on the server whenever the server reboots. This does not appear to occur for either regular stub zones or Active Directory-integrated primary zones.

Resolution: Alerts automatically closed when server was fully back online.

▶ **Alert: DNS 2008 Resolution Time Alert.**

Issue: The DNS 2008 response time monitor checks for the speed of DNS resolutions every 15 minutes. If the response time is greater than 1 second, it generates an alert. The server responded to the DNS query in 1.061 seconds.

Resolution: Tracked the performance of this counter (object = DNS Server, Counter = Response Time), available by right-clicking on alert and opening the performance view; then setting the Look For to select Items by Text Search and typing in Response. This counter tracked between 0–10 seconds over a 7-day timeframe. The environment being tested is a brand-new environment with no user load currently. Created an override for all DNS servers to increase the ThresholdsSeconds counter from 1 second to 20 seconds and stored it in the management pack created to store the DNS overrides (DNSServer_Overrides). This now matches the override created for the same alert in the DNS 2003 management pack (DNS 2003 Resolution Time Alert). Kevin Holman discusses this in more detail at http://blogs.technet.com/kevinholman/archive/2009/02/24/dns-mp-noisy-resolution-time-alerts-and-how-to-deal-with-them.aspx.

▶ **Alert: DNS 2008 Server External Addresses Resolution Alert.**

Issue: The firewall product was blocking external connectivity to the forwarders that were defined for the DNS server.

Resolution: Removed firewall restriction to block the IPs defined as forwarders for the DNS server.

▶ **Alert: DNS 2008 Troubleshoot AD DS And Restart DNS Server Alert.**

Issue: DNS was not functional until the domain controller was back online. This domain controller running DNS has been rebooted and this warning was reported.

Resolution: Closed error after verifying via nslookup that DNS was working. This monitor (DNS 2008 Troubleshoot AD DS and restart the DNS service Server Service monitor) does not appear to return to green state automatically.

▶ **Alert: DNS 2008 Check Zone File Alert.**

Issue: Removal of the cache.dns file was taking place as part of the process to remove the root hints for this server.

Resolution: Closed the alerts, as this was an expected situation as part of the process to remove the root hints for the DNS server.

▶ **Alert: DNS 2008 Zone Not Running Alert.**

Issue: Occurs for each DNS zone hosted on the server whenever server is rebooted for each Active Directory stub zone on the server. This does not appear to occur for regular stub zones or Active Directory-integrated primary zones.

Resolution: Alerts automatically closed when server was fully back online.

▶ **Alert: Resolution Time Alert.**

Issue: The DNS 2008 response time monitor checks for the speed of DNS resolutions every 15 minutes. If the response time is greater than 1 second, it generates an alert. The server responded to the DNS query in 1.061 seconds.

Resolution: Tracked performance of this counter (Object = DNS Server, Counter = Response Time), available by right-clicking on the alert and opening performance view, then setting the Look For to select Items by Text Search and typing in Response. This counter tracked between 0–3.5 seconds over a 7-day timeframe. The environment tested is a brand-new environment with no user load currently. Created an override for all DNS servers to increase ThresholdsSeconds counter from 1 second to 5 seconds and stored it in the management pack created to store the DNS overrides (MicrosoftWindowsDNS2008Server_Overrides).

▶ **Alert: Script or Executable Failed to run.**

Issue: For the script DNS2008ComponentDiscovery.vbs.

Resolution: Requires DNS server(s) to have agent proxy configured (set in the OpsMgr console -> Administration -> Device Management -> Agent Managed -> Properties of the system; check the box on the Security tab).

DNS Management Pack Evolution

The default settings for DNS response time should most likely be increased from 1 second to more like 20 seconds due to average DNS response times.

Additionally, the ability to compare what zones exist on each DNS server and report inconsistencies in what zones exist on what servers would be very useful when attempting to debug inconsistencies in name resolution.

Group Policy MP

The Windows Server Group Policy management pack is available as a single download that contains different libraries to monitor Windows Server Group Policy on Server 2003 and 2008 Operating Systems. This article is available online at http://tinyurl.com/GroupPolicyMP-ByExample.

How to Install the Group Policy MP

Perform the following steps to install the Group Policy MP:

1. Download the Windows Server Group Policy management pack from the Management Pack Catalog at http://pinpoint.microsoft.com/en-US/systemcenter/managementpackcatalog. The Windows Server Group Policy Management Pack Guide is included in the download and is labeled "OM2007_MP_GP2008.doc."

2. Read the Management Pack Guide, which points out solid tips like the installation order (Windows Server management packs, Group Policy 2008 management packs, and then Group Policy 2003 management packs).

3. Import the Group Policy 2008 management pack (using either the Operations console or PowerShell), and then the Group Policy 2003 management pack.

4. Create a GroupPolicy_Overrides management pack to contain any overrides required for the MP.

Agentless monitoring is not supported by the Windows Server Group Policy management pack.

Group Policy MP Tuning/Alerts to Look for

The following alerts were encountered and resolved while tuning the various Group Policy management packs (listed in alphabetical order by alert name):

▶ **Alert: Application of Group Policy Alert.**

Issue: The alert monitor on the alert was the Time Skew Monitor. The computer in question was in the wrong time zone.

Resolution: Changed the time zone on the server reporting the alert.

▶ **Alert: Application of Group Policy Alert.**

Issue: Alert that a user in a different forest than the computer account is logging on and that group policy from the other forest is not currently allowed.

Resolution: This environment has two different forests. One of them is a new replacement forest, and group policies for it are being built to replace the group policies used in the original forest. Although users will log into the new forest with credentials for the old forest, the old forest group policies should not apply. This will eventually be resolved when the old forest is decommissioned. In the interim, the monitor was overridden to not be enabled (override, parameter enabled = false) for all objects of type: Group Policy 2008 Runtime.

▶ **Alert: Folder Redirection CSE ProcessedWithErrors.**

Issue: Group policy client failed 1085 and event 107 (which showed the user that had the issue) before it. This was occurring on a terminal server (Citrix).

Resolution: User did not have his or her home folder mapped correctly.

▶ **Alert: GPO Data Retrieval Error.**

Issue: Event log (application) userenv 1058 error on group policy.

Resolution: Found article Microsoft KB article 828760 that implies that ACSL sysvol had issues with the domain controllers and Windows 2003 SP 1. Used gpupdate /force on the system to see if could recreate the event. Found that it creates a 1704 message in the event log (information) that it succeeded. Tested accessing of this path from the domain name, and from each of the domain controllers that it should be using to authenticate. There were differences in the dates of the folders indicated within the error message itself. The actual content was consistent, however. This was occurring on the all-domain computers policy. No indication that this occurred because of a WAN outage.

▶ **Alert: GPO Data Retrieval Error.**

Issue: Every 5 minutes, errors were occurring in the application log for Userenv for 1058 and then 1030.

Resolution: Determined that the domain controller had not been patched or rebooted in over six months (checked the system log for the event source of eventlog). Patched and rebooted the DC, and the group policy errors stopped occurring.

▶ **Alert: Group Policy Preprocessing (Active Directory) Alert.**

Issue: DNS issues occurred in the environment, causing an inability to resolve names in the environment.

Resolution: Fixed the DNS resolution issue so the environment could resolve names.

▶ **Alert: Group Policy Preprocessing (Networking) Alert.**

Issue: This alert occurs when an event of 1058 is created in the system log for the source of GroupPolicy. This occurs when the system is unable to connect to \\abc.com\SysVol\Policies\abc.com\Policies\<*guid*>\gpt.ini (where abc.com is the domain name, and guid is the guid provided in the alert). Issues like this are caused by network connectivity or network resolution, or FRS latency, or if the DFS client is not running (per the knowledge in the alert). Information on this event is available at http://technet.microsoft.com/en-us/library/cc727259(WS.10).aspx.

Resolution: In this case, this was an errorcode number of 5, which is "access is denied." From the details on the event, copied the file path and verified that the system could open the file with notepad. Logged into a server that had the last event in the System log from the source of GroupPolicy, opened a command prompt (Run-as administrator), and did a gpupdate /force. Verified successful creation of a 1502, and 1503. Verified that the majority of these alerts all occurred at the same time. Closed this alert.

Also verified that DNS was providing this information correctly. Opened nslookup and did a resolution for abc.com. Copied the name of the file shown (the gpt.ini file), replaced the abc.com domain name with the actual IP address (\\1.1.1.1\SysVol\Policies\abc.com\Policies\<*guid*>\gpt.ini), and verified that each of the domain controllers not only had the gpt.ini file but that it was readable from the path specified.

► **Alert: Group Policy Preprocessing (Security) Alert.**

Issue: This alert appears to occur when there is an inability to resolve DNS from the system identified or group policy fails to apply. It is stating that the specified domain either does not exist or could not be contacted.

Resolution: Researching this alert from the system log event number 1054 found this article from Microsoft at http://technet.microsoft.com/en-us/library/cc727331(WS.10).aspx. After researching, it appears that an event 1500 that has occurred since the 1054 occurred indicates that group policy is now functional.

Copied the name of the server from the alert detail pane, changed the view to Monitoring -> Computers, and pasted the name of the server into the filter. Used the Computer Management task to connect and remotely review the event logs for the server. Closed the alert after verifying that the 1500 has occurred since the 1054 occurred in the system log where the alert occurred.

Logged into a server that had the last event in the System log from the source of GroupPolicy, opened a command prompt (Run as administrator), and did a gpupdate /force. Verified successful creation of a 1502 and 1503. Closed this alert.

Group Policy Management Pack Evolution

The Group Policy File Access Monitor in the Group Policy 2008 management pack version 6.0.6648.0 should be a two-state monitor with a health condition of the 1500 event (or 1051, 1052, or 1053) and a warning or critical for the 1058 event. This could be accomplished by creating a new custom monitor and disabling the original monitor included in the management pack.

The Machine Account Determination Monitor in the Group Policy 2008 management pack version 6.0.6648.0 should be a two-state monitor with a health condition of the 1500 event (or 1051, 1052, or 1053) and a warning or critical for the 1054 event. This could be accomplished by creating a new custom monitor and disabling the original monitor included in the management pack.

DHCP MP

The Windows DHCP Server management pack is available as a single download that contains different libraries to monitor Windows DHCP on Windows Server 2000, 2003, and 2008 operating systems. This article is available online at http://tinyurl.com/DHCPMP-ByExample.

How to Install the DHCP MP

Perform the following steps to install the DHCP MP:

1. Download the Windows DHCP Server management pack from the Management Pack Catalog at http://pinpoint.microsoft.com/en-US/systemcenter/managementpackcatalog. The Windows DHCP Server Management Pack Guide is included in the download and labeled "OM2007_MP_DHCP_2003_2008 QFE110408.doc."

2. Read the Management Pack Guide as this covers items to be aware of with the DHCP, such as how DHCP clustering and multicast scopes are not supported.

3. Import the Windows DHCP Server management pack (using either the Operations console or PowerShell).

4. Create a DHCPServer_Overrides management pack to contain any overrides required for the MP.

DHCP MP Tuning/Alerts to Look for

The following alerts were encountered and resolved while tuning the various DHCP management packs (listed in alphabetical order by alert name):

▶ **Alert: DHCP IPv4 Runtime Authorization Needed Alert.**

Issue: DHCP scopes (both IPv4 and IPv6) were showing up as turned off offline/not authorized. This server had been authorized and then the IP address of the server was changed. The authorization was listing the previous IP address.

Resolution: Unauthorized the current server name/wrong IP address and re-authorized it with the correct IP address. This was occurring on a domain controller in a child domain. To do this change, logged into the root domain and authorized/re-authorized the server, and then restarted services on the domain controller after a short period of time.

► **Alert: DHCP Scope Addresses Available Monitor.**

Issue: Alert description is that the available scope addresses have fallen below the specified threshold. This is raised by the DHCP Scope Addresses Available Monitor. This monitor goes to warning level when there are less than 10 available IP addresses in the pool, and to critical when there are no remaining IP addresses in the pool. This environment originally had one DHCP server that contained the entire scope of available addresses. To provide redundancy, the scope was split between two different DHCP servers. This unfortunately leads to a tendency for the original DHCP server scope to fill while the other scope remains with a large number of available addresses in the range.

Resolution: For this environment, it was necessary to match up the two different scopes to determine if the lack of addresses was really a lack of addresses or just half of the scope filled while the half remained open. Performed the following actions to make this more readily apparent:

  ► Configured the warning states on this monitor to go to yellow when there are less than two available IP addresses in the scope.

  ► Monitored within the Microsoft Windows DHCP Server -> Scope Health view and ordered by display name to validate that the address range was not critical on both halves of the scope.

  ► Used the Microsoft Windows DHCP Server -> DHCP Performance Views -> Scopes & Superscopes -> Scope Free Addresses view sorted by instance and color coded to match the colors for each half of the scope (so that, as an example, both halves of the data network on floor three show up as blue). Added this to the My Workspace view with the Y access limited to a maximum of 10 (to more easily identify scopes with less than 10 available addresses). This is useable but pretty unwieldy with a large number of DHCP scopes.

► **Alert: DHCP Service Bound to Static IP Address.**

Issue: The alert description on the Alert Context tab shows that "The DHCP service is not servicing any clients because none of the active network interfaces have statically configured IP addresses, or there are no active interfaces."

Resolution: The product knowledge provided an effective resolution for this issue. The DHCP service was not bound to any IP addresses on the system. In this case, this DHCP scope was not required, and as it was the only DHCP scope on the system, removing the DHCP service from the system was an acceptable solution after deactivating the DHCP scope for a period of time.

► **Alert: Performance Threshold: Process\Working Set threshold exceeded.**

Issue: DHCP management pack error. Occurring sporadically on the DHCP server in the environment, but not seeing any errors or issues as a result of the condition. The rule (Performance Threshold: Process\Working Set threshold exceeded) is configured to work over a 5-minute interval, and to measure over three samples by default (per the overrides). The management pack says that the utilization is measured over five samples. In a 24-hour period, there were approximately 22 of these alerts occurring and self-closing. Increased the number of samples to measure over from three to five and tracking the result (as these were usually closing with 5–10 minutes automatically). This did not help the issue.

Resolution: In this particular environment, this alert is NOT affecting the ability of the DHCP server to function, but could affect it at higher-level values. This value is in place because exceeding this threshold can be an issue, so do not disable or override this rule unless you are sure that it is NOT impacting your environment.

Determined the trend of this value based upon the alerts in the environment (tried tracking it by monitoring the performance counter for this variable with no luck, as there does not appear to be one). For each alert, went to the alert context tab and tracked the values that appeared (17806131, 17780028, 17809408, 17823061, 17793024, 17788928, 17791658, 17800330, 17786197, 17787562, 17828522, 17772544, 17783466, 17824426, 17829888, 17821696, 17788928, and 17870028). Determined the average, maximum (17870028), and minimum (17772544) values to determine where this threshold should be for the environment; found that closed alerts were not relevant as they showed values less than the threshold.

Created an override to change this value for this server (on the monitor) from the default of 17830000 to 18070000.

▶ **Alert: Script or Executable Failed to run.**

Issue: Script failure for Nslookuptest.js. Reporting for tests to Microsoft.com, localhost ip address, and the fully qualified name of the server. All three failed at the same date and time.

Resolution: Noted the alert and the date/time to see if a root cause could be tracked back. Reviewed the event logs on the system to track back potential issues; none were found. Reviewed the performance counters gathered by OpsMgr, but no bottlenecks were identified during that timeframe. Closed the alerts.

▶ **Alert: The DHCP service has determined that it is not authorized on this domain.**

Issue: Description says the DHCP/Binl service on the local machine belonging to the windows administrative domain (domain name) has determined that it is authorized to start. It is servicing clients now. This appears as a critical alert, but is actually stating that the DHCP server is working.

Resolution: The only option for the override on this is to disable it, so the criticality of the alert cannot be changed. This should actually be an informational level alert. The only alternative currently is either to close the alerts or to disable the alert.

▶ **Alert: The DHCP service is not servicing any clients because none of the active network interfaces have statically configured IP addresses, or there are no active interfaces.**

Issue: DHCP server cannot be a DHCP client.

Resolution: Hard-coded an IP address for the DHCP server.

DHCP Management Pack Evolution

It would be extremely useful if, in future revisions of this management pack, it could effectively match scopes (based upon name, or matching subnet potentially) and gather the information to provide a critical alert when each of the different scopes was nearing empty.

Another useful enhancement would be to provide the number of available addresses in the range within the alert description text.

Print Server MP

The Windows Print Server management pack is available as a single download that contains different libraries to monitor Windows Print services on Windows Server 2000, 2003, and 2008 operating systems. This article is available online at http://tinyurl.com/PrintServer-ByExample.

How to Install the Windows Print Server MP

Perform the following steps to install the Print Server MP:

1. Download the Windows Print Server management pack from the Management Pack Catalog at http://pinpoint.microsoft.com/en-US/systemcenter/managementpackcatalog. The Management Pack Guide is included and labeled "OM2007_MP_PrintSvr.doc."

2. Read the Management Pack Guide to gather additional information, such as that the current version only supports monitoring clustered instances of the Print Server role on Windows Server 2008.

3. Import the Print Server management pack (using either the Operations console or PowerShell) after importing the Windows Server management pack.

4. Create a PrintServer_Overrides management pack to contain any overrides required for the MP.

The Windows Print Server MP supports agentless monitoring with the exception of tasks.

Windows Print Server MP Tuning/Alerts to Look for

The following alerts were encountered and resolved while tuning the various print server management packs (listed in alphabetical order by alert name):

▶   **Alert: Document failed to print.**

  Issue: Document failed to print; this is categorized as a critical alert.

Resolution: This should not be a critical alert. Downgraded to a warning level alert through an override in the PrintServer_Overrides management pack.

▶ **Alert: Printer: Publish Error.**

Issue: The print server had a single DNS server defined for its location, and the DNS server was down.

Resolution: The DNS server was brought back online and a second DNS server configured for the system that reported this error. Manually closed alert.

▶ **Alert: Shared Printer Availability Alert.**

Issue: An error was generated for each of the shared printers on the server. These were generated by the "Shared printer: Restart the print spooler, fix sharing problems, and check group policy" alert.

Resolution: This is an alert generated by a rule, not a monitor, so it does not automatically resolve itself. There does not appear to be an equivalent number for the same source in the event logs, which indicates that the print spool is back online (which may be why this is an alert rather than a monitor).

Per the knowledge base, restarted the spooler service on the server with the issues when this was caused by a situation that was not a reboot.

This also occurred when the print server was rebooted. Verified the ability to print to the printer specified after the reboot completed.

Print Server Management Pack Evolution

Although the Windows Server 2008 version of this management pack functions well, earlier versions of this management pack do not work well on a clustered server (either Windows 2000 or 2003). There are also issues with the approach to discovery on Windows 2000/2003 servers so that many servers are identified as being print servers that may not actually be print servers. The evolution of this set of management packs would be to bring the same functionality now available in the Windows Server 2008 management pack to the Windows 2000 and 2003 versions.

SharePoint MP

The Office SharePoint Server 2007 management pack and SharePoint Portal Server 2003 management pack are separate management packs. This discussion focuses on the Office SharePoint Server 2007 management pack, as this is the more current version of the two. This article is available online at http://tinyurl.com/SharePoint-ByExample.

How to Install the SharePoint MP

Perform the following steps to install the SharePoint MP:

1. If running SharePoint 2007, download the Office SharePoint Server 2007 management pack from the Management Pack Catalog. The Office SharePoint Server 2007 Management Pack Guide is included in the download and labeled "Microsoft_Office_SharePoint_Server_Management_Pack_Guide.doc."

2. Read the Management Pack Guide, which includes tips such as resizing the Windows System and Application logs to at least 10240 in size.

3. Import the Office SharePoint Server 2007 management pack (using either the Operations console or PowerShell).

4. Create a SharePoint_Overrides management pack to contain any overrides required for the MP.

The Office SharePoint 2007 management pack does not support agentless monitoring.

SharePoint MP Tuning/Alerts to Look for

The following alerts were encountered and resolved when tuning the various SharePoint management packs (listed alphabetically by alert name). Alerts from the SharePoint Portal Server 2003 management pack are also provided as additional information should similar issues be found in the SharePoint 2007 version of the management pack:

▶ **Alert: Cannot load virus scanner.**

Issue: SharePoint 2003 alert. This looks for event number 1000 from the source of Windows SharePoint Services 2.0 containing the description.

Resolution: There is no virus scanner on this system specifically for SharePoint, so disabled this rule for this system.

▶ **Alert: Failed to load index.**

Issue: This appears to be a side effect of an underlying corruption that occurred on an index. See http://objectmix.com/sharepoint/298641-sharepoint-search-index-corrupt.html.

Resolution: This environment had three SharePoint servers: two of them for SharePoint content and the third server to provide indexing. In SharePoint Central administration, it was determined that there was no indexing server. Configured third server to perform indexing, and these issues no longer occurred.

▶ **Alert: Failure in loading assembly.**

Issue: Per the Management Pack Guide: Discovery for the SharePoint Portal Server management pack relies on the file wssDiscovery.exe. This file runs automatically when you import the management pack. You must configure the agent action account so it has administrative access to the SharePoint Portal Server API and administrator rights to the SQL Server databases.

Resolution: For this to work correctly, you must enable Proxy. Be sure to enable Proxy for each of the SharePoint (including SharePoint 2003) servers.

▶ **Alert: IIS Stop Command.**

Issue: IIS was stopped on the server while a portal protection program was installed on the system. This action was performed by a system administrator. This is an alert rule, so it will not close automatically.

Resolution: Created a web monitor for the SharePoint website. Changed the severity of this item from 2 to 1 (critical to warning), as this is by itself is not a critical situation. If the website was down as a result, that would be a critical situation, but these are checked separately with web monitors.

▶ **Alert: Index is corrupt.**

Issue: Index corruption identified on multiple SharePoint servers.

Resolution: This environment had three SharePoint servers: two for SharePoint content and the third to provide indexing. In SharePoint Central administration, it was determined that there was no indexing server. Configured the third server to perform indexing, and these issues no longer occurred.

▶ **Alert: Query server removed from rotation.**

Issue: This appears to be a side effect of an underlying corruption that occurred on an index. See http://objectmix.com/sharepoint/298641-sharepoint-search-index-corrupt.html.

Resolution: This environment had three SharePoint servers: two for SharePoint content and the third to provide indexing. In SharePoint Central administration, it was determined that there was no indexing server. Configured the third server to perform indexing, and these issues no longer occurred.

▶ **Alert: Sweep Synch failed.**

Issue: Errors reported on various SharePoint servers in the server farm; it appears to be a side effect of an underlying corruption that occurred on an index; see http://objectmix.com/sharepoint/298641-sharepoint-search-index-corrupt.html.

Resolution: This environment had three SharePoint servers: two for SharePoint content and the third to provide indexing. In SharePoint Central administration, it was determined that there was no indexing server. Configured the third server to perform indexing, and these issues no longer occurred.

▶ **Alert: The Microsoft Single Sign-on Service State.**

Issue: This service is not running on the SharePoint 2007 servers in the environment. This service is used to store login credentials for third-party applications so you can create links from SharePoint to those apps and auto-login users not using Windows authentication. That is the only reason you would need to have it running.

Resolution: This functionality was not being used, so created an override to disable the alert, and stored it in a Sharepoint_Overrides management pack.

▶ **Alert: The Office SharePoint Server Search Service State.**

Issue: Office SharePoint Server Search is not running. This appears to be a side effect of an underlying corruption that occurred on an index. See http://objectmix.com/sharepoint/298641-sharepoint-search-index-corrupt.html.

Resolution: This environment had three SharePoint servers: two for Share-Point content and the third to provide indexing. In SharePoint Central administration, it was determined that there was no indexing server. Configured the third server to perform indexing, and these issues no longer occurred.

▶ **Alert: Unable to discovery SharePoint components.**

Issue: Per the Management Pack Guide: Discovery for the SharePoint Portal Server management pack relies on the file wss Discovery.exe. This file is run automatically when you import the management pack. You must configure the agent action account so that it has administrative access to the SharePoint Portal Server API and administrator rights to the SQL Server databases.

Resolution: For discovery to work correctly, you must enable Proxy. Be sure to enable Proxy for each SharePoint server (including SharePoint 2003).

Configuration Manager MP

The Configuration Manager management pack now adds support for monitoring Configuration Manager 2007 SP 2 in a 64-bit environment with Operations Manager 2007 R2 or Operations Manager 2007 SP 1 with hotfix (KB 971541) installed. This enables the Configuration Manager 2007 SP 2 management pack to work with either the 32-bit or the 64-bit Operations Manager 2007 agent. You can also find this article online at http://tinyurl.com/ConfigMgrMP-ByExample.

How to Install the Configuration Manager MP

Perform the following steps to install the Configuration Manager MP:

1. Download the Configuration Manager (ConfigMgr) management pack from the Management Pack Catalog. The Configuration Manager 2007 Management Pack Guide is available at the same URL as the download and is labeled "CM07_OM07_MPGuide.doc."

2. Review the Management Pack Guide—cover to cover. This document spells out some important pieces of information you will need to know.

3. Import the Configuration Manager MP (using either the Operations console or PowerShell).

4. Deploy the OpsMgr agent to all ConfigMgr servers.

5. Enable Agent Proxy configuration on all ConfigMgr primary site servers. This is in the Administration node, under Administration -> Device Management -> Agent Managed. Right-click each primary site server, select Properties, click the Security tab, and then check the box labeled "Allow this agent to act as a proxy and discover managed objects on other computers."

6. Create a ConfigurationManager_Overrides management pack to contain any overrides required for the MP.

How to Configure the Configuration Manager MP

After installing the Configuration Manager management pack, there is additional configuration and tuning to adjust management pack settings to your particular environment. The following sections discuss configuration tasks for the Configuration Manager management pack.

Create Groups Needed for Overriding Targets with Common Requirements

As with other management packs, the groups needed for management pack tuning depend on the specifics of your deployment and the support model for your organization. As an example, a group of logical disks on Configuration Manager distribution point servers may require a lower threshold for disk space monitoring.

Configure Wake On LAN (WOL) Performance Monitoring Rules

If WOL is in use in your Configuration Manager environment, you should enable monitoring of this feature. Several management pack rules, including performance measuring counters and rules monitoring the WOL feature, are disabled by default. To use the data collected by these rules, you must enable them by using overrides. WOL rules disabled by default in the Configuration Manager 2007 management pack include the following:

▶ **ConfigMgr 2007 Perf Threshold**—Site Server Inbox WOLCMGR.box Backlog > 20 over 1 hour

▶ **ConfigMgr 2007 Perf Threshold**—Site Server Inbox WOLCMGR.box\data Backlog > 100 over 1 hour

▶ **ConfigMgr 2007 Perf Threshold**—SMS Wake On LAN Communication Manager Total Number of Packets Failed > 100 over 15 minutes

▶ **ConfigMgr 2007 Perf Threshold**—SMS Wake On LAN Communication Manager Total Number of Requests Pending > 10,000 over 3 hours

Create Custom Inbox Monitoring Rules

Most performance rules monitoring inbox backlogs have default thresholds of 10,000 messages for 3 hours. The threshold is not exposed as an overridable parameter in these monitors, meaning you must disable the monitor and create a replacement recurring threshold unit monitor with threshold, interval, and repeat count settings appropriate to the environment being monitored.

This step is necessary only if the default thresholds are not acceptable for your environment. You can make this determination based on the normal levels in your specific environment—collecting and viewing data from inbox performance counters to understand the performance baseline better.

Configure Sender Connectivity Monitoring

If the sender cannot connect to its parent site, status messages do not flow up the Configuration Manager hierarchy and the management pack does not generate an alert on those status messages. For these rules to work, create the *%SMS_INSTALL_DIR_ PATH%* environment variable on your site server with the installation path previously specified for your site installation.

Configure Configuration Manager Integration with Operations Manager

You can use the Configuration Manager console to configure how Configuration Manager responds during software distribution activities. These settings are not enabled by default.

Enable maintenance mode for Configuration Manager software distribution—when enabled, this allows Configuration Manager to enact the maintenance mode for the Operations Manager agent during software deployment operations.

Enable Operations Manager 2007 alerts if a Configuration Manager 2007 program fails to run—if enabled, this allows event logging resulting in alerts being raised in Operations Manager 2007 if a program fails to run.

Define the SMS Environment Variable to Support Log-Based Rules

A number of rules in the ConfigMgr management pack read Configuration Manager-based log files (sender.log, distmgr.log, and policypv.log) to check for errors. To monitor these logs, specify the location of the Configuration Manager installation folder by creating the *%SMS_INSTALL_DIR_PATH%* system environment variable on a site server. This enables the MOM/OpsMgr agent running under Local System or a local administrator user context to have access to the log files in the *%SMS_INSTALL_DIR_ PATH%*\Logs folder.

Note that the *%SMS_INSTALL_DIR_PATH%* variable is not present on ConfigMgr systems by default. For the Operations Manager Health Agent to use this system environment variable, you may need to restart the Configuration Manager site server.

TIP: CONFIGURING ENVIRONMENT VARIABLES

Steps for configuring system environment variables will vary by operating system. For detailed instructions on setting system environment variables on Windows 2008, refer to the system environment variable web page at http://technet.microsoft.com/en-us/library/cc772047.aspx.

Define Configuration Manager Admin UI Variable to Support Console Tasks

If the Configuration Manager 2007 console is collocated with an installation of the Operations Manager 2007 Operations console, the OpsMgr console will be able to launch the following Configuration Manager 2007 UI components, using the following console tasks presented in the Actions pane of the Operations console:

► Resource Explorer
► Configuration Manager console

▶ Service Manager

▶ Status Message

Define the system environment variable %*SMS_ADMIN_UI_PATH*% as the path to the folder containing the Configuration Manager 2007 console. This system environment variable is used to launch the console. The environment variable points to the folder containing the Configuration Manager console, <*ConfigMgrInstallationPath*>\AdminUI\bin\i386, by default.

NOTE: %*SMS_ADMIN_UI_PATH*% VARIABLE

The %*SMS_ADMIN_UI_PATH*% variable should be present on any system where the Configuration Manager console is installed. However, for the Operations Manager Health Agent to use this system environment variable, you may need to restart the system after completing the Configuration Manager console installation.

Enable General Health Monitoring

When enabled, general health monitoring for ConfigMgr servers is implemented through four unit monitors, all of which generate alerts when a health metric on a Configuration Manager server is above a certain threshold over a period of time. Here are the metrics checked by the unit monitors that implement general health monitoring:

▶ Processor Time at 95% over 3 hours

▶ Smsexec

▶ Ccmexec

▶ Total

▶ Paging File Usage at 98% over 3 hours

General health monitoring in the Configuration Manager 2007 management pack is disabled by default. If desired, use overrides to enable the following unit monitors:

▶ **ConfigMgr 2007 Perf Threshold**—Paging File %Usage > 98% over 3 hours

▶ **ConfigMgr 2007 Perf Threshold**—% Processor time(ccmexec) > 95% over 3 hours

▶ **ConfigMgr 2007 Perf Threshold**—% Processor time(smsexec) > 95% over 3 hours

▶ **ConfigMgr 2007 Perf Threshold**—% Processor time(_Total) > 95% over 3 hours

Disable Unused Performance and Non-Critical Event Collection Rules

As mentioned in the previous discussion of the Active Directory management pack ("Active Directory MP"), disable any non-critical collection rules in the Configuration Manager management pack to free up database space, bandwidth, and processor cycles.

Configuration Management MP Tuning/Alerts to Look for

The rules and monitors generating false (or otherwise non-actionable) alerts will vary from one environment to another. For the alert rules mentioned here, the issues do not appear immediately after importing the management pack but rather over time during normal product use:

▶ **Alert: ConfigMgr 2007 Status: Distribution Manager failed to process a package.**

Issue: The alert generated by this rule indicates that the Distribution Manager failed to copy a package from its source folder to its destination folder on a distribution point. This is usually indicative of permissions on the folder, which you can resolve by granting permissions to the share for the server attempting to copy.

Resolution: Disabled due to false alerts generated from the management pack.

▶ **Alert: ConfigMgr 2007 Status: Distribution Manager does not have enough free disk space to copy a package.**

Issue: The alert generated by this rule indicates that the Distribution Manager failed to copy a package from its source folder to its destination folder on a distribution point. This may indicate a true space issue, but it can also be triggered by permissions on the folder, which you can resolve by granting permissions to the share for the server attempting to copy.

Resolution: Disabled due to false alerts generated from the management pack.

TMG MP

The Threat Management Gateway (TMG) management pack adds support for monitoring Forefront TMG with Operations Manager 2007. TMG runs only on the X64 versions of Windows Server 2008 and Windows Server 2008 R2. All versions of TMG are monitored including TMG Medium Business Edition (MBE) and Forefront TMG 2010 Enterprise and Standard editions. You can also find this article online at http://tinyurl.com/TMGMP-ByExample.

How to Install the TMG MP

Perform the following steps to install the TMG MP:

1. Download the TMG management pack from the Management Pack Catalog. The TMG Management Pack Guide is available on the same URL as the download and is labeled "OM2007_MP_TMG.DOC."

2. Review the Management Pack Guide—cover to cover. This document spells out some important pieces of information you will need to know.

3. Import the TMG MP (using either the Operations console or PowerShell).

4. Deploy the OpsMgr agent to all TMG servers. Agentless monitoring for TMG servers is not supported.

5. Enable Agent Proxy configuration on all TMG servers. This is in the Administration node, under Administration -> Device Management -> Agent Managed. Right-click each TMG server, select Properties, click the Security tab, then check the box labeled Allow this agent to act as a proxy and discover managed objects on other computers. (If you have a large number of agents to enable this setting for, the TMG MP guide contains a script to automate this task.)

6. Create a TMG_Overrides management pack to contain any overrides required for the MP.

How to Configure the TMG MP

After installing the TMG management pack, additional configuration and tuning is necessary to adjust management pack settings to your particular environment. The next sections discuss configuration tasks for the TMG management pack.

Create Groups Needed for Overriding Targets with Common Requirements in Your Environment

As with other management packs, the groups needed for management pack tuning depend on the specifics of your deployment and the support model for your organization.

In the case of management groups monitoring TMG firewalls as well as SQL 2008 databases, there are two SQL 2008 database monitors, enabled by default, which should not be running on TMG firewalls. Resolve this issue by creating a group such as "TMG ISARS Databases." Populate this group with the ISARS SQL database objects discovered on each TMG server, and then create overrides in each of these SQL 2008 database monitors to disable monitoring for the group you created:

► SQL Server Full Text Search Service Monitor

► Blocking SPIDs

Install TMG Console, Stage Utilities, and Configure Security to Support Tasks

If the TMG console is collocated with an installation of the Operations Manager 2007 Operations console, the OpsMgr console will be able to launch the TMG console. To support this feature, add the OpsMgr operator to one of the following Forefront TMG roles:

► **Forefront TMG Administrator (Array or Enterprise Administrator in Enterprise Edition)**—Allows full access to Forefront TMG monitoring and configuration.

> ▶ **Forefront TMG Auditor (Array or Enterprise Auditor in Enterprise Edition)**—Allows full access to Forefront TMG monitoring, able to view Forefront TMG configuration, and able to configure logging and alerting.

> ▶ **Forefront TMG Monitoring Auditor (Array or Enterprise Monitoring Auditor in Enterprise Edition)**—Allows full access to Forefront TMG monitoring only.

In addition, you should add the OpsMgr operator's computer to either the Remote Management Computers or Enterprise Remote Management Computers Forefront TMG computer sets.

Here are two other utilities that need to be staged on the managed TMG server to be launched correctly by tasks in the console:

> ▶ **AdamSites.exe (http://go.microsoft.com/fwlink/?LinkId=168771)**—Install in the *%ProgramFiles%*\Microsoft Forefront TMG folder of the Forefront TMG computer hosting the configuration storage server (CSS) role.

> ▶ **Dnstools.exe (http://go.microsoft.com/fwlink/?LinkId=168772)**—Install in the *%ProgramFiles%*\Microsoft Forefront TMG folder of the Forefront TMG computer hosting the Firewall role.

Create a Firewall Access Rule on the TMG Firewall Configuration

You must configure an access rule in Forefront TMG to allow the Forefront TMG computer to communicate with the management servers. This will be from the Local Host network to an "SCOM Set" computer set that contains all management or gateway servers on TCP port 5723. The access rule is per-array for Forefront TMG Enterprise Edition and per-server for Forefront TMG Standard Edition and TMG Medium Business Edition.

TIP: ENABLING AUTOMATIC OPSMGR AGENT INSTALL ON TMG FIREWALLS

Steps to create a firewall access rule that supports monitoring, but not automatic agent install, are included in the TMG MP guide. The TMG MP guide covers only manual agent install. If you have a large number of firewalls that require installing the OpsMgr agent, consider allowing automatic agent install as follows:

> ▶ Extend the rule created according to the TMG MP guide to include the protocols needed for automatic agent installation, and disable strict RPC checking in the rule properties.

> ▶ Exclude the "SCOM Set" computer set from the built-in system policy for Active Directory communications.

Figure A.2 illustrates an Enterprise-level rule that permits the necessary access (remember to disable strict RPC checking on this rule), as well as the edited system policy for an array excluding the "SCOM Set" from the system policy rule.

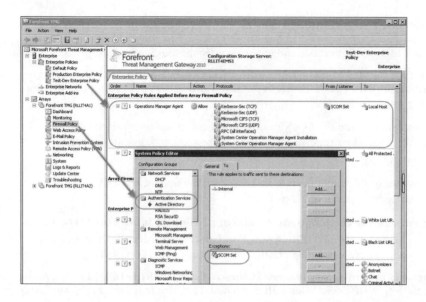

FIGURE A.2 Firewall rule and system policy exceptions to support automatic OpsMgr agent installation

Install the Network Load Balancing Management Pack if Using TMG NLB

If your TMG 2010 Enterprise Edition firewalls will be running in array configuration with NLB enabled, import the Windows Server 2008 Network Load Balancing management pack for Operations Manager 2007 as well as the TMG MP. While TMG does control all NLB functions on a TMG array member, the NLB MP provides a useful performance view to help you confirm that all members of an NLB team are about equally loaded.

Figure A.3 charts the load distribution across nodes (received and sent packets per second) on the Internet interfaces of a three-node TMG enterprise array.

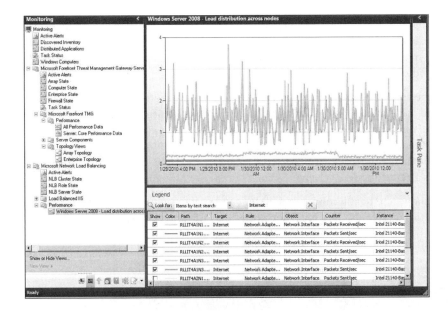

FIGURE A.3 Leverage the NLB management pack to confirm equal load distribution across TMG array nodes.

Perform General Health and Configuration Monitoring

Implement general health monitoring for TMG firewall computers by watching these 13 TMG server components, each of which has its own state view folder and is exposed in columns of the top-level Firewall state view:

- ▶ Cache State View
- ▶ Publishing-Enabled TMG Servers State
- ▶ E-Mail Protection State
- ▶ Reporting State
- ▶ HTTPS Inspection State
- ▶ SIP State
- ▶ ISP Redundancy State
- ▶ URL Filtering State
- ▶ Malware Inspection State
- ▶ VPN State
- ▶ Network Inspection System State
- ▶ Web Proxy State
- ▶ Network Load Balancing State

Performance views in the TMG MP are simplified, with the primary view being a single dashboard view named Server: Core Performance Data. This view is optimized to compare the overall CPU time and firewall service CPU time across TMG array members or individual servers.

The TMG enterprise health topology diagram validates the Active Directory Lightweight Directory Services (ADAM) instance supporting the organization's firewall arrays, and is represented by the health of each CSS component (known in TMG as the Enterprise Management Server [EMS]) and the health of each managed firewall array. The health of each multi-node array is represented by the NLB-redundant services running on each firewall node.

Figure A.4 shows the health model of a TMG enterprise with two CSS (EMS) servers and two multi-node arrays. The NLB service of the first array is expanded to the node level.

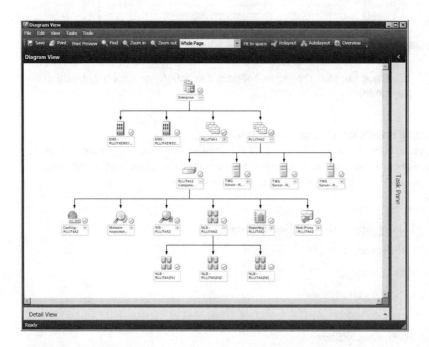

FIGURE A.4 Firewall services running on multiple NLB nodes are the focus of TMG enterprise monitoring.

The TMG MP adds eight reports to the OpsMgr Reporting space. Two report on top alerts and events, two target TMG performance counters, and four reports are on TMG configuration data from the CSS, enterprise, array, and server perspectives. The array report, when targeted at multiple arrays in the enterprise, is a useful way to audit which TMG enterprise policy is applied to each TMG array. Figure A.5 is an example of this report, invoked from the Tasks area in the Monitoring space.

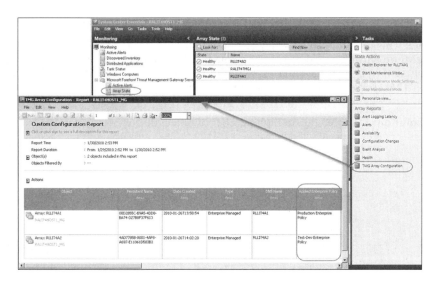

FIGURE A.5 TMG reports assist with security configuration auditing.

TMG MP Tuning/Alerts to Look for

The rules and monitors generating false (or otherwise non-actionable) alerts will vary from one environment to another. For the alert rules mentioned here, the issues do not appear immediately after importing the management pack, but rather over time during normal product use:

► **Alert: The SQL Server Service Broker or Database Mirroring transport is disabled or not configured.**

Issue: The SQL Server MP does this check on all SQL Servers. Any alert generated by this rule does not apply to TMG computers.

Resolution: Created an override disabling this rule for the class Microsoft Forefront TMG Computers.

► **Alert: Forefront TMG Server: Web Proxy—Current Direct Fetches Avg Ms Per Request Performance Monitor.**

Issue: Busy TMG servers can be noisy with this rule. You can modify the default threshold of 20 seconds per request to a higher setting to reduce alert volume.

Resolution: Disabled due to false alerts generated from the management pack.

► **Alert: Forefront TMG Server: Cache—Current Cache Fetches Avg Ms Per Request Performance Monitor.**

Issue: Busy TMG servers can be noisy with this rule. You can modify the default threshold of 0.3 seconds per request to a higher setting to reduce alert volume.

Resolution: Disabled due to false alerts generated from the management pack.

▶ **Monitor: Forefront TMG Server: Configuration State Monitor.**

Issue: This monitor can be a source of configuration churn in very large OpsMgr environments that are also managing large numbers of TMG servers. Each new version of the enterprise configuration triggers a new discovery for each TMG server. This is an issue only in very large environments and is only indicated when symptoms of configuration churn are detected.

Resolution: Disabled due to high number of object discoveries generated from the management pack.

APPENDIX B

Reference URLs

This appendix includes a number of reference URLs associated with System Center Operations Manager 2007 (OpsMgr). A list of URLs was previously included in Appendix E, "Reference URLs," in the predecessor to this book, *System Center Operations Manager 2007 Unleashed*, and is updated here to include references pertinent to OpsMgr 2007 R2 (Release 2). Links are also available "live" with the online content available for with this book. URLs do change—although the authors have made every effort to verify the references in this appendix as working links, there is no guarantee that they will remain current.

General Resources

A number of websites provide excellent resources for OpsMgr, as follows:

▶ Ian Blyth wrote an article on OpsMgr 2007 architecture at http://ianblythmanagement.wordpress.com/2006/08/01/scom-2007-architecture/. This includes some compare/contrast with MOM 2005, if you are familiar with that platform.

▶ Also architecture-related is an article by Brian Wren at http://blogs.technet.com/ati/archive/2007/05/14/targeting-rules-and-monitors.aspx. The article talks about how to target rules and monitors, and the difference between groups in MOM 2005 and OpsMgr 2007. This is also discussed at length in Chapter 9, "Unleashing Operations Manager 2007."

You may also want to check Jonobie Ford's article at http://blogs.technet.com/momteam/archive/2007/10/31/targeting-series-part-1-differences-between-2005-and-2007.aspx.

▶ The ReSearch This! management pack troubleshooting tool is hosted by System Center Central. You can download the management pack at http://www.systemcentercentral.com/PackCatalog/PackCatalogDetails/tabid/145/IndexID/21716/Default.aspx.

► A list of the top KB articles published for Operations Manager 2007 is available at http://kbalertz.com/Technology.aspx?tec=533.

If you're not already receiving email notifications of new articles in the Microsoft Knowledge Base from kbAlertz, you can sign up for them at http://kbalertz.com/. You just need to create an account and select the technologies you want to be alerted about.

► Here are some articles on Audit Collection Services (ACS) in OpsMgr 2007:

For a white paper on auditing using ACS and optimizing that experience with Secure Vantage, see http://www.securevantage.com/docs/Secure%20Vantage%20WhitePaper%20Enterprise%20Auditing%20with%20ACS.pdf.

Read Microsoft's ACS white paper at http://download.microsoft.com/download/E/E/7/EE797D69-02B2-420D-B0F2-196906CCE063/Whitepaper-Audit_Collection_with_System_Center_Operations_Manager_2007_final.pdf.

Secure Vantage offers an ACS resource kit as a free community download, available at http://www.securevantage.com/Products/ACSResourceKit.aspx.

Maarten Goet (OpsMgr MVP) provides an overview of ACS-related information at http://opsmgr2007.wikidot.com/system:audit-collection-services.

Maarten also has a series of ACS Deep Dive articles at System Center Central:

► http://www.systemcentercentral.com/BlogDetails/tabid/143/IndexID/13052/Default.aspx

► http://systemcentercentral.com/BlogDetails/tabid/143/indexid/13112/Default.aspx

► http://www.systemcentercentral.com/tabid/143/indexid/53717/Default.aspx

You can find an ACS disk and database planning calculator at http://www.systemcentercentral.com/Downloads/DownloadsDetails/tabid/144/IndexID/7425/Default.aspx.

ACS Windows 2008 and Vista audit reports are listed at http://blogs.technet.com/momteam/archive/2009/05/08/acs-reports-for-windows-2008-and-windows-2008-r2.aspx.

http://securevantage.spaces.live.com/Blog/cns!905E136EE69247B4!454.entry provides information about routine ACS health checks.

Eric Fitzgerald (an original Microsoft ACS Program Manager) documents and demystifies ACS Event Transformation at http://blogs.msdn.com/ericfitz/archive/2008/02/27/acs-event-transformation-demystified.aspx.

For information on configuring ACS to use certificate-based authentication, a good place to start is Clive Eastwood's article at http://blogs.technet.com/cliveeastwood/archive/2007/05/11/how-to-configure-audit-collection-system-acs-to-use-certificate-based-authenication.aspx.

Although Service Pack (SP) 1 lets you enable the ACS forwarder on a management server or the RMS (root management server), Jeff Skelton of Rede Consulting documents doing it in the base version of OpsMgr 2007 at http://helpmemanage.blogspot.com/.

Find a summary of ACS support for CrossPlat systems at http://blogs.technet.com/momteam/archive/2009/05/11/solution-summary-acs-support-for-unix-and-linux-systems.aspx.

Maarten Goet presents a preview of R2 and Cross Platform ACS at http://www.systemcentercentral.com/BlogDetails/tabid/143/IndexID/13046/Default.aspx.

Three downloadable components are required for Cross Platform Audit Collection Services:

- ▶ **R2 CrossPlat updated management packs**—
  http://www.microsoft.com/downloads/details.aspx?displaylang=en&FamilyID=b15fef5c-e331-4006-8913-be376bb0e0c1

- ▶ **CrossPlat ACS management packs**—
  http://www.microsoft.com/downloads/details.aspx?displaylang=en&FamilyID=24081923-a92f-449f-a182-48ad81ccaf14

- ▶ **CrossPlat ACS installer**—
  http://www.microsoft.com/downloads/details.aspx?displaylang=en&FamilyID=68590cff-453f-4822-b9e4-140824c76486

▶ Here are some resources regarding the Gateway Server Component:

http://www.techlog.org/archive/2007/02/14/operations_manager_2007_gateway is an article by Maarten Goet on the gateway server approval process.

Pete Zerger (OpsMgr MVP) and Ian Jirka of Microsoft copresented at MMS 2008 on using the Gateway Server role. This included key use scenarios and troubleshooting; you can download their presentation at http://www.systemcentercentral.com/Downloads/DownloadsDetails/tabid/144/IndexID/6224/Default.aspx (sign into System Center Central to download).

Mutual authentication takes one of two forms in Operations Manager—Kerberos or certificate authentication. http://www.systemcentercentral.com/BlogDetails/tabid/143/IndexID/32926/Default.aspx is Pete's master list of mutual authentication-related errors for OpsMgr 2007 (also applicable to System Center Essentials).

Pete also has a three-part series on PKI and gateway scenarios here, as follows:

- ▶ http://www.systemcentercentral.com/BlogDetails/tabid/143/indexid/19101/Default.aspx

- ▶ http://www.systemcentercentral.com/BlogDetails/tabid/143/IndexID/19102/Default.aspx

- ▶ http://www.systemcentercentral.com/BlogDetails/tabid/143/IndexID/31342/Default.aspx

Rory McCaw, OpsMgr MVP and technical editor of this book, documents R2 changes to gateway server configuration with Windows Server 2008 at http://www.systemcentercentral.com/BlogDetails/tabid/143/IndexID/20563/Default.aspx. Brian Daniel writes more about this at http://www.systemcentercentral.com/BlogDetails/tabid/143/IndexID/19171/Default.aspx.

► An RTM bug—If you install additional management servers after installing OpsMgr reporting, the new management servers will not be able to write to the data warehouse until you create profiles. Documentation is at http://blogs.technet.com/momteam/archive/2007/08/29/if-you-install-opsmgr-2007-reporting-and-then-install-secondary-ms-then-it-will-not-be-able-to-write-dw-data-as-profiles-are-not-created.aspx, and the bug is fixed in SP 1.

► Walter Chomak of Microsoft has done some research on OpsMgr 2007 I/O considerations. Read about his results at http://wchomak.spaces.live.com/blog/cns!F56EFE25599555EC!610.entry.

► Satya Vel of the OpsMgr team has an article on network bandwidth utilization for OpsMgr roles at http://blogs.technet.com/momteam/archive/2007/10/22/network-bandwidth-utilization-for-the-various-opsmgr-2007-roles.aspx. A related chart by Jeff Skelton comparing bandwidth between OpsMgr 2007 and MOM 2005 is at http://helpmemanage.googlepages.com/MOMvsSCOMUsageovertime.JPG.

► Gartner Group has Operations Manager 2007 firmly in the Challenger's quadrant. See their December 2007 and 2009 reports http://mediaproducts.gartner.com/reprints/microsoft/vol10/article2and3/article2and3.html and https://h10078.www1.hp.com/bto/download/Gartner_Magic_Quadrant_IT_Event_Corr_Analysis.pdf, respectively.

► Ready to dig into MP authoring? Check out Chapter 8, "Management Pack Authoring," and you also should read Pete Zerger's article at http://www.systemcentercentral.com/Details/tabid/147/IndexID/24878/Default.aspx:

The Operations Manager R2 MP Module Reference is at http://technet.microsoft.com/en-us/library/dd391800.aspx.

Check out the Management Pack University at http://74.52.12.162/~microsft/conference_agenda.php?cid=19.

Download the OpsMgr 2007 MP Authoring Guide from http://download.microsoft.com/download/7/4/d/74deff5e-449f-4a6b-91dd-ffbc117869a2/OM2007_AuthGuide.doc.

You will also find a great website on management pack authoring, maintained by Steve Wilson of Microsoft, at http://www.authormps.com/dnn/.

Here's a four-part series on creating a two-state PowerShell script monitor using the authoring console by Stefan Koell (code4ward.net). The series comes with a sample MP you can use to check your work and see the intended end result at http://www.systemcentercentral.com/tabid/144/IndexId/50087/Default.aspx:

► http://www.systemcentercentral.com/BlogDetails/tabid/143/IndexID/44971/Default.aspx

- http://www.systemcentercentral.com/BlogDetails/tabid/143/IndexID/46908/Default.aspx

- http://www.systemcentercentral.com/BlogDetails/tabid/143/IndexID/48469/Default.aspx

- http://www.systemcentercentral.com/BlogDetails/tabid/143/IndexID/50085/Default.aspx

Here's a posting on how to create a PowerShell task for OpsMgr using the Authoring console by Andreas Zuckerhut, at http://www.systemcentercentral.com/BlogDetails/tabid/143/IndexID/41687/Default.aspx.

Creating a PowerShell Script discovery including on-demand discovery task with the Authoring console, also by Andreas Zuckerhat, is at http://www.systemcentercentral.com/BlogDetails/tabid/143/IndexId/50020/Default.aspx.

- Tools for MP authors include the following:

  - **System Center Operations Manager 2007 R2 Authoring Resource Kit**— http://www.microsoft.com/downloads/details.aspx?FamilyID=9104af8b-ff87-45a1-81cd-b73e6f6b51f0&displaylang=en.

  - **Log Smith for Operations Manager 2007**—By Stefan Koell. A great tool for identifying event parameters when authoring event rules. For the feature list, go to http://www.code4ward.net/main/LogSmith/Features.aspx; download it at http://www.code4ward.net/main/LogSmith/Download.aspx.

  - **OpsMgr Community Toolkit**—A complete list of community-authored tools for OpsMgr 2007 is at http://systemcentercentral.com/tools.

- Looking for community-authored management packs? For a complete list, see http://www.systemcentercentral.com/mps. Here are some recently released community-authored MPs of note:

  - **PowerShell 2-State-Monitor Sample**—Sample MP leveraging the R2 OpsMgr PowerShell modules by Stefan Koell at http://www.systemcentercentral.com/tabid/144/IndexId/50087/Default.aspx.

  - **PKI Certificate Verification MP**—By Raphael Burri at http://www.systemcentercentral.com/PackCatalog/PackCatalogDetails/tabid/145/IndexID/24860/Default.aspx.

  - **Service Pack 1 Edition of the Cisco Management Pack, v1.0.2.6**— By Kris Bash at http://operatingquadrant.com/2009/09/26/scom-sp1-edition-of-the-cisco-management-pack-v1-0-2-6/.

- The OpsMgr Reporting Authoring Guide is available at http://technet.microsoft.com/en-us/opsmgr/bb498235.aspx.

► Brian Wren of Microsoft talks about programmatically creating groups at http://blogs.technet.com/brianwren/archive/2008/11/18/programmatically-creating-groups.aspx.

► Want to know how to combine a System.SnmpProbe and System.Performance.DeltaValueCondition module to calculate SNMP counter delta values? See Kris Bash's post at http://operatingquadrant.com/2009/10/14/scom-combining-a-system-snmpprobe-and-system-performance-deltavaluecondition-modules-to-calculate-snmp-counter-delta-values/.

► Looking for training? This is not an exhaustive list, but here are several places that offer courses on OpsMgr 2007:

InFront Consulting Group's training is at http://www.infrontconsulting.com/training.php.

Secure Vantage offers free online training on ACS; see http://www.securevantage.com/ACSTraining.aspx for information on the Masters Class series.

http://learning.microsoft.com/Manager/Catalog.aspx?clang=en-US&dtype=Table&Sort=Relevancy&page=1&search=operations%20manager will get you a listing of Microsoft-developed training.

Training videos are available at http://technet.microsoft.com/en-us/opsmgr/bb498237.aspx. To download these videos (webcasts), go to http://www.microsoft.com/downloads/details.aspx?FamilyID=1276a840-671f-4452-98c7-5599c0d3ff9c&DisplayLang=en.

You may also want to invest a couple of hours viewing the TechNet Support Webcast by Brian Wren, Troubleshooting Microsoft Operations Manager Top Issues, found online at http://support.microsoft.com/kb/828936.

Other training videos and demos are available at http://www.microsoft.com/events/series/technetmms.aspx?tab=webcasts&id=42365.

Microsoft now provides the System Center Ramp Up Series at http://systemcenter.vlabcenter.com/. This includes the material on architecting a cross platform solution and managing your Unix/Linux systems.

JCA Academy (Telindus) also has material, described at http://www.jcacademy.be/_media/pdf_cursus/_en/MOC138%20-%20Opsmgr%202007%20training.pdf and taught by Rory McCaw. The main web page is http://www.jcacademy.be/.

http://www.cbtplanet.com/microsoft-it/microsoft-system-center-operations-manager-training-video.htm is a collection of OpsMgr training videos on CD.

There is also https://www.learnitstuff.com/pc-16-7-operations-manager-2007-and-mom-2005.aspx.

► Satya Vel and one of his coworkers adapted the MOM 2005 Resource Kit MOMNetCheck utility for command-line use in OpsMgr 2007. You can use the tool to remotely check installation prerequisites. Information and a download are available at http://blogs.technet.com/momteam/archive/2007/11/20/remote-agent-prerequisite-checker-tool-for-opsmgr-2007.aspx.

▶ Do you want to move the OpsMgr databases to another server? The authors researched the requirements and documented the steps in Chapter 12, "Backup and Recovery," of *System Center Operations Manager 2007 Unleashed*. Blog articles discussing this are also available at http://ops-mgr.spaces.live.com/blog/cns!3D3B8489FCAA9B51!177.entry and http://ops-mgr.spaces.live.com/blog/cns!3D3B8489FCAA9B51!225.entry for information on moving the Operational database; and http://ops-mgr.spaces.live.com/Blog/cns!3D3B8489FCAA9B51!235.entry for the steps to move the OpsMgr data warehouse.

▶ Microsoft discusses virtualizing SQL Server 2008 at http://www.microsoft.com/sqlserver/2008/en/us/virtualization.aspx. An article on using SQL Server 2005 in a virtual environment is available at http://download.microsoft.com/download/a/c/d/acd8e043-d69b-4f09-bc9e-4168b65aaa71/SQLVirtualization.doc.

▶ Michael Pearson has an excellent article discussing SRS Recovery Planning, available online from the SQL Server Central community at http://www.sqlservercentral.com/columnists/mpearson/recoveryplanningforsql reportingservices.asp. You must register with SQLServerCentral to view the full article.

▶ For information on the types of SQL maintenance to perform on your OpsMgr databases, check Kevin Holman's posting at http://blogs.technet.com/kevinholman/archive/2008/04/12/what-sql-maintenance-should-i-perform-on-my-opsmgr-databases.aspx.

▶ For steps on setting up a SQL Server cluster, read Microsoft's article at http://msdn.microsoft.com/en-us/library/ms179530.aspx.

▶ Trying to set up a virtual server cluster? See http://blogs.technet.com/pfe-ireland/archive/2008/05/16/how-to-create-a-windows-server-2008-cluster-within-hyper-v-using-simulated-iscsi-storage.aspx to create a virtual cluster on Windows 2008/Hyper-V.

▶ Coauthor Cameron Fuller wrote a (humorous) piece on the Clustering MP at http://www.systemcentercentral.com/BlogDetails/tabid/143/IndexId/51752/Default.aspx, emphasizing major steps to remember when working with clustered resources in OpsMgr.

▶ For a discussion of agent discovery hanging after enabling the SQL Broker Service, see Steve Rachui's posting at http://blogs.msdn.com/steverac/archive/2009/08/30/opsmgr-agent-discovery-hanging-after-enabling-broker-service.aspx. Steve is a contributor to this book.

▶ What's new in the OpsMgr R2 Software Development Kit (SDK)? Check the article at http://msdn.microsoft.com/en-us/library/bb437542.aspx. A diagram showing an architecture overview is available at http://msdn.microsoft.com/en-us/library/bb437500.aspx.

▶ Have an interesting experience when trying to delete an agentless system? This happens if you first install agentless and then install as a managed agent without first deleting the agentless configuration. This information is discussed in Chapter 9, "Installing and Configuring Agents," of *System Center Operations Manager 2007 Unleashed*, with full details available at http://ops-mgr.spaces.live.com/default.aspx?_c01_BlogPart=blogentry&_c=BlogPart&handle=cns!3D3B8489FCAA9B51!163.

► For information on debugging the infamous alert, the "Script or Executable Failed to Run," see http://cameronfuller.spaces.live.com/blog/cns!A231E4EB0417CB76!1006.entry.

► Steve Rachui has a two-part series on understanding monitors, as follows:

http://blogs.msdn.com/steverac/archive/2009/08/30/understanding-monitors-in-opsmgr-2007-part-i-unit-monitors.aspx

http://blogs.msdn.com/steverac/archive/2009/09/06/understanding-monitors-in-opsmgr-2007-part-ii-aggregate-monitors.aspx

► The System Center Virtual Machine Manager (VMM) 2007 scripting guide is available for download at http://go.microsoft.com/fwlink/?LinkId=104290. "How-to" videos for managing VMM with PowerShell are at http://go.microsoft.com/fwlink/?LinkId=98846.

► Download Boris Yanushpolsky's Override Explorer from http://blogs.msdn.com/boris_yanushpolsky/attachment/4301837.ashx.

► Several people have done some work on helping you put computers into maintenance mode in batch.

This includes Clive Eastwood's command-line tool, documented at http://blogs.technet.com/cliveeastwood/archive/2007/09/18/agentmm-a-command-line-tool-to-place-opsmgr-agents-into-maintenance-mode.aspx.

Andrzej Lipka enhances Clive's approach using the PsExec Tool. See http://blogs.technet.com/alipka/archive/2007/12/20/opsmgr-2007-putting-computers-in-maintenance-mode-remotely.aspx. PsExec is available at http://technet.microsoft.com/en-us/sysinternals/bb897553.aspx.

See a discussion on running PowerShell from a batch file for maintenance mode at http://social.technet.microsoft.com/Forums/en/operationsmanagergeneral/thread/33d0ee92-2c1d-4f2d-a656-834877de565d.

► Want to mass-create computer groups? Use XML to do this easily. See http://cameronfuller.spaces.live.com/blog/cns!A231E4EB0417CB76!982.entry.

► If you can't get your reports to send email subscriptions, check out http://blogs.msdn.com/ketaanhs/archive/2005/09/05/461055.aspx on how to configure the PermittedHosts entry in the RSReportServer.config file.

► You can download a tool that enables you to test emails from the command line; this lets you see how the message will look prior to configuring a mail server. The tool is available at https://blogs.pointbridge.com/Blogs/morse_matt/Lists/Posts/Post.aspx?ID=24.

► If you do a Help -> About in the Operations console, it displays a version (build) number. The MOM team provides a cross-reference of version numbers to "common names" (although only through SP 1 RC) at http://blogs.technet.com/momteam/archive/2008/01/10/versioning-in-opsmgr.aspx. For more recent build numbers, see a thread at http://www.systemcentercentral.com/Forums/ForumPost/tabid/177/IndexID/45009/Default.aspx.

▶ David Wallis wrote an application allowing OpsMgr admins to acknowledge and resolve alerts via email—download it at http://www.systemcentercentral.com/Downloads/DownloadsDetails/tabid/144/IndexID/44253/Default.aspx.

▶ Use PowerShell to resolve rule-generated alerts older than X days; download the script at http://www.systemcentercentral.com/Downloads/DownloadsDetails/tabid/144/IndexID/19968/Default.aspx.

▶ http://www.systemcentercentral.com/Details/tabid/147/IndexID/35783/Default.aspx discusses using Process Monitor to identify which discovery and monitoring script is using more resources than expected.

▶ Need help to configure notifications?

Check out the Microsoft website at http://technet.microsoft.com/en-us/library/dd440890.aspx.

Here's a post on configuring IM notifications: http://blogs.technet.com/operationsmgr/archive/2009/04/15/configuring-im-notifications-in-system-center-operations-manager-2007.aspx.

Kevin Holman writes about configuring notifications at http://blogs.technet.com/kevinholman/archive/2008/06/26/using-opsmgr-notifications-in-the-real-world-part-1.aspx.

To see how to configure notifications to include alerts from specific groups and classes, read http://blogs.technet.com/kevinholman/archive/2008/02/01/configuring-notifications-to-include-specific-alerts-from-specific-groups-and-classes.aspx.

Use PowerShell to create individual notification subscriptions for individual rules and monitors. Read how to do so at http://blogs.technet.com/kevinholman/archive/2008/10/12/creating-granular-alert-notifications-rule-by-rule-monitor-by-monitor.aspx.

▶ Appendix A, "OpsMgr R2 by Example," is a compilation of previously posted blog articles on tuning management packs. Find these posts "green" and online at:

http://tinyurl.com/ActiveDirectoryMP-ByExample

http://tinyurl.com/ExchangeMP-ByExample

http://tinyurl.com/SQLMP-ByExample

http://tinyurl.com/WindowsServerMP-ByExample

http://tinyurl.com/OperationsManagerMP-ByExample

http://tinyurl.com/DNSMP-ByExample

http://tinyurl.com/GroupPolicyMP-ByExample

http://tinyurl.com/DHCPMP-ByExample

http://tinyurl.com/PrintServerMP-ByExample

http://tinyurl.com/SharePointMP-ByExample

http://tinyurl.com/ConfigMgrMP-ByExample

http://tinyurl.com/TMGMP-ByExample

► Wondering how to use a property bag? See
http://blogs.msdn.com/mariussutara/archive/2008/01/24/momscriptapi-createtypedpropertybag-method.aspx and
http://www.systemcentercentral.com/Downloads/DownloadsDetails/tabid/144/indexID/7803/Default.aspx.

Microsoft's OpsMgr Resources

The following list includes some general Microsoft resources available for OpsMgr 2007:

► **Microsoft's Operations Manager website**—
http://go.microsoft.com/fwlink/?LinkId=86432.

► **Microsoft's System Center website**—
http://www.microsoft.com/systemcenter/.

► **System Center Operations Manager 2007 Catalog**—
http://go.microsoft.com/fwlink/?LinkId=82105 or
http://pinpoint.microsoft.com/en-US/systemcenter/managementpackcatalog.

► Microsoft's System Center Pack Catalog has multiple pages for all things OpsMgr and ConfigMgr. The catalog incorporates the following pages:

All packs for all products—
https://www.microsoft.com/technet/prodtechnol/scp/catalog.aspx
(http://go.microsoft.com/fwlink/?Linkid=71124).

Operations Manager 2007—
https://www.microsoft.com/technet/prodtechnol/scp/opsmgr07.aspx
(http://go.microsoft.com/fwlink/?LinkId=82105). With OpsMgr 2007 R2, you can also download management packs from within the Operations console!

Operations Manager 2005—
https://www.microsoft.com/technet/prodtechnol/scp/opsmgr05.aspx.

Operations Manager 2000—
https://www.microsoft.com/technet/prodtechnol/scp/opsmgr00.aspx.

Configuration Manager 2007 Configuration Packs—
https://www.microsoft.com/technet/prodtechnol/scp/configmgr07.aspx.

Virtual Machine Manager 2008 PRO Packs—
http://technet.microsoft.com/en-us/systemcenter/cc462790.aspx.

TIP: FINDING THE SYSTEM CENTER PACK CATALOG

In late 2009, the System Center Pack Catalog was moved to the Pinpoint platform. The links listed here should redirect you to Pinpoint, or you can access the System Center Pack Catalog directly at http://pinpoint.microsoft.com/en-US/systemcenter/managementpackcatalog.

▶ **Operations Manager 2007 management pack guides**—
http://go.microsoft.com/fwlink/?LinkId=85414.

▶ **Operations Manager 2007 management pack guides for server products**—http://go.microsoft.com/fwlink/?linkid=83259.

▶ **Microsoft download site for SP 1 documentation for Operations Manager 2007**—
http://www.microsoft.com/downloads/details.aspx?familyid=d826b836-59e5-4628-939e-2b852ed79859&displaylang=en&tm.

▶ **OpsMgr 2007 R2 documentation**—http://technet.microsoft.com/en-us/opsmgr/bb498235.aspx.

▶ What's OpsMgr all about, anyway? Microsoft has published "Key Concepts for Operations Manager 2007." You can download the document at http://www.microsoft.com/downloads/details.aspx?FamilyID=3a633532-1dde-49b6-930f-7df50b69b77b&DisplayLang=en. This document describes how OpsMgr 2007 implements modeling.

▶ **Operations Manager 2007 online help**—http://technet.microsoft.com/en-us/library/bb381409.aspx.

▶ **Operations Manager 2007 Technical Library**—
http://technet.microsoft.com/library/bb310604.aspx.

▶ Find a great Microsoft discussion on processor bottlenecks at http://technet.microsoft.com/en-us/library/aa995907.aspx.

▶ The "Operations Manager 2007 Performance and Scalability" white paper is at http://www.microsoft.com/DOWNLOADS/details.aspx?FamilyID=a1b7610d-3dbe-4e51-bcb3-446d50dadf14&displaylang=en.

▶ The Operations Manager 2007 Rule and Monitor Targeting Poster is available at http://download.microsoft.com/download/f/a/7/fa73e146-ab8a-4002-9311-bfe69a570d28/BestPractices_Rule_Monitor_REV_110607.pdf.

▶ **TechNet Manageability Center**—Links to resources and *TechNet* magazine articles at http://technet.microsoft.com/en-us/manageability/default.aspx.

▶ **Virtual hands-on labs**—Virtual labs for System Center products including Operations Manager, Essentials, and Configuration Manager at http://technet.microsoft.com/en-us/bb539977.aspx.

▶ **All about OpsMgr licensing for customers with Software Assurance (SA)**—The volume licensing brief for OpsMgr 2007 is at http://go.microsoft.com/fwlink/?linkid=87480.

▶ **Operations Manager 2007 R2 SDK**—http://msdn.microsoft.com/en-us/library/cc268402.aspx. The pre-SP2 version is at http://msdn2.microsoft.com/en-us/library/bb437575.aspx.

▶ XML Notepad 2007 is an intuitive tool for browsing and editing XML documents. Read about it at http://msdn2.microsoft.com/en-us/library/aa905339.aspx, and download the tool from http://www.microsoft.com/downloads/details.aspx?familyid=72d6aa49-787d-4118-ba5f-4f30fe913628&displaylang=en.

▶ **System Center Operations Manager 2007 tools and utilities**—This is a link to the catalog and listing of resource kit tools, at http://go.microsoft.com/fwlink/?LinkId=94593.

▶ Interested in learning more about the Microsoft Operations Framework? Check out version 4.0 of the MOF at http://go.microsoft.com/fwlink/?LinkId=50015.

▶ Information on the Infrastructure Optimization (IO) model is available at http://www.microsoft.com/technet/infrastructure.

▶ Details about the Microsoft Solutions Framework (MSF) are located at http://www.microsoft.com/downloads/details.aspx?familyid=50DBFFFE-3A65-434A-A1DD-29652AB4600F&displaylang=en and http://www.microsoft.com/downloads/details.aspx?familyid=a71ac896-1d28-45a4-880c-8b0cc8265c63&displaylang=en.

▶ To create company knowledge, one of the required pieces of software is the Visual Studio 2005 Tools for Office Second Edition Runtime. This is available at http://www.microsoft.com/downloads/details.aspx?FamilyID=F5539A90-DC41-4792-8EF8-F4DE62FF1E81&displaylang=en. (Microsoft Word is also required.)

▶ View a TechNet webcast on Microsoft IT's implementation of OpsMgr 2007 at http://msevents.microsoft.com/CUI/WebCastEventDetails.aspx?culture=en-US&EventID=1032322478&CountryCode=US.

Read the related white paper online at http://technet.microsoft.com/en-us/library/bb735238.aspx.

There is also an accompanying PowerPoint presentation, available for download at http://download.microsoft.com/download/6/8/4/6848d1c4-227c-4831-936b-98c10fec6c55/ImpSysCtrOpsMgr2007updatePPT.ppt.

▶ Download a 180-day evaluation copy of Operations Manager 2007 R2 from http://www.microsoft.com/technet/prodtechnol/eval/scom/default.mspx. You can also download an evaluation copy and get information about the R2 release at http://technet.microsoft.com/en-us/opsmgr/dd239186.aspx.

Information about bug fixes in R2 is at http://support.microsoft.com/kb/971410/.

▶ Cumulative Update 1 for R2 is available at the Microsoft Download Center at http://www.microsoft.com/downloads/details.aspx?FamilyID=05d30779-2ddc-48dc-aa91-a23167ee2cad&displaylang=en. This contains a number of fixes for the Operations Manager 2007 R2 release. The corresponding Knowledge Base (KB) article is published at http://support.microsoft.com/kb/974144.

▶ Cumulative Update 2 for R2 CrossPlat is available at http://www.microsoft.com/downloads/details.aspx?FamilyID=befb326c-67fb-4449-b7f8-3cbb64d61f19&displaylang=en, along with updates to affected management packs at http://www.microsoft.com/downloads/details.aspx?FamilyID=b15fef5c-e331-4006-8913-be376bb0e0c1&displaylang=en. KB article 979790 at http://support.microsoft.com/kb/979490 explains the changes.

▶ http://technet.microsoft.com/en-us/opsmgr/cc280350.aspx lets you download the slipstreamed evaluation copy of SP 1 and the SP 1 upgrade bits for existing installations.

Bugs fixed with the SP 1 release are listed in KB article 944443, at http://support.microsoft.com/default.aspx/kb/944443.

The update rollup for SP 1 is available at http://www.microsoft.com/downloads/details.aspx?FamilyID=05d7785d-fe69-48bc-8dfa-72a77c8936bf&displaylang=en.

▶ There are resource kits for the various versions of Operations Manager:

  ▶ OpsMgr 2007 ResKit is at the System Center Operations Manager TechCenter (http://go.microsoft.com/fwlink/?LinkId=94593).

  ▶ The MOM 2005 Resource Kit is available at http://go.microsoft.com/fwlink/?LinkId=34629 and http://technet.microsoft.com/en-us/opsmgr/bb498240.aspx.

Blogs

There has been an explosion of blogs with information regarding OpsMgr. Where previously you might be directed to websites and papers, now most information seems to appear on the blogs. Here are some blogs the authors have used. Some are more active than others are, and new blogs seem to spring up overnight!

▶ A great source of information is System Center Central (http://www.systemcentercentral.com); managed by three OpsMgr MVPs—Pete Zerger, Rory McCaw, and Maarten Goet. (Pete contributed the material on management pack authoring for this book, and Rory is our technical editor.)

▶ The OpsMgr team has a blog at http://blogs.technet.com/operationsmgr/. You can find older postings at http://blogs.technet.com/smsandmom/.

▶ If you're interested in keeping up with VMM, the VMM team has a blog at http://blogs.technet.com/scvmm/.

▶ http://www.contoso.se/blog/ is the Operations Manager blog by Anders Bengtsson, an OpsMgr MVP.

▶ See a blog by Stephan Stranger (former MVP and now at Microsoft) at http://blogs.technet.com/stefan_stranger/.

▶ http://blogs.msdn.com/incarnato is Justin Incarnato's "Mother" blog. Justin is a senior program manager on OpsMgr team.

▶ http://blogs.technet.com/cliveeastwood is an OpsMgr, SCE, and MOM blog by Clive Eastwood, a Microsoft OpsMgr Supportability Program Manager.

▶ Kevin Sullivan's Management blog is at https://blogs.technet.com/kevinsul_blog/. (Kevin is a Technology Specialist at Microsoft focusing on management products.)

- ► http://blogs.msdn.com/boris_yanushpolsky is Boris Yanushpolsky's OpsMgr++ blog. Boris is an OpsMgr Program Manager.

- ► http://blogs.msdn.com/mariussutara contains notes by Marius Sutura on Operations Manager, including troubleshooting, development information, and comments.

- ► http://blogs.technet.com/kevinholman is Kevin Holman's OpsMgr blog.

- ► http://alipka.wordpress.com/experience/ is a blog by Andrzej Lipka on IT management and operations. Andrzej, formerly at Microsoft, is now at Dell. http://blogs.technet.com/alipka contains his earlier postings, which he has thoughtfully posted at his new site.

- ► http://blogs.msdn.com/rslaten is a blog by Russ Slaten, a Microsoft Escalation Engineer supporting management products.

- ► http://blogs.msdn.com/steverac is Steve Rachui's manageability blog. Steve is a Support Escalation Engineer at Microsoft, concentrating on OpsMgr and ConfigMgr. Steve contributed the material on targeting in this book, and was the technical reviewer for *System Center Configuration Manager 2007 Unleashed*.

- ► http://blogs.msdn.com/sampatton is a blog by Steve Patton, an OpsMgr developer.

- ► http://www.systemcentercommunity.com/ is an OpsMgr 2007 forum with questions and answers about OpsMgr. You will need to create a user ID to reply to the posts.

- ► http://blogs.msdn.com/jakuboleksy is by Jakub Oleksy, previously an OpsMgr developer and now working on Service Manager.

- ► http://blogs.technet.com/mgoedtel/ is a blog by Matt Goedtel, a Microsoft MCS consultant focusing on Operations Manager.

- ► http://discussitnow.spaces.live.com/ is by Blake Mengotto, an OpsMgr MVP and self-described "MOM dude."

- ► Secure Vantage has a blog on Windows Live; see http://securevantage.spaces.live.com.

- ► http://blogs.msdn.com/eugenebykov/ is a great source of information on authoring OpsMgr reports by Eugene Bykov, an OpsMgr developer responsible for the reporting user interface.

- ► http://www.technotesblog.com/ is Dustin Hannifin's Tech Notes blog, which has a section dedicated to OpsMgr 2007.

- ► http://www.scom2k7.com/, by Timothy McFadden, is titled "Everything System Center Operations Manager 2007."

- ► http://www.techlog.org/ is all about everything Microsoft, by Maarten Goet (OpsMgr MVP), Kenneth van Surksum, Steven van Loef, and Sander Klaassen in the Netherlands.

- ► http://advisec.wordpress.com/ is by Bjorn Axell, an OpsMgr MVP and senior consultant focusing on Microsoft infrastructure products.

- ► www.systemcenterguide.com is a System Center blog by Duncan McAlynn.

- ▶ Gordon McKenna's blog is available at
  http://wmug.co.uk/blogs/gordons_blog/default.aspx. Gordon is an OpsMgr
  MVP, has worked with the software since its Mission Critical Software days,
  and is extremely knowledgeable on the product.

- ▶ http://thoughtsonopsmgr.blogspot.com is maintained by Marnix Wolf, an
  OpsMgr MVP.

- ▶ Check out http://myitforum.com/cs2/blogs/smoss/default.aspx, a blog by
  OpsMgr MVP Scott Moss.

- ▶ http://blogs.technet.com/momteam/default.aspx is a blog by the OpsMgr team.

- ▶ Walter Chomak's blog on OpsMgr design and capacity planning is at
  http://blogs.technet.com/wchomak/. Walter is a Senior Consultant with Microsoft MCS and a great technical resource.

- ▶ Ian Blyth, previously a Lead Technical Specialist in Microsoft UK, blogs at
  http://ianblythmanagement.wordpress.com/ on System Center Technologies.

Here are our own blogs:

- ▶ Our Operations Manager and MOM blog is located at http://ops-
  mgr.spaces.live.com. New articles are also posted to
  http://www.systemcentercentral.com/opsmgr.

- ▶ http://cameronfuller.spaces.live.com is where Cameron discusses his technical
  theories, ramblings, and rants. Cameron currently cross-publishes to System
  Center Central at http://www.systemcentercentral.com/CameronFuller and to
  his employer blog at http://blogs.catapultsystems.com/cfuller.

- ▶ http://www.networkworld.com/community/meyler is a blog by Kerrie, with
  more general discussion topics, but concentrating on OpsMgr and Microsoft
  management.

- ▶ And finally, the OpsMgr/MOM blog by Andy Dominey
  (http://myitforum.com/cs2/blogs/adominey/).

OpsMgr Shell

An extension to PowerShell, the Operations Shell (known as the Command Shell prior
to the OpsMgr 2007 R2 release) enables you to do most everything you would ever
want to for OpsMgr in a batch or scripted mode. Here are some useful links:

- ▶ http://blogs.msdn.com/scshell/ is about getting started with the OpsMgr Shell.
  Robert Sprague, a PowerShell guru on the OpsMgr team, maintains this site.

- ▶ For the video recording of Marco Shaw's presentation on Operations Manager
  2007 and PowerShell/Command Shell for the System Center Virtual User
  Group's inaugural meeting, go to
  http://marcoshaw.blogspot.com/2008/06/operations-manager-2007-and-
  powershell.html.

- ▶ http://www.systemcentercentral.com/WIKI/WIKIDetails/tabid/146/IndexID/2
  0507/Default.aspx is an alphabetical reference of OpsMgr 2007 cmdlets, including syntax and sample scripts.

► An online article on PowerShell in OpsMgr that appeared in Microsoft's TechNet Magazine is at http://technet.microsoft.com/en-ca/magazine/2008.08.scom.aspx.

► SystemCenterCentral.com provides a tutorial on using PowerShell scripts in custom console tasks at http://www.systemcentercentral.com/Downloads/DownloadsDetails/tabid/144/IndexID/7880/Default.aspx (login and hit the Download button for the pdf file).

► To see how to create a PowerShell task for OpsMgr using the R2 Authoring console, check out the tutorial at http://www.systemcentercentral.com/BlogDetails/tabid/143/IndexID/41687/Default.aspx, contributed by Stefan Koell.

► To create an OpsMgr group in PowerShell, Marco Shaw provides a script at http://www.systemcentercentral.com/BlogDetails/tabid/143/IndexID/14790/Default.aspx. Also, see http://www.systemcentercentral.com/Details/tabid/147/IndexID/32917/Default.aspx.

► Microsoft TechNet social forum covering Operations Manager extensions, such as the SDK and PowerShell integration, is located at http://social.technet.microsoft.com/Forums/en-US/operationsmanagerextensibility/threads.

► Andreas Zuckerhut has several postings, as follows:

  ► A generic performance data connector using .csv files at http://systemcentercentral.com/BlogDetails/tabid/143/IndexId/45313/Default.aspx.

  ► Eventcollection with Floodingprevention at http://www.systemcentercentral.com/BlogDetails/tabid/143/IndexID/32955/Default.aspx.

  ► Discovery Write Action Modules for On-Demand Discovery Agent Tasks, at http://www.systemcentercentral.com/BlogDetails/tabid/143/IndexId/50850/Default.aspx.

PowerShell Information

You can find information on PowerShell itself at the following sites:

► The official PowerShell site is at http://www.microsoft.com/powershell.

► http://social.technet.microsoft.com/Forums/en-US/operationsmanagerextensibility/thread/a3d09372-1a93-418a-a93c-9bc9ddd075b9—Unofficial PowerShell FAQ by Marco Shaw, who contributed material on PowerShell and the Command Shell to this book. Marco updates this FAQ on an as-needed ("irregular") basis.

► The Microsoft TechNet social forum covering general PowerShell discussions is at http://social.technet.microsoft.com/Forums/en-US/winserverpowershell/threads.

► Marco Shaw maintains his own blog at http://marcoshaw.blogspot.com. To look only at the OpsMgr-related postings, check out http://marcoshaw.blogspot.com/search/label/opsmgr.

► You may want to check all the PowerShell webcasts by the Scripting Guys at http://www.microsoft.com/technet/scriptcenter/webcasts/ps.mspx.

► Direct from the PowerShell guy himself (Marc van Orsouw, PowerShell MVP), is located at http://thepowershellguy.com/blogs/posh/default.aspx.

► Find a PowerShell cheat sheet at http://blogs.msdn.com/powershell/archive/2007/01/25/powershell-cheat-sheet-redux-the-pdf-version.aspx.

► The Windows PowerShell team has its blog at http://blogs.msdn.com/powershell/.

► Find PowerShell script examples at http://www.microsoft.com/technet/scriptcenter/hubs/msh.mspx.

► PowerShell+ is a free PowerShell editing and debugging environment. You can get a free personal copy at http://www.powershell.com/downloads/psp1.zip.

► Even more about PowerShell and examples of some of the constructs are available in an article by Don Jones at http://www.microsoft.com/technet/technetmag/issues/2007/01/PowerShell/default.aspx.

Cross Platform

One of the most visible changes in the R2 version of OpsMgr 2007 is its integrated monitoring of cross platform environments. Here are some references on Cross Platform (also known as CrossPlat or X-Plat).

► The Cross Platform team recently released a very useful MP authoring guide dedicated to the IT Pro type scenarios around extending their monitoring on Cross Platform systems. The guide and downloadable sample are available at http://technet.microsoft.com/en-us/opsmgr/bb498235.aspx.

► MP Guides for the Cross Platform agents are located at http://technet.microsoft.com/en-us/library/ee346642.aspx.

► http://technet.microsoft.com/en-us/library/dd789030.aspx lists the platforms supported by CrossPlat and prerequisites.

► Find Cross Platform PowerShell scripts to help automate discovery of UNIX/Linux servers, install and upgrade cross platform agents for Operations Manager 2007 R2, sign certificates, and change the management server managing the UNIX/Linux server at http://blogs.msdn.com/scxplat/archive/2009/12/11/cross-platform-powershell-scripts-released.aspx.

► Marnix Wolf maintains a compilation of resources on X-Plat at http://thoughtsonopsmgr.blogspot.com/2009/07/opsmgr-r2-xplat.html.

► http://blog.xplatxperts.com/xplat-xperts/ is maintained by Rob Doucette and Michael Guthrie, who work on the Bridgeways management packs at Xandros.

Connectors

Connectors are covered in Chapter 2, "Unix/Linux Management: Cross Platform Extensions." Here are some useful references:

► The Cross Platform team documents the connectors for OpsMgr 2007 R2 at http://blogs.msdn.com/scxplat/archive/2009/07/28/announcing-rtm-of-the-system-center-operations-manager-2007-r2-connectors.aspx.

► http://msdn.microsoft.com/en-us/library/bb437511.aspx can get you started on developing your own connectors.

The System Center Family

Here are some references and articles regarding other components of Microsoft's System Center family:

► For System Center Essentials deployment planning and installation, see http://go.microsoft.com/fwlink/?LinkId=94444.

► Here are some blogs on System Center Essentials (Essentials) and Remote Operations Manager (ROM):

   ► **Remote Managed Services blog**—http://blogs.technet.com/dustinj/.

   ► **The System Center Essentials Team Blog (by the product group)**—http://blogs.technet.com/systemcenteressentials/.

   ► **SCE Setup, Policy, and Reporting**—http://blogs.technet.com/rtammana/.

► The System Center Essentials Community TechCenter can be found at http://technet.microsoft.com/en-us/sce/bb677155.aspx.

► One scenario for System Center Essentials is as a means for managing and monitoring assets of small organizations, tied to a centralized Operations Manager server. Read John Joyner's take on Microsoft's direction for management tools in the midsized market at http://www.eweek.com/article2/0,1895,1905780,00.asp.

► Is it System Essentials or is it Operations Manager? It's both—the Remote Operations Manager! Download the Deployment Guide from http://www.microsoft.com/downloads/details.aspx?FamilyId=4B621EB7-01BB-45F5-9A77-52853F06EEC9%20&displaylang=en.

► Microsoft's Service Manager page is at http://www.microsoft.com/systemcenter/en/us/service-manager.aspx. Webcasts are available at http://msevents.microsoft.com/CUI/WebCastEventDetails.aspx?culture=en-US&EventID=1032416974 and http://msevents.microsoft.com/CUI/WebCastEventDetails.aspx?culture=en-US&EventID=1032424297&CountryCode=US.

▶ Tim Vanderderkoii writes about his experiences with the Service Manager test releases through December 2008 in the midsized business at http://timvanderkooi.wordpress.com/2008/12/05/service-managergreat-product-but-has-microsoft-missed-the-mid-sized-boat-again/.

Public Forums

If you need an answer to a question, the first place to check is the Microsoft public forums, which replaced the newsgroups used prior to the R2 release of OpsMgr 2007. Here's a list of the current OpsMgr forums:

▶ **General**—http://social.technet.microsoft.com/Forums/en-US/operationsmanagergeneral/.

▶ **Deployment**—http://social.technet.microsoft.com/Forums/en-US/operationsmanagerdeployment/.

▶ **Management Packs**—http://social.technet.microsoft.com/Forums/en-US/operationsmanagermgmtpacks/.

▶ **Reporting**—http://social.technet.microsoft.com/Forums/en-US/operationsmanagerreporting/.

▶ **Authoring**—http://social.technet.microsoft.com/Forums/en-US/operationsmanagerauthoring/threads.

▶ **Extensibility (SDK, Connectors, and PowerShell)**—http://social.technet.microsoft.com/Forums/en-US/operationsmanagerextensibility

Here are the public forums for CrossPlat and Interoperability:

▶ **Cross Platform – General**—http://social.technet.microsoft.com/Forums/en-US/crossplatformgeneral/.

▶ **Cross Platform – HPUX**—http://social.technet.microsoft.com/Forums/en-US/crossplatformmupux/.

▶ **Cross Platform – Solaris**—http://social.technet.microsoft.com/Forums/en-US/crossplatformsolaris/.

▶ **Cross Platform – Red Hat**—http://social.technet.microsoft.com/Forums/en-US/crossplatformredhat/.

▶ **Cross Platform – SLES**—http://social.technet.microsoft.com/Forums/en-US/crossplatformsles/.

▶ **Interoperability – General**—http://social.technet.microsoft.com/Forums/en-US/interopgeneral/.

▶ **Interoperability – Tivoli Connector**—http://social.technet.microsoft.com/Forums/en-US/interoptivoli/.

▶ **Interoperability – HP Connector—**
http://social.technet.microsoft.com/Forums/en-US/interophpoperationsmanager/.

▶ **Interoperability – Universal Connector—**
http://social.technet.microsoft.com/Forums/en-US/interopuniversalconnector/.

▶ **Interoperability – BMC Remedy ARS Connector—**
http://social.technet.microsoft.com/Forums/en-US/interopremedy/.

APPENDIX C

Available Online

Online content is available to provide add-on value to readers of *System Center Operations Manager 2007 R2 Unleashed*. This material, organized by chapter, can be downloaded from http://www.informit.com/store/product.aspx?isbn=0672331179. This content is not available elsewhere. Note that the authors and publisher do not guarantee or provide technical support for the material.

SQL Server Resources

Chapter 4, "Using SQL 2008 in OpsMgr 2007 R2," refers to a number of scripts that are included as online content:

▶ **SRS Upgrade Script (srsupgradescript.vbs)**—An updated VBS script for the SQL Reporting Services (SRS) Upgrade Tool, used when upgrading the SRS database used by Operations Manager (OpsMgr) Reporting from SQL Server 2005 to SQL Server 2008.

▶ **Cleanup (cleanup.sql)**—Cleans up the localized text table. This was an issue in Service Pack (SP) 1 with converted Microsoft Operations Manager (MOM) 2005 management packs running backward compatibility scripts. Each event wrote additional data to the localized text table, which is not groomed. The issue is resolved with R2, and the script cleans up the database.

▶ **Reduce Fragmentation (Reindex_Database.sql)**—This script can be used to reduce fragmentation in the Operational database.

▶ **Optimization Results (Optimization_Results.sql)**—This script, used with the data warehouse, displays the optimization method applied to each table and levels of fragmentation before and after the data ware house optimization jobs.

► **Noisiest Monitor (Noisiest_Monitor.sql)**—Identifies the monitor in the Operational database that is making the most "noise" and will eventually need tuning.

► **Listing Groups (Listing_Groups.sql)**—Lists all groups for a given computer.

► **General Performance Overview (General_Performance_Overview.sql)**—This query returns performance data for the logical disk, network interface, processor, and memory for all Windows computers. You can use this query to build a report displaying this information.

Authoring Resources

Chapter 8, "Management Pack Authoring," comes with PowerShell scripts, exTended Markup Language (xml), and Visual Basic scripts to help you do the exercises referred to in this chapter, as follows:

► **Readme (Readme.rtf)**—Provides a detailed guide to the files used with the exercises.

► **CreatePOSJobDistServer.ps1**—PowerShell script to install the "Software\ACME\POSBatchProcess\Version" representing the sample Point-of-Sale Job Server role.

► **CreatePOSJobProcessServer.ps1**—This PowerShell script installs the "C:\Program Files\ACME\POSBatchProcess\Processing" representing the sample Point-of-Sale Processing Server.

► **PerfView.xml**—XML to support the practice management pack authoring exercises.

► **POSFolderSizeCookDown.vbs**—Visual Basic script to support the practice management pack authoring exercises.

► **POSJobProcessDisc.vbs**—Visual Basic script to support the practice management pack authoring exercises.

► **Report_ParameterBlock.xml**—XML to support the practice management pack authoring exercises.

► **Unleashed.POSBatchProcess.Version1.xml**—XML to support the practice management pack authoring exercises.

ACS Resources

Several files are available as part of the ACS discussion in Chapter 9, "Unleashing Operations Manager 2007." These files reference a GPO HTML report for locking down the forwarder service and include PowerShell scripts for locking down audit reports, as follows:

► **Lockdown ACS Forwarder Service.htm**—Provides a sample Group Policy report with lockdown settings for the ACS Forwarder service.

► **CreateSecRptRole.PS1**—This script creates a new OpsMgr security role to associate with ACS reports.

► **ListRoles.PS1**—Lists the OpsMgr security roles.

Also included are accompanying print screens, specifically the following:

► **SQLServer2008Audit_AuditProperties.jpg**—Sample configuration screen for a SQL Audit policy.

► **SQLServer2008Audit_ExplorerView.jpg**—Sample screen shot of SQL Explorer view revealing Audit policy and Audit Specification policy.

► **SQLServer2008Audit_SecurityEvent.jpg**—Sample of q SQL Server security audit event written to local Windows Security log.

► **SQLServer2008Audit_AuditServerSpecificationProperties.jpg**—Sample screen shot for a SQL Audit Specification policy where you define what to audit.

Reference URLs

Reference URLs (see Appendix B, "Reference URLs") are provided as Live Links. These include nearly 300 (clickable) hypertext links and references to materials and sites related to Operations Manager.

A disclaimer and unpleasant fact regarding Live Links: URLs change! Companies are subject to mergers and acquisitions, pages move and change on websites, and so on. Although these links were accurate in early 2010, it is possible some will change or be "dead" by the time you read this book. Sometimes the Wayback Machine (http://www.archive.org/index.php) can rescue you from dead or broken links. This site is an Internet archive, and it will take you back to an archived version of a site—sometimes.

Index

Symbols & Numbers

A

F

G

H

X-Y-Z

UNLEASHED

Unleashed takes you beyond the basics, providing an exhaustive, technically sophisticated reference for professionals who need to exploit a technology to its fullest potential. It's the best resource for practical advice from the experts, and the most in-depth coverage of the latest technologies.

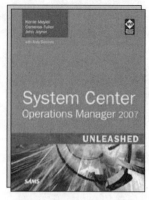

System Center Operations Manager 2007 Unleashed
ISBN-13: 9780672329555

OTHER UNLEASHED TITLES

Microsoft Dynamics CRM 4 Integration Unleashed
ISBN-13: 9780672330544

Microsoft Exchange Server 2010 Unleashed
ISBN-13: 9780672330469

WPF Control Development Unleashed
ISBN-13: 9780672330339

Microsoft SQL Server 2008 Reporting Services Unleashed
ISBN-13: 9780672330261

ASP.NET MVC Framework Unleashed
ISBN-13: 9780672329982

SAP Implementation Unleashed
ISBN-13: 9780672330049

Microsoft XNA Game Studio 3.0 Unleashed
ISBN-13: 9780672330223

Microsoft SQL Server 2008 Integration Services Unleashed
ISBN-13: 9780672330322

IronRuby Unleashed
ISBN-13: 9780672330780

Microsoft SQL Server 2008 Integration Services Unleashed
ISBN-13: 9780672330322

Microsoft SQL Server 2008 Analysis Services Unleashed
ISBN-13: 9780672330018

ASP.NET 3.5 AJAX Unleashed
ISBN-13: 9780672329739

Windows PowerShell Unleashed
ISBN-13: 9780672329883

Windows Small Business Server 2008 Unleashed
ISBN-13: 9780672329579

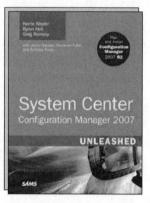

System Center Configuration Manager 2007 Unleashed
ISBN-13: 9780672330230

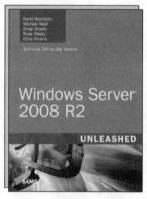

Windows Server 2008 R2 Unleashed
ISBN-13: 9780672330926

SAMS

informit.com/sams

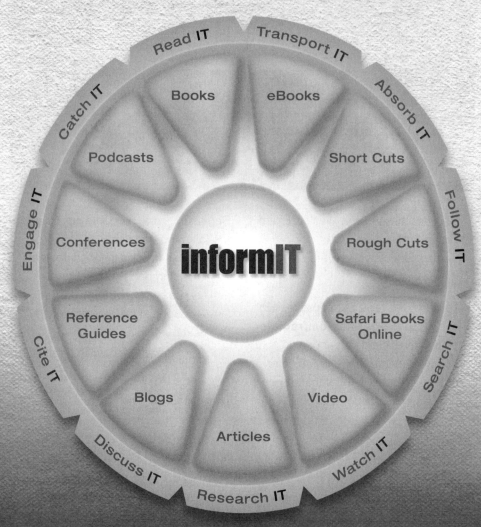

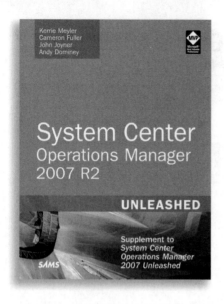